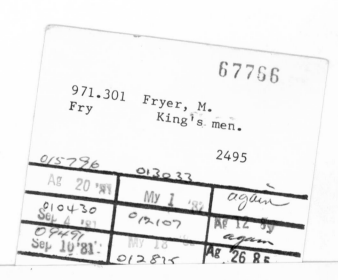

King's Men

the Soldier Founders of Ontario

by Mary Beacock Fryer

Cover:
*King's Rangers or Loyal
Rangers, foreground*

Burgoyne's provincials

design by ron & ron design photography

King's Rangers in motley garb

Butler's Ranger in parade dress

*Privates, Royal Highland
Emigrants*

*Officer, King's Royal Regiment
of New York*

King's Men

the Soldier Founders
of Ontario

King's Men

the Soldier Founders of Ontario

by Mary Beacock Fryer

Toronto and Charlottetown
Dundurn Press Limited
1980

In memory of my loyalist ancestor, Private Caleb Seaman, New York Volunteers, (Third American Regiment).

Design: Ron and Ron Design Consultants

Dundurn Press Limited
P.O. Box 245, Station F
Toronto, Canada
M4Y 2L5

The author and publisher wish to acknowledge the generous assistance of the Canada Council and the Ontario Arts Council.

We especially wish to acknowledge the Ontario Heritage Foundation, Ministry of Culture and Recreation whose grant-in-aid of publication made this book possible.

Printed and bound in Canada by T. H. Best Printing Company Limited

Canadian Cataloguing in Publication Data

Fryer, Mary Beacock, 1929-
  King's men

Includes index.
ISBN 0-919670-51-2 (bound)

1. United Empire Loyalists.* 2. Canada - History -
1763-1791. 3. Canada - History, Military - To 1900.*
I. Title.

FC3070.L6F79   971.3'01   C81-094163-5
F1058.F79

Table of Contents

Part Three: Afterwards

List of Maps

List of Illustrations

Preface

During the American Revolution, thousands of men in Britain's North American colonies enlisted in what were called Provincial Corps of the British Army. Originally this work was to be a history of those American loyalists who joined provincial regiments in the Province of Canada, but such an approach was too narrow. One group of provincials on duty in Canada from 1775 until 1784, the first battalion Royal Highland Emigrants, consisted for the most part of colonials who were resident in Canada or Newfoundland before the war began. Yet because some of the men in this corps were American loyalists it could not be excluded.

Another complication arose over the status and function of the Indian Department, and its relationship to two of the corps, the King's Royal Regiment of New York and Butler's Rangers. The history of both these regiments is intrinsically bound to that of the officers and men who were recruited under the auspices of the Superintendent of Indian Affairs, whose establishment was separate and distinct from the provincial corps. It was neither feasible nor desirable to recount the actions of these regiments in isolation from those of the Indian Department. Then, too, some of the men who enlisted in provincial corps served in the naval establishment, as artificers and as crews on the ships of the Provincial Marine.

This study seeks to unearth the neglected period in the lives of the founding fathers of the Province of Ontario and their families. The myth, related in countless versions, tells that after the revolution ended, thousands of the King's friends in the former Thirteen Colonies left their homes to settle in the wilds of Canada. Such a statement has some validity for loyalists who gathered at New York City and were transported to the Maritime provinces, but it will not suffice for Ontario. While the migration of loyalists into British territory continued until the end of the century, many of Ontario's founding families were in Canada all through the war. The men served in provincial corps, certain of the woman doing the housekeeping, while mothers with small children, the elderly and infirm, were encamped around Montreal and along the lower St. Lawrence years before the war ended. Some refugees fled directly to the British garrisons at Fort Niagara and Carleton Island, and a few made their way to Detroit. At Niagara they were settling years in advance of the main migration up the St. Lawrence that occurred in the spring of 1784.

Engrained mythology that envisages loyalists, both provincial

9

troops and civilians, marching out of the United States at the close of the revolution denies Ontario's founders their place in Canadian history prior to 1784. While there is drama in the story of how they attacked the forest primeval and coped with the cruel land, surviving the Hungry Year, it pales in the light of what they endured and strived to achieve before they faced up to the reality that their future lay in Canada. The story of their efforts to regain the colonies, the intrigue, subversion and individual acts of derring-do is information that captures the imagination.

For Canadian history, the importance of the loyalists is that some of them became the refugee founders of English-speaking Canada, the interesting part the years they spent fighting a war. Our history has been accused of being dull, and in truth, because historians have often seen fit to concentrate on events of significance, omitting the trivial but stimulating, it often appears to be drab. Yet the unimportant ought to precede the event of moment if it is interesting. See what this approach can do for Butler's Rangers. It is best to begin with the news that they vanquished that coonskin-hatted American folk hero, Daniel Boone, before admitting that their contribution to Canadian history was the founding of Niagara-on-the-Lake.

Typical of any young country, Canadian history had to be too good to be true at first. Myth-makers have transformed the loyalists from losers into upholders of empire: from homeless refugees into a nobility. Because they did not want independence, they have been miscast as imperialists – today a dirty word and one with irrelevant overtones for loyalists of the American Revolution. In fact, they merely wanted to retain the rights they enjoyed as British subjects. Their empire was not the powerful force of Queen Victoria's day, the era when the myth-makers were at work. Then, too, it should not be forgotten that Canada, for loyalists, was second best. They really wanted to return to their homes, to take up their old lives among loved ones. No British colony, with the exception of Australia, ever had less willing founding fathers than Ontario or New Brunswick.

Another aspect of the loyalist myth recounts that loyalists were the wealthiest and most influential people in American colonial society. Biographical material on the corps commanders incorporated into this work tends to support this myth, because such were leaders among men. The reader should not overlook the fact that the average loyalist was a follower, a man of modest means with little or no formal education.

I am grateful to the countless people who have guided and en-

10

couraged me in the course of preparing this work. Notable are the staffs of the Public Archives of Canada, the Ontario Department of Public Records and Archives, and the Metropolitan Toronto Central Library, all of which have fine collections, and the British Museum and Public Record Office in London, for permission to publish muster rolls of several of the regiments. I want to thank in particular Professor Kenneth McNaught, of the University of Toronto, President Ian MacDonald of York University, Mr. Lorne Ste. Croix and Professor Sydney Wise, of the Ontario Heritage Foundation, Colonel Ralph Harper, of the MacDonald Stewart Foundation, and Alwyne Compton Farquharson of Torloisk. I am grateful to Norah Hugo-Brunt for the hours she spent in typing the manuscript.

I also want to thank Glenn Steppler and Victor Suthren, who command period units and belong to the Museum of Applied Military History, and I especially appreciate the assistance of Gavin Watt, the president of the museum as well as the commander of the re-created King's Royal Regiment of New York. When I first met Gavin, on the Plains of Abraham in 1976, he was dressed as a sergeant, carrying a seven-foot long halbert. Now he marches as a commissioned officer, and in the phrases of the eighteenth century, may be said to 'carry the halbert in his face.'

Because the members of the Museum of Applied Military History and the Brigade of the American Revolution have established period units and carefully researched their uniforms and equipment, I have been able to photograph them at various re-enactments of the military actions of the war. Without their realistic demonstrations of eighteenth-century tactics, my understanding of such events would have been inadequate to the task I have undertaken.

Part One: Background and Perspective

Chapter 1: Circumstances Surrounding the Revolution

The reasons why certain residents of Britain's Thirteen Colonies decided to revolt against the mother country have been stated in many sources. Two of the chief causes were the Quebec Act, which closed the territory beyond the Allegheny Mountains to settlers, and the contentious issue of taxation without representation. Yet behind a smoke screen of rhetoric lay the outcome of the Seven Years' War. In North America the war had lasted from 1756 until the capitulation of Montreal in 1760, although the Peace Treaty between Britain and France was not signed until the war ended in Europe three years later.

For the American colonists this war was a turning point in their lives. It removed the menace of France's presence from the Northern part of their continent and left them feeling self-assured. In jig time enterprising businessmen, many of them from New England, flocked into Montreal in search of opportunities, while down Lake Champlain and the Richelieu River came timber rafts in search of a market. Meanwhile, the colonial legislatures were active. The Thirteen Colonies had three types of government – Crown, Proprietary and Corporate. Massachusetts, Connecticut and Rhode Island were Corporate provinces, each with its own charter, and in the latter two the Governor was elected by a limited number of freemen who met the stiff property qualification. Maryland, Delaware and Pennsylvania were Proprietary provinces, while the remainder were Crown provinces which, like Massachusetts, had appointed royal governors with sweeping powers over the elected assemblies of freemen.

The population of the Thirteen Colonies on the eve of the revolution was approximately 2.5 million. Since 1760, tension had mounted between the appointed governors and the assemblies that were ambitious to run more of their own affairs. Into this delicate situation the British government tossed the inflammatory Intolerable Acts, which, from the point of view of Parliament and the King were entirely reasonable. Britain had expended vast sums and thousands of lives on the late war and felt justified in imposing taxes to help recover the enormous cost of securing the future of the colonies. The local people felt differently. If their assemblies raised taxes that was acceptable, but it was quite another matter to have them imposed by a Parliament to which they could not send elected representatives. Revolutionaries in the various colonies set up Committees of Correspondence, which kept in communication with one another. Then in 1774, the first Continental Congress met in Philadelphia, and it gradually evolved into a provisional government. Two years later it passed the Declaration of Independence, although years would pass before the separation of the United States of America became official.

The populace was far from united behind the Continental Congress. About one third of the people supported the rebellion and independence, another third was indifferent, the remaining third loyal to the mother country. Thus, as with most revolutions, this one was prosecuted by a vocal, hard-working minority. The revolutionary elements took control of the colonial assemblies, turning them into revolutionary governments, setting up Committees of Public Safety (for the safety of the state, not the individual) which had serious overtones for loyalists. In the case of New York, the bodies persecuting 'Tories' were Boards of Commissioners for Detecting and Defeating Conspiracies, and they were established in each county for the purpose of harassing those opposing independence. Because of the activities of the revolutionary committees, by 1775 loyalists began leaving the colonies to seek refuge in the parts of British North America that had not joined the Continental Congress; they left for Nova Scotia and Canada, and no doubt some would have gone to Newfoundland had it not been too remote. The other places that offered sanctuary were Florida, which had strong British garrisons, and the New York City area after British troops occupied it in the autumn of 1776.

The other important elements to the success of the revolution were considerable sympathy in Britain for the colonists' aspirations, and the participation of France. The latter formed a military alliance with the rebels in 1778, and dispatched an army of regular troops to assist George Washington's Continental Army. Without French help, and Spain's declaration of war that threatened Gibraltar, the poorly equipped Continental Army and the various rebel militia regiments could never have staved off the British regulars in most of the campaigns of the war.

Chapter 2: British Administration in Canada

Provincial Troops

Had Britain established a firm, sensible policy on the use of troops raised in her colonies at the outset of the revolution, the outcome of the war might easily have been different. By the end of the war when George Washington's Continental Army numbered scarcely more than 8,000 men, records show that more than 10,000 men were serving in provincial regiments in some category or other.[1] But from the outset British policy with respect to provincials was ambivalent and confused. On the one hand, the home government assumed that loyalists would come forth and help; on the other, many high-ranking British regular officers were hostile to the suggestion of any favours being granted to provincials – whom they looked upon as mere colonial farmers who lacked military bearing and were utterly unprofessional. This dichotomy had an adverse effect on the recruitment and use of provincials in Britain's North American colonies throughout the revolution.

Upon the outbreak of hostilities, loyalists tended to flock to the nearest royal standard, often a fort where a few British regulars were on duty, or to their royal governors, and where feasible, to the commander-in-chief, General Thomas Gage. Some colonial governors established loyal militia units, but Gage, and his successor, General Sir William Howe, were operating under vague guidelines emanating from the Secretary of State for the Colonies, Lord George Germain, and the War Office. In addition to the militia, men of stature in the provinces – frequently officers who were veterans of provincial or regular units from the Seven Years' War – were issued with beating warrants to raise new Provincial Corps of the British Army.

The name 'beating warrant' implied raising men by travelling through the country accompanied by a drummer, but in the case of colonies in a state of rebellion, something more furtive was necessary. A provincial corps was to be similar to a British regular regiment of foot, at least numerically. A regiment usually consisted of one battalion of ten companies, approximately 500 men. One company was of grenadiers, and one of light infantry, while the others were referred to as battalion companies. A provincial corps included a light company, but in place of grenadiers, one company was often of artificers employed in construction under an officer of the Royal

14

Engineers. At that time no corps of Engineers existed. Officers held their commissions from the Board of Ordnance, and were assigned artificers from established regiments.

The terms of the various beating warrants seemed destined to produce numbers rather than competence among the officers of provincials. A man of wealth who received permission to raise a corps was usually responsible for nominating his officers, who were to receive commissions upon raising a specified number of recruits. A captain had to raise a full company, and numerical strength varied from 50 to 60 men, depending on the terms set forth in the commanding officer's warrant. A lieutenant was required to raise half a company, an ensign a quarter. Sometimes, bounties were paid to recruits, or a man might be promised 50 acres in lieu of cash. Enlistments were for two years or until the end of the war. All provincials were to receive the same pay as officers and men in regular infantry regiments, but no provision was made for the gratuity pay allowed regular officers.

When provincial corps were serving with regulars, their officers were ranked as junior to officers the grade below them. Thus, a captain of provincials was considered a lieutenant when his unit was operating with regulars, but he was subordinate to lieutenants of regulars. Officers of provincials were not entitled to hold permanent rank, nor receive half pay when their regiments were reduced. These provisions arose in part because British regular officers declined to be placed under the command of untrained provincials of higher rank, while the prohibition on half pay was a matter of economy, a measure to prevent enlarging the lists of reduced officers.

The terms applying to provincial corps were not alluring. No provision was made for the care that was automatically part of any plan for regular regiments when these were established, namely regimental orderly rooms, hospital and nursing care, and gratuity pay for maimed and wounded officers. Discouraging to potential officers and enlisted men alike, the provincial corps were to be inferior to the regular units, intended as auxiliaries, leaving the serious fighting to the professionals. The prospect of spending their days chopping down trees to build barracks and fortifications, or cutting hay to feed the army's livestock, had scant appeal to loyalists whom the rebels had failed to identify.[2]

The consequence of such ungenerous terms was predictable. Men resident in the colonies were reluctant to serve, and the system of granting commissions led to abuses and quarrelling that were a burden on British commanders in all four departments organized for conducting the war. In the beginning, while the British government expected help from loyalists, it saw no need to offer enducements, because regular soldiers would deal with the rebels. General John Burgoyne's surrender of 5,000 troops at Saratoga in the autumn of 1777, forced a change in the approach to colonials.

Once the rebels had demonstrated their success in coping with a British army, France formed an alliance with the Continental Congress in February 1778 and Spain soon declared war on the mother country in the hope of grabbing Gibraltar. A new policy on provincial troops was imperative, for they had become indispensible. Yet, even under this pressure, the changes were slow in the making. On January 23, 1779, Lord George Germain wrote to General Sir Henry Clinton, then the commander-in-chief at New York City, with new orders for the provincial corps. Officers were to have permanent rank, and half pay upon reduction of their corps, as long as these were completed to the same strength as applied to British regiments of foot. A provincial officer who was maimed, or lost a limb, was permitted one year's pay in advance.[3]

Each recruit was entitled to a bounty of 22 shillings and 6 pence. In Canada the records show that many provincials received care in the hospitals established at Fort St. Johns and at other bases, while a surgeon and sometimes a surgeon's mate were shown on the muster rolls for some of the largest corps. Also, in all departments, the practice of downgrading provincial officers one rank was discontinued, although an officer of provincials remained inferior to an officer of regulars of like rank.

The new recruiting policy proved to be disappointing; in Canada, under General Frederick Haldimand, it was hardly implemented until 1781. Other concerns influenced Canada's Governor-in-Chief. For one thing, King George III disapproved of establishing too many new corps, whether regular or provincial. In his opinion it was better to augment existing regiments, and in any case, he was suspicious of provincials who should be 'raised for rank'. By this, he meant that colonials should serve in the ranks, while officers for the provincial corps would be drawn from among the regulars.[4] Secondly, Haldimand had serious difficulties over provisions. The population of Canada was about 100,000 when the war began, the local agriculture inefficient. Thus he was forced to import vast quantities of food, and military actions were frequently curtailed until supply fleets arrived from the mother country.

When the new policy was launched early in 1779, regiments of promise might be accepted for the British regular establishment, or placed on a special American establishment that is best described as British regulars second class. Under these provisions, the Royal

16

Highland Emigrants, with one battalion serving in Canada, joined the British regular establishment as the 84th Foot. By 1781, five corps of provincials had been put on the American establishment and numbered. The Queen's Rangers, led by Colonel John Graves Simcoe, became the 1st American Regiment; the Volunteers of Ireland was the 2nd; the New York Volunteers the 3rd; the King's American Regiment the 4th; and the British Legion the 5th. All five American regiments fought in the southern campaign, and no corps in Canada was ever elevated to this category.[5] Later the Volunteers of Ireland, 2nd American Regiment, was placed on the Irish regular establishment as the 105th Foot.[6]

By the time the revolution ended, there were four types of provincial units – militia, Provincial Corps of the British Army, regulars of the American establishment, and regulars of the British establishment.

The policies of 1779 failed to achieve the hoped for results, mainly because they were formulated too late. Many loyalists who might have come forward to enlist had decided, in order to survive, to lie low and await the outcome. Those who had been hounded and required sanctuary were inclined to serve, but others felt let down by the home government, and were disenchanted by the time the new policy was launched. Had the British government known that provincial support was vital to the execution of the war in the first months, and permitted regiments of the American establishment in the beginning, the mother country might well have succeeded in quelling the rebellion and restoring order.

Two Governors

During the revolution, two governors occupied the Chateau St. Louis, the official residence of the King's representatives in Quebec City – Sir Guy Carleton and General Frederick Haldimand. Both served Canada well, and both had disappointments. They belonged to an era when governors were meant to govern, and neither had much sympathy for democracy. Carleton was the governor at the beginning of the war, and for a second time after it ended. From the viewpoint of officers in provincial corps, Carleton was the more sympathetic superior. Haldimand viewed most provincials with misgivings and suspicion.

Guy Carleton was something of a paradox. He was cool and aloof towards his subordinates, yet he treated many of them with understanding and sympathy. He could be ruthless with an underling who exposed his faults. He was a man of vision whose actions

17

fell short when he came to implement his designs. Nevertheless, to many of his officers of the provincials, behind the chilling facade lurked a man who acted in what they felt was their best interests.

Despite valid criticisms of Carleton's shortcomings as a military commander and administrator, many provincials had a healthy respect for him. In turn, he placed more confidence in the abilities of colonials than did his successor, General Frederick Haldimand. Had Carleton remained on duty in Canada, he might have made more effective use of his provincial troops. When he left the province in 1778, the frontier war in the north, fought mainly by loyalists, was only beginning, and upon his return in 1786 he was dealing with them as settlers, not fighting men.

Guy Carleton was born in 1724 of Anglo-Irish parents. The future governor of Canada chose a military career and became a close friend of James Wolfe, who wanted him for his expedition against Louisbourg in 1758. Carleton was a lieutenant-colonel in the 72nd Regiment, but he was sent instead to Germany.[7] Wolfe was annoyed, but Carleton had spoken disparagingly of Hanovarian troops which had offended King George II.

When Wolfe was preparing his expedition against Quebec, he again asked for Carleton, and the King relented. Guy served as Wolfe's quartermaster-general; at the Battle of the Plains of Abraham he was wounded, although not seriously. In 1761, Carleton returned to Britain, but five years later he came back to Quebec as Governor James Murray's deputy. In January 1768 he succeeded Murray as Governor of Canada.[8]

Carleton's early years as Governor of Canada were a highlight in his career, as he sought to win the friendship of the French-speaking subjects for his King. He argued that Canada deserved special status, that her own traditions should be respected. To implement English civil law was impracticable, and it would be cruel to follow the practice of denying Roman Catholics the right to hold public office. Carleton fought for these principles, and for a constitution that would recognize the right of Roman Catholics to practice their religion and to perpetuate their own institutions. The achievement of this constitution did not come easily. Not until the summer of 1774 did the Quebec Act receive final assent.

Unfortunately, once the Quebec Act became law, Carleton was unable to implement the constitution to the satisfaction of his subjects. He failed to grasp certain facts about the people he governed, possibly because he equated the seigneurs of Canada with the Irish landed gentry from which he had sprung. The French seigneurial system had been a failure for the seigneurs. As landlords they were unable to prosper because the seigneuries were under-populated, and the tenants had alternatives not available to peasants in France. In Canada, a tenant who did not get on with his seigneur could move, or turn to lumbering or the fur trade. The real leaders of the people were captains of militia, elected by the residents of the parishes.

Carleton failed to recognize the impotence of the seigneurs on their more than half-empty estates. When he appointed his first Legislative Council, he retained some Protestant members and added seven Roman Catholics, all seigneurs. Such were remote from the common folk, and by allying himself with the seigneurs, Carleton alienated the good will of the militia captains and the masses.

Next Carleton alienated another group that might have served him well. Since the fall of New France, English-speaking merchants and traders had moved into Canada. Some were from British colonies, some from the mother country. The Quebec Act guaranteed the continuance of French civil law, but the British government intended that English civil law be used in cases where an English resident was involved, and to preserve the right of habeas corpus. [8] In failing to implement limited use of English civil law, Carleton lost the sympathy of the English residents by creating the impression that the mother country had denied them their rights as British subjects. Oblivious to the rising resentment, Carleton was convinced that his province stood as a bastion of loyalty against the swelling tide of rebellion to the south. He readily agreed to send two regiments to Boston in 1774 in response to an urgent appeal from General Thomas Gage. When the rebels led by Montgomery and Benedict Arnold arrived on his doorstep the following year, Carleton was taken by surprise. Attempting to marshall support, he found that most of the Canadian militia would not turn out, while some of the English-speaking residents sympathized with the aims of the Continental Congress. Carleton rallied enough support to keep the rebels at bay, but he had to call upon Britain for reinforcements. Not until General John Burgoyne arrived with fresh troops was Carleton able to drive the rebels from his province and seize the initiative. [9]

As a soldier, Carleton demonstrated a gap between theory and practice. In February 1767, he urged the strengthening of the Lake Champlain and Lake George routes by restoring Crown Point, Ticonderoga and Fort George. Had his advice been accepted, Britain would have kept her colonies divided, making communication by land awkward. Yet when Carleton led his expedition against the

19

rebels in the autumn of 1776, he did not follow his own advice. He occupied Crown Point with a strong army, but failed to push on and take Fort Ticonderoga, which he could have done. Instead, he decided that the season was too far advanced and took his army back to Canada for the winter, intending to try again. When a British army re-entered New York State in the spring of 1777, the rebels were better prepared to meet it.

Carleton could have captured the entire force that invaded Canada, but his pursuit of the rebels was so leisurely that he let them escape. One excuse offered is that he wanted to be lenient with people who were themselves British, even though temporarily misguided. Later Sir Guy felt compelled to defend himself in the face of charges that he had been soft on the rebels. Having promised, if he were reinforced, to occupy the posts along Lake Champlain, once he got the troops he failed to deliver.

Sir Guy also had no love for the Colonial Secretary, Lord George Germain, and many versions blame the latter. Because Germain was cashiered in 1759, Carleton despised him, and his dispatches were not cordial. When Burgoyne reached Canada from Britain in the spring of 1777, Carleton resigned, not because he was no longer the commander of the expedition, but because Burgoyne had superseded him as military governor. Affronted by the demotion to civil governor, Carleton agreed to remain in Canada until his replacement arrived. When Burgoyne was in New York State with his floundering army, he admitted that Carleton could not have been more helpful. Although angry with the home government, Carleton stood by his brother officers. [10]

Carleton's successor in 1778 was General Frederick Haldimand. The new Governor lacked Carleton's self-confidence, partly because he was a foreigner in the service of Britain, partly from shyness. He was more comfortable with a few intimates than before a crowd. Although unimaginative he was meticulous, paid close attention to detail, and left very complete records of his administration. He viewed all colonials with misgivings be they Canadian or American. Haldimand adhered to the policy he brought with him, that new regiments were not to be formed but established ones might be enlarged. He was unhappy over some of the situations he inherited and had to accept. To officers of provincial corps, he was more frustrating to deal with than Sir Guy Carleton.

Frederick Haldimand was a Swiss professional soldier, born in 1718 at Neuchatel, into a French-speaking Protestant family. Switzerland encouraged her sons to seek service in foreign armies. Young Frederick began his military career in Prussia, and later he was in the Swiss Guards serving in the Netherlands.

With the approach of the Seven Years' War, Britain decided to raise provincial troops in her American colonies. In Pennsylvania and other provinces were Swiss and German Protestant settlers who were potential recruits. Officers conversant in German were needed, although the colonel must be British. In 1756, forty German-speaking officers arrived at New York City to serve under Lord Loudoun, the colonel-in-chief of a new regiment, the 60th Foot or Royal American Regiment. Frederick Haldimand received the command of a battalion with the rank of lieutenant-colonel. He accompanied General James Abercromby on his abortive attempt to capture Fort Ticonderoga. Haldimand led the grenadiers in the assault and was wounded. Later, with his battalion he was sent to rebuild the forts at Oswego, which the French had destroyed three years earlier.[11]

Haldimand went with General John Prideaux on the expedition to capture Fort Niagara in 1759. Prideaux was killed, and Haldimand, the highest ranking regular officer, expected to assume command. Sir William Johnson declared himself the leader, and Haldimand was too astute to challenge the Mohawk Valley potentate. He wrote to Lord Jeffrey Amherst, the commander-in-chief, explaining that he would rather serve under Johnson than cause unpleasantness. The other approved, for Johnson's support was essential to keep the Six Nations Indians on Britain's side.[12] The Swiss officer was on Amherst's expedition down the St. Lawrence to the capitulation of Montreal in 1760, and on that journey he acquired information valuable when the defence of Canada became his responsibility.

After Montreal surrendered, Haldimand was the military governor of Trois Rivières. He carried out many useful works, improving the road from Montreal to Quebec City and increasing the output of bog iron smelted at the forges of St. Maurice. His next posting was as governor of West Florida, exchanged with Spain for Havana in 1763. Haldimand remained on duty from 1767 until 1773, when General Thomas Gage wanted a leave of absence. That spring Haldimand took up residence in New York City. By that time he had become a naturalized British subject. While in New York, the Boston Tea Party occurred, and he scornfully described it as that 'Indian caper.' He was having his first experience with people who expected to govern themselves and he was not impressed. [13]

With the worsening situation in the colonies, General Thomas Gage returned with troops and occupied Boston, leaving Haldimand on duty in New York, where restive rebels burned Lord North in effigy. Late in the autumn of 1774, Haldimand joined Gage in Boston with reinforcements and moral support. He was also concerned for the safety of his property. Everywhere he went Haldimand acquired belongings, in this case a house, poultry and a garden in New York City. During his absence the mob stole everything movable, and General Washington occupied the house. [14]

In 1775, Haldimand was recalled. General Gage wanted to retire, and the Swiss professional was a logical successor. The home government wanted the post to go to a native-born officer, and appointed Sir William Howe. For three years Haldimand was on duty in England. When Sir Guy Carleton resigned in 1777, Haldimand was appointed governor-in-chief of Canada.

On his arrival at Quebec in June 1778 Haldimand immediately seized the reins. He was responsible for a vast sweep of territory – as far west as Michilimackinac – and his regular troops amounted to some 4,000 British and 2,000 Germans. He also had three below-strength provincial corps – the Royal Highland Emigrants, the King's Royal Regiment of New York and Butler's Rangers – but all other provincials in Canada were not his concern. To Haldimand these provincials were refugees, entitled to provisions, but they were not part of his Northern Department.

Although his own garrison was weak, Haldimand was a stickler for rules. He could not afford to allow recruits to join regiments that might one day be removed to their proper departments. Haldimand's experience during the Seven Years' War had left him wary of all colonials, both for their political allegiance and their fighting abilities. He feared that loyalists in Canada might have spies among them, sent by the rebels to serve as informers. For the same reason he ordered refugee families to be housed in the nearly vacant parish of Machiche on the north shore of the St. Lawrence opposite Sorel. There they were separate from the French speaking inhabitants, making communication between the two groups awkward. In Haldimand's opinion too much seditious literature was circulating in the seigneuries and he wanted to render impotent any rebel spies hiding among the loyalists. [15]

The governor was equally suspicious of the French, within and without his province. The military alliance France made with the Continental Congress worried him. He thought he might marshal enough support to repel a rebel attack, but he feared the story would be different if they arrived accompanied by French regulars. Naturally, the Canadians would resume their former allegiance. Haldimand reckoned that his hold on Canada was tenuous.

His fears seemed justified because Moses Hazen, a veteran of

Rogers' Rangers living near Fort St. Johns, had joined the rebels and raised a battalion of disenchanted Canadians for service with the Continental Congress. [16] He was further disturbed when Pierre du Calvet, of Montreal, was caught exchanging messages with the rebels. Because his province seemed so insecure, Haldimand was cautious about allowing provincials to act, lest the rebels retaliate and force him to defend his territory. The safety of Canada, and Haldimand's innate thrift, were to bedevil the efforts of provincial troops wanting to strike back at their enemies throughout the last five years of the war.

The governor also fretted over money, fearful of reprimands for spending more than London authorized. On many occasions he pointed out to provincial officers that he did not operate under the same rules as the Central Department of New York, although he never explained why he could not avail himself of directives sent from London that were implemented at New York City. As he explained to Sir John Johnson, there were differences:

> To the Southward, Subscriptions are Successfully carried on for these purposes – here the Whole Burdon falls upon Government, and it is not a light one, nor have I the authority to incur the expence attending it. [17]

He was replying to a request that a loyalist be put on the subsistence list and provisioned. The governor pointed out that wealthy people in New York City had the resources to aid loyalists, while such bounty was not available in his department.

Haldimand's stance was generally defensive; Canada's security came first. But in 1780, he was more amenable to allowing his provincials some latitude. He authorized Sir John Johnson's raids into the Mohawk Valley, and he did not try to restrain Butler's Rangers along the frontier. He also relented and allowed recruiting in the hope of completing other corps and independent companies. By the autumn of 1781, he was willing to increase the numbers of provincials in his department because he feared an attack on Canada. Unable to obtain large numbers of regulars to reinforce his garrison, Haldimand resolved to take second-best, loyalists from the colonies. But he continued to keep a close watch on their activities. Resounding in the ears of officers who consulted with Haldimand were exhortations to treat all prisoners with the greatest civility and humanity. No matter what the rebels did, Haldimand would tolerate no breaches of the rules of war by his provincials. Yet despite the governor's warning, some outrages were perpetrated by loyalists in his service.

Haldimand was rarely impressed by his provincial troops, yet he was humane in caring for helpless refugees, taking on responsi-

Northern Department Sphere of Operations 1775-83

1781 ✳
✳ **1718**
Forts at Michilimackinac

lake michigan

lake huron

lake ontario

Fort Niagara ✳

buffalo creek

genesee river

Fort Detroit ✳

lake erie

N.Y.

Penna.

sandusky river

allegheny river

Territory Ceded to Canada, Quebec Act, 1774

Fort Pitt
✳ **(Pittsburgh)**

ohio river

monongahela river

potomac river

licking river

Blue Licks

kentucky river

Boone's Station

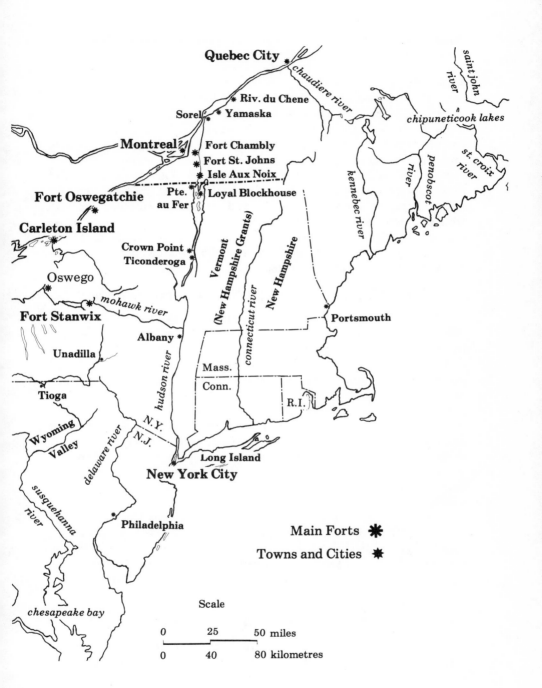

Quebec City

Riv. du Chene
Sorel *Yamaska*

Montreal
Fort Chambly
Fort St. Johns
Isle Aux Noix
Fort Oswegatchie
Pte. Loyal Blockhouse
au Fer
Carleton Island

Crown Point
Ticonderoga

Oswego

Fort Stanwix

mohawk river

Albany

Unadilla

Tioga

Wyoming
Valley

delaware river

*susquehanna
river*

New York City

Philadelphia

Long Island

chaudiere river

*saint john
river*

chipuneticook lakes

*st. croix
river*

kennebec river

*penobscot
river*

Vermont
(New Hampshire Grants)

New Hampshire

connecticut river

hudson river

Portsmouth

Mass.

Conn.

R.I.

N.Y.

N.J.

Main Forts ✱

Towns and Cities ✱

chesapeake bay

Scale

| 0 | 25 | 50 miles |

| 0 | 40 | 80 kilometres |

25

bilities for which he had no authority. People without clothing and shelter could not await orders from far off London. A bachelor, the governor fostered the careers of numerous nephews, and he treated some of the families of his subordinates as though they were his own. He was godfather to Kanada von Riedesel, the daughter of the German Commander-in-chief, born at Sorel in 1783, who lived only a few months. In the spring of 1783, when Haldimand ordered Justus Sherwood to come to Quebec City, that officer brought his wife and three children in order to show them to the governor.

As he had following the Seven Years' War, Haldimand did many constructive things. He had a shallow canal dug at Côteau du Lac to bypass the Cedars Rapids, and he wanted to obtain priests from countries other than France for his Canadians. He established a postal service, and schools for Canadians and loyalists' children. He ordered the first census of Canada, which showed 113,012 people, with 28,000 fit to bear arms.

The Northern and Indian Departments

With the approach of overt hostilities, there existed in North America the skeletons of two potential military establishments – the British regular army and the Indian Department. Detachments of British soldiers under the command of General Thomas Gage guarded the colonies' military installations. Within the colonies were two sources of support for the regulars: the veterans of the Seven Years' War who had settled in the new world afterward, and the local militia units. However, both these sources were divided and supplied talent to each side in the conflict. Horatio Gates, for example, was a former British officer who joined the Continental Army, the rebels' regular troops, while that army's commander-in-chief, George Washington, had been a colonel in the Virginia Militia.

The other potential military organization was the Indian Department. Because of the existence of this department, with its own established traditions, the responsibility for the operations in the northern theatre of the war was divided between the Governor-in-Chief of Canada, and the Superintendent of Indian Affairs, Northern District.

The Northern Department

To conduct the operations for quelling the rebellion in the Thirteen Colonies, the War Office organized four military departments in key locations where it was possible to establish bases that were difficult for the rebels to capture. The Central Department was at New York City, which the British army occupied in the autumn of 1776, and held until after the peace treaty was signed in 1783. There the commander-in-chief was in residence – in succession, Generals Thomas Gage, Sir William Howe, Sir Henry Clinton, and Sir Guy Carleton. The governors of the other three divisions were usually subordinate to the commander at New York. These departments were the Southern, based on Florida, the Eastern (or Northeastern) which was Nova Scotia, and the Northern, which was the Canadian (or Quebec) sector.

The headquarters of the Northern Department was the Chateau St. Louis, the residence of the governor-in-chief, in Quebec City. Commanded by Governor Carleton from 1774 until 1778, and by Governor Haldimand for the remainder of the war, the territory of the Northern Department was vast, including as it did all the land placed under British rule by the Quebec Act of 1774. The only densely settled parts lay along the lower St. Lawrence and Richelieu rivers, which were protected by a string of fortified sites: Quebec City, Montreal, Chambly, St. Johns and Isle aux Noix. As the war progressed, Sorel became a stronghold, and blockhouses were added at Rivière du Chene, Yamaska, Pointe au Fer and at North Hero Island on Lake Champlain. In the largely unsettled wilderness to the west was a chain of forts: Oswegatchie on the upper St. Lawrence, Niagara, Detroit and Michilimackinac along the Great Lakes and inland at Pittsburgh, where the Allegheny and Monongahela rivers enter the Ohio. There Fort Pitt was captured by the rebels and held throughout the war.[19] To these forts, Governor Haldimand added Carleton Island in 1778; and in 1782 Oswego, empty since the Seven Years' War, was reoccupied.

Present at each of what Haldimand called his upper posts – those to the west of the settled parts of the province – were Indian agents or commissaries, and traders as well as troops. The presence of representatives of the Indian Department complicated the military jurisdictions by dividing them, and posed a dilemma for the commander-in-chief of the Northern Department. The Indian Department had a measure of independence, but the security of the far-flung posts was the responsibility of the governor. However, the Indian Department was a source of wealth, for individuals and the government; the governors hesitated to interfere with it.

In the autumn of 1782, for the better administration of his sprawling domain, Governor Haldimand divided the province into six military districts each under a commandant. Quebec District encompassed the north shore of the St. Lawrence to a point west of

Machiche, under Major-General Alured Clarke. Kamouraska was the south shore of the river as far west as Beancour, under Major General de Loos. Beancour District included the north end of Lake Champlain, La Prairie on the St. Lawrence, and Sorel under Major-General the Baron Friedrich von Riedesel. Machiche was the north shore west to Montreal, under Brigadier Ernst von Speth. Montreal District included the island and Ile Jesus and part of both shores, under Brigadier Barry St. Leger. Oswegatchie took in all the western posts from that fort to Michilimackinac, and was commanded by Brigadier Allan Maclean, who made Fort Niagara his home base. In addition to the district commanders, the Provincial Marine, of which William Chambers, R.N. was the commanding captain, assisted all the district officials and reported directly to the commander-in-chief.[20]

The Indian Department

At the onset of the revolution the headquarters of the Northern District of the Indian Department was Fort Niagara, where the superintendent had his official residence – the stone building the Indians called the French Castle, because the French had built it. References to the Indian Department in documents are legion, but very little information exists on exactly how it was constituted, and where its powers began and ended. A policy of having agents who represented the British government among the Indians had begun years earlier at behest of the Lords of Trade and Plantations, the administrative body formed during the reign of King Charles II to supervise the British colonies in America.[21]

The Indian Department evolved gradually. In the beginning it was a joint project, a less than holy alliance between the Lords of Trade and the Society for the Propagation of the Gospel. For the former, profit was the issue, for the latter, missions to Christianize the native peoples who came to the various frontier posts to trade their furs. As the rivalry between Britain and France for the control of the fur trade intensified, Indian Affairs began to take on military overtones. The man who emerged with considerable prestige among the natives was William Johnson. In 1738, at the age of twenty-three, he had left his native Ireland and settled in the Mohawk Valley. He entered the fur trade, and acquired vast holdings from the Mohawk Indians, allowing the former owners such free access to it that they did not realize they had been deprived of their property. Once Johnson's own fortune was assured, he became the defender of the sanctity of Indian lands, often standing in the way of other white men who sought to emulate him.

In 1746, the Lords of Trade appointed Johnson a Commissary for Indian Affairs, to bring in trade goods and distribute them, and on August 28 of that year he was named 'Colonel of the Forces to be raised out of the Six Nations.'[22] In 1755, on the eve of the Seven Years' War, General Edward Braddock, then the commander of British forces in North America, appointed William Johnson Superintendent of Indian Affairs, Northern District. He would deal mainly with the Iroquois and their allies who lived between the British colonies and New France.[23]

In 1764, Sir William was knighted for his part in the late war. But the military role of Indian Affairs did not end with the Peace Treaty of 1763. There remained French residents near several of the frontier posts who might stir up mischief, and the famous Ottawa chief, Pontiac, was formenting unrest among the tribes to the west. Johnson's commissaries at the various forts were known by military ranks, although it is not clear who authorized these commissions. Johnson may have had permission from the Lords of Trade, or perhaps his agents were addressed by ranks they held in the militia. Sir Guy Carleton, as Governor-in-Chief of Canada in 1775, may have originated the practice of granting commissions within the Indian Department as an emergency measure. Later, Governor Haldimand informed Lord Townsend, of the Lords of Trade, that Carleton had to give temporary appointments which his successor could not reduce, owing to the nature of the times.[24]

When Guy Johnson became the Superintendent in 1774 after the death of Sir William, one of his deputies was Daniel Claus. Both men were Sir William's sons-in-law. Alexander McKee was the deputy stationed at Fort Pitt, near the village of Pittsburgh. As the winds of discontent began to blow along the Mohawk River, the stage was set for the valley to become a battleground between the rebels and the supporters of the powerful Johnson family. Of the latter faction, Guy Johnson was the weakest link, Sir William's widow, Molly Brant, his heir, Sir John, and John Butler the strongest. With Molly at the several posts where she stayed were her six daughters, Elizabeth, Magdalene, Margaret, Mary, Susannah and Anne. Her son George, probably the youngest, attended school in Montreal, while her other son Peter held a commission in the 26th Regiment of Foot.

When the rebel invasion of 1775-76, threatened the security of Canada, Governor Guy Carleton, with the collusion of John Butler, organized the Indian Department into a military force, granting commissions to officers within that establishment, to lead native warriors into action. Trade was still important, but for the safety of commerce as well as the defeat of the rebels, Carleton felt he had to ensure that the natives would remain neutral, or actively assist Britain. The relationship between the Northern Department and the Indian Department, Northern District, was a complex one, for General Haldimand, Carleton's successor, and for students of the period. Haldimand's records indicate that the men who led the Indians, both native and white, were on the same footing as officers in provincial corps.[25]

Part Two: The Provincial Corps, Northern Department

Chapter 3: The Role of the Provincials

At the time of the Declaration of Independence, on July 4, 1776, one Provincial Corps of the British Army had been attached to the Northern Department for nearly a year. By the time the Treaty of Separation had been signed on September 3, 1783, there were five: the Royal Highland Emigrants, the King's Royal Regiment of New York, Butler's Rangers, the Loyal Rangers and the King's Rangers.

The title, Provincial Corps of the British Army, is explicit, and the history of these regiments' role in the American Revolution on behalf of the Northern Department does not encompass the full participation by loyal colonials in the defence of Canada and excursions there-from into rebel territory. The governor-in-chief of Canada could also call upon the services of two militia forces, one anglophone, referred to as the British militia in the records, and one francophone, called the Canadian militia in the same sources. The role of the militia is beyond the purview of this work, yet some groups must, at least, be defined or many important questions would go unanswered, especially concerning the American loyalists who came to Canada before, during and after the war.

These loyalists have been classified as incorporated, unincorporated, or members of associations. Those called incorporated were serving in the provincial corps. Certain of the unincorporated ones came into Canada as refugees, and were assigned to provincial units for provisioning, but did not enlist. Other unincorporated men formed small, informal units which may have aspired to the status of provincial corps, but never became large enough. The term associated loyalists is the most ambiguous of all, and it meant different things at different times. The name occurs most often in the records of the Central Department to apply to a group at New York City not in the provincial corps who asked for permission to harry the rebels along the coast. The King approved, allowing commissions, but 'without Pay or Rank in the Army or Command over other Corps.'[1]

Serving in the Northern Department in addition to the militia and the five provincial corps were four units whose names crop up in correspondence and other sources with no information as to their status. One such was Joseph Brant's Volunteers, a hint that the Mohawk leader aspired to raise a provincial corps. It was composed of Indians and white settlers from the Mohawk Valley. A second was the Loyal Foresters, who were mentioned with Brant's men on a 'Return of Persons under the Description of Loyalists encamped near Fort Niagara' on December 1, 1783.[2] The third mysterious group was the Detroit Volunteers, raised among the residents in that neighbourhood.[3] Many were francophones, whose families had been there since before the Seven Years' War, or disbanded British regulars who chose to remain in the vicinity afterward. The fort commanders instituted compulsory service in the militia, and the denomination 'volunteer' seems to imply willingness, as against coercion. The French-speaking volunteers may account for references in some of the mythology on Daniel Boone wherein French Canadians invaded the Kentucky country during the revolution.[4]

Lastly are the references to Colonel Daniel Claus's rangers. In April 1781, writing to Sir John Johnson on the need for accurate information about developments within the rebelling colonies, Governor Haldimand asked him to look for reliable men 'in your Corps, or among the Rangers Colonel Claus employs.'[5] His references leave no doubt that Claus's rangers were a separate group from the provincial corps, and from the Mohawks who gathered near Montreal after fleeing from their homeland.

Brant's Volunteers, the Loyal Foresters, and Claus's rangers were closely associated with the Indian Department, and the first two groups went to Fort Niagara. Later, they were resettled among the men of butler's Rangers when the war ended. Many of Claus's men were residents of Montreal who had not lost their homes. The Detroit Volunteers had homes intact, although many shifted to the east side of the Detroit River to make sure they would be inside British territory.

Another activity was the bateau service. One company of King's Loyal Americans was drafted for that service during Burgoyne's campaign. With Colonel St. Leger's smaller expedition through the Mohawk Valley at that time, the bateaux were in charge of Hon Jost Herkimer, a brother of rebel General Nicholas Herkimer whose column was ambushed at Oriskany. Later, in September 1780, Hon received the command of a company of bateaumen at Côteau du Lac.

Since none of these units was official, the men must have been regarded as unincorporated loyalists. Those who were refugees after the Peace Treaty was signed were entitled to land as heads of families, but not military grants.

Some American Loyalists and many Canadians served as officers and seamen in the ships of the Provincial Marine. Senior officers were seconded from the Royal Navy, but the vessels and bateaux were manned in part by colonials. When the revolution began, such men were also required as artificiers to help construct the fleets. Vessels were keelboats, rigged as sloops, snows or brigantines. A gunboat was flat-bottomed and oared; a bateau was also oared and flat-bottomed, and usually carried a lateen sail. The actual number of provincials in the Naval Department can not be determined accurately, for most records apply to the men seconded from the Royal Navy. A safe estimate would be approximately 300 residents of Canada or loyalists from the rebelling colonies. This service will be described in more detail in chapter 11.

Chapter 4: The Royal Highland Emigrants (84th Foot)

The first battalion, Royal Highland Emigrants, was the earliest provincial corps to be attached to the Northern Department, and the only one serving in Canada that was put on the British regular establishment. This corps was different because the majority of the men who enlisted were residents of Canada. In the other regiments the enlistments were nearly all American loyalists driven from the Thirteen Colonies, or volunteers recruited by agents who visited them clandestinely in their homes. Some Royal Highland Emigrants were veterans of the Seven Years' War who had settled along the lower St. Lawrence. A few were rebel prisoners who chose service as an alternative to confinement, and a detachment hailed from Newfoundland. For a time the regiment also included a 'French Company,' maintaining that traditional Franco-Scottish friendship. A return of His Majesty's 84th Regiment of Foot dated January 1, 1783, at Carleton Island, states that of a total of 520 officers and men, 94 were English, 119 'Scotch,' 174 Irish, and 133 were 'Foreign.'[1] Thus the name given the corps was rather misleading.

Some who joined had come to North America to serve in the Fraser Highlanders, 78th Foot, and elected to settle in Canada when the regiment was disbanded after the Seven Years' War. Often Roman Catholic, they inter-married with the Canadians. Their offspring grew up bilingual in French and Gaelic, thereby making the corps trilingual. Those who joined from the rebelling colonies, generally the Mohawk Valley, were Highlanders who had settled there in 1773, as tenants of the Johnson family.

The commanding officer, Allan Maclean, and some junior officers, were seconded from British regular regiments, and some returned to Britain when the war ended. The safe location of the homes of most rank and file, and the fact that many were veteran-regulars made them less unruly than other provincials, and more satisfactory in the opinion of a professional soldier like Haldimand. Not one native-born Highlander deserted, and only one was brought to the halberts for punishment.[2]

Allan Maclean

Allan Maclean, the commanding officer of the Royal Highland Emigrants, was the third son of Major Donald Maclean, fifth laird of Torloisk, Isle of Mull, Scotland.

Margaret Clephane, Maclean's great-niece, wrote to a friend:

*Allan Maclean, commander of the 84th Foot Royal Highland
Emigrants. From a miniature in Duart Castle. In regiments
permitted Highland dress, officers and sergeants ran their sashes
through the epaulette. In other regiments sashes were worn round
the waist. Allan married Janet Maclean of Brolass. Her brother
and half brother were chiefs of clan Maclean, which may explain
why the miniature is in the Duart collection. Courtesy: The Right
Honourable Lord Maclean, K.T., G.C.V.O., K.B.E., the 27th chief.*

his history would make a novel; he once passed through the American Camp in the disguise of a quack doctor, and sold a whole box of physic to the Yankees, and reached the British headquarters.[3]

Allan was born in 1725, when the population of the Highlands was still smoldering over the defeat of the Jacobites ten years before. Under the English General, George Wade, the clansmen had been disarmed and pacified by force. Clan Maclean was defeated in 1691 by clan Campbell, its lands forfeited to the Duke of Argyll, from whom Allan's family leased Torloisk. The clan rose for the Old Pretender, and again when the son, Prince Charles, landed and planted his standard at Glenfinnan in 1745. Allan was twenty years old and he served as a lieutenant in a battalion of clan Maclean at the Battle of Culloden in 1746. The following year Allan Maclean was in the service of the Netherlands, in the Scots Brigade, at a time when his fellow Highlanders were being pacified even more brutally than after the rising of 1715. Because he had joined Bonnie Prince Charlie, Maclean had gone into exile. The armies of many European powers offered a means of survival to the warlike Highlanders.

Maclean served in the Scots Brigade until 1750, when King George II offered amnesty to Jacobite officers who pledged allegiance to the House of Hanover. Once the Seven Years' War became a certainty, the British government began raising troops, especially seasoned veterans. Having the quarrelsome Highlanders fight Britain's wars provided a solution to keeping them out of mischief in their own country. On January 8, 1756, Maclean was commissioned a lieutenant in the 62nd Regiment of Foot, later renumbered the 60th. The following year Maclean received a captaincy to command an independent company of New York provincials, and he served on the frontiers of North America that lay between New York and New France.[4]

He was severely wounded in the summer of 1758, during General Abercromby's failure to capture Fort Ticonderoga, when that incompetent man tried a frontal assault without adequate artillery. The following year, he was wounded again while with the expedition led by Sir William Johnson that captured Fort Niagara from its French garrison.[5] When the war ended in North America in 1760, Maclean returned to Britain and was appointed the major commandant of another new regiment, the Royal Highland Volunteers, 114th Foot. With his corps he sailed to North America and served until the war ended in 1763.

Allan was bilingual, and probably spoke French as well. Gaelic was the mother tongue of the Highlanders, and he used it to command men who in many instances knew no other language. He acquired English from tutors, or at a boarding school on the mainland, for he wrote it correctly and with some zest. The elaborate phrases in his letters must have brightened the day for many a jaded superior during the American Revolution. Towards the end of the war he informed Governor Haldimand that Butler's Ratgers 'would rather go to Japan than go among the Americans, where they could never live in peace.'[6]

After so much experience Maclean was well qualified for the commission he received in 1775 to raise the Royal Highland Emigrants. He was aware of the many Highlanders who had served in North America and had remained there, taking advantage of the chance to start afresh, away from their now desolate, impoverished homeland. To the British government, Maclean pointed out that his people could be a bulwark of loyalty against the American rebels. He thought that:

the Associations then beginning to be formed by the Rebels might receive a very Effectual check by engaging proper persons who had influence among the aforesaid Emigrants to form Counter-Associations which, with the assistance of the Loyal part of the Natives, and both being properly supported by His Majesty's Governors and the Commanders might, if adopted in time, have produced very salutary Effects without having recourse to arms.[7]

King George III approved a commission for Maclean, who embarked in May to report to General Thomas Gage, the commander-in-chief of His Majesty's forces, who was then in Boston.

Maclean was commissioned to raise five battalions from the British provinces, and as an inducement, each man who enlisted was to receive 50 shillings bounty money. A battalion was to consist of 10 companies, and each company required the following: 1 field officer or captain, 2 subalterns, 3 sergeants, 3 corporals, 2 drummers and 50 private men.

Each battalion was entitled to the following officers: 1 colonel-in-chief, 1 lieutenant-colonel commandant, 2 major commandants, 17 captains, 20 lieutenants, 18 ensigns, 2 adjutants, 2 quartermasters, 2 surgeons, 2 surgeon's mates and 1 chaplain.[8] Full strength for each battalion was to be 648 all ranks, and when completed the regiment would have 3,240 officers and men.

To be known as the Royal Highland Emigrants, the men were to be uniformed according to His Majesty's Highland regiments, in this case, the kilt of Black Watch tartan with matching plaid, described as 'Old Government Tartan.' The red coat was faced with dark blue, denoting a Royal regiment, the bonnet dark blue and flat with a royal blue tourie. After 1778, the raised bonnet was introduced, with a red pompom and red/white, blue/red, and red/white dicing round the headband. The hose were red and white in Argyle pattern, the sporran, normally of badger pelt, was racoon, possibly because that animal was more plentiful in the new world.

The uniform was a not very subtle lure. Few sons of the Highland glens, or grandsons fed on tales of the past, could resist the chance to don the well loved native dress, proscribed since the public airing it had had at Culloden Moor in 1746. A man willing to serve the Hanoverian monarch, 'German Geordie,' could sport the kilt once more. Highlanders had grabbed the bait during the Seven Years' War, and could be relied upon to repeat their performance. Fighting was second nature to them, and almost any excuse to take up the claymore and go to war was sufficient. The men were issued at first with the fuzee, then a newer flintlock musket, and eventually with Brown Bess, the pride of the regulars. Pistols and dirks were permitted, but the officers and men had to provide their own.[9] A list of the materials for an officer's uniform, gold lace and gold accoutrements, showed that the cost of his clothing was £14. 4s. 3½d., for the arms £10. 8s. 6d.; and for his tent £0. 19s. 2½d.

The first loyal colonial who offered his services to Maclean was John Munro, a resident of Shaftesbury, in the part of Charlotte County, New York, that later was included in Vermont.[10] From New York City Maclean sailed for Boston, leaving Munro behind with instructions to seek out recruits. After General Gage gave Maclean his commission for the five battalions, he ordered him to assemble his men near Lake Champlain and march them to Boston, but 'should they be formed in Canada you will act under Command of General Carleton until further orders.'

A monumental task faced the energetic, no-nonsense Maclean, and he wasted no time. By June 14 he had signed more than twenty officers, of which seven were Macleans.[10] Some of the men had come to Boston in anticipation of receiving commissions, while others were seconded from regular regiments in the neighbourhood. Maclean issued them with beating warrants authorizing them to go in quest of recruits throughout the colonies. The warrant implied marching through the countryside accompanied by a drummer thumping to attract attention. For agents operating in colonies on the verge of erupting in rebellion something more furtive might have been less hazardous.

Maclean sent his officers out singly or in pairs, and entered into a summer of cloak and dagger intrigue. First he headed back to New York City where John Munro warned him that he was in great danger of being taken prisoner. Maclean wrote:

I divested myself of every military appearance, and secured my papers, etc., on board the Asia man-of-war, and at the risk of his life he [Munro] conducted me

Not long after, Munro was captured and clapped in Albany gaol.

Two officers were taken prisoner by the rebels while recruiting in North Carolina. Major Donald McDonald and the battalion's chaplain, the Reverend John Bethune, were apprehended and taken to Philadelphia. Both were freed in 1777 when General Sir William Howe, Gage's successor, occupied that city and drove the rebels inland. Eventually both McDonald and Bethune joined the regiment in Canada. Mentioned in the same report was a Captain Macleod, whose name does not appear on any extant list of officers. Ambushed while he was leading a party of recruits towards Canada, Macleod and his men were killed.

Allan Maclean found that he could not assemble his corps near Lake Champlain for the march to Boston. Ethan Allen and his Green Mountain Boys had seized the forts at Ticonderoga and Crown Point in May 1775, and the lake was controlled by his people. Maclean chose a logical alternative, well known to him from the Seven Years' War, and turned his steps towards the Mohawk Valley. He led his officers into Tryon County where, under the leadership of the Johnson family, the populace was supposed to be loyal. Maclean hoped to get recruits, but even there he found he had to be cautious. Settlers from Connecticut had formed a Committee of Safety and begun harassing local loyalists. Sir John Johnson, guarded by loyal, brawny Highland tenants, received Maclean's party, but his cousin, Guy Johnson, the Superintendent of Indian Affairs, had left for Oswego with several officers of his department.

Around Johnstown Maclean recruited 400 men, most of them Highlanders who had settled in the vicinity in 1773, at the invitation of Sir John's father, Sir William Johnson. Conveying them to Canada was as risky as trying to march to Boston, for the rebels had disarmed the local loyalists. Stripped of the means to protect themselves, Maclean realized he would lose many of them along the way. With his officers he headed for Oswego and descended the St. Lawrence River. He left some of the officers in Montreal to get recruits and went on to Quebec City to meet Governor Carleton.[12]

The colonel from Scotland did not come unannounced. On July 20, the *Quebec Gazette* had reported that Maclean would be raising two battalions of Royal Highland Emigrants, and on August 19 it published the terms of enlistment to attract recruits.[13] In its earlier statement the newspaper was prophetic. The five battalions envisaged by General Gage turned out to be too optimistic. Maclean raised only one battalion, and it was attached to the Northern Department for the whole of the revolutionary war. A second battalion was raised, mainly in Nova Scotia, Prince Edward Island and Newfoundland, and was part of the Eastern (Northeastern) Department. Consisting of ten companies, each of 75 men, five companies did duty in Nova Scotia, while five were sent to the armies commanded by Sir Henry Clinton, General Howe's successor at New York City, and to Lord Charles Cornwallis, in charge of the southern campaign. Men of the second battalion were present at the Battle of Eutaw Springs, the capture of Savannah, Georgia, and the surrender at Yorktown, Virginia. After the war ended this battalion was given the Township of Douglas in Nova Scotia.[14]

The Defence of Quebec, 1775-1776

Lieutenant-Colonel Allan Maclean reached Quebec City at the beginning of September 1775. Governor Carleton, desperately short of troops, was very relieved to see him, and after taking his measure made the seasoned Highland officer his second-in-command. In short order Maclean had enlisted 100 men from among the Highlanders along the lower St. Lawrence, and the issue of the *Quebec Gazette* for September 14 announced that the colonel had marched for Montreal on September 9.[15]

Almost immediately Carleton sent orders to Maclean to leave his men and return to Quebec City. Ominous rumours of a large rebel expedition advancing down Lake Champlain had alarmed the Governor. He wanted to be on hand if Montreal was endangered, and he needed a competent military mind in the province's stronghold. Carleton's deputy, Hector Cramahe was a civilian with little insight into the requirements for defending Quebec City should the rebels menace that position. The situation might call for the utmost exploitation of every loyal man. Carleton's army consisted of two below-strength regular regiments – the 7th Royal Fusiliers and the 26th Cameronians – Maclean's fledgling battalion, and whatever militia, francophone or anglophone, the governor could cajole into serving. The British hold on Canada was fragile since Carleton, mistakenly convinced that his militia would help, had sent two regiments to Boston at the request of General Gage.

Towards the end of September, Carleton ordered Maclean to muster as large a force as possible and set sail for Sorel, at the mouth of the Richelieu River. From there he was to march up the river to reinforce Fort St. Johns, where a captain and 19 privates of the Royal Highland Emigrants were already on duty as part of the garrison.[16] A rebel force had encircled this fort and captured Fort

Royal Highland Emigrants taking part in a military pageant at Fort Wellington, Prescott.

View of Fort St. Johns by Ensign James Peachey, 60th Regiment. To the right of the blockhouse, foreground, are abattis of tree branches. The second vessel from the left is the frigate Royal George. *Courtesy: Metropolitan Toronto Library.*

Chambly, twelve miles to the north. Maclean was to retake the post at Chambly, and Carleton would join him from Montreal with more reinforcements to relieve Fort St. Johns.

Maclean worked fast, sending recruiting agents among the Highlanders living at Murray Bay. Sad to relate, not all the men who enlisted proved trustworthy. On October 6, Lieutenant-Governor Cramahé wrote to Lord George Germain, the Colonial Secretary, to inform him that he was sending 17 deserters from the Royal Highland Emigrants to Britain. They had elected to serve in Africa, rather than face a general court martial in Quebec City.

Despite this minor setback, by the 14th Maclean reached Sorel with 220 Royal Highland Emigrants, 60 Royal Fusiliers, and some Canadian militiamen. There he scrounged about and brought his force to 400 men. At the head of his little column Maclean marched southward, expecting Carleton to reinforce him before the rebels learned that he was on their trail. The rebel force menacing Fort St. Johns, commanded by General Richard Montgomery, was said to be 1,900 strong. Unknown to either Maclean or Carleton, another rebel expeditionary force under Colonel Benedict Arnold was on its way overland towards Quebec City.

On St. Helen's Island, near Montreal, Carleton had assembled 800 Canadian militiamen, a combined party of 130 Royal Highland Emigrants and Royal Fusiliers, and 80 Indians. On October 30, he had an unnerving brush with the rebels – an ambush by Colonel Seth Warner and 350 of his Green Mountain Boys. While Carleton's boats were nearing Longueil, on the south shore, Warner's men opened fire. Carleton hesitated after beating off the attack, then withdrew. Maclean was already on the Richelieu River, and when he received word that Carleton would not be joining him, he, too, turned back. His 400 men were insufficient to deal with the rebels holding Fort Chambly, or save the beleaguered garrison at Fort St. Johns. The hasty journey from Quebec City had been in vain, and 20 of his own men were as good as lost. The road to Montreal from Lake Champlain would soon lie open to the enemy, the city inadequately fortified and weakly defended must fall.

Carleton now turned his attention to Quebec City, the fortress that could be defended and the key to retaking the rest of Canada. Should that stronghold fall, the rebels might capture the entire province. From Sorel Maclean hurried with the men of his regiment and the regulars down the St. Lawrence, reaching Quebec City on November 12. Behind him Fort St. Johns fell on the 3rd, and by the 13th the rebel army had occupied Montreal. Upon his arrival in the city Maclean found a timorous Cramahé talking of surrender.

Brusquely, the Highlander ordered all defeatist chatter to cease. With Maclean's support, Cramahé stiffened his own resolve, and the two made plans for the defence of the city. Anxiously they wondered how Carleton was faring near Montreal, but November 14 brought more immediate problems. Benedict Arnold appeared on the Plains of Abraham tagged by 600 wretched, starving followers. The fiery Arnold had force marched them up the Kennebec River and down the Chaudière Valley, a feat that has been likened to Hannibal crossing the Alps. After obtaining provisions from Canadian sympathizers on the south shore of the St. Lawrence, the rebels had crossed the river in every conveyance they could appropriate. Lacking artillery, Arnold encamped to await the arrival of General Richard Montgomery and reinforcements from Montreal.[17]

Fortunately for Maclean, the frigate *Lizard* arrived a few days before his own return, bringing accoutrements and clothing for 6,000 men and £20,000 in specie to pay the troops. Also aboard was Captain Malcolm Fraser, the paymaster, who arrived from Newfoundland with 150 recruits, men of Irish extraction who had embarked at St. John's. Maclean mustered his small garrison and intimidated the militia with grisly pictures of the fate awaiting them and their families if the rapacious Americans succeeded in entering the fortress.

On November 19 Carleton arrived at Quebec City. Leaving his forces under Colonel Prescott to surrender to the Americans, he had embarked from Montreal on November 11 with 130 regulars and Royal Highland Emigrants on ships and bateaux. But near Sorel the wind swung to the east, threatening to blow the flotilla ashore where the rebels had erected a gun battery. Then the wind dropped and the fleet lay becalmed. The rebels sent a flag of truce to demand that Carleton surrender his entire force or watch while his ships were sunk by rebel cannon.

Carleton was far from helpless, but he decided not to run the gauntlet of the rebel position. Among his ships were some thirty guns, and while his gunners fired on the rebel position, Jean Baptiste Bouchette, the captain of one of the vessels, agreed to row Carleton to safety in a small boat. In darkness, oars muffled, Bouchette's whaleboat carried the governor past the rebels and on into Trois Rivières. They continued downstream, fearful because of reports that some of Benedict Arnold's men were lurking at Pointe aux Trembles, about twenty miles west of Quebec City. They found the snow *Fell* and Captain Napier ran the governor past the ragged rebel army on the Plains of Abraham and safely into the stronghold's harbour.

Maclean and Carleton prepared for the siege. Anyone who might be disloyal was ordered to leave the city for security and to save rations. Soon word arrived of Prescott's surrender, and both commanders knew that the men left near Sorel would not be joining the garrison. The defenders made themselves as ready as possible, and some 1,800 men were under arms, listed as follows by Captain Thomas Ainslie, of the British militia:

70 Royal Fusiliers.
230 Royal Emigrants.
22 Royal Artillery fire workers etc.
330 British Militia.
543 Canadian Militia.
400 Seamen.
50 Masters and Mates of trading Vessels.
35 Marines.
120 Artificiers.
1800 Men bearing Arms.
The number of souls within the wall computed at 500 – eight months provisions in town. Firewood, hay, oats scarce.[18]

A 'Return of Men for the Defence of the Town of Quebec this 16th November 1775' preserved in the War Office was more detailed and conservative:

	Officers	Privates
Royal Artillery	1	5
Recruits belonging to Royal Emigrant Regiment	14	186
Lizard Frigate Marines	2	35
" Seamen effective	19	114
Hunter Sloop	8	60
Magdaline arm'd Schooner	4	16
Charlotte arm'd Ship	4	46
Masters, Mates, Carpenters & Seamen belonging to the Transports & Merchant Ships that have not been impressed	0	74
Artificiers & Carpenters	0	80
British Militia, including Officers.		200
Canadian Militia including Officers.		300
	52	1,116
Royal Fuseleers on board the Fell & Providence arm'd Vessels expected to arrive soon	3	60
Seamen belonging to said Vessels.	18	72
	63	1,248

```
Return of Provisions in the Garrison

Flour ──────────────────────────────── 1950 Barrels.
Wheat 7,840 Bushells will make
in Flour ─────────────────────────── 1500    "
Rice in Tierces about 450 lb
each ─────────────────────────────── 146
Bisket ──────────────────────────── 1100 Quintals.
Butter ──────────────────────────── 406 Firkins
Pease ───────────────────────────── 800 Bushells.

Endorsed:  In Cap'n. Hamilton's of the 20th November. (19)
```

On December 3, General Montgomery, the rebel commander, reached Pointe aux Trembles with 600 reinforcements for Benedict Arnold, and the eagerly awaited artillery. Ironically, they had travelled aboard the ships captured at Sorel a fortnight before. The siege seemed about to commence. Maclean and Carleton slept in the Recollet Convent fully clothed and the garrison did likewise, arms close at hand. Now everyone waited for Montgomery and Arnold to make their move. Days passed, the defenders watching warily.

The bastions along Quebec's walls that protected the Upper Town had been improved and were manned. Two fences obstructed the route round the southern side of the rock into the Lower Town, along a path called Près de Ville. To block the rebels should they attempt coming round the north side of the peninsula by way of the suburb of St. Roch into the Lower Town, two barricades had been erected. The first stood near the entrance to Sault au Matelot Street, the second at the end of this street where Rue de la Montagne, from the Upper Town, joined it. The houses along Sault au Matelot had been evacuated, except for one belonging to a merchant named Simon Fraser, which had two 3-pounder cannon and 30 men – Canadians under Captain Chabot, seamen led by Captain Barnsfare, and John Coffin, a refugee loyalist from Boston.

In the rebel camp on the Plains of Abraham, Montgomery and Arnold planned a two-pronged attack. Montgomery would lead one force round the southern side of the rock, while his second-in-command took a larger body through St. Roch, by the northern route.

Defence of Quebec Dec. 31 1775

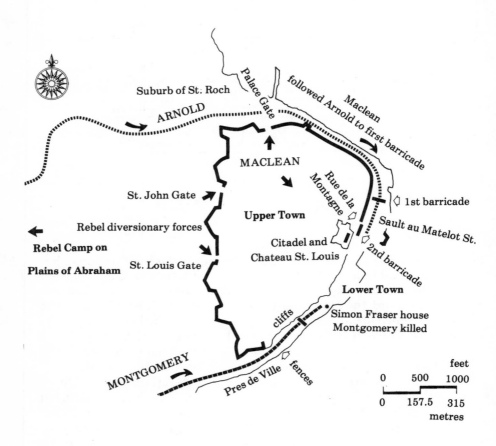

Suburb of St. Roch

ARNOLD

Palace Gate

Maclean followed Arnold to first barricade

MACLEAN

St. John Gate

Rue de la Montagne

Upper Town

1st barricade

Rebel diversionary forces

Sault au Matelot St.

Rebel Camp on

Citadel and
Chateau St. Louis

2nd barricade

Plains of Abraham

St. Louis Gate

Lower Town

cliffs

Simon Fraser house
Montgomery killed

MONTGOMERY

Pres de Ville

fences

feet		
0	500	1000
0	157.5	315
		metres

The two commanders would join forces inside the Lower Town, find a way into the Upper Town, try to rush the defenders and take them by surprise. While this was taking place, two small bands of rebels would keep up a lively fire near the St. Jean and St. Louis gates, to distract the occupants and assure that not too much strength was thrown against the real striking force.

The weather remained maddeningly mild, the nights clear; Montgomery wanted falling snow, or at the very least clouds to obscure his attack. He was getting edgy, for many of his enlistments would expire on January 1, 1776. Before dawn on December 31, in the nick of time, conditions seemed right – a blizzard was raging that certainly interfered with the visibility. Montgomery set out with 500 men for Près de Ville, and he broke through the two fences without difficulty. Meanwhile, Arnold was leading his section of 700 men through St. Roch along the northern route past the rock of Quebec. Captain Ainslie recorded the next events:

> About 4 o'clock in the Morning Capt. Malcolm Fraser of the Royal Emigrants being on his rounds, saw many flashes of fire without hearing any reports; the sentries inform'd him that they had perceived them for some time on the heights of Abraham, the sentinels between Port Louis and Cape Diamond had seen fix'd lights like lamps in a street – the appearance being very uncommon and the night favouring the designs of the enemy, Capt. Fraser order'd the Guards and Pickets on the ramparts to stand to their arms. The drums beat, the bells rang the alarm, and in a few minutes the whole Garrison was under arms – even old men of seventy were forward to oppose the attackers.

Carleton gave Maclean the command of the coming battle. It was Arnold's men Fraser had spotted; Montgomery's furtive approach along the south side of the rock was still undetected, but not for long.

When Montgomery's force was in front of Simon Fraser's house overlooking Près de Ville, the occupants released a hail of grape shot from the two 3-pounder guns. Montgomery fell dead, and two dozen other rebels died with him. The remainder turned and fled pell-mell. About the same time Arnold's vanguard reached the edge of the Lower Town, under steady fire from the ramparts above. On they crawled, stumbling in the oblivion created by the swirling snow, carrying scaling ladders to the first barricade in Sault au Matelot Street. Here Arnold fell, wounded below the knee, and was helped away by two of his men, while Colonel Daniel Morgan took command. This six-foot-four giant from the Kentucky Valley who led a corps of frontier riflemen in fringed shirts, had been anti-British since receiving 500 lashes for striking a regular officer during Braddock's campaign of 1755.

Brashly, Morgan and his riflemen smashed through the first barricade and halted farther up the street, waiting for the artillery to be brought forward. Soon chaos reigned in Sault au Matelot, and outside it. Some of the rebels following got lost; others retreated at the sight of wounded men trying to escape. In the Upper Town, Maclean had the situation well in hand. The defenders knew better than to take the small groups of rebels firing near the St. Jean and St. Louis gates seriously. Maclean ordered a body of troops to march down Rue de la Montagne to reinforce the second barricade. Next, he sent 200 more out of the Palace Gate to march to the rear of the American position in Sault au Matelot Street. Both detachments included men from his regiment.

Daniel Morgan's rebels were trying to mount the second barricade, but Captain John Nairne of the Royal Highland Emigrants and some of his men wrested a scaling ladder from the rebels and used it to enter the second storey of a house. After chasing out some rebels who had taken shelter on the ground floor, they commenced firing upon the men trapped in the street below. Then the troops who had left the Upper Town by the Palace Gate closed in, bottling up Morgan and some 400 others in Sault au Matelot. They sought refuge in houses, but their line of retreat was cut off. In tears, Daniel Morgan handed his sword to a black-robed priest rather than surrender it to a hated redcoat.

Rebel losses were some 400 captured, 42 wounded but safely back in camp, and 30 killed. Later, Arnold counted 700 survivors, but many rebels were not accounted for by either side. Ainslie put the number captured at 426, including 44 wounded officers and other ranks. In the spring Maclean reported finding 20 bodies once the snow had melted.[20]

By contrast, Maclean's casualties had been light. Carleton reported one captain of the navy killed, and five rank and file wounded, of which two died later. The captured rebel officers were housed in the seminary, and after a short stay in the monastery and the college of the Recollets, the rank and file were sent to the Dauphin gaol for safe keeping. Carleton decided to gamble, and he allowed the captives of British birth to recant and enlist in the Royal Highland Emigrants. In all 94 did, and most of those who accepted the governor's offer were Irish. Later, Maclean discovered that some were trying to desert, and in March, Carleton ordered the suspects to turn their uniforms and arms in. The more obvious turncoats were sent to the holds of ships in the harbour to be confined.

The rebels lingered in their encampment on the Plains of Abraham. Eventually, on May 6 the *Surprise* , the first British ship of the spring fleet, sailed into the harbour bringing a detachment of reinforcements. Now Carleton had the resources he needed to chase the small army of rebels from the neighbourhood. Carleton and Maclean led a sortie outside the city gates, and the rebels offered no resistance. In their flight, Ainslie noted that they abandoned most of their belongings:

> they left cannon, mortars, field pieces, muskets and even their cloaths behind them. As we pursued them we found the road strew'd with arms, cartridges, cloaths, bread, pork &cc.

Gleefully Maclean reported that his regiment partook of a meal laid out for the rebel officers, who were interruped by the sudden appearance of his vanguard.[21] With that the tone of the Scottish veteran of many campaigns waxed caustic over the way Carleton was behaving. The governor was treating the rebels leniently despite the damage they had done, and deliberately refusing to pursue them and capture their army. Had the second-in-command had his way, Montreal might have been cleared of its nest of rebels days sooner. At Trois Rivières Carleton learned that General John Burgoyne and the Baron von Riedesel had reached Quebec on June 1, with the rest of the reinforcements of British and German regulars. He left to greet his colleague, ordering Maclean to remain where he was until further orders.

That the reinforcement was of British regulars was not surprising, but a word of explanation is in order concerning the arrival of the German troops. American sources invariably refer to these men as mercenaries, and imply that they were raised through harsh impressment so that the rulers of the four principalities from which they were drawn could receive £7 per recruit from Britain, as well as a lump sum. In fact, while some men were raised expressly for service in North America, and there were abuses in recruiting, the German soldiers were, by and large, well-trained professionals, proud of their abilities and their, regiments. The troops, from Brunswick, Hesse-Hanau, Anhalt-Zerbst and Hesse-Cassel, were members of regular regiments that were rented by Britain, not, as often suggested, purchased country boys torn from their families and shipped off to do Britain's dirty work. These professionals had one serious defect, shared to some extent by the British regulars; they were unable to adapt their style of conducting warfare to the exigencies of the forested frontiers.[22]

While Maclean and his force remained at Trois Rivières, the rebels withdrew as far as Sorel and encamped with reinforcements that had arrived there. During the winter, what the Continental Congress called its Army of the St. Lawrence had received some 4,000 fresh troops, which were posted to Montreal, Fort St. Johns, Sorel, Berthier and the Cedars Rapids. The western-most detachment had fallen into British hands. Regulars, loyalists and Canadian volunteers, and a party of Indians with Walter Butler, led by Captain George Forster, the commandant of Fort Oswegatchie, had descended from that post and laid seige to the rebel position at the Cedars. Forster's men took 400 captives and negotiated the exchange of the prisoners captured with Colonel Prescott at Sorel the previous November, after Carleton's narrow escape.

Here was news that should have spurred Carleton to close in while the rebels at Montreal were off balance, but neither Carleton nor Burgoyne, the new arrival, were in a rush. The newly arrived soldiers were not very fit after weeks at sea, and arrangements for moving provisions up the St. Lawrence took time. Maclean must have been even more distressed when the good report from the Cedars reached him as he sat kicking his heels at Trois Rivières. Meanwhile, at Sorel, rumours circulating among the rebels suggested that Maclean had only 300 men with him. General John Sullivan, in command there and hoping for another chance to seize Quebec, ordered an attack on Maclean's position. Unknown to Sullivan, the Highlander had been joined by Lieutenant-Colonel Simon Fraser of the 24th Regiment with four fresh battalions. Furthermore, Fraser and Maclean were in a neighbourhood where the Canadians were loyal.

Unaware of the real situation Sullivan – later to achieve notoriety by leading the expedition that desolated the Iroquois lands – sent Brigadier William Thompson forward with 2,000 men, and this expedition landed seven miles above Trois Rivières. An accommodating Canadian agreed to guide the rebels to Maclean's camp. Instead of taking the road, the Canadian guided them into a swamp through which the rebels floundered to the point of exhaustion. Emerging from the swamp into the open they were confronted with Fraser's men, drawn up in battle formation. A loyal militia officer, one Captain Landron, had seen the rebels landing and hastened to inform Maclean. The rebel force broke and fled, but Fraser's men captured 200 prisoners, including Thompson, and his deputy. The survivors escaped by taking to the swamp again. On June 14 Carleton returned to Trois Rivières accompanied by General Burgoyne, Baron von Riedesel and enough British and German regulars to bring his expedition to 8,000 men. For the rebel Army of the St. Lawrence the denouement had begun.

Carleton divided his army into two sections. Burgoyne, Brigadier William Phillips and Colonel Fraser landed with 4,000 troops at Sorel, which was deserted. Sullivan had advance warning of the fleet's approach; and was hustling his demoralized, disheartened force towards Fort Chambly, making the most of a 24-hour start. He had 2,500 effectives, but the rest were wounded or suffering from smallpox.

While Burgoyne followed Sullivan, Carleton sailed on, with Maclean, von Riedesel and the remaining 4,000 troops to deal with Benedict Arnold's rebels in Montreal. An aide warned Arnold of Carleton's impending arrival, and like Sullivan he wasted no time. In four hours the rebels had left the city, making for Fort St. Johns, the loyal militia preparing to welcome Carleton. By June 17 the governor was in Montreal, while Sullivan and Arnold, who had joined forces at Fort St. Johns, were withdrawing towards Isle aux Noix. Burgoyne's light infantrymen could have outflanked the rebels and his troops might have captured the entire force, for many were ill. However, Burgoyne never did put on a burst of speed through his entire service in the war.

From headquarters in Montreal, Carleton spent a few days inspecting his advance posts. Then, leaving Maclean in command, he returned to Quebec City. The Royal Highland Emigrants stayed with their commanding officer, and including the prisoners of war, the regiment stood at about 400 men. Maclean sent out patrols towards Fort St. Johns, and one duty was to bring back deserters. For American prisoners who had joined the corps, the temptation to escape was overwhelming, now that they were closer to the New York frontier.

Guardians of the Border

Apart from a sortie into New York in the autumn of 1777, and two small detachments that were part of larger expeditions, the defeat of the rebel invaders in 1775-1776 marked the end of the Royal Highland Emigrants' active participation in the war. Henceforth the corps was used to guard the frontiers of Canada. In the autumn of 1776, when Carleton was ready to deal with the rebel fleet commanded by Benedict Arnold on Lake Champlain, the Royal Highland Emigrants were left on duty around Montreal and at the outposts along the Richelieu River. That winter the corps was quartered at La Chénage, Terre Bonne, and Rivière du Chene.[23]

Serving as an ensign in the regiment was 26-year-old John MacDonell, whose home was in the Mohawk Valley. He was in the employ of a Montreal merchant when the recruits for the regiment were being raised in the autumn of 1775.[24] In the spring of 1777, John MacDonell Sr., the ensign's father, arrived in Montreal with 100 recruits, some for Sir John Johnson's regiment, the others for

Maclean.[25] In June General Burgoyne prepared to set out with his expedition 9,000 strong, to invade New York, and he took several groups of provincials, but not Maclean and his Royal Highland Emigrants.

Making his plans, Burgoyne recommended that the corps be left behind as part of the Canadian garrison:

I.propose Maclean's corps, because I very much apprehend desertion from such parts of it as are composed of Americans, should they come near the enemy. . . In Canada, whatsoever may be their disposition, it is not easy to effect it.[26]

Desertion was Burgoyne's stated excuse for refusing to include the Royal Highland Emigrants, yet, he may have harboured a private reason. To most English officers, those kilted provincials were Jacobites. Like the prisoners of war, they were not to be trusted. Nor was Burgoyne reassured by the knowledge that their commanding officer had served in the post-1746 refuge for Highland supporters of Bonnie Prince Charlie, the Scots Brigade in the Netherlands. Thus Maclean and his regiment remained at Montreal when Burgoyne embarked on his disastrous expedition. Both officers and men were disgruntled at being denied the opportunity to win battle honours, but they soon saw that they were the lucky provincials. Small detachments were at the forward posts, and a full company, presumably of the most reliable elements, was at Fort St. Johns. Carleton promoted Maclean to the provincial rank of brigadier-general, the usual practice to ensure that regular officers could never be inferior to mere colonials.[27] This meant that Maclean was a brigadier general in Canada, although he remained a lieutenant-colonel in the regular establishment and also in the Royal Highland Emigrants. Despite Burgoyne's low opinion of Maclean's corps, on March 26, 1777, Lord Germain wrote to Carleton praising the zeal demonstrated by the Royal Highland Emigrants, noting that these men were being considered for the regular establishment.

In October 1777, while Burgoyne was being forced to surrender his army at Saratoga, Carleton, who still hoped the expeditionary force would escape, ordered Maclean and his regiment forward to Chimney Point, on Lake Champlain near Crown Point. The Royal Highland Emigrants marched, accompanied by a detachment of the 31st Regiment, hoping to meet Burgoyne on Lake Champlain, and to keep in communication with Brigadier Watson Powell and the British garrison that Burgoyne had left to secure Fort Ticonderoga. As winter approached, Carleton sent instructions to Maclean for the evacuation of his post and Ticonderoga. Maclean relayed the message to Powell, who destroyed anything of value to the rebels and burned the fort before retiring to Fort St. Johns. As November drew to a close, Maclean asked for leave of absence to go to London to obtain medical treatment. The cause of his suffering was a badly wasted leg which made walking almost impossible, riding an agony because of acute pain in the sole of his foot. The difficulty could have originated from wounds he had received during the earlier war. Carleton gave his consent but Maclean's ship was driven ashore by ice and he had to return to Montreal.[28]

A return dated December 24, 1777 for the first battalion Royal Highland Emigrants showed that the regiment had, in addition to the lieutenant-colonel and major, 8 captains, 11 lieutenants, 8 ensigns, a chaplain, adjutant, quartermaster, surgeon and surgeon's mate, 30 sergeants, 30 corporals, 20 drummers and 394 privates. It was, therefore, the largest and most nearly completed of any provincial corps attached to the Northern Department at that time.[29]

A list of 16 new recruits for Captain Alexander Fraser's company showed that the youngest was 16, the eldest 50, the shortest five feet four inches, the tallest six feet. One was born in France, 5 in Canada, 6 in Ireland, and the other 4 in Britain.[30] Each man had drawn a bounty of from £2. 5s. 6d. to £2. 11s. 8d. and under the heading 'Complexion' a recruit was described as fair, brown or swarthy.

A 'Return of Officers of the First Battalion of His Majesty's Regiment of Royal Highland Emigrants' dated Isle aux Noix, April 15, 1778, shows Lieutenant-Colonel Allan Maclean, Major Donald McDonald, 7 captains, 8 lieutenants, 7 ensigns and 4 staff officers on duty at that post or around Montreal. Lieutenants Neil McLean, Francois Dambourges and Alexander Stratton, Ensign Hector McLean and the Reverend John Bethune are listed as prisoners of the rebels. However, other evidence shows that Major McDonald, captured with Bethune in the summer of 1775 in North Carolina, had not reached Canada. Soon after he had arrived as Carleton's successor, Governor Frederick Haldimand, granted Maclean's request for leave, and Maclean was absent from Canada from the autumn of 1778 until the following October. In his absence the governor appointed Captain John Nairne to command the corps with the temporary rank of major.[31]

Nairne was a veteran of the Scots Brigade in the Netherlands, and a reduced captain from the old 78th Regiment.[32] That Haldimand appointed Nairne is proof that Major McDonald had not reached Canada after imprisonment in Philadelphia, although he had been free since General Sir William Howe had freed the city from the rebels in 1777. Informing Lord George Germain, Haldimand wrote:

with the departure of Lt.Col. Maclean command of his battalion fell to a Capt. Nairne, a very able officer and who distinguished himself very much at the seige of Quebec. . . to prevent the Mortification of him of being commanded occasionally by Majors of Provincials, I have given him Nominal Rank of Major till further orders[33]

Haldimand took this step because Nairne was a former regular officer, and the governor had plans for the Royal Highland Emigrants. In December 1778, obeying a directive from the Colonial Office, Haldimand ordered the battalion placed on the regular establishment as the 84th Foot, and brought up to strength. The difficulty over obtaining recruits had caused Maclean, and now Nairne, no small worry. Some of the men who had agreed to join Maclean when he was in the Mohawk Valley before coming into Canada preferred Sir John Johnson's King's Royal Regiment of New York after he received permission to raise it. Also, some potential recruits and men already in the regiment chafed over the inactive role it had been assigned, especially if they were American loyalists.

One such was Ensign John MacDonell. He became acquainted with Walter Butler when the young man was convalescing in Quebec City during the summer of 1778, after harsh confinement in Albany gaol. Hearing of the exploits of Butler's Rangers, MacDonell applied for a transfer to that corps. On July 31 Haldimand gave his consent, and MacDonell was awarded a captaincy by Walter's father, Major John Butler.[34] Other one-time Royal Highland Emigrants who became Butler's officers were Captain George Dame, Lieutenant Alexander MacDonell, and Lieutenant David Sutherland.[35]

In the autumn of 1778, only a small detachment of Royal Highland Emigrants was on duty at Montreal. The rest were at Sorel, where Haldimand ordered his provincials to build strong fortifications, to forestall another invasion of Canada from the Richelieu River. In July 1779, Haldimand sent Nairne to Carleton Island to succeed Captain George MacDougall as the commandant of Fort Haldimand on the island. With Nairne went 50 Royal Highland Emigrants to strengthen the garrison.

When the regiment became part of the regular establishment as the 84th Foot, Sir Henry Clinton, then the commander-in-chief at New York City, was the Honorary Colonel. Allan Maclean, on leave of absence, was the lieutenant-colonel commandant, with Donald McDonald and John Nairne as the majors. In addition there were 7 captains, 11 lieutenants, 8 ensigns, an adjutant, quartermaster, surgeon and the chaplain.[36] Notable among the officers was Lieutenant François Dambourgès, a Canadian commissioned on

54

February 27th, 1776, during the rebel seige of Quebec City. Dambourgès was particularly useful directing the francophones in the rank and file. In the spring of 1779, before the arrival of Major Nairne, Captain George MacDougall asked that the 'French Company' of the Royal Highland Emigrants be sent to him at Carleton Island because they were such good workers.[37]

A muster roll dated April 16, 1781, at Sorel, suggests that the French Company was broken up, the members distributed among other companies. At that time Dambourgès was in Nairne's company.

The recruiting drive to bring the Royal Highland Emigrants up to strength met with success. On August 30, 1779, soon after Maclean returned to Canada, Governor Haldimand signed a 'Beating order for the 84th Regiment.' Maclean, the lieutenant-colonel commandant, was authorized to augment his battalion with 20 private men to each company, 'by Beat of Drum or otherwise,' and 'as a due encouragement, Three guineas pr. man and no more will be allowed for every recruit approved of.' Maclean had hand bills printed with this information, adding that exclusive of the bounty money, each man should receive 200 acres for himself, and an additional 50 acres for his wife and each of his children. On October 22, 1779, Haldimand appointed a third major to the corps, John Adolphus Harris.[38] Maclean was occupied with his duties as commander at Montreal, John Nairne was at Carleton Island, and the corps needed additional leadership at a trying time.

General John Sullivan's 5,000 strong expedition was ravaging the lands of the Iroquois Confederacy. Governor Haldimand ordered a reinforcement of 90 men of the 32nd Regiment and the Royal Highland Emigrants to join Colonel John Butler and his Rangers at Canawagoras (near Lake Ontario) as part of the force that was harrying the rebel expedition.[39] Before these men could reach Fort Niagara, the rebels had begun to withdraw. Maclean's men were able to resume their usual duties at Carleton Island, Sorel and Montreal. By the autumn of 1779, the first battalion of the regiment was completed to 500 privates, 8 captains, 10 lieutenants, 10 ensigns, 20 drummers, 60 non-commissioned officers, the lieutenant-colonel, 2 majors, adjutant, quartermaster, surgeon, surgeon's mate and chaplain, for a total of 626 all ranks.[40]

In the autumn of 1780, one company of Royal Highland Emigrants went with Major Christopher Carleton's expedition to destroy the New York outposts along Lake Champlain that penetrated rebel territory below Fort Edward. Lieutenant John Enys, of the 29th Regiment – Major Carleton's own – kept a journal, and he recorded the composition of the force as follows:

	Ma.	Capt.	Lieut.	Ensn.	Sert.	Corpl.	Drum	Privates
29th Regt.	1	2	3	2	5	5	1	182
34th "	-	1	2	1	4	4	1	100
53rd "	-	1	2	1	4	4	1	100
84th "	-	1	2	0	2	2	0	50
Chassures		1	0	1	1	1	30
Royalists	2	4	8	22	9	0	0	125
Savages		1						108 (41)

By Royalists, Enys meant a detachment of King's Loyal Americans, and another of King's Rangers; the first led by Major Edward Jessup, the second by Major James Rogers.

The expedition left Isle aux Noix on September 27, 1780, in bateaux, and was ready to return by October 26. However, Major Carleton received a dispatch from Haldimand,

> ...ordering us to keep on the Lake as long as possible; which Order however disagreeable to us all we were obliged to Comply with for which purpose we again return'd to our old Station at Mill Bay. As Soon as we had Arrived in our camp one Capt. Sherwood of the Royalists, was sent with a flag of truce to the State of Vert Mont.

Allan Maclean's correspondence provides an insight into the problem he and all the other corps commanders encountered in uniforming and accoutring their officers and men. In 1775 and 1776, despite instructions that his battalion was to be dressed in the same manner as other Highland Regiments, his men wore whatever they had, and as far as is known, at the defence of Quebec City their coats were green. Not until the end of 1776 did they have full uniform and red coats faced with blue. They still retained their kilts with pride. Writing to Haldimand in 1780, Maclean asked for one hundred jackets and waistcoats, adding 'Breeches we do not want!'[42] Once they had their proper attire, the thrifty Maclean, as penny-pinching as Haldimand himself, ordered the men not to dispose of their older clothing, and to keep it for doing fatigue duty.[43] Much as Maclean loved to see his men in Highland dress, he admitted in October 1781 that breeches were more suitable in the Canadian climate, both to keep out the cold, and as a protection against the many stinging insects flying about. For a time the men wore canvas trousers under their kilts.

At the time of writing Maclean was about to depart for his second leave of absence, but for what reason he did not say. When he left for England, General Ernst von Speth, the Lieutenant-Colonel of the Regiment von Riedesel, assumed the command of Montreal.[44] Meanwhile, the Royal Highland Emigrants were on duty at various posts. Since the winter of 1780, Captain Patrick Sinclair, his sergeant, John Hay, and 22 rank and file had been at Michilimackinac, the detachment farthest from headquarters. In 1781, the garrison built a new fort on Mackinac Island, a safer position than the old fort built by the French on the mainland.

Shortly before Maclean sailed for home, Major John Ross, then the commandant at Carleton Island, was leading his expedition against the rebels in the Mohawk Valley, and one source claims that 36 Royal Highland Emigrants were part of a force that numbered nearly 700 men. The detachment with Ross would have been from the men on duty at Carleton Island.[45]

During the Ross expedition Lieutenant Francois Dambourgès was in command at Carleton Island. John Nairne, Ross's predecessor, had transferred to the 53rd Regiment and been posted to Isle aux Noix as the commandant of that fort. Nairne was responsible for overseeing all the provincial troops in the area.

When Maclean returned to Canada in the autumn of 1782, Haldimand ordered him to Fort Niagara to take over all the upper posts from Brigadier Watson Powell, who had been in command of them for two years and wanted to be relieved. On his upward journey, the veteran Highlander inspected the forts along the way which came under his care – Oswegatchie, Carleton Island and Oswego, recently occupied by Ross. Some of Maclean's Royal Highland Emigrants were with him at Niagara, and others were scattered from Montreal to Michilimackinac, but their commanding officer was at least as preoccupied by the affairs of Butler's Rangers as with his own regiment. On November 17, 1782, by which time Sir Henry Clinton had resigned his command at New York City and returned to Britain, Allan Maclean succeeded him as the brevet-colonel of the Royal Highland Emigrants, a mark of distinction that recognized the value of his service. Donald McDonald, the senior major, succeeded Maclean as the lieutenant-colonel commandant of the regiment.

Late in the autumn of 1783; Maclean was again requesting leave to attend to his private affairs in Britain. His argument must have been compelling, for Haldimand concurred at a time when he was very worried about the security of the western forts. Maclean left in October and never returned to Canada. The men of his corps were then reinforcing the upper posts, except for a few who were at Isle aux Noix with Nairne. Since April 1782 a detachment had been at Oswego, reinforcing Major Ross, in command at that post.[46]

The colours of the Royal Highland Emigrants. Each flag measures six feet six inches flying, six feet deep on the pike. They do not conform to the specifications for regular regiments. Maclean had them made before setting out for the colonies to raise his corps. Silk colours were expensive, and his regiment carried the originals after it was placed on the British establishment as the 84th Foot. Courtesy: Alwyne Compton Farquharson of Torloisk; photograph by Dr. W. H. Clegg.

For the safety of the fur trade and the Indians, Haldimand wanted his frontier posts held at all costs, and the Royal Highland Emigrants were more suitable for this task than other provincials. About the time Brigadier Maclean was inspecting his posts on his way to Niagara, Major Ross wrote from Oswego suggesting that British soldiers were necessary to guard the forts, because morale was low among the troops 'raised from the Colonies.'[47] With a strong component of former regulars, the homes of many unmolested, the Royal Highland Emigrants were more dependable, once the news that Britain was making peace terms unfavourable to American loyalists became widely known.

On August 9, 1783, a month before the peace treaty was signed in Paris, Lord North at Whitehall sent an order to Governor Haldimand to disband all his Provincial troops, including the 84th Regiment. The packet did not reach Quebec City until November, too late to be implemented that season for the men on duty at the upper posts.[48] Thus the Royal Highland Emigrants and two other battalions of provincials were not disbanded until June 1784. Haldimand was amenable to paying the men of the 84th longer, because their presence might help restrain some of the more bloody reprisals against the Indians by the victorious American rebels.

The Governor hoped that the provincials stationed far to the west would settle in the neighbourhood of the posts where they had been on duty. Such a measure would save the cost of transporting them elsewhere, to the gratification of the parsimonious Haldimand. A few of the Royal Highland Emigrants did so, but most had families awaiting their return along the lower St. Lawrence or in Newfoundland. Others, notably the MacDonells and the Reverend John Bethune, elected to settle among friends and relatives in the townships beside the upper St. Lawrence that were assigned to the first battalion, King's Royal Regiment of New York. Lieutenant Neil Maclean stayed at Cataraqui, and several others settled across the river from Fort Detroit.[49]

A paper kept in Torloisk House, Isle of Mull, states that Maclean died in 1797. Allan and his wife Janet lived in London after the revolution ended, but he made at least one visit to Mull and the house where he was born. With him went a prized possession, the colours of his battalion, described thus: 'There are two colours at Torloisk which were the colours of the 84th Regiment. One of them is a blue ensign which has in its centre a thistle in a circle surmounted by a crown, with the motto 'Nemo me impune lacessit'; and below this is a riband bearing the words 'Royal Highland Emigrants' The second flag is a Union Jack with similar devices in the centre. With the flag is preserved a note written in the hand of Mrs. Clephane (daughter of Lachlan Maclean, 7th of Torloisk and niece of the General). It runs as follows 'The colours of the 84th Regiment of Royal Highland Emigrants – at the close of the War for American Independence were brought to Torloisk and Deposited by their Colonel, Allen Maclean, Lieutenant-General in the Service, in the hands of his niece, and the representative who was to succeed her father, elder brother of the General. He raised this Corps among his emigrated countrymen, when the defence of Canada could not in any other way be effected, when the Americans under Montgomery came in force and besieged Quebec, which he, with his Corps which he had newly raised, defended successfully, till the fall of their brave leader and the little impression they had made, occasioned their retreat. Conscious that my uncle left me, by that deposit, the best possession he had, his military renoun, I should not deserve the trust, if I left his Banners without making the future possessor aware of the value of them'

M.D. Maclean Clephane,

Torloisk, 24th July, 1819.

Allan's branch of the clan was not very prolific. According to the family, Allan and Janet left no issue. An item found in the British Museum indicates that Maclean was to be allowed £100 per year for his wife in the event of his death – double the usual pension for a Colonel's widow – and a grant of land for his children.[50] He did receive 5,000 acres on the north side of the Ottawa River in 1788,[51] but if he had children it may be that none lived to maturity. His brother Lachlan left only one daughter Marianne, who inherited his possessions and Torloisk.

Sad to relate, Allan did not live to see an event that would have gladdened his heart. In 1800, three years after his death, the Duke of Argyll put his lands on Mull up for sale, and the family bought back the estate.[52]

Of all the provincial troops in the Northern Department, the Royal Highland Emigrants were the most professional and caused Governor Haldimand the least trouble. Yet with the exception of the King's Rangers, these men saw the least action. Commanded in part by British regular officers, and with many veterans of regular regiments in the ranks, they were more manageable than their brothers in arms. They had less cause for discontent, since the homes of many were secure. Men who had not lost their possessions had less grounds for bitterness, and were able to act according to the gentlemanly rules of war so important to Haldimand.

After the regiment was placed on the British establishment,

Camp colour, Royal Highland Emigrants, sixteen inches flying, fourteen inches deep on the pike. The flag is blue worsted, to match the facings on the uniforms, the edges bound with red tape. Copied from original in the Canadian War Museum. Courtesy: Royal Highland Emigrants Regimental Association. Redrawn by G. R. D. Fryer.

Prices of Commissions in Regular Regiments, 1775
Marching Regiments of Foot

Lieutenant Colonel	£3,500
Major	2,600
Captain	1,500
Captain-Lieutenant	950
Lieutenant	550
Ensign	400

Fusiliers with 1st and 2nd Lieutenants

1st Lieutenant	500
2nd Lieutenant	450

some of the promotions may have followed the practice in other regular regiments. Evidence hints that some commissions were purchased. A list published at the Château St. Louis in Quebec City on October 17, 1782, shows that Volunteer James MacDougall had become an Ensign on June 25 of that year, and Duncan MacDougall was shown as the vice – the man from whom the commission was obtained.[53] In other provincial corps the officers' commissions were usually awarded according to the number of men recruited.

The achievements of the first battalion, Royal Highland Emigrants were less spectacular than those of Butler's Rangers, the King's Royal Regiment of New York, and certain members of the Loyal Rangers. The duties assigned them gave the 84th Foot few opportunities for the kind of action undertaken by the provincials who entered rebel territory with Burgoyne, or went on raids staged later in the war. Yet the stature of the commanding officer, Allan Maclean, went far beyond the leadership of his battalion, and the regiment performed valuable service. Its assignments were routine, but the men accomplished much by their sheer presence at the outposts where they served. Their contribution to the safety of Haldimand's sprawling domain was of vital significance throughout the nine years of the regiment's life.

Chapter 5:The King's Royal Regiment of New York

Sir John Johnson's King's Royal Regiment of New York and John Butler's corps of rangers did a great deal of damage to the rebel war effort along the frontiers of New York and Pennsylvania from the Battle of Oriskany in August of 1777, until the autumn of 1782. In every action both provincial corps were accompanied by detachments of native warriors led by their own chiefs and by officers of the Indian Department. The native contribution varied from small parties of scouts to a majority of the participants. The main purpose of most of the raids was to destroy the rebels' food supply, in order to restrict the effectiveness of the Continental Army and the militia units. Although detachments of British regulars were usually present as well, this was a guerilla war between loyalist and rebel, a bitter and highly personal fight.

For posterity the King's Royal Regiment of New York had an unfortunate name, one that implies that it was in one location, while another was more closely associated with it. If any place on the map may be selected as the most significant for the regiment, it is Montreal, where the first battalion was based for nearly the whole of the revolutionary war. In spite of the cumbersome title, the King's Royal Regiment of New York was never quartered in any part of that province – or state, as it was known once the Continental Congress named the new republic by its declaration of 1776. This awkward title accounts for the corps being known by so many nicknames – the Royal Yorkers, the Royal Greens or simply, Sir John Johnson's Corps.

The second provincial corps to be raised for service with the Northern Department, the King's Royal Regiment of New York was also the largest, the only one to comprise two battalions, although the second was never completed. As a fighting unit it was severely under-used. The men spent the lion's share of their time employed in fatigue duty, building fortifications and barracks, and houses for refugee loyalist families. Governor Haldimand once wrote to his superior, Sir Henry Clinton at New York City: 'Sir John Johnson's Regiment tho' a usefull Corps with the Ax, are not altogether to be Depended on with the Firelock.'

The Corps' commander, Sir John Johnson, was an experienced officer, a veteran from the Seven Years' War, and a major-general of militia in New York province before the revolution. He was also a very frustrated man, with a driving ambition to see his corps ele-

63

vated to the British regular establishment. His repeated requests to Haldimand fell upon deaf ears, or were adroitly parried by the conservative Swiss governor. On the few occasions when Johnson had the opportunity of taking his men into action, they proved themselves as capable with the firelock as the axe.

Sir John Johnson

No biography of Sir John Johnson would be possible without some reference to his father, Sir William, his brothers-in-law, Guy Johnson and Daniel Claus, and a miscellany of other relatives. To comprehend the forces that shaped Sir John, it is necessary to look behind his father's public image to his domestic life. Sir William's track record as a parent was impressive. He is known to have sired at least fourteen children, by three different women; and similiarity in stature and personality hints that Joseph Brant might be his son also, since he received the same treatment in Sir William's will as other children not recognized as legitimate by white man's laws.[1]

The first-born son was William of Canajoharie. William and his two sisters were the children of Caroline Peters, a niece of the baronet's good friend, the Mohawk sachem, King Hendrick. Since that union was by Indian rites, it did not preclude marriage to a German girl named Catherine Weisenberg, who had entered Sir William's house as an endentured servant, and presented him with three children – Ann, John and Mary. By the time young Johnny was about three years old his mother was in failing health. Sir William suspected that if these three offspring were ever to be legitimate he should not dawdle. After the deathbed wedding to Catherine, Sir William consoled himself with Molly Brant, a sister of Joseph, the Mohawk warrior who, as we have seen, might have been more closely related. Known as Brown Lady Johnson, Molly gave Sir William eight more children – six daughters and two sons – and she was instrumental in keeping her people on Britain's side during the revolution. In this somewhat unorthodox household, Johhny was the crown prince, cock of the walk.

After Sir William died in 1774, Guy Johnson, his nephew, became the Superintendent of Indian Affairs, Northern District. Guy was an opportunist who had left Ireland to better himself, and he married Mary, Sir William's younger daughter by Catherine Weisenberg. Daniel Claus, a half-pay Captain in the 60th Regiment who married Catherine's elder daughter Ann, was the deputy in charge of the Indians in Canada. At that stage, Johnny was something of an unknown quantity among the residents of the Mohawk Valley, for from 1765 until 1773, he spent most of his time in Albany, New York City, or England, occupied on business and social matters. During his many absences his brothers-in-law became the successors to his father in dealing with the Indians. Nevertheless, Johnny was the principal heir to the feudal barony.

He was born in 1742, in a large frame house known as Mount Johnson, presided over by his mother. By 1749, the widowed Sir William had moved his motherless children to Fort Johnson, a substantial stone mansion of Georgian design that is now the headquarters of the Montgomery County Historical Society. Johnny was raised to think of himself as special, and treated with deference by his half-brothers and sisters. The children, and some of their young neighbours, were taught in a school established by Sir William. The master was notorious for his severity, but he dared not lay a hand on young Johnny, lest he incur the wrath of the father.[2]

Otherwise, the evidence on Johnny's education is skimpy, although it is known that he attended school in Philadelphia. At age thirteen we know he was with his father on the expedition to Crown Point in 1755. Four years later he was with the party sent to capture Fort Niagara from its French garrison, and in 1760 he was on the Amherst expedition that sailed from Oswego. Like John Butler, he was a witness to the Battle of the Thousand Islands, when some 600 French regulars, sailors and Canadian militia delayed a British force 10,000 strong for more than a week before it could proceed down the St. Lawrence to the capitulation of Montreal. With that schedule, it is difficult to determine when Johnny had time to be in school in Philadelphia.

He also served as a captain of militia during the Pontiac uprising.[3] By the end of that war, the Johnson family was living in a splendid new mansion, Johnson Hall, which Sir William had begun to build in 1761. Of square timbers, painted white and today a museum owned by New York State, it is symmetrical, and flanked by stone fortifications. This Georgian edifice on the frontier was the hub of the Indian trade, where native people were always welcome, and the social centre for gentry willing to tolerate the presence of Brown Lady Johnson and her half-Mohawk brood. One shocked visitor was Lord Amherst, who disapproved of Molly's elder son having been named Peter Warren Johnson, in honour of Sir William's auspicious uncle, Admiral Sir Peter Warren.

A favourite pastime of Johnny's was fox-hunting, with hounds imported from England by Daniel Claus, acting on behalf of his father-in-law.[4] This is an indication that Johnson Hall and the Mohawk Valley in the 1760s was hardly the forest primeval. The Iroquois Indians had cleared considerable land in the course of their corn, beans and squash cultivation before they sold these acreages to Sir William Johnson. Young John was an excellent horseman, much given to using flamboyant, imported tack. In particular, he possessed an ornate saddle, trimmed with blue leather and decorated with silver motifs. For a time he led a troop of horse, and in 1763 he galloped off at the head of his column to punish one Kanestio, whose defiance of convention had irritated Sir William.[4]

In 1765, the devoted Sir William sent 23-year-old Johnny to broaden his social contacts in England. The heir was well received by London society, and was presented at court as the protege of Lord Adam Gordon, who had met Sir William while on a business trip to acquire land in the Mohawk Valley.[5] For reasons that are now obscure, he was knighted by King George III, and was therefore addressed as Sir John before his father's death made him the Second Baronet of New York. The young man remained in England two years, his activities not purely social. A letter from his father showed that he was taking care of business affairs while living the life of a London buck. It hinted that Sir William was not overly fond of Guy, his nephew, and contained some orders for Johnny to fill:

You would laugh to see Guy drive his Skeletons with all his Family in a Sled. I hope you will be verry careful in ye choice of ye glasses I wrote for as my Eyes grow verry weak, and bring me 3 or 4 pound of Coarse English Rappe Snuff.[6]

Following his return from England, Johnny was somewhat at a loose end. His brothers-in-law were assisting his father with Indian affairs, and he soon acquired a mistress, Clarissa Putnam. They had two children, William and Margaret, and an abiding fondness for each other, although it did not lead to marriage. In the autumn of 1772, he met his true love, or at any rate one with better connections than Clarissa. She was Mary, usually called Polly, a daughter of John Watts, a wealthy merchant in New York City. Her mother was a member of the powerful DeLancey family, and she married Johnny in June 1773. Sir William, unwell at the time, sent a letter to remind John Watts that a generous dowry was in order, for Johnny was a fine catch who was bestowing a title on Miss Mary. After proffering this bit of advice, Sir William apologized for being unable to attend the wedding.

Marriage settled Johnny down, and the young couple made their home at Fort Johnson until Sir William's death. Then they moved into Johnson Hall, and Molly took her children to live at Fort Johnson. Their first child arrived in 1775, and they named him William.

By that time the situation in the Mohawk Valley was becoming

Sir John Johnson, the commander of the King's Royal Regiment of New York. Courtesy: Metropolitan Toronto Library.

Johnson Hall, Johnstown, N.Y. The wooden mansion was confiscated after Johnson fled to Canada, and is now a museum.

tense. Sir John had a great deal at stake. His inheritance comprised 240,000 acres, with granaries, mills, stables and hundreds of tenants. Certain of the latter caused resentment in Tryon County, which commenced ten miles east of Johnstown, the county seat, and extended beyond the frontier into Indian territory. To populate some of his lands and also alleviate poverty in the Scottish Highlands caused by the uprising of 1745, Sir William had brought over some 600 Gaelic-speaking Roman Catholic settlers. Their arrival in the autumn of 1773 did little to endear Sir William or his heir to the settlers from Germany's Palatinate. Staunchly Protestant, they had been uprooted from their homes through fear of Roman Catholicism when France invaded the Rhineland, and they were appalled by the rough-looking Highlanders, gibbering their outlandish tongue, trampling the countryside, dirks shoved in their stockings.

At first the Palatines felt helpless, for the Johnsons held Tryon County in a firm grip. Sir John was a member of the legislative assembly, having defeated the almost equally wealthy landowner from Albany, Philip Schuyler, a major-general in the militia wherein John Butler, a faithful but unloved subordinate, was the lieutenant-colonel commandant of a regiment and Guy Johnson was his superior as honorary colonel. Administration, be it civil, military or Indian, was solidly in the hands of the Johnson family. Gradually, however, some of the Palatine settlers, who under normal circumstances were apolitical and had no use for Yankees, formed an alliance with the New England settlers, because both were anti-Roman Catholic.

In May 1775, amidst some disorder, these factions established the Tryon County Committee of Safety, and while their liberty pole was pulled down, opponents to the rule of the Johnsons were closing ranks. Guy Johnson responded by fortifying his fine mansion, Guy Park, the gift of his late father-in-law, when rumours spread that a plan was afoot in Philadelphia and Albany to have him kidnapped. Upon hearing from the commander-in-chief, General Thomas Gage, holed up in Boston with his army, that every available Indian had been recruited by the rebels for the seige of the city, Guy decided to act.[7]

Assembling some 250 friends, among them John and Walter Butler, Joseph Brant, Gilbert Tice and John Deserontyn (like Brant a Mohawk), Guy set off up the Mohawk, arriving at Oswego on June 17, 1775. Other Indians and officers of the Indian Department joined him along his route, and behind him Mayor Abraham Cuyler of Albany attempted to send boatloads of supplies, but these were stopped by the rebels. (Later Cuyler fled to the British garrison at

New York City for safety.)[8] After sending to Fort Oswegatchie, on the upper St. Lawrence, for provisions and bateaux, Guy's party, then 220 strong because some of the Indians had turned back, descended the St. Lawrence to Montreal. Most of the men joined Governor Carleton's defence force, but Guy Johnson left for England, accompanied by Daniel Claus, and Indian Department officers Gilbert Tice, Joseph Brant, and John Deserontyn. Guy was in a huff because Carleton had refused to allow him to turn the Indians loose against the rebels. In the void left by the superintendent's departure, Carleton sent John Butler to Fort Niagara as the deputy to stand in for Johnson.

The departure of so many leaders of the Indian Department greatly weakened the position of the loyalists in the Mohawk Valley, as Allan Maclean discovered when he arrived that summer in search of recruits for his Royal Highland Emigrants. Sir John Johnson received Maclean at Johnson Hall, guarded by his Highland tenants. Outside this enclave, reinforced by troops from New England, the rebels were disarming Sir John's tenants, Butler's and those of other loyalist leaders who had left the valley with Guy Johnson. Sir John's own days at home were numbered.

On September 7, a letter from the Tryon County Committee of Safety to the New York Provincial Congress roundly denounced Sir John and the Scots Highlanders who were protecting the man who had, in effect, become their chief. Johnson sent Allan MacDonell, one of his most trusted tenants, with a letter for Governor William Tryon, who had taken refuge on the H.M.S. *Duchess of Gordon*, in New York harbour, out of reach of the rebels who were marching through the city's streets. There MacDonell delivered the letter, and a verbal message, on January 3, 1776. Sir John was offering to form a battalion of loyalists, had already selected his officers, and was asking the governor to supply him with the necessary armaments.

Tryon forwarded this letter to Lord George Germain, the Colonial Secretary, informing him that Sir John could muster 500 Indians who, with the support of a few regulars, could be used to recapture the forts at Ticonderoga and Crown Point, which Ethan Allen and his Green Mountain Boys had seized from their British garrisons in May 1775. The rebels got wind of the plan. Philip Schuyler, Johnson's political rival and now the commander of the rebel military department in Albany, marched up the Mohawk with a force estimated at 3,000 men.[9] At Schenectady they halted, and Schuyler sent a message to Sir John requesting that he come to a meeting promising that the baronet and anyone accompanying him would be allowed to return home.

The rendez-vous was staged sixteen miles west of Schenectady, and in the face of such overwhelming odds, Johnson's back was against the wall. He had to agree to allow his Highlanders to be disarmed, and he signed his parole to take no further part in hostilities against the Continental Congress and the New York Provincial Congress. He was also restricted to the eastern portion of Tryon County, but he could go into other states as long as he stayed away from all seaports. Allan MacDonell and five of the latter's kinsmen were surrendered as hostages for the good conduct of the rest. These six were sent under guard to Lancaster, Pennsylvania. The Tryon County militia was organized under officers selected by Schuyler, and a regiment of men from New England took possession of Fort Stanwix, strategically located at the bend in the Mohawk on the portage to Lake Oneida, that had been empty since the Seven Years' War.[10]

For nearly three months Sir John Johnson sat tight, abiding by the humiliating terms Schuyler had pressed on him. Then, after the rebel defeat at the Cedars, near Montreal, by Captain George Forster, assisted by Indians and others sent by John Butler from Niagara, Schuyler ordered Johnson arrested. But some Indians warned their friend of the rebel commander's intention.

Johnson wasted no time. Gathering together about 200 friends and tenants, with provisions and blankets, he buried his papers and silver plate close to Johnson Hall. Guided by Indians his party marched along trails where the rebels would not expect to find them. Their path took them into the Adirondack Mountains, well away from the more travelled routes, and they dragged a brass 3-pounder cannon that had escaped the rebels' notice when they were collecting weapons. High in the mountains, out of provisions, and without strength to drag the gun the men abandoned it. (Some years ago a party of hikers found the gun, and now it graces the front of Johnson Hall.) The refugees were nineteen days in the wilderness, with little food and no shelter, subsisting on what game they could catch without firearms, wild onions, roots, berries and the leaves of beech trees.

Exhausted and half starved, shoes through at the soles, Johnson's party reached Montreal on June 18, 1776, one day after Governor Carleton had repossessed the city from the rebels. Carleton received Sir John at his headquarters, and the other immediately asked for permission to raise a regiment of loyalists from among his friends in New York State. Carleton agreed readily, possibly because this was in accordance with the then vague British policy of having loyalists defeat the rebels, more likely because the governor was unnerved at the spectacle of an irate, dishevelled Sir John, backed by his big brawny Highland farmers, following their laird as earnestly as their fathers had followed Bonnie Prince Charlie's standard a generation before. At that time Carleton had no clear idea as to how he would pay them, but he decided that the corps would be called the King's Royal Regiment of New York. It would be similar to other marching regiments serving in America, and Johnson was appointed the lieutenant-colonel commandant.[11]

When winter was upon him, Johnson felt he could do little towards recruitment, and he went by sea to New York City, where Governor Tryon was back in his mansion. The British army under Sir William Howe, the new commander-in-chief, had occupied the city that September. As matters turned out, Sir John was in the right place at the right time, for Lady Johnson had been having adventures of her own.

Finding Sir John had made good his escape, the rebels sprang into action. Polly, her 15-month-old son William, some servants and the members of the Butler family that had not gone to Niagara were escorted to Albany as hostages. Polly was pregnant, and after some nerve-wracking interrogation she was taken to a country house outside the town and kept under guard. In dead of winter, her second son only a few weeks old, Polly escaped from the house with the help of a black servant – the word slave was never found in contemporary usage – named Long. They set off down the Hudson Valley, bound for New York City, now a haven in British hands and closer than Montreal. The story handed down through the Johnson family shows Polly searching for a way to cross the Hudson through broken ice, her baby clutched to her breast, the servant Long carrying young William. When they spotted a boat some way out, Long suggested they hop from one block of ice to the next, and on reaching the boatman ask to be taken to the opposite shore. When Polly offered him a substantial reward, the boatman agreed to drop them on Manhatten Island, and thus they reached New York City.

A party of Indians who had escorted Sir John to the city was the first to discover Polly and the black man Long, making their way through the snow. The 140-mile trek had been too much for the young babe, and the small body was cold and still by the time Polly was able to place him in his father's arms.[12] When Sir John returned to Canada by sea, Polly, the servant Long, little William and her brother Stephen Watts went with him, leaving a small grave for her New York relatives to tend. From then until after the war the family's home was at Lachine, in a large frame house overlooking the rapids.[13] There, other children were born to Sir John and Lady Johnson.

Oriskany, 1777

The warrant Sir John Johnson received from Governor Carleton on June 19, 1776 was to raise a regiment of ten companies. Each company was to consist of 1 captain, 1 lieutenant, 1 ensign, 3 sergeants, 3 corporals, 2 drummers and 53 rank and file, as well as staff officers, a lieutenant-colonel commandant and a major.[14] Called the King's Royal Regiment of New York by Carleton, it was the second provincial corps to be raised for service in the Northern Department, preceded only by the first battalion, Royal Highland Emigrants.

Ultimately to consist of two battalions, the first was uniformed in green coats, faced with the dark blue that signified a royal regiment. The corps was soon dubbed the Royal Yorkers, or the Royal Greens, and this last may have applied to the colour of the coats. Yet it was customary to attach such a nickname to the facings, which implied that for a time these may have been green. The officers' uniforms were trimmed with silver lace, and they carried silver accoutrements, while the men's buttons were pewter. The battalion companies wore bicorne hats, while the light companies had close-fitting forage caps and shorter coats. The second battalion, established in 1780, wore red coats with dark blue facings, and the officers had gold lace and accoutrements.[15] As their uniforms wore out, the first battalion was gradually equipped with red coats, the officers with gold lace and accoutrements.

There are indications that Carleton had jumped the gun in giving Johnson his warrant, because at the time the governor had no firm directives from London on what to do with loyalists who sought shelter to Canada and were asking to join the King's troops, nor on what authority such men should be paid. Carleton apparently assumed that Sir John, with all his wealth, was in a position to clothe and equip his battalion without recourse to public funds. Such was inferred in a letter written to Johnson by General Burgoyne. First, Burgoyne denied that any bounty should be paid to men who enlisted, an inducement that had been promised to the men who joined the Royal Highland Emigrants, but which did not apply in the case of the King's Royal Regiment of New York:

The light in which your proposal, Sir, is regarded is that of a great opulent, distinguished subject, who after the example of a most honourable predecessor, steps forward in a time of difficulty and danger to vindicate the rights of His Majesty's Crown and restore the blessings of legal government.

Burgoyne went on to explain that Sir John's regiment would not be removed from America, and it was the intention that the corps members not be marched from their own province. This was specious. The men were already out of their own province, in Canada. Nevertheless, Burgoyne plunged on:

It is presumed that upon the representation of taking arms pro aris et focis, and, under the influence of so respectable a chief as yourself, the enlistments will be made with little expence.

Burgoyne sought to appeal to Sir John's vanity, a waste of time, for that gentleman was a pragmatist. Any expectation of motivating men by the highest principles of patriotism was sheer wishful thinking. Johnson was, rightly, chagrined, for he had hoped to be reimbursed to the extent of £375. 17s. 0d. for arms and equipment already purchased for his men. With his few soldiers Sir John joined Carleton's expedition up Lake Champlain that autumn, when the rebel fleet was defeated and the enemy forced to withdraw into Fort Ticonderoga. After Carleton decided not to attempt the capture of this fort so late in the season, the men of the fledgling King's Royal Regiment of New York returned with the army to Canada, and were assigned winter quarters in billets at Lachine, Pointe Claire and Ste. Anne, on the Island of Montreal.[16]

As winter drew near, Carleton dumped a troublesome matter in Johnson's lap. He had reported to Lord George Germain, the Colonial Secretary, on November 17:

During my stay at Crown Point several parties some with arms, of the inhabitants of the Province of New York came into us for refuge, and I have joined them to the Corps commanded by Sir John Johnson, who, after the Campaign, desired leave to go to New York, which I have permitted.

The inhabitants to whom Carleton alluded were those led by the Jessup brothers and Justus Sherwood, who expected to be commanded by leaders of their own choosing, and who took a dim view of being placed under Johnson's command. Sir John avoided the first round of dissent by going to New York City to meet his wife. Back in Canada his second-in-command, Major James Gray, faced the music. Gray was a veteran of the Seven Years' War, who had served as a captain in the Royal Highland Regiment, 42nd Foot. At the end of that war he sold his commission and settled in New York province, seeking shelter in Canada when the rebels became too overbearing.

In Johnson's absence, Gray kept assuring the Jessups that they would not be forced to join the King's Royal Regiment of New York, and that they had only been placed under Sir John's command in order to receive billets and rations – a matter of convenience, not commitment. He was immensely relieved when Johnson landed at Quebec City on May 27, 1777, and hurried on to Montreal.

By March, several parties of Royal Yorkers were out scouting, in quest of information on rebel plans, and more recruits had arrived. Captain John MacDonell, Royal Highland Emigrants, came in from the Mohawk Valley with 100 men, all Highlanders, some for his own regiment, some for the King's Royal Regiment of New York. In June, when General Burgoyne was preparing his invasion of New York by way of Lake Champlain, he delegated Lieutenant-Colonel Barry St. Leger, of the 34th Regiment, to make a diversion through the Mohawk Valley from Oswego and meet the main force at Albany. This expedition was to liberate loyalists in the valley and to capture Fort Stanwix, east of the carrying place between the Mohawk River and Wood Creek, which drained to Lake Oneida, and which in turn drained to Lake Ontario by the Onondaga River. (This latter stream is often called the Oswego River in primary accounts.)

Early in June, Burgoyne placed the King's Royal Regiment of New York under St. Leger, in preparation for the coming expedition. The Royal Yorkers were assigned 48 bateaux, to be delivered to the men's quarters, with 45 felling axes and three broad axes, as well as 75 felling axes and two broad axes for the use of the 34th Regiment. Each boat was entitled to two fishing lines and hooks, and Johnson's contingent was allowed 440 barrels of provisions (mainly pork and flour) with 10 barrels for each of 44 boats. The rum and brandy would ride in the officers' boats for security. Captain René de Rouville was given command of a company of Canadians who were to accompany St. Leger, because their original officer, Captain Samuel McKay, a veteran of the 60th Regiment during the Seven Years' War, had resigned in order to go with Burgoyne's main force.

The flotilla of boats set out from Lachine about June 26, and by July 8 it had reached Buck Island, at the foot of Lake Ontario. With the men went some tailors, who were still working on uniforms for the provincials. St. Leger, who had been given the rank of acting brigadier-general for the expedition, ordered a space cleared so that his army would have room to exercise, Colonel Daniel Claus, Johnson's brother-in-law, was along as the superintendent of the Indians, and with the help of Major John Butler, then at Fort Niagara, Claus was to raise a large body of warriors to assist St. Leger's regulars and provincials.

To conserve ammunition, St. Leger ordered that no soldier was to discharge his firelock without permission, except after a period of bad weather to ensure that it was in working order. On July 14, he

Provincials advancing. The Union Jack is of the period; the cross of St. Patrick was added in 1802.

An officer's sword hilt was silver or gold, depending on regulations. Officers' sashes were crimson silk; sergeants' of red worsted with a stripe along the centre that matched the facings. For corps with red facings the stripe was white.

appointed Sergeant Killigrew, of the 34th Regiment, as the provost marshal at 2s. 6d. per day. His duties were to care for all prisoners captured, deal with spies and deserters, all disorders in camp, send out patrols after marauders and stragglers, control the sale of liquor, and report all infringements to the quartermaster-general. His powers under martial law were equal to a country sheriff under civil law. He was also the executioner when required, and where a condemned man deserved an honourable death by a firing party – as opposed to hanging – the provost marshal was to give the word of command.

All tents were to be opened, the rears pulled up for four hours each day, to air them, and no activities were permitted that would render them filthy. Each morning the King's Royal Regiment of New York was to spend some time 'firing at marks,' and the officers were to pay their men to August 24, inclusive. On July 17, St. Leger announced to his men that Burgoyne had captured Fort Ticonderoga. The troops were then preparing to embark, taking 40 days' provisions for 500 men, and ammunition for two 6-pounder cannon, two 'Cohorns,' 50 ball cartridges per man, and the ovens were to bake six days' supply of bread. All units without sufficient ammunition were to apply to the artillery, and all officers were to provide cases to keep the men's firelocks dry. A case was made of leather, and could be tied over the lock to protect it. St. Leger also had two old ships, the *Colwheel* and the sloop *Charity* surveyed to see how much repair they required. Whether he actually used these vessels is in doubt, and they are not on the lists of vessels belonging to the Provincial Marine.

By July 19 the expedition was starting for Oswego, with each corps carrying the necessities in one bateau, while some Canadians under Captain de Rouville would bring up the other supplies. The vanguard under Lieutenant Henry Bird, 8th Regiment, would take twenty days' provisions, in case the supply bateaux were slow. Three rebel prisoners captured by scouting parties would be allowed to assist the bateaumen after giving their paroles, and ten of Sir John Johnson's men would stay behind to help carry supplies. St. Leger, who had a tidy military mind, would lead the flotilla in his bateau, the others following in '2 lines dressing.' After the commanding officer, St. Leger ordered the artillery, the 8th King's Regiment and a detachment of Rouville's men. Another detachment of artillery, the King's Royal Regiment of New York, a company of 'Chasseurs' (which meant German riflemen), and the officers and rangers of the Indian Department and the remaining Canadians were to embark on July 20, at four o'clock in the morning. An ensign hoisted in the bow and one musket shot was the signal for all boats to put ashore. Any boat in distress was to fire three musket shots.

Beforehand, at Fort Niagara, Lieutenant Bird, Major John Butler and Colonel Claus were making arrangements for the detachments from that quarter to join St. Leger at Oswego. The members of the King's Regiment were on duty at Niagara, while Butler and Claus were persuading Indians to accompany them. Butler went a step farther, by placing some loyalist refugees on the payroll of the Indian Department and bringing them along. By the time St. Leger left Oswego on July 25, his force consisted of these units:

```
King's Royal Regiment of New York — 133 — (Sir John Johnson)
Rangers from the Indian Department — 67 — (Col. John Butler)
Canadians ———————————————— 50 — (Capt. René de Rouville)
8th Regiment ——————————————— 100 — (Lieut. Henry Bird)
34th Regiment ——————————————— 100 — (Capt. Richard Lernoult)
Hesse Hanau Jaegers ————————— 50 — (1st Lieut. Jacob Hildebrand)

                                   500 men

Indian Department Officers ————— 15 — (Col. Daniel Claus, Capt
                                        Wm. Johnson).

Indians  Senecas ——————————— 200 — (Sayenqueraghta - Old Smoke)
         Cayugas ——————————— 200
         Mississaugas ———————— 150
         Mohawks ——————————— 400 — (Capt. Joseph Brant).
         Delawares ——————————  ?

                                 1,000 approximately
```

Also present were an indefinite number of local loyalists, many recruited by Walter Butler who had made a journey through the Mohawk Valley while St. Leger was making his way from Montreal. Opposing St. Leger at Fort Stanwix were 750 Continental soldiers, some from New York under Colonel Peter Gansevoort, and others from Massachusetts, led by Colonel Marinius Willett, a Long Islander by birth. St. Leger's men would travel in their bateaux as far as the carrying place between Wood Creek and the Mohawk. The two 6-pounder cannon rode in the boats, together with some 'royals.' (A royal was a short-barrelled gun that was unmounted, but which could be fitted on the same carriage as a 6-pounder). The Indians, who had brought some horses, were following trails through the woods.

By July 31, the expedition reached Oswego Falls on the Onondaga River, and two days later St. Leger had received a letter from Lieutenant Henry Bird, advising him that the advance party was investing Fort Stanwix. Replying, St. Leger urged Bird to prevent acts of barbarity and carnage by the Indians, and said he expected to be at the entrance to Wood Creek by that afternoon. The following day, the commander reached the fort, and the entire expedition was soon reinforcing Bird outside the walls. Captain Gilbert Tice, of the Indian Department, went forward with a message from St. Leger enjoining the rebels to surrender. Atop the fort flew a new flag with thirteen stripes of alternating red and white, with a constellation of thirteen white stars on a blue background in the upper left corner. According to records at the fort, now rebuilt as a museum, this was the first occasion when Old Glory flew over an American base.

St. Leger soon found that his artillery was not heavy enough to affect the British-built wooden batteries and the sod walls of Fort Stanwix, and his men waited stymied. Scouts sent by Molly Brant, then at Canajoharie, warned St. Leger that a relief column was approaching the fort. The body of Tryon County militiamen was 800 strong, led by General Nicholas Herkimer, who had a nephew, brother and brother-in-law serving with the Indian Department.[17] St. Leger ordered Sir John Johnson forward with a detachment to intercept Herkimer, who, with the commander's consent, chose the light company of his regiment under his brother-in-law, Stephen Watts; John Butler and 30 of his rangers; Sayenqueraghta (Old Smoke) and his 200 Seneca warriors; and 100 Mohawks and other Indians under Captain Joseph Brant.

In consultation with Butler and Brant, Johnson selected a ravine near the Indian village of Oriskany, six miles east of Fort Stanwix. There the only road available wound through the small ravine, and the column, which was accompanied by supply wagons, had to pass that way. Johnson and Butler positioned their force hoping that a confrontation would not be necessary, and that they would be able to persuade Herkimer to turn back without bloodshed. Many of the men in their force had brothers and cousins marching with Tryon County Militia, and blood was thicker than water. Brant and the other Indians were opposed to any quarter, and on August 6, as the unwary Herkimer led his men into the ravine the warriors opened fire, followed by the loyalists. In one of the bloodiest small encounters of the revolution, the rebel column was dispersed. St. Leger reported to Burgoyne:

The compleat victory was obtained; above 400 lay dead upon the field, amongst the number of whom were almost all the principal movers of rebellion in that country.[18]

Among the fallen lay Nicholas Herkimer, a leg shattered, who would die a few days later following an amputation. His rebel casualties were higher than St. Leger had reported. John Butler put them at over 500 in a letter he wrote to Governor Carleton on August 15, a week after the Indians and loyalists had finished combing the battlefield for their own dead and wounded. The Indians had borne the brunt of the rebel defence, with 33 killed and 29 wounded, including 5 chiefs. White casualties were negligible. Major Butler reported one private and Captains James Wilson and John Hare killed. The latter had joined the expedition during the march and was not on the list Butler made on June 15 before he left Niagara.[19] Captain MacDonell and three privates of Johnson's corps were killed. One private, an unnamed subaltern and Captain Stephen Watts were wounded, while Lieutenant George Singleton was captured. Butler said that Captain Watts:

whose amiable qualities deserved a better fate, lay wounded in three places upon the field two days before he was discovered, however, it is thought he will recover.[20]

Meanwhile, back at Fort Stanwix, St. Leger heard the firing of the loyalists and Indians, and a scout came in claiming that Sir John was in trouble. The commander dispatched Lieutenant Bird at the head of a detachment to march to Johnson's relief. Inside Fort Stanwix, Colonel Marinius Willett chose that moment to send a sortie of 350 men outside. They attacked the camp of the absent Indians and provincials, seizing many belongings left there. St. Leger sent Captain Robert Hoyes and a company of the 34th Regiment after them, and at the sight of opposition the rebels ran back inside the fort.

The Indians, who had gone into battle stripped to the waist, in breechclouts and leggings, lost their blankets, while Sir John Johnson's orderly book was captured, along with other secret papers.[21] For eighteen days the siege of Fort Stanwix continued, and St. Leger's artillery made many attempts to reduce the walls. He reported to Carleton:

It was found that our cannon had not the least effect on the sod work of the Fort and that our Royals only had the power of teizing [teasing] as a six inch plank was sufficient security for their powder magazine as we learnt from deserters.

They tried to convert the royals into howitzers, but their fire was no more effective. What they needed was a ship's mortar that could fire shells with deadly accuracy, and had a high but short trajectory. Such a piece could have fired the shells over the walls, causing panic among the garrison. The artillerymen attempted to place a mine under the fort's main bastion, but this too failed. Standing about while these futile efforts were taking place, the Indians lost patience and wanted to return to their villages. In spite of all power of persuasion by John Butler, Daniel Claus and Sir John Johnson, some began to decamp, amidst rumours that a rebel force of 3,000 men under Benedict Arnold was marching towards Fort Stanwix. On August 11, St. Leger wrote to inform General Burgoyne that he was withdrawing to Oswego until heavier guns could be brought from Fort Niagara.

At the waterfall on the Onondaga River, St. Leger received Burgoyne's reply, informing him that the report of an enemy advance on Fort Stanwix was false. However, Burgoyne's main army, then on the Hudson River had suffered heavy losses. St. Leger was to choose the most sensible of four alternatives: compel the fort to surrender; remain where he was until Burgoyne was in a position to give him a reinforcement; send off his guns by water under escort and march through the woods to meet the army on the Hudson; or return to Montreal and join the commander-in-chief by way of Isle aux Noix and Ticonderoga. St. Leger chose the last course, and from Oswego he set out for the St. Lawrence. The officers and men of the 8th Regiment and the Indian Department returned to Fort Niagara taking all the surplus provisions and powder. Johnson and his regiment accompanied St. Leger, who, as he wrote to Carleton, had to pause in Montreal to:

procure necessaries for the men, who are in the most deplorable situation from the plunder of the Savages, that no time may be lost to join General Burgoyne by Lake Champlain.

The savages in question were Indian allies who had helped themselves to some of St. Leger's supplies before they left for their villages.

The Battle of Oriskany was proclaimed a victory by both sides, despite the fact that the Indians and loyalists won the day and were in command of the field afterward while the rebels suffered horrendous casualties. The American claim rests on St. Leger's withdrawal. Certainly none of his officers regarded the entire expedition as a failure, and for them the retreat was merely a postponement to fetch artillery. Until Burgoyne gave St. Leger different orders, his men fully expected to return and challenge Fort Stanwix again. Daniel Claus explained:

The Chiefs advised the Brigr to retreat to Oswego and get better artillery at Niagara, and more men, and so return and renew the siege (to which St. Leger agreed). . . All the good done by the expedn was that the Ringleaders and principle men of the rebels of Tryon County were put out of the way.[22]

Carleton, concerned over the fate of the beleaguered Burgoyne, left Quebec City and reached Montreal on September 23, where he arranged for reinforcements to go up Lake Champlain. St. Leger advanced as soon as his men were equipped, taking the King's Royal Regiment of New York with him under the command of Major James Gray, an indication that Sir John may have been among the indisposed when his men reached Montreal from Oswego. St. Leger left the Royal Yorkers and Hesse Hanau Jaegers to reinforce Fort St. Johns, while he continued on towards Lake Champlain at the head of the regulars of his own 34th Regiment. He reached Lake George, discovered that Burgoyne had surrendered at Saratoga on October 17, and retraced his steps down the Richelieu River.

Burgoyne's surrender was a turning point in the war. The British expeditionary force failed in its attempt to penetrate deep into the northern colonies, a disaster which had enormous ramifications not foreseen by the provincials at the time. Soon afterwards France formed a military alliance with the United States and in due course sent troops to bolster Washington's Continental Army. Spain followed France in a declaration of war, and Britain's capacity to supply troops to North America was drastically curtailed.

The King's Royal Regiment of New York returned to the villages around Montreal where the men had wintered the year before, and were employed on fatigue duty, working on the fortifications for the defence of the city. Building such works was to occupy the corps for the next three years, although small parties of men were constantly out scouting in search of intelligence and recruits, and the regiment was mobilized in the autumn of 1779.

Guarding the Home Front.

The earliest extant return of the regiment is dated at Quebec, June 1, 1778. It shows 1 lieutenant-colonel (Sir John), 1 major (James Gray), 8 captains, 10 first lieutenants, 7 ensigns, 1 chaplain, 1 adjutant, 1 surgeon and 1 surgeon's mate, 30 sergeants, 10 drummers and 298 rank and file fit for duty. Another 23 were prisoners of the rebels, captured the autumn before while serving with Colonel St. Leger, 20 rank and file were sick, and 8 were in confinement. Thus Johnson lacked 2 captains, 3 ensigns, 10 drummers and 181 rank and file to complete his battalion. No mention was made of corporals on this return, and these may have been included with the rank and file. Compared with the record of enlistments for other provincial corps, Sir John was an impressive recruiter, bounty or not.

On June 26, 1778, General Frederick Haldimand arrived in Quebec City as Sir Guy Carleton's successor, and his first duty was the strengthening of his posts. To Haldimand, the matter was urgent because France had formed her military alliance with the rebels that February. The new governor-in-chief decided to use provincial troops to improve the defences of Fort Oswegatchie, on the upper St. Lawrence, and to build a new base on Buck Island at the foot of Lake Ontario. Haldimand had seen the spot in 1760, while on the Amherst expedition, and he renamed it Carleton Island in honour of his predecessor. The new fort would be called Haldimand in deference to himself.

On July 22, Brigadier Watson Powell, then on duty in Montreal, informed Haldimand that Captain MacDonell, of Sir John Johnson's Corps, found that the entire company under his command was refusing to go to Fort Oswegatchie to work as artificers. Speaking with them, Powell found that they objected because the whole regiment was not being sent there. Powell was able to placate them, and they went off with their captain. A few men were employed as scouts along Lake Champlain, but the regiment's most important task of the summer of 1778 was the work at Carleton Island. By July 28, Haldimand had sent three companies of the 47th Regiment under Captain Thomas Ancrum, with two companies of the King's Royal Regiment of New York and 28 artificers, up the St. Lawrence in bateaux to begin constructing Fort Haldimand. The men were accompanied by a few soldiers' wives who were to perform housekeeping duties.[23]

This expedition included Lieutenant William Twiss, an able officer in the Royal Engineers, to plan the defences, and Lieutenant John Schanck, Royal Navy, to design the docks and found a naval base for the Provincial Marine. The regulars of the 47th Regiment were formed into work parties or assigned garrison duty, while the provincials were expected to cut timber and work with the Indians. Haldimand intended that the fort bearing his name would serve as a trading post and mission to the Iroquois as well as a defence post.[24]

For all these purposes Fort Oswegatchie was unsuitable. Built by the French in 1749, it was badly sited, set low and an easy prey as well as in bad repair. The work Captain MacDonell's company was doing would make the fort a suitable staging post for supplies moving inland, but in contrast Fort Haldimand, on two-mile-long and one-mile-wide Carleton Island, was being built on a secure site. On a bluff overlooking a low isthmus to an elongated peninsula, the fort faced two good harbours, one at either side of the narrow neck of land. Guns placed facing these bays could protect ships anchoring below, and the naval construction area was on the low isthmus between the two shores.

While the regulars sawed boards, made shingles, burned lime for mortar and built a stone pier, the loyalists cleared a field of fire to ensure that no enemy force landing on the far side of the island could approach without warning. Lieutenant Twiss complained

Southwest Portion of Carleton Island

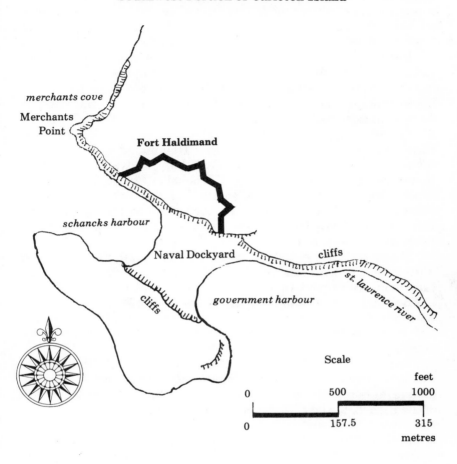

merchants cove

Merchants
Point

Fort Haldimand

schancks harbour

Naval Dockyard

cliffs

st. lawrence river

cliffs

government harbour

Scale

feet

| 0 | 500 | 1000 |

| 0 | 157.5 | 315 |

metres

about having no rum for men on fatigue duty, a situation remedied a year later when Captain Alexander Fraser, regiment not identified, arrived as the Indian agent. During the winter of 1779-1780, from 600 to 800 gallons of rum were sold at Carleton Island every week.[25] At the same time Governor Haldimand was constantly worried about supplying provisions to some of the upper posts and urging the troops and refugees to grow their own food. Rum for the important Indian trade took precedence over provisions when bateaux were being assigned to carry goods.

In the autumn of 1778, Sir John Johnson's detachment returned to the Montreal area. Governor Haldimand was planning a review of his provincial corps at Sorel, but in advance he ordered some of them to accompany Major Christopher Carleton on an expedition against several settlements along the east side of Lake Champlain, in Vermont Territory. According to Lieutenant John Enys, of 19 officers and 376 rank and file, 1 lieutenant and 30 privates were 'Royalists' from Sir John's Royal Yorkers.[26]

Another reliable source indicates that loyalists from other units were also with this expedition. Mentioned by name were Captain Justus Sherwood, then of the Queen's Loyal Rangers, Lieutenant Solomon Johns, who later joined the King's Rangers, and William and Thomas Fraser, brothers who farmed near Ballstown, a village across the Mohawk some eight miles to the north of Schenectady.

On October 16, all the provincials, except Butler's Rangers and the detachments serving with Major Carleton, paraded before Haldimand at Sorel. The governor decided that this town, at the mouth of the Richelieu River, would be the headquarters for all his provincial corps, and as well as the other units a large fatigue party of the King's Royal Regiment of New York was to spend the winter there, making the site as secure as possible, to seal off the invasion route some of the rebels had used in 1776 to penetrate Canada. Before Haldimand departed for Quebec City, the provincials who had accompanied Major Carleton reached Sorel.

Although Johnson's battalion was at barely two-thirds strength, Haldimand toyed with the idea of establishing a second one from among the remnants of Burgoyne's provincial troops. On October 19, he postponed any such plan, suspecting there would be too much dissent among the loyalist leaders. He admitted in a letter to Johnson that he had decided to:

> leave them under the same predicament as ordered by Sir Guy Carleton in hopes that some account from England will soon enable me to rid you of the trouble they have already given you; or make them in a more effectual manner attached to your Regiment.

84

British policy on provincial corps soon changed, and officers were entitled to permanent rank and half pay, but Haldimand was slow to act on these new terms. His only decision, possibly prompted by Lord Germain, was to place the Royal Highland Emigrants on the British regular establishment, which had no bearing in improving the status of other provincials in his department.

In October, Lieutenants William Byrne and William Redford Crawford led a party of provincials and Indians from Sorel to the Mohawk Valley to retrieve valuable belongings of Sir John that were buried near Johnson Hall. On November 24, Johnson informed Haldimand:

> the Ruins of my Papers, none of which are legible; my loss in consequence of the destruction of my Papers at the lowest computation twenty thousand Pounds, which is all the Intelligence I have been able to obtain; the Indians and six Prisoners that they took are gone to Colonel Claus, who, I suppose, will give Your Excellency all the information they have brought.

It became standard practice for recruits from rather dubious sources to be accepted into provincial corps. The first were men who deserted from rebel units, both the Continental Army and the militia. Sir John asked whether they should be regarded as sincere or as spies. Two brothers named Harper, from Massachusetts, confined in Quebec City by the provost marshal, asked to join the Royal Yorkers. Haldimand decided they could, as long as men already enlisted would vouch for their loyalty. The other doubtful source of recruits was prisoners of war who professed loyalty and pointed to coercion by the rebel committees of safety. The practice of permitting prisoners whom officers thought reliable to join provincial corps became commonplace as the war went on. Johnson frequently reported that men detained in Canada, and deserters from the rebels, were asking to join him. Haldimand found most acceptable.

The First Raid on the Mohawk Valley, Spring 1780

As the spring of 1779 approached, Sir John Johnson sent out many parties of his men on scouting missions, and on May 4 he confidently informed Governor Haldimand that reports of a rebel expedition against the Six Nations were without foundation. John Dafoe (later a captain in the King's Rangers) brought the message to Montreal, and Haldimand ordered the scout to come on to Quebec City to discuss the import of the intelligence he had gathered.[27] Dafoe's information was incorrect. A few days later the governor received a verbal report from John Walden Meyers (a captain in the Loyal Rangers when that corps was formed) who had reached Fort

St. Johns with a letter from Sir Henry Clinton in New York City, and a verbal report that the rebels had attacked the Onondaga Indians' villages. Much baffled, Brigadier Watson Powell, the commandant of Fort St. Johns, sent the scout to Quebec City to discuss his intelligence with His Excellency.

Meyers was convinced that the rebels were about to attack all the Iroquois, except the Oneidas, but Sir Henry Clinton's message, a duplicate of one he had sent to John Butler at Niagara read:

> I have reason to imagine that the Rebels mean to make an Attack upon Detroit this Spring, and I am informed they intend to make a feint on the Susquehannah, in order to draw the attention of Colonel Butler and the Indians from the other quarter.[28]

The rebels had successfully leaked false information to scouts operating from New York City. For months Haldimand would remain convinced that the troop movements which alarmed the Iroquois and Butler were only a feint. Detroit was in more danger, and so was Quebec, which remained the key to holding Canada. The rebels had succeeded in duping both Clinton and Haldimand, and were thus free to destroy the homeland of the Iroquois Confederacy, opposed by the Indians and Butler's Rangers (see pages 122-129).

Convinced that the rebels' activities on the frontier were not serious, Haldimand took time to reorganize the provincials who had accompanied General Burgoyne's expedition two years before. Thus far they had remained on a temporary list, assigned to Sir John Johnson, who regarded them as a nuisance. On May 16, the governor appointed Captain Daniel McAlpin to take command of them, with the exception of the men serving with Captain Robert Leake. Both men had been lieutenants in the 60th Regiment during the Seven Years' War, and as former regulars Haldimand had some respect for their capacities.[29]

McAlpin, who would hold the rank of major of provincials, was at Sorel, and Haldimand asked Johnson to meet him there and arrange to hand over the men. Leake was ordered to form his men into an independent company of from 70 to 80 strong and to select four or five good officers. Leake and his men would be quartered at Lachine, and he was not to keep any millwrights in his ranks, since the engineers had need of them. Not more than four or five women were to be quartered with this company, and no children, an indication that Haldimand intended Leake's command to be mobile.[30]

Meanwhile, rumours that the rebels had sent a large expedition up the Susquehanna persisted, and scouts arrived with word that other Iroquois villages had been burnt. Colonel John Butler was asking for reinforcements, and some chiefs met with Major John Campbell, the Indian agent at Montreal, asking that Sir John

Johnson, their son, be sent immediately to help them. Haldimand remained adamant, convinced that this rebel action was more fiction than real, and he feared that the French fleet would sail into the harbour of Quebec at any moment. His supply ships from England had not arrived, although he had been expecting them ever since the ice left the st. Lawrence, and he suspected a French attack. His victuallers, as he called them, finally came on August 19, but still he hesitated.[31]

At length, on September 1, 1779, the governor admitted that something ominous was indeed happening in the Iroquois country, and he ordered Johnson, then in Montreal, to take from 100 to 200 men of his regiment and Captain Robert Leake with 50 of his company, and proceed up the St. Lawrence in bateaux. They would accompany a force of 100 regulars and meet Butler and his rangers on the Genesee River, or any other convenient place. The gesture was too little, too late. Haldimand apparently had no notion of the strength of the expedition that was destroying the lands of the Iroquois. General Sullivan's army was more than 5,000 strong, and Butler's Rangers and the Indians were desperately trying to whittle down its numbers by hit and run tactics.

While making his arrangements to move westward, Johnson asked Haldimand for permission to claim recruits pledged to him that were serving with Butler, but the governor advised him to avoid making a fuss that might backfire. After admitting that he found both John and Walter Butler little to his taste, Haldimand added:

> Much had been lost upon former occasions for want of Cordiality . . . as Major Butler and his Son have by the success fallen in their way acquired great Credit at Home and I have the King's Orders to signify to them his Royal approbation of their Conduct; so that by any miscarriage which might happen in the course of Events and that possibly could be placed to your Account.

Johnson replied by reassuring the governor that he would not rock the boat. He would forbear, hoping to recover his men at the end of the campaign. More to the point, a third of the detachment he wanted to take to Carleton Island, en route to the Genesee, were without arms, and he had been refused any at Montreal. He asked that these be sent after him, and his force would soon be moving up the St. Lawrence in four divisions. Replying on the 13th, Haldimand wrote:

> my instructions to you must be reduced to very general terms. The object of your Expedition being to drive the Rebels out of the Indian Country, and to distress them by every possible means, falling upon their Troops whenever there is a probability of advantage – cutting off their Supplies and destroying their Stores of every Kind.

The season being well advanced, Haldimand explained, John-

Members of the King's Royal Regiment of New York, attended by Iroquois warriors, await the approach of some rebels.

Light infantrymen, King's Royal Regiment of New York. The coats were shorter, hats and cartridge cases smaller than in battalion companies.

son should not waste time trying to pursue the rebels. Rather, he should attempt to cut them off from the supplies they were supposed to have cached along their march. By denying them their source of food, Sir John might induce the rebels to abandon the Iroquois country.

By September 14 Johnson had assembled 12 officers and 201 men of his corps, but he wrote to Haldimand complaining that in spite of the intentions of Sir Guy Carleton, and assurances from His Excellency, his expectation of having the King's Royal Regiment of New York put on the British regular establishment had thus far come to nothing; the regiment was still a provincial corps. Haldimand, who had no intention of promoting Johnson's amateurs, some of them former rebels, nevertheless felt that a concession was indicated. He gave Johnson the command of the entire relief expedition, making the detachment of regulars that he planned to send subordinate to him. These were 50 from the 34th Regiment, and 50 from the 47th, as well as Butler and all his rangers. Only Colonel Mason Bolton, the commandant of Fort Niagara, would remain Sir John's superior. Here was some salve for Johnson's wounds.

The governor claimed that he did not have the authority to put the regiment on his regular establishment, which may have been true; yet he informed Johnson that making him a brigadier-general of provincials would not give him any advantages he did not then enjoy. Haldimand wrote to Colonel Bolton, apprising him of Sir John's ambitions, and pleading with that officer to be tactful. Johnson and his expedition set out in bateaux, in the four divisions he had mentioned, and on September 30 all but the men of the 47th Regiment had reached Carleton Island, where Major John Nairne, Royal Highland Emigrants, was the commandant. Writing from Fort Haldimand, Sir John reported:

I take with me in the Mohawk and in twenty Batteaux from hence provisions for fifteen hundred men for six weeks, and that I might not detain the Vessels from the Transport of provisions I have ordered a Detachment of one hundred and forty men from the 34th and my own Regiment to go round in Batteaux by Oswego in company with the Indians . . . The Detachment of the 47th remain here till the Shipping return.

From Carleton Island, which he left on October 4, Johnson hoped to meet John Butler and his rangers at a place he called Ascerotus, which from his description was on the shore of Lake Ontario, near the south of the Genesee River. A gale struck, and the *Mohawk* had to take shelter the following day in the Niagara River close to the fort. Ashore, Sir John learned from Colonel Bolton that Sullivan had turned back, and that Butler and most of his rangers had returned to the fort. Johnson was detained there for a meeting with the Indians, and they agreed to assemble at Oswego for an attack on the Oneida settlements, to punish that nation for the help it had rendered to Sullivan. Accompanied by Colonel Butler and one company of his rangers, Sir John set out along the shore in bateaux. The soldiers he had brought to Niagara were on the *Mohawk*, and he was planning to intercept the men making for Ascerotus in the bateaux.

By October 15 the entire force was at Oswego – 213 King's Royal Regiment of New York, Captain Leake's 50 men, the 100 British regulars and 50 German Jaegers. Late in September, Bolton had sent the Germans stationed at Niagara to Carleton Island because they refused to do fatigue duty. Such menial work was beneath the dignity of professional sharp-shooters. Nairne decided to send them with Johnson, who would soon be in a position to make good use of them. The Indians who joined Sir John were mostly Iroquois, but some were from Canada.

Johnson planned to move part of his force in bateaux up the Onondaga River while the Indians rode in their canoes, and a detachment marched through the woods with the horses. The preparations took a week, and by that time Johnson discovered that his prey had been alerted. A Cayuga Indian who had left Fort Niagara when the expedition was setting out from that base had reached the Oneida villages and warned their chiefs. Since a surprise attack was out of the question and the season too advanced to permit the men to wait at Oswego in the hope of sneaking up on the Oneidas before the snow fell, the expedition returned to Carleton Island.

Johnson and the men of his corps, with some of the regulars, returned to Montreal. He planned to take a leave of absence in England, to argue his case for higher status for his corps in person, but he was too late to find passage that year. During the winter, parties of Royal Yorkers were employed at Sorel and Côteau du Lac, helping complete fortifications at these points. On March 23, 1780, Haldimand informed Johnson that clothing and provisions would be supplied for the refugee families of the men serving in his regiment, a question the baronet had raised a few weeks earlier. The governor also told him that a scout named Sutherland had returned from the Mohawk Valley and reported that all the loyalists around Johnstown were to be formed into three companies of rangers by the beginning of May. Any who refused to join the rebel service were to be sent to Albany in irons, their homes burnt, and all their property sold for the benefit of the Continental Congress. Loyalists had sent messages to Haldimand begging for a pilot to lead them to safety before the rebels' deadline fell.

Johnson offered to lead an expedition to bring out the loyalists, and had already chosen two trusty men to go to the vicinity of Johnstown. He also planned to ask Colonel Daniel Claus to recommend an Indian guide for the scouts. Haldimand liked these suggestions, and on March 30, gave his approval for the expedition, stressing the need for secrecy and asking for more recommendations. However, the governor thought the expedition should wait until navigation opened and vessels could be made ready to carry the loyalists. A longer march through the woods might be hazardous for many of them.

Johnson replied that he wanted to go by Lake Champlain, southwestward to his own estate at Johnstown, where the local people could assist him by giving the expedition provisions and information. Next he proposed to make a night march to Stone Arabia, nine miles distant, to destroy the grain stored there, and continue along the Mohawk, while a party of Indians destroyed the settlement of Caughnawaga, four miles from Johnstown. Afterward he wanted to withdraw towards St. Regis, an Iroquois settlement on the upper St. Lawrence, keeping a jump ahead of the rebels who were certain to follow in pursuit. He recommended that a mixed force of loyalists and regulars accompany him, and he specifically requested the services of four men from his company of artificers then on duty at Sorel – Luke Bowen, Michael Carman, Jacob Coon and George Shaver. If the detachments he requested were sent to posts along Lake Champlain under the pretence of scouting up the lake, and for the protection of the loyalists reaching those shores, his overall design might be kept secret from the rebels' scouts.

Haldimand approved these plans but he decided that the expedition should wait until the ice was cleared from Lake Champlain and he cautioned Johnson to keep his plans dark until nearer the time of departure. He appointed Captain Thomas Scott of the 53rd Regiment to command the regular troops accompanying him into the Mohawk Valley. The governor cautioned Johnson to take as many Mohawks as he could persuade to join him, but to exclude all other Iroquois lest word be leaked to the Oneidas, as had happened the autumn before.

By the beginning of May the expedition was ready to set out, and it consisted of the following units:

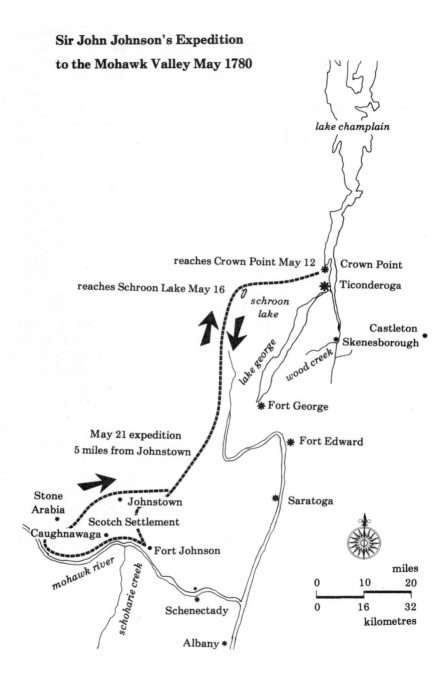

**Sir John Johnson's Expedition
to the Mohawk Valley May 1780**

lake champlain

reaches Crown Point May 12   ✳ Crown Point

reaches Schroon Lake May 16   ✳ Ticonderoga

*schroon
lake*

Castleton
✳ Skenesborough ✳

lake george

wood creek

✳ Fort George

May 21 expedition
5 miles from Johnstown   ✳ Fort Edward

Stone
Arabia   • Johnstown   ✳ Saratoga
•
Scotch Settlement
Caughnawaga •   • Fort Johnson

mohawk river

schoharie creek

•
✳ Schenectady

Albany ✳

miles

| 0 | 10 | 20 |

| 0 | 16 | 32 |

kilometres

```
King's Royal Regiment of New York (3 Companies) — 150 — (Sir John Johnson)
Captain Leake's detachment ————————————————— 50 — (Capt. Robt. Leake)
53rd Regiment ———————————————————————————————— 36 — (Capt. Thos. Scott)
29th Regiment (Light Infantry) ———————————————— 36
34th Regiment ———————————————————————————————— 36
Creutzburg's Regiment (German Regulars) ——————— 21

Mohawk Indians ———————————————————————————————— 130
Lake of Two Mountains Indians (Canadian) ——————— 80
                                                589
Total including Johnson, Leake & Scott ————————— 592 (32)
```

Although Haldimand wanted all Iroquois except the Mohawks excluded, he had no objections to Johnson's taking some from Canada, for such had little communication with those still living in the Mohawk Valley. Sir John was also to attach five of his Royal Yorkers to each party of regulars to act as guides should they become separated on the march. Lastly, as the expedition was forming the governor decreed that should any man desert, the Indians were to go after him and would be rewarded for bringing back his scalp: 'I believe this to be essential to Your Safety, and therefore should be Executed universally without respect to Corps.'

Normally Haldimand abhorred such a measure, but on this occasion he knew that a deserter, whether provincial or regular, reaching the rebels or their Indian friends, could lead to the slaughter of the entire force. In his last minute instructions, he beseeched Johnson to restrain his Indians:

It might be difficult, particularly after the recent misfortunes experienced by the Mohawks, to restrain them from Acts of Cruelty which I am persuaded would be as repugnant to your feeling as to mine, I therefore wish to Express to you my apprehensions of this Evil and Bad Consequences, which in a political view might result from it. I trust it will be in your power effectually to prevent the Destruction of women and Children.

The main body assembled at Lachine on May 3, while 80 Indians from Lake of Two Mountains went ahead as scouts, ready to capture rebel patrols to prevent them reporting on the impending raid. The regulars and loyalists followed in the vessels of the Provincial Marine as far as Crown Point, their powder in canteens wrapped in oilcloth or pieces of bladder to protect it from damp. They reached the outpost on May 12, after being delayed by contrary winds. By the 16th, Johnson reported that he was at Lake Schroon, and would be another four days reaching Johnstown. He promised to curb excesses by his Indians, and noted that his force then numbered 528. Apparently some had fallen ill and been sent back.

By May 21, the expedition was within five miles of Johnstown, but the Indians had their own ideas, and Johnson was unable to carry out his original plan. His native followers refused to allow the expedition to split into two parts, so that the regulars and loyalists could attack Stone Arabia while they marched on Caughnawaga. Instead, the entire force remained as one body, marched to Fort Johnson and everyone proceeded to Caughnawaga,

> destroying all before us as we marched along. From thence we proceeded to within a mile of the Nose, where a halt was found absolutely necessary, the Troops and Indians being much fatigued and in want of Refreshment having marched from Six in the morning of the 21st till ten in the morning of the day following; some of the Indians and Rangers continued Burning and laying Waste everything before them until they got above the Nose. Most of the Inhabitants fled to the opposite shore with their best Effects, securing their Boats which prevented us from crossing the River.[33]

Johnson suggested marching to Stone Arabia, but the Indians objected, claiming that the troops were too fatigued to go further. Besides, there was little point, because the inhabitants had all fled into their forts taking their possessions. Empty houses were not worth the trouble, since these would not yield much plunder. Some began moving off with the booty they had already lifted, and Johnson admitted that he had no choice but to follow them. The expedition moved back towards Johnstown, burning several houses en route, and after obtaining provisions from loyalists in the neighbourhood marched to what Johnson called the Scotch Settlement. There they burned 120 houses, barns and mills, and to Sir John's relief the Indians killed only eleven people:

> The Prisoners taken amount to Twenty-seven, fourteen of them I suffered to Return, being either too old or too young to march, and I was induced by the earnest desire of the Loyal families left behind to set at Liberty two of the Principal Prisoners we had taken to protect them from the Violence of the People, which they most solemnly promised to do and in Order to make them pay the utmost attention to their engagements I assured them that the rest of the Prisoners would be detained as Hostages for the performance of their promise.

Then the withdrawal began, and the men headed back towards Crown Point where the vessels of the Provincial Marine were waiting. Sir John did not go ahead with his early plan to retreat towards St. Regis – a difficult route, as he well knew. With the men on the march towards Lake Champlain went the rescued loyalists that had prompted the expedition in the first place. These were described as 143 men, some women and children, and 30 black slaves, of which 17 belonged to Sir John Johnson, Guy Johnson and Daniel Claus. Vast quantities of flour, bread, Indian corn and other provisions were seized or burnt in the houses and mills, while Sir John's men also appropriated arms and cash, killed many cattle and brought away 70 horses. They reached Fort St. Johns, having suffered almost no casualties. As Haldimand had hoped, Sir John appeared to have conducted the raid in total secrecy, and with such speed that

Musicians on drum and fife were identified as drummers on muster rolls. The chevrons on their sleeves made them easy to spot through the smoke of battle. Musicians in royal regiments wore the same colours as the ranks; in other corps their colours were reversed.

opposition to the expedition rallied too late to have any effect.

The whole affair was unsavoury, and Johnson's matter-of-fact recital is horrifying, but then so was the Sullivan expedition against the Iroquois of the season before. Sir John was not a man to turn the other cheek. Satisfied with what he read, Haldimand reported to the Colonial Secretary:

> In order to favor the Escape of those desiring to take Refuge in this Province which he effected by his Activity in a march of 19 days through the Woods, having brought off 150 Loyalists fit to carry Arms, first destroying a considerable number of Houses, Mills, &c., and a great quantity of Provisions and Stores of all kinds, 1700 men were collected but too late to oppose Him for the day after he Embarked at Crown Point on his Return, they arrived at that Place.

After this sweep of the eastern Mohawk Valley, the first battalion King's Royal Regiment of New York was nearly complete. On July 13, 1780, Haldimand authorized Johnson to form another battalion, empowering him:

> by beat of Drum or otherwise forthwith to raise a second Battalion consisting of Ten Companies, that is to say, One Major & Captain, nine Captains more, twelve Lieuts., eight Ensigns, one Chaplain, one Adjutant, one Quarter Mr., one Surgeon, one Mate, Thirty Sergeants, Thirty Corporals, Twenty-six Drummers or Fifers, and Five hundred and thirty Privates, to be paid, clothed and accounted in the same manner as the First and called the Second Battalion of the Royal Yorkers, to both of which you are hereby appointed Lieut. Colonel Commandant.

Captain John Ross, 34th Regiment, was appointed the major, with Robert Leake as the senior captain. His independent company was incorporated into the battalion, and Ensign Humphrey Arden, 34th Regiment, was the adjutant. While the affairs of his own regiment were satisfactory, the problem of the below-strength corps which Haldimand did not consider part of his Northern Department returned to haunt Johnson. Major Daniel McAlpin, whom Haldimand had placed in command of these units, died suddenly. Once more the men were under Johnson's command, although the governor allowed recruiting which might lead to some of them becoming full battalions.

Most of these small units were incorporated into the Loyal Rangers under Major Edward Jessup in 1781, but a few were absorbed into Sir John Johnson's second battalion. For the time being, these units remained at Sorel, and no doubt Johnson was happy to keep them at arm's length. The autumn of 1780 promised to be a very full one for the King's Royal Regiment of New York as the provincials retaliated for the rebel's destruction of the Iroquois lands in 1779.

Second Expedition through the Mohawk Valley, Autumn 1780.

In August 1780, Major John Ross took most of the men in his battalion to Côteau du Lac for fatigue duty. William Twiss, now a captain in the Royal Engineers, was supervising the construction of a shallow canal to bypass the Cedars Rapids. From Montreal, Sir John Johnson sent out parties of scouts who returned with intelligence, newspapers and recruits. One party who had been in the Mohawk Valley reported that the Oneida Indians had prevented the members from getting more than fifteen recruits, and when this information reached Governor Haldimand, he decided to force these Indians to change their allegiance. Writing to Johnson on August 24, Haldimand authorized him to lead another expedition to the Indian and rebel settlements near the Mohawk:

> The Treachery of the Onidas and constant obstacles they present to our Scouts in any attempt upon the Mohawk River makes it a matter of serious consideration to compel them to relinquish the Rebel interest, or to cut them off. The present seems a favourable opportunity for the undertaking.

The crop, Haldimand continued, had been good, and the rebels were not in a position to send a large reinforcement after any expedition that might enter the country around Johnson's former home. The governor was taking a calculated risk, for he did not want to reduce the strength of his garrison; but the grain was ripening and it should be destroyed before the rebels had time to remove it for the use of the Continental Army. He asked Johnson for advice on the best way of achieving the double objective of punishing the Oneidas and burning the crops. Again, Haldimand cautioned that the utmost secrecy was implicit.

Ideally the proposed expedition should be accompanied by a large force of Indians from Carleton Island and Niagara, but the governor was apprehensive over using them. After Sir John's safe return on June 3, Haldimand discovered that news of the impending raid had been known at Fort Stanwix on May 6 although the men did not leave Fort St. Johns until between the 8th and 10th. Despite Haldimand's earlier warnings, someone managed to slip away and alert the rebels. That they had forewarning had not hindered Sir John, but Haldimand was anxious to make certain that he would not be sending men into New York State only to be captured and lost to his garrison at a time when the security of Canada might be in jeopardy:

> By the Accounts I have from England and Concurring Reports I have from the Southward, some attempt is meditated against the Province, so situated the Impropriety of Risking the Flower of our Little Army (which must compose your Expedition) will evidently occur to you unless we are pretty Certain that the Indians will not abandon us in case of being obliged to fall back, the advantage expected would by no means atone for the Loss to be apprehended from the Onidas in case of a Retreat.[34]

Johnson heartily concurred with Haldimand. The Oneidas should be chastised, the grain crop destroyed, and the safety of Cabada must not be endangered. He proposed to have the expedition assemble at Oswego. From there he wanted to move well to the south, avoiding the settlements in the valleys, and burst from the forest at Schoharie, surprising the inhabitants. Next he proposed to sweep along the Mohawk, across the Oneidas' lands, and back to Oswego. However, if the pursuit was too close it might be judicious to allow part of his force to escape to Fort Oswegatchie. As for armaments:

> Two Royals and the Grass Hopper might be found serviceable, and can be easily conveyed on Horses for which there are good Roads all the way. I shall be happy with the assistance of Captain Scott and the same Detachments as I had before, but think that British in lieu of Chasseurs will answer better as they are not accustomed to Wood marches or carrying large Packs.

Grasshopper was the nickname used by both Johnson and John Butler for a small brass 3-pounder gun on a carriage. The Chasseurs were German Jaegers, who had not found favour with many of the British or provincial officers. From the experience he had gained on the earlier expedition, Sir John had some recommendations for improving the clothing of the men:

> from the nature of the Service the Troops destroy their Cloaths surprisingly. The Indian Shoes they received for the last Expedition were scarcely worth accepting. Blankets, overalls, and Shoes are necessary, which I hope Your Excellency will order for them as an Encouragement to go through the Service with cheerfulness. I shall observe the strictest secrecy on my Part and our Route will serve to conceal our real destination or intentions.

A contingent of rangers and regulars from Fort Niagara would meet him at Oswego.

> I expect it will take about fifteen days from the time we leave La Chine to get to Oswego from which the movement of the Troops from Niagara may be regulated, those who arrive first to wait the arrival of the other Division. Ten or a dozen Horses will be wanted from Niagara.

A scout should be sent from Carleton Island as soon as Haldimand could send the order, and Johnson intended dispatching a scouting party from Montreal at once, to bring back intelligence from the Mohawk Valley. For greater secrecy, Allan Maclean, the commandant at Montreal, was informed only that some men of the first battalion, King's Royal Regiment of New York were being sent to reinforce the garrison at Carleton Island. The governor decided not to send any regular troops from the lower St. Lawrence, partly for secrecy, partly because he was fearful of reducing his strength at Montreal. On August 31 he informed Johnson:

> You will find at Oswego the Light Companies of the King's and 34th Regts., and about 80 picked men of the same with 250 Rangers. Two men of the Royal Artillery, the whole about 440 men, which, with your own Corps will I suppose Complete a Body of about 750 fine Troops. I cannot pretend to say the number of Indians, but I imagine when collected at Oswego they must be considerable – in that

98

Officer's gorget, of gold or silver, was about five inches wide, worn on the chest. Officers of battalion companies had a single epaulette on the right shoulder; those in grenadier and light companies wore two epaulettes. Courtesy: Gaven K. Watt; photograph by Jean LaCroix.

Business I am the most apprehensive of a Discovery . . . Captain Scott shall accompany you and Captain Parke, who will take Command of the Detachment of the King's Regiment at Oswego; they can follow with you in the Light boat. I shall not mention to them a word of the Expedition.

By September 1, Haldimand had decided that only 150 of the first battalion, King's Royal Regiment of New York should be sent on the expedition, instead of the 310 he had earlier envisaged. At Carleton Island Johnson was to pick up part of Captain Robert Leake's company, leaving an equal number of the first battalion in lieu of them. Also, he was to choose men not employed in essential work at Côteau du Lac. Haldimand sent orders to Colonels Mason Bolton and Guy Johnson at Fort Niagara to prepare 140 of the King's (8th) Regiment, and 80 of the 34th Regiment, and 200 of Butler's Rangers for embarkation to Oswego, fewer men than he had specified earlier. The guns and horses would accompany them, and Colonel Guy Johnson was to recruit the Indians.[35]

On September 1, Sir John Johnson drew up a return of his first battalion which showed that 32 officers and 453 other ranks were fit for duty, of which 139 were occupied with essential work. Another 34 were sick in their quarters, 4 were sick in hospital, and 46 were on leave, while 15 were prisoners of the rebels. Within a week Sir John inadvertently incurred the wrath of Allan Maclean. Maclean had been ordered by the governor to dispatch 200 Royal Yorkers to Carleton Island and he was disconcerted to discover that Major James Gray had left Lachine for that base with only 150 men. Furthermore, a captain from Sir John's corps had told Maclean that an excursion to the Mohawk Valley would soon depart from Carleton Island. Maclean was annoyed that he had not been informed through more conventional channels – the governor or his secretary for English correspondence, Captain Robert Mathews of the 53rd Regiment.

For his part, Sir John was disturbed because Haldimand had reduced the strength of his detachment for the expedition. He had other men fit for duty, although his second battalion lacked winter clothing and arms, and a few of the first battalion were in the same condition. In the interest of security, Mathews wrote to Maclean on September 7, reiterating that the troops were only intended for Carleton Island. Deeply offended, Maclean took Sir John Johnson to task, and said that since he and his regiment were part of the District of Montreal, and therefore his subordinates, Sir John should have informed him of any orders he received from headquarters. To Mathews the peeved Maclean wrote:

I would however humbly beg leave to say that sending orders to inferior officers to execute without any Communication to the Commanding Officer of the District, may contribute to create an opinion that the Commanding Officer is not of any consideration whatever.

Mathews' reply was a mild reprimand. Maclean ought to have guessed that secrecy was His Excellency's only motive for excluding him, and the secretary ordered him to co-operate by sending a small diversionary expedition from Fort St. Johns towards Saratoga. In fact, two expeditions left at the same time. One, led by Major Christopher Carleton, was intended to pressure Vermont into becoming neutral – by destroying the outposts on New York territory near Lake Champlain. The other was to be led by Captain John Munro, of the first battalion, Royal Yorkers, and was to be organized by Brigadier Maclean. The captain was no stranger to Maclean, for he had piloted the Highlander through New York State in 1775 in quest of recruits for his Royal Highland Emigrants.

On September 28, Haldimand sent Maclean instructions to dispatch Munro with from 80 to 100 men from Isle aux Noix. The purpose of Munro's expedition was to draw attention away from what Sir John Johnson would be doing from Oswego. Ultimately, it consisted of two companies of the King's Royal Regiment of New York; 34 of Daniel Claus' Rangers, and 100 Mohawks from Fort Hunter in the Mohawk Valley, who had taken refuge near Lachine. From the vicinity of Saratoga, Munro was to swing southward and, if practicable, link up with Sir John's main force moving eastward from Oswego.

Meanwhile, Johnson had sailed from Carleton Island on September 20, reaching Oswego the following day. Then he was delayed, awaiting the arrival of a part of his force that was held up by poor winds, and the Indians, regulars and rangers coming from Fort Niagara with the grasshopper and one royal. The number of Indians, and the size of the Niagara contingent were disappointing. Johnson reported that sickness in that garrison was widespread. When he left Oswego he commanded these troops:

```
3 companies, first battalion, King's Royal
   Regiment of New York ─────────────── 150 ─ (Maj. James Gray)
Part of Leake's company ──────────────   50 ─ (Capt. Robert Leake)
Light Company, 8th Regiment ──────────   50 ─ (Capt. Andrew Parke)
Light Company 34th Regiment ──────────   50
Battalion Companies, 8th Regiment ────   90 ─ (Capt. Thomas Scott)
Battalion Companies, 34th Regiment ───   30
4 Companies, Butler's Rangers ──────── 200 ─ (Col. John Butler)
Artillery detachment ─────────────────   10
                                         ───
                                         630

Indians ────────────────────────────── 150 ─ (Capt. Joseph Brant)[36]
```

The force reached the Onondaga villages, near the river of the same name on October 5, and after crossing Lake Oneida concealed the boats and some provisions near Oneida Creek. There a scouting party brought word that a large rebel force had been assembling at Sacondaga, to the east, expecting the attack to come from Lake Champlain. Unruffled, Johnson marched his men, with the guns on sleds drawn by horses, close to the Oneida villages, where a scout of fifteen Indians with four prisoners joined him. From the prisoners Sir John learned that two Oneidas had gone to Albany to report that Colonel Butler and Captain Brant had left Niagara with 800 men for the Mohawk River. At that the Indians became alarmed,

Sir John Johnson's Raid on the Mohawk Valley
September-October 1780

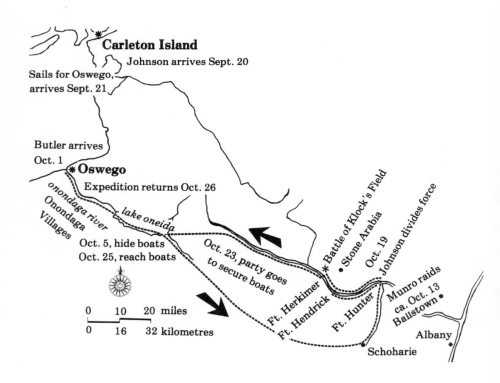

Carleton Island
Johnson arrives Sept. 20
Sails for Oswego, arrives Sept. 21
Butler arrives Oct. 1
Oswego
Expedition returns Oct. 26
Onondaga river
Onondaga Villages
lake oneida
Oct. 5, hide boats
Oct. 25, reach boats
Oct. 23, party goes to secure boats
Battle of Klock's Field
Stone Arabia
Oct. 19
Johnson divides force
Ft. Herkimer
Ft. Hendrick
Ft. Hunter
Munro raids ca. Oct. 13
Ballstown
Albany
Schoharie

0   10   20 miles
0   16   32 kilometres

and said they were not happy about penetrating settled country at Schoharie. Johnson was hard pressed to prevent them vanishing in small groups, and they were further disturbed by reports that 2,000 rebels might gather to oppose them.[37]

Johnson pushed on and, finding himself short of provisions, ordered some cattle brought from the nearby settlements. Then he turned towards Schoharie. Before dawn on October 17, his men were passing what he called the upper fort at Schoharie, where he ordered the field piece and the royal brought forward:

I soon had the mortification to see [the guns] were of no use, the men not understanding their business sufficiently to do the Enemy any Injury – finding that it was only losing time and hearing that the Country was alarmed, Captn Thompson of the Rangers was sent with a Flag to summons them to surrender, to which they paid no other attention but that of firing upon him.

Johnson left the settlers in their forts, while his men scoured the countryside for fifty yards around each of the fortified sites; then they turned towards the Mohawk by the road along the west shore of Schoharie Creek. Finding the road muddy and nearly impassable for the sleds, he ordered the royal slung across a horse, but word arrived that the rebels were gathering close by, and Major Gray had the gun, with all its shells, buried in a swamp. While some of the men struggled with the grasshopper, Captains Joseph Brant and Andrew Thompson went forward with 150 rangers and Indians and burned the settlement at Fort Hunter. The force was divided into two detachments, which marched westward along both sides of the Mohawk, burning everything in their path until they were just east of Stone Arabia, on the north shore. Then Johnson, with the detachment on the south shore, learned that the other detachment was about to be attacked.

At that point, there occurred an incident which proved that Haldimand had been injudicious in yielding to the wishes of his provincial officer and allowing deserters and prisoners to enlist. Making camp at midnight, the expedition scoured the narrow passes on both sides of the Mohawk:

Two of the men who had deserted from Fort Stanwix this spring left us and went over to the Enemy at Stone Arabia and informed Colonel Brown, who commanded there that the Detachment on that side of the River was very weak, which induced him to march out the next morning with three Hundred and sixty men to attack them. I meant to have crossed over to them in the night but the Troops were too fatigued to attempt it till the morning.

At dawn on October 19, in thick fog, Johnson and his force crossed the river to reinforce the detachment on the north shore, and the entire expedition marched towards Stone Arabia. They discovered some horsemen watching their movements from a height of land, and going in pursuit came upon the rebels' advance guard.

103

About 50 Indians attacked, supported by regulars and rangers. The rebels stayed in the woods; but Johnson's men were in an open field, too exposed to enemy fire for his liking.

Johnson ordered Captain John MacDonell, of the rangers, around to the left of the rebel position. In the ensuing skirmish the rebels fled, and in the pursuit, the rebel commander, Colonel John Brown, and 100 others were killed. Of MacDonell's force, one private and three Indians were killed, and Joseph Brant received a wound in the foot. From papers found on Brown's body, Johnson learned that General Robert van Rensslaer and 600 rebel militiamen had reached Fort Hunter the day before and could not be far behind. He ordered the settlement burnt and withdrew westward twelve miles until he was opposite Fort Hendrick, which stood on the south shore.

Here his expedition took to the woods to avoid three or four fortified houses which had commanding views of the ford across the Mohawk. The Indians fled to the south shore. Leaving a strong rearguard on the heights, Johnson led his main body of troops downhill towards the river, the enemy firing upon them. He tried to seek shelter in a house and some barns, but the fire was heavy, and some of the 34th Regiment and Royal Yorkers had to give way. Then the grasshopper was loaded with grape shot, which soon silenced the rebels. In local history this skirmish has been remembered as the Battle of Klock's Field, from the nearby fortified house called Fort Klock, but it was too minor to be included in general histories of the war. Under cover of darkness Johnson led his forces across the ford to the south shore of the Mohawk, and along the road towards Fort Herkimer, at German Flatts.

The expedition marched westward until October 23, without incident. Then it took a prisoner who said he had left Fort Stanwix with a party of rebels bent on destroying the boats the expedition had left concealed on the Oneida Creek. Johnson dispatched a party of six Indians and troops to safeguard them, and two days later the entire force was assembled at the spot. By nightfall the men reached the Oneida Falls on the Onondaga River and Oswego the following day. There the expedition dispersed, Butler's Rangers and the regulars making for Fort Niagara, while Johnson, Robert Leake and their men sailed for Carleton Island, arriving late in the evening of the 26th in the sloop *Caldwell*. With them went 64 prisoners. Johnson and part of the force that had come from Lachine left the outpost at two o'clock in the morning of October 27, and reached Montreal on the 30th. In his report written the following day Johnson said that he lost 9 men killed, 2 wounded, and had 52 missing.

104

Several of them were disabled by wounds, but he thought that the Indians would bring many out safely, or else keep them in their villages until they were fit to travel. He expected Major James Gray to reach Montreal with the rest of the Royal Yorkers and the prisoners within the next day or two.

While Johnson and his force of provincials, regulars and Indians had penetrated the Mohawk Valley from the western end, Major Christopher Carleton had successfully destroyed all the New York posts near Lake Champlain. Captain Munro reported that his party of provincials, rangers and refugee Mohawks had accompanied Carleton as far as Crown Point. Then, after sinking his boats to hide them, Munro marched his party westward on October 7. Seven miles into the woods, his men were complaining of the weight of the provisions and ammunition in their packs. Munro ordered a quantity of both cached, and with each man carrying 50 rounds and thirty days' supply of food, they continued their march. On the sixth day out from Crown Point, scouts returning informed Munro that the countryside was alarmed because a deserter from Major Rogers' King's Rangers had informed the rebels of Munro's intent. The militia from Schenectady had been rushed to Ballstown, a village eight miles to the north. The unflappable Munro sent out other scouts, and kept on marching towards Ballstown, the road 'the worst I ever travelled, and the night being very dark.' Then, with some bravado, Munro decided to take possession of the home of Colonel James Gordon, the commandant of the Ballstown Militia:

> I ordered Lieut. Langan with the Rangers and Indians to rush in at once on the House, while I drew up my men at two paces from each other, with shouldered Arms & fixed Bayonets, the moon shining so bright upon the mens arms & forming the Line so large a Person not Acquainted with our numbers would imagine them much greater than they realy were – The Coll. and all his family were soon secured.[38]

According to Lieutenant John Enys, the rangers with Munro belonged to Daniel Claus, and the officer mentioned was Patrick Langan, later a captain in the second battalion, King's Royal Regiment of New York.[39] Munro was tempted to take up a position in a church at Ballstown, but thinking it might be imprudent, he concentrated instead on burning all the rebel houses in the neighbourhood. Unable to find out where Sir John Johnson was, Munro withdrew, rejoining Major Carleton near Crown Point on October 23. His men were desperate for provisions, for those they had cached had been found by what he described as 'some Parties coming to this Province, and the rest of what we left was eat up by the vermin.' Hungry refugees were the beneficiaries of Munro's foresight, while his men had to proceed with empty bellies.

In a report, dated November 20 at Lachine, Munro felt a need to justify his actions, explaining that he had done all his small force permitted without endangering his men, and that he was unable to go to Saratoga, as ordered. Like Johnson, Munro stated that forest warfare was hard on clothing and his party 'was distressed for everything having wore out all their Shoes, Mockosins, Trowsers, Leggings, &c.' He also explained why he had been unable to carry out all his orders, for fear of acquiring some undesirable reinforcements:

My reason for not striking on Saratoga as directed was owing to the great number of Women & Children which were lodged in the Barracks and having their Husbands in my Detachment, would of course follow them, and also not knowing that General Schyler was arrived there; these considerations induced me to get as near Schenectady as possible in order to join Sir John Johnson in which I was disappointed.

The women and children in Saratoga were interned by the rebels, who had removed them from their homes, and naturally if Munro's party had struck that village the dependants would have wanted to be taken away. Munro's report also sheds light on how loyalists still in their homes were a help to provincials marauding in rebel-controlled territory. He explained that he had marched ten miles across friendly country, guided by local men through darkness which left even the Indians helpless. As he withdrew, these local loyalists told the rebels who pursued him that his force was 500 strong, which induced them to turn back. From his informants Munro learned that 400 'Negros' around Albany and Schenectady were anxious to join the King's troops, but he warned Haldimand not to trust:

those Gentlemen Called the Green Mountain Boys, I have been at open War with them these Sixteen years past – they have been a pest to the Government of New York since the last war, they are a Collection of Malefactors.

Munro scornfully informed Haldimand that 'some of these People who came in on pretence of Terms of Reconciliation to Major Carleton at Crown Point . . . were my Wood cutters at Home.'

Once, after a fierce argument Seth Warner drew his sword and smote Munro over the head. According to Ira Allen, the Scotsman's thick hair and skull saved his brains and broke Warner's sword. Ira, the smallest and most devious of the Allen brothers, described the day when the Green Mountain Boys tried Munro for his 'crimes' and sentenced him to what was called 'chastisement by twigs of the wilderness.' He was tied to a tree and flayed on the bare back with a green beech rod until he fainted. He was revived and the flogging resumed until he fainted again. After he fainted and was revived a third time, Munro's wounds were dressed and he was banished from the Green Mountain forever.[40]

Ira Allen's account is vivid rather than accurate. Munro was imprisoned twice, and prior to his first incarceration he had assisted Allan Maclean who was recruiting in New York for his Royal Highland Emigrants.[41] Maclean had promised Munro a commission but when the latter reached Canada he chose the King's Royal Regiment of New York, possibly because he found that Maclean's men would not be very active against the rebels.

Before Sir John Johnson left with his force for Oswego, Governor Haldimand had suggested that he might leave some men at Carleton Island for the winter and he offered Johnson the command of Fort Haldimand. Sir John declined, informing Haldimand that he thought the first battalion would be of more service in 'Canada' while the second battalion, although far from complete, would suffice for Carleton Island, where Major Ross could take command of the garrison. Haldimand accepted Sir John's recommendations, and Ross left Côteau du Lac that November with 100 Royal Yorkers. On Carleton Island Ross' detachment began strengthening Fort Haldimand's defences, which were far from satisfactory.

On November 15th, Governor Haldimand reported to Sir Henry Clinton at New York City on Johnson's expedition from Oswego:

> The Crops at Schohary and the Mohawk River were never known to be so great and so little had been sent to Market and every grain destroyed for near 50 miles, it is thought that the Enemy's Loss at a moderate computation cannot be less than 600,000 bushels of grain. This with the damage done by the Detachment under Major Carleton and another of above 200 Indians which marched at the same time for the Connecticut River & Destroyed 32 barns full of grain and a Quantity of Live Stock will have greatly impoverished those Parts but will probably be an additional motive for the Enemy to attempt the Reduction of this Province for the security of their frontiers.

The first battalion, King's Royal Regiment of New York was ordered into winter quarters at Sorel, along with the Royal Highland Emigrants, which had become the 84th Foot. Johnson, perturbed that he could not achieve the same status for his corps, applied to Haldimand again for leave to go to England, so that he could plead his case for inclusion on the regular establishment. He told the governor that he regretted not going to New York City to raise his regiment, for he was aware that Oliver DeLancey and Cortlandt Skinner, two gentlemen hardly of the same social standing as himself, had been raising brigades. DeLancey, a distant relative of Lady Johnson, had raised three battalions, while Skinner ultimately commanded five battalions of New Jersey Volunteers – the largest provincial corps in any department. Both men were brigadier-generals, and Sir John was feeling ill used.

Haldimand, who must have been aware that the status of his provincials could be raised, indulged in some double talk. He assured Sir John that all regiments enlisted in North America were provincial corps, as was the 84th until put on the British establishment. Johnson was not deceived:

> It would appear that I have been unjustly dealt with, and because I began to act much earlier and have hitherto not had that assistance in the Raising of my Regiment that all others to the Southward have, I am not even to enjoy the same Rank and consequently the same emoluments as they do.

By assistance he meant a brigadier-general's pay, the right to a bounty for his recruits from public funds, and half pay for his officers when the corps was reduced, all of which were permissible under the British government's policies by 1780. Clearly Sir Henry Clinton was abiding by the more recent directives from London, whereas Haldimand, with his dark suspicion of all colonials, was withholding favours.

That autumn of 1780 brought another blow to Sir John Johnson's ego. On October 9, the New York Provincial Congress passed an Act of Attainder outlawing most of the loyalist leaders from that state and making their estates forfeited. Johnson hoped to ask for compensation from the home government, but he could not find passage on a suitable vessel. Relieved, the governor told Johnson that should he fall into rebel hands, he would be lost to the cause and to his family. Next Sir John asked that the men of his second battalion, most of whom were at Côteau du Lac, be issued with decent firearms. Thus far they had only 'Indian muskets.' Haldimand declined because he had no more arms to spare for provincials.

Johnson's resentment over Haldimand's restrictions smouldered as the snows began to fall. Messrs Peters and Jessup, the leaders of two below-strength provincial corps, he noted, understood from warrants signed by Sir Guy Carleton that their officers' commissions would be approved when their corps reached two-thirds strength. Haldimand had held out no such hope for the officers of the second battalion, King's Royal Regiment of New York. In an angry protest Sir John wrote:

> I have the Vanity to think that Had I been so fortunate as to have gone to New York, in place of coming to Canada, and met with the same Countenance and encouragement that the New Levies in every other part of the Continent have done . . . I would have had at least three Battalions in place of one; and still without taking the unwarrantable means that others seem to be countenanced in, of handing Enlistments through Prison Grates to be signed by any Person who may chuse to be enlarged upon so easy terms without regard to their principles or Character. I hope to compleat my Second Battalion but I must beg to Know what numbers are necessary to justify the appointment of the Officers.

He also enquired when he would receive warrant money due him, but Haldimand's reply was crusty. He denied that recruiting officers were raising new levies by enlisting jailbirds. Furthermore, no matter what Jessup and Peters said, their officers would be ap-

108

pointed to each company as it was completed. He also added:

I cannot consistently with the authority transmitted to me from Home and consequently with my duty declare your Regiment any other than a Provincial Corps, I am only left to regret it – and upon the latter I must desire you will in future avoid all Reflections of the kind.

Despite Johnson's frustrations, a return of his regiment before the year ended showed that, in addition to commissioned officers, the first battalion had 30 sergeants, 30 corporals, 20 drummers and 485 privates, with 137 listed as casualties. There were 301 effectives in the second battalion, making a total of 1,003 rank and file and non-commissioned officers. The first battalion had a full compliment of commissioned officers. Haldimand informed Sir John that payment for casualties would have to be handled with discretion:

The matter of Casualties you may be assured of it shall be made as easy for you as possible, but it is a subject which must rest entirely between us – Mr. Peters affirms that he had lost 210 killed at Bennington and 30 made Prisoners, others in Proportion, if these were to be allowed, little should be expected of the New Levies.

In other words, if all casualties were to be compensated, the governor would be short of funds to pay the newer recruits.

Major John Ross's Expedition, Autumn 1781

During the winter of 1780-81, parties of the Royal Yorkers were active in the Mohawk Valley acquiring intelligence for Governor Haldimand. One of Sir John Johnson's contacts was the Reverend John Stuart, the Anglican missionary to the Mohawks at Fort Hunter, who had been hired by Sir William Johnson. Many of Stuart's flock had fled to Lachine, and the rebels had marched the clergyman to Schenectady and placed him under house arrest. Nevertheless, on March 15, Johnson reported the return of a scouting party led by John Parker, who brought back some newspapers provided by Stuart. Parker (hanged a year later after the rebels captured him near Albany) had visited his father, whose house was near Johnstown. In his letter to Haldimand, Sir John asked for clemency on behalf of Parker's brother, who had been convicted of theft and sentenced to be executed.[42]

Haldimand was quick to oblige, being grateful for Parker's intelligence, which warned him that the high-ranking officers in Albany might be planning an invasion of Canada. Parker's source was a Mr. Dawson, who served as an engineer with the rebels. In April, Johnson lost his most valuable contact in that town when Dr. George Smyth, the erudite 'Hudibras,' was forced to flee to evade arrest. A man identified as Hewson, a volunteer serving with Joseph Brant, had defected to the rebels at Fort Stanwix, and had been escorted to Albany to give testimony against Smyth who, upon discovering that a warrant for his apprehension had been issued, had vanished.[43]

Although Haldimand had other sources of information – Captain Justus Sherwood, then operating from Isle aux Noix, Major John Ross at Carleton Island, and Colonel John Butler at Niagara, as well as scouts going out from many frontier posts – he depended on Johnson for important intelligence at that time. Towards the end of April, Haldimand ordered him to come to Quebec City for a conference on a variety of subjects, one being ways and means of completing the second battalion, King's Royal Regiment of New York.

A return of the first battalion, taken in March showed the following:

Rank and file fit for duty 379
Sick in quarters 23
On Command (i.e., fatigue duty)58
Sick in hospital 5
On furlough 20
Prisoners with the enemy 31
Total 556
Needed to complete the establishment, 44

This return does not show why 44 men were still needed. All rank and file was supposed to amount to 530, not 560. Possibly the 30 corporals were included with the ranks, which would make up the difference between the requirements and the terms of Sir John Johnson's warrant.

It is not known what Haldimand and Johnson discussed together at Quebec, but by June 4 Johnson was back in Montreal and reporting that 12 recruits had arrived, and that he anticipated the scouts then in rebel territory would shortly bring in 30 more. However, he was perturbed to discover that in his absence Brigadier Allan Maclean had censured Captain John Munro. Major James Gray was on leave, and Munro had been in command of a detachment of the first battalion on duty at Côteau du Lac. Johnson's letter reveals another task performed by the regiment that is rarely alluded to in secondary sources. Munro's men were guarding prisoners of war. Compounds and private homes around Montreal were used to house such prisoners. In her diary Mrs. Simcoe described an incident on Prison Island: 'Rebels having been confined on it during the last War, some of whom escaped by swimming across the Rapids by which it is surrounded.'[44]

It may have been this incident that upset Maclean. He called Munro derelict in his duty and upbraided the entire regiment. Johnson sprang to the defence of his men. He wrote to the governor, enclosing a copy of Maclean's irate letter to Munro:

[I] must beg to intreat that Your Excellency will be pleased to remove us from under the Command of a Person capable of such severe censure upon a set of men whose only wishes are and ever have been to serve their Sovereign and Country as far as their abilities and interests will permit them.

Haldimand's reply is more enlightening. Munro failed to report the escape of some prisoners to Maclean, which he ought to have done since the brigadier was the commandant of the district. The governor began by agreeing that the regiment should be removed from 'its present situation' but this was not feasible for the time being. Nonetheless, Munro had not acted with propriety:

The omission of not reporting the affair at Coteau du Lac to the Brigadier and Receiving his orders theron was certainly very Reprehensible in whoever commanded the Regiment and if an Old Soldier still more so, a proper rebuke from the Brigadier I should imagine would have been well received . . . I am sorry he should have adopted a method of rebuking Individuals that is capable of giving umbrage to a Body, tho' I am persuaded he wishes too well to the Service and to you to have intended any.

Writing the same day to Maclean, Haldimand scolded him for being too quick to condemn an entire corps when only Munro was at fault:

There is a tenderness and delicacy to Sir John Johnson who cannot be expected to have a minute acquaintance with military forms and consequently cannot teach them, demands not to say anything of what is due to his meritorious conduct. Young Corps stand in need of admonition & indulgence and naturally commit many errors which in old ones could be faults.

Meanwhile, several parties of Royal Yorkers were out scouting. That season the New York State revolutionary government passed a law aimed at interfering with the recruitment of loyalists still in their homes. Parents of young men who had gone to join the British were subjected to fines. Where one son had gone, the penalty was ninepence in the pound to the whole value of their property, and where two or more sons were known to be serving with the King's troops, the sum was to be doubled or tripled.[45] This law proved nearly impossible to enforce, and the agents recruiting for Johnson and the other provincial corps commanders continued bringing in men.

On July 16, Haldimand asked Johnson to straighten out some confusion surrounding 'Negros brought into Canada by scouting parties.' Most came expecting to be given their freedom in return for promising to join a provincial corps. The baronet was to make a return of all the black men and submit it to Maclean. Those belonging to loyalists in Canada were to be sent to their owners, but those belonging to rebels posed a dilemma, although some might be permitted to enlist. The list was to show the names of all owners, whether loyalist or rebel. Where a man had been sold to a new owner, the price paid and his present whereabouts were to be recorded.

111

Johnson soon sent a recommendation that Colonel James Gordon, captured at Ballstown by Munro's men the autumn before, be exchanged for the Reverend John Stuart, still under house arrest in Schenectady. Haldimand refused, because Gordon had tried to foment a revolt among the prisoners of war around Montreal and had been removed to Quebec City for safe keeping. In fact, in October the rebels allowed Stuart to leave for Lake Champlain with a party of refugees. Haldimand admitted that the refugee problem had become unwieldy, and he hoped that the Reverend Stuart would remain in Schenectady as long as possible, supplying scouts with intelligence:

> The Public Good will in the end reap the benefit . . . as to the Families of the soldiers now in the Colonies, I must in Confidence acquaint you that every Ration of Provisions that can be saved in our present situation is an object – It is a Declaration I cannot make to all, but those to whom I do make it, I persuade myself will give every assistance in their Power to promote that economy which I am sorry is so necessary. . . . Such are my apprehensions for a Scarcity of Provisions that I propose sending to the Colonies by the Returning Flag all the women and children considered as Prisoners from the Rebels.[46]

Haldimand was referring to the wives and children of rebel sympathizers living in Montreal, most of them Yankee businessmen who had moved there following the Seven Years' War in search of commercial gain. The businessmen were generally interned until they could be exchanged for prisoners the rebels were holding. The governor therefore asked Johnson to make a list of all the women and children who were to be exchanged and Maclean was to hold them in readiness to depart. All were to promise under oath to refrain from taking up arms against His Majesty as a condition of their being allowed to leave Canada.

On September 24, Johnson wrote to the governor for the third time to request his leave of absence in England, pleading the need to look after his private affairs, and place his eldest children in suitable schools there. He felt that the season was too far advanced for any more excursions against the rebels. His paper work was up to date, and the corps ready to go into winter quarters. This time Haldimand relented, although he did have plans to use part of the regiment for an offensive into New York State:

> Tho' I cannot help regretting the loss of so Zealous an officer even for the short Time you propose staying . . . Private concerns, which you represent now so pressingly to require your attendance in England induced me to comply with your request and you have my permission to go the first opportunity. . . . If you have not made an arrangement for your passage I shall be happy to accommodate you and Lady Johnson in one of the Transport Vessels which are equally safe and less expensive.

With the Johnson family on the high seas for England, Haldimand authorized one more expedition against the rebels in the Mohawk Valley. Major John Ross would command it, using men from his own second battalion, King's Royal Regiment of New York, some regulars and Indians. Ross, the commandant at Carleton Island since the previous November, was the recipient of considerable intelligence brought to his post by scouts working from that quarter. In June he heard that the rebels had withdrawn from Fort Stanwix. He dispatched a party led by Lieutenant William Redford Crawford to verify this report. Returning, Crawford announced that the fort had indeed been evacuated by the rebels, and the timbers burnt.

John Ross, a veteran who had served on the frontiers during the Seven Years' War, was an inventive officer. In May, he sent out John Servos, a one-time rebel soldier who had been captured during Johnson's raid the autumn before and had enlisted in Ross's battalion. Ross instructed Servos to give himself up to the rebels as a deserter, and he was taken to Albany and questioned by Governor George Clinton and the members of his executive council, who were meeting in the town at that time. Servos gave them an inaccurate report on the defences at Carleton Island that had been prepared by Ross, who joyously reported the return of his spy in August:

I was lucky in my choice. He had been in every fort on the Mohawk river, one excepted, and brought in detail of the strength of the whole. After fulfilling everything requisite he obtained a pass to go to the Jerseys, but returned to join his regiment a few days ago with six young recruits for Sir John Johnson's 2nd Battalion. He says the inhabitants are in expectation of a visit from Sir John, and in some places are secreting Provisions for him.

Ross sent Servos to Montreal to be examined again, and Haldimand awarded him a gratuity of $20 in return for such valuable services. In the meantime, Lieutenant Crawford and Adjutant Humphrey Arden had been in the Mohawk Valley with small parties of the second battalion and some Indians to capture cattle. Towards the end of August they returned and reported that they had driven superior numbers of rebels to seek shelter in their forts. The two officers and their men attacked a settlement fifteen miles below Fort Herkimer, destroying a mill, other buildings and much grain, and had killed some cattle.

Haldimand's letter to Ross, ordering him to command an expedition into the Mohawk Valley was dated September 6, and marked private. Ross would lead troops from the garrisons at Fort Niagara and Carleton Island, to avoid the publicity attendant with moving troops from Montreal; and for added security only Ross, Brigadier Watson Powell, then the commandant of the upper posts and resident at Fort Niagara, would know of their intentions. As on Johnson's last raid, this expedition would assemble at Oswego, where the governor recommended leaving a cache of provisions. At the same time, an expedition led by Colonel St. Leger was to occupy Crown Point. Haldimand advised Sir Henry Clinton that both these excursions against the rebels in New York were intended to influence the Vermont politicians, to make them see the benefits of neutrality and declare for Britain:

> Vermont Assembly is to meet the 1st Oct. I shall send a large detachment about that time to take Post and remain while the Season will permit at Crown Point. Strong Parties will likewise appear upon the Mohawk River and Frontier of Pennsylvania – I have Hopes from the Assurance of those whose Loyalty and Knowledge I have the greatest Confidence that this step will produce a favourable decision in the Affairs of Vermont – If your Excellency can derive any Advantages from it in your present Situation it will afford me infinite Pleasure.

Clinton did not avail himself of the opportunity to move out from New York City towards the Mohawk Valley.

To Powell at Fort Niagara, Haldimand sent instructions to co-operate with Major Ross, by sending some of Butler's Rangers and ordering Colonel Guy Johnson to gather together a large body of Indians:

> You will give these parties orders effectively to destroy all kinds of grains &c. Forrage, Mills &c., cattle and all articles which can contribute to the support of the enemy. They will as usual have the strongest Injunctions to avoid the destruction of women and children and every species of cruelty. This opportunity should if possible be taken to extirpate the remaining unfriendly Oneidas who much impede our scouts and recruiting Parties and are in many respects very useful to the Rebels.

As always, speed and secrecy were the essence of the attack. Haldimand wanted Ross to be close to his prey before news that St. Leger had reached Crown Point could be relayed to the rebels. The contingent from Fort Niagara was delayed by contrary winds and slow communication, and it did not reach Oswego until October 10, a week after Ross's men arrived from Carleton Island. The combined expedition consisted of these units:

```
FROM CARLETON ISLAND:

4 companies, 2nd batt. King's Royal
Regiment of New York, including Leake's — 198   (Maj. John Ross)
34th Regiment ————————————————————————— 76    (Capt. Wm. Ancrum)
84th Regiment, Royal Highland Emigrants — 36
German Jaegers ———————————————————————— 12
                                         322

FROM NIAGARA:

3 companies Butler's Rangers ——————————— 167   (Capt. Walter Butler)
8th Regiment (King's) —————————————————— 36    (Lieut. Thos. Coote)

Indians, mixed tribes ————————————————— 109    (Capt. Gilbert Tice)

Indians from the Genesee River country
    who joined Ross at Oswego ————————— 100  (47)
Total commanded by Ross                  734
```

Ross was destined to meet stiffer opposition, and to find less to destroy than Johnson had on his last sweep of the Mohawk Valley. Many people had left the area, and those who remained were able to

Ross's Expedition to the Mohawk Valley October 1781

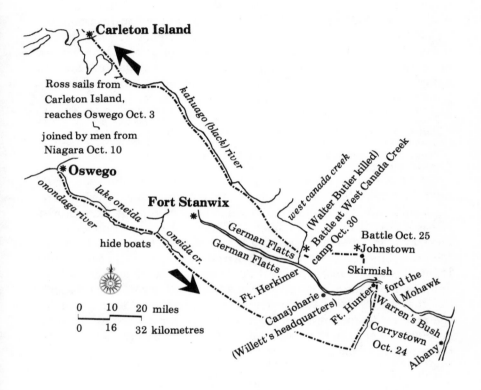

Carleton Island

Ross sails from
Carleton Island,
reaches Oswego Oct. 3

joined by men from
Niagara Oct. 10

*Oswego

onondaga river

lake oneida

kahuago (black) river

Fort Stanwix

hide boats

oneida cr.

0   10   20 miles

0   16   32 kilometres

German Flatts
German Flatts

Ft. Herkimer

Canajoharie

(Willett's headquarters)

west canada creek

(Walter Butler killed)
* Battle at West Canada Creek
camp Oct. 30

Battle Oct. 25
*Johnstown

Skirmish

Ft. Hunter

ford the Mohawk

Warren's Bush

Corrystown
Oct. 24

Albany*

take refuge in strong posts. Between Schenectady and German Flatts, some 63 miles, were twenty-four fortified camps, each capable of sheltering many families with their cattle and horses, grain and implements. In command of the rebel troops was Colonel Marinius Willett, who had established his headquarters at Canajoharie after the rebels abandoned Fort Stanwix. Small parties of regulars from his detachment of two regiments of Continental soldiers were constantly on the march, to reassure the remaining inhabitants. As well as his 1,200 regulars, Willett could call out 800 militiamen.

Ross's report on his venture is dated October 7, 1781, but he must have written it nearly a month later, for at that time he had not even set out from Oswego. He complained that the Indians who joined him from Niagara were a poor-spirited group, but Captain Gilbert Tice, who led them, sprang to their defence:

This is worth your observation, the Indians did not attempt to meddle with any Women, Children, old men or men not in arms, neither was any man or person killed by them, or striped of what they had on, only the engagement, except one man who fired his piece at an Indian that Broke open the Door of his House, they took him out, and shot him, but did not as much as Scalp him, which I think is remarkable.[48]

In his report, after stating that Colonel Guy Johnson could have sent more Indians, and men of better character from Niagara, Ross said that his expedition reached the vicinity of Corrystown, south of Fort Hunter on October 24. They had left their boats at Canasarago, on Oneida Creek and marched well to the south of the Mohawk. His first objective was Warrensborough, to the east of Fort Hunter, and he was apprised that the rebels were expecting him, and had more than 2,000 men in readiness. Ross resolved on speed, but the weather had turned frightful – heavy rain that converted the road into a quagmire. A night march took his force to Warrensborough, where the men rested until daylight. Before noon, despite the rain, the whole settlement was in flames:

Near one hundred farms, three mills and a large Granary for Public service were reduced to Ashes, the Cattle and Stock of all kinds were likewise destroyed. The Inhabitants fled precipitately in the Night. The Troops joined according to orders within 12 miles of Schenectady . . . from Prisoners and others I learned that the Rebels were on their march from every Quarter far superior to my numbers. . . . I always in my own breast designed retreating to Carleton Island but imparted it to none, so that the Prisoners who fell into Enemy's hands the night before could make no discovery; to retreat as I came must give the Enemy every advantage, they having command of the River could get in my front at pleasure.[49]

Ross suspected that the rebels might easily find the cache of provisions hidden back on Oneida Creek, and a journey from there to Niagara and Carleton Island, with empty bellies and worn footwear at that time of year 'presented a disagreeable Prospect.' A more direct withdrawal towards his own post seemed the wisest course, and accordingly at one o'clock on the afternoon of October 25, his men began fording the Mohawk, making for Johnstown. Rain teemed down, and the rebel militia began appearing along the river bank before he got his whole force across. After a skirmish with the garrison of the rebel fort at Johnstown, Ross resolved to march through the forest to the part of German Flatts that lay north of the Mohawk, from which place a trail led northward, directly to Carleton Island. Entering the woods east of Johnstown at four o'clock in the afternoon, Ross's scouts warned him that the rebels were right behind him. Fearing he could not outmarch them he determined to make a stand.

Although the ground was not to his advantage, he formed up his men. Colonel Willett's advance party appeared, and when fired upon retreated. Then Willett himself came forward with the main body of his troops. Ross's men stood their ground. The rebels wavered, and Ross ordered an advance, carrying a running fight until his men were at the edge of some woods. Willett's men broke and fled for more than a mile, and Ross wrote:

I lamented the want of a good Body of Indians, (few of those present venturing to engage), in which Had I been so fortunate, it would in all probability have crushed the Spirit of Rebellion on the Mohawk River, on our left the Rebels had planted a Field Piece with another Body of men, and in our following the Enemy out of the Woods they kept up a brisk fire, the Troops advanced to attack, the very countenance of which made the Rebels give way.

The rebels abandoned their field piece, but still another body of their troops came on from the right. Ross ordered their own 3-pounder turned on them while his troops almost surrounded them. Nightfall prevented further action. In the darkness Willett made his escape. Ross's men destroyed the ammunition the rebels had abandoned, hid in the woods for the night, and resumed their march towards the trail north from German Flatts. During the battle Ross said his men acquitted themselves well, and he reported that more than 1,200 rebels pursued them, 400 of them Continentals. His casualties were negligible, while the enemy lost many officers and at least 20 men where he had time to make a count.

The weather was appalling. Not until October 29 were Ross's scouts able to find the trail north. Then the Indians from Niagara decided to go straight home, regardless of the safety of the rest of the force. A day's march from German Flatts, snow fell, and Ross was forced to make camp. The next morning, Ross reported:

we parted with the Indians leaving them in the Camp. I still thought that from our late delays we should have a visit from the Enemy, nor was I disappointed, they were in our Camp soon after we sett off, and before the Indians left it, who had just time to save themselves in the Woods, an Indian officer was taken.

(The officer was Lieutenant John Ryckman.) Next, the rebel ad-

117

vance parties fired upon an Indian in Ross's rearguard. The major ordered his men across the West Canada Creek with all dispatch. The crossing was completed by two o'clock in the afternoon:

> Just as the Troops had all got over, the Rebels made their appearance and fired upon our Rear, the fire was returned. Captain Butler, who commanded the Rangers covering the Line of March was unfortunately killed, several men were also killed and wounded. The Enemy had greatly the advantage of Ground and their favourite object of firing at a distance, wherefore I ordered the Troops to move forward in order to take possession of the first favourable Spot that offered which was accordingly done, the sick and wounded were sent on.

Ross's men waited nearly an hour, then he concluded the rebels had no stomach for pursuit. The march resumed, after the battle, although the men were exhausted and short of provisions; but they reached Carleton Island on November 6, without abandoning a single prisoner they had taken. Ross promised to recover the provisions left at Oswego, and if possible the cache beside Oneida Creek.

Naturally, Colonel Willett belittled Ross's accomplishment, although he grudgingly admired the major's performance and the way his men escaped. Willett claimed a mild victory, and put the rebels' losses at thirty farms, not the hundred reported by Ross. He also wondered why such a good body of troops had been sent to so little effect – for he did not know that one reason for the show was to impress Vermont. The rebel officer noted with approval:

> Although they had been four days in the wilderness with only half a pound of horseflesh per man, yet they ran thirty miles in their famished condition before they stopped.[50]

By November 16, Ross was able to report the safe arrival of the men he had sent to retrieve the supplies from Oneida Creek and Oswego at Carleton Island. From a loyalist who returned with two men of the second battalion who had been scouting, Ross heard that 42 rebels had been killed at West Canada Creek. To his superiors Colonel Willett reported only 13 killed and 24 wounded. Initially, Ross's return showed that he had lost 74 all ranks, but 50 were reported missing. Of these, 13 were Butler's Rangers who reached Oswego safely, and many others turned up at Niagara and Carleton Island as the days passed. Whether Ross's men destroyed as much property as he claimed or not, their withdrawal under frightful conditions, pursued by a superior force, must stand as one of the more remarkable achievements by provincials and regulars of the revolutionary war.

The Occupation of Oswego, Spring 1782

Sir John Johnson's active leadership of the King's Royal Regiment of New York ended with his departure for England in the autumn of 1781. He remained nominally the lieutenant-colonel commandant, but the command passed to his two majors. James Gray and the first battalion were on duty around Montreal, and a detachment was still used to guard prisoners of war at Côteau du Lac. Indirectly – diplomatically – Governor Haldimand had solved Johnson's difficulties with Allan Maclean, who had also taken a leave of absence and was on his way to England. Haldimand gave the command of the district of Montreal to Brigadier Ernst von Speth, a German regular officer. Once Maclean's leave was up, he was sent to replace Brigadier Watson Powell as commandant of the upper posts.

Soon after taking up his post, Brigadier von Speth ordered Captain Samuel Anderson of the first battalion to take 80 ranks and two other officers and reinforce the garrison at Côteau du Lac. Shortly afterward Major Gray reported that the threat of an outbreak of prisoners was exaggerated, but he placed one subaltern and 30 men in the barracks on Prison Island, while Anderson, one subaltern and the other 50 men were quartered in a fort on the north shore of the St. Lawrence.

Major Ross expected to have the most of his second battalion at Carleton Island to reinforce his garrison, but some of these men did not reach Fort Haldimand until mid December. Meanwhile, disquietening rumours from Virginia hinting that Lord Charles Cornwallis had surrendered were reaching the various posts and Quebec City. Ross had strengthened his defences in case the rebels should attack his base once the ice on the St. Lawrence was thick enough to take the weight. He asked the governor to let him have the rest of the second battalion in the spring; he disliked having his command scattered as he could not administer to the needs of his men satisfactorily.

Near Montreal, the number of wives and children was increasing as more loyalists fled their homes, or the rebels deported or exchanged families. The enemy was as anxious as Governor Haldimand to have fewer mouths to feed, and families of the men serving in Canada were destitute and a drain on the public purse.[51] Many such families who had been escorted to the border were quartered in barracks on Ile Jesus.

As the year 1782 opened, Haldimand's fears that Cornwallis had capitulated were confirmed, and he looked to the defences of Canada anew. George Washington and his French allies were now in a position to turn the might of their combined forces northward, and Haldimand suspected that he could not rely on his francophone subjects should their former countrymen march on his province. Although the rebels were virtually defeated in the north, Haldimand suspected that Britain might grant the Thirteen Colonies their independence, which prompted him to comply with a demand the Indians had been making for years, the occupation of Oswego. For the security of the fur trade the three crumbling forts left from the Seven Years' War ought to be rebuilt and strongly garrisoned without delay. Oswego must form part of Haldimand's chain of forts remaining in British hands should a Peace Treaty be signed, since possession was nine points of the law. Therefore the governor ordered Major Ross to prepare to take over the decayed forts with a strong detachment and supplies as soon as possible in the spring. For greater secrecy, Ross was to spread the word that the extra men and supplies reaching Carleton Island were destined for Fort Niagara, where they were needed by the many refugees who had come to that post.

On March 6, Haldimand issued his order for Ross to set out from Carleton Island, and the major took 170 men of his own battalion of Royal Yorkers and 80 of the 8th (King's) Regiment. In the same letter the governor's secretary, Robert Mathews, now a major, informed Ross that he would soon be receiving four companies of Butler's Rangers. Mathews' subsequent letters to Ross showed that Haldimand was fussing over reports that the rebels were assembling arms and clothing for 10,000 men at Albany, and that French commisaries were buying all the pork and flour that was available. Many rebel families, feeling more secure since Cornwallis's fall, were returning to their farms and might be in a position to supply an army on the march with provisions. Ross was to look to the state of his food supply, for should the rebels enter the lower part of the province the St. Lawrence, the lifeline, would be cut and all transport to the upper posts cease.

Ross left Carleton Island, his men in bateaux, and the command of Fort Haldimand passed to Captain William Ancrum, 53rd Regiment. The men had to pole their boats through blocks of floating ice, but they reached Oswego the day after they set out. On March 16, some ships followed on a fair wind. The snow *Seneca*, commanded by Captain René LaForce, went on to Niagara and returned with 27 soldiers of the 8th Regiment and 7 officers and 185 men of Butler's Rangers. Ross then sent a request to Brigadier Powell at Niagara to dispatch some Indians to work as scouts, and he received 20 warriors.

In the interval, Captain Ancrum had been complaining that his garrison had too many invalids and elderly men to fulfill the duties expected of them at Carleton Island. Governor Haldimand agreed to send the rest of the second battalion, King's Royal Regiment of New

York, and two companies of Royal Highland Emigrants to reinforce that post. He also authorized Ross to open a trading station at Oswego, and he granted licences to two prominent merchants at Fort Niagara, Robert Hamilton and Richard Cartwright. To operate the station at Oswego and supply the garrison and Indian allies, Hamilton and Cartwright sent Robert Dickson as their agent.

By June 26, Joseph Brant, for whom Ross had been watching ever since he reached Oswego, arrived with 300 Indians. All pitched in to help Ross's troops build fortifications. By that time Brant knew that the North ministry in London had fallen, and he was very worried about the policies the new Prime Minister, Lord Rockingham, might adopt. Ross reported that Brant had had an experience in London which indicated clearly the sympathy many Englishmen felt for the rebels:

The Change of Ministry affects him much nor does he like it, he says that the Indians can expect no friendship from them and starts several questions which I own I am puzzled to answer.
He recited an Event which happened at a Masquerade in London. An English Nobleman came up to him and asked him if ever he intended to lift the tomahawk which he held in his hand against the Americans. Joseph guessing at his Sentiments, answered no on which the Nobleman replied that he was glad to hear it, he hoped all the Indians were of the same way of thinking for the Americans were an injured people, and with a seeming degree of satisfaction kissed his Tomahawk.

The following day, Ross was lavish in his praise of Brant:

I can assure your Excellency that we are much indebted to the Indians for assisting us to work, a Circumstance which I believe never before happened. Joseph showed them the Example. I never saw men work so hard and it greatly encouraged the Troops.

Soon after Ross wrote this letter he reported on what was destined to be the last foray into the Mohawk Valley by the men of the King's Royal Regiment of New York. He informed Haldimand that Captain Brant had set off on July 5, with 460 of his warriors and the light company of the second battalion led by Captain George Singleton (promoted from the first battalion). Brant hoped to 'make a great Stroke' but Ross doubted whether the different tribes, who were seriously divided, would co-operate with him. Again Ross praised Brant for helping him manage the Indians:

He used often to come to me at nights and get what little things I had to give them, and distribute them privately to the needy & no man could study more the economy of Provisions and Rum than he did.

Ross admitted that he had stripped many of the Mississauga Indians of their half-worn moccasins, to prevent numbers from returning discontented to their villages. Haldimand had been in Montreal inspecting the city's defences, and by June 20, he had returned to Quebec City. There, instructions from Sir Guy Carleton, who had replaced Sir Henry Clinton as the commander-in-chief at

New York City, awaited him. The home government was about to seek an accommodation with the rebels, and all future operations were to be confined solely to defence. Brant had set out before Haldimand's orders reached Oswego, but, with great disappointment, Ross recalled him. Captain Singleton, who accompanied Brant with his detachment of Royal Yorkers, kept a journal on what transpired during the aborted expedition.

On July 9, Singleton recorded, 13 Indians were sent to capture a prisoner in order to obtain intelligence. By the 13th, the main body had reached Fort Stanwix, where the Indians insisted on following a main road because of the bad condition of their moccasins. The whole force marched eastward on the north side of the Mohawk towards Fort Dayton, camping during the night. On the 15th, a Monday, they reached Fort Herkimer, on the south shore, at four o'-clock in the afternoon, where a decoy of 20 men lured 40 rebels from the fort under cover of their cannon. Some of Singleton's troops and Brant's Indians circled to cut off the line of retreat, while others captured cattle and horses. The rebels succeeded in regaining the fort, although 8 or 9 were killed, including an Oneida scout. Unable to lure any more rebels outside, Brant and Singleton marched back to Fort Dayton, but they could not find any cattle or horses there. On hearing the boom of Fort Herkimer's guns, the local people took shelter in their fort with their livestock. The two officers then marched towards German Town, in the German Flatts settlement, where their advance party had taken the cattle captured near Fort Herkimer. Some of the Indians broke off into small parties, intent on taking prisoners and returning to their own country.

> I did not think it my duty to interfere with them nor consistent with my orders to make myself a party to such enterprise. When I arrived at German Town found the Indians were bent upon making a property of the whole of the Cattle without paying any attention to my men and it was with great difficulty with the assistance of Capt. Brant that I got twenty five head (out of two hundred and twenty four) which I brought to this place, with the Troops all in good health and Spirits without the smallest accident accompanied with a few Indians. All the rest of the Cattle were drove to Niagara in spite of every argument to the Contrary.

By 'this place' Singleton meant Oswego. In his letter of August 3 to Haldimand, Ross said that 100 of Butler's Rangers had been recalled to Fort Niagara, to the detriment of his security, and he was expecting a reinforcement of Royal Highland Emigrants from Carleton Island. Once again he expressed his enthusiasm for Joseph Brant's conduct:

> On my sending to Captain Brant when upon the Frontiers your Excellency's pleasure for relinquishing (for a time) Hostilities, he like himself, obeyed the orders and called in the Indians, he highly merits the good opinion your Excellency is pleased to entertain of him and besides his abilities as a Partizan, I think I do not say too much in his favour if I presume to give him great praise in his disin-

terested and exemplary management of the Department.

Apart from small scouting parties who were keeping track of rebel movements for signs of preparation against Canada, the war was over for the men of the King's Royal Regiment of New York. Sir John Johnson had returned from England, reaching Quebec City on July 14.[52] While on leave he had been appointed the Superintendent of Indian Affairs, replacing his cousin Guy, and he was much too preoccupied with the need to reassure the natives that Britain would not wholly abandon them to resume the command of his regiment. Haldimand kept issuing instructions that there must be no predatory excursions into rebel territory from any of his posts, a cruel blow to the aspirations of the Indians. As soon as the rebels were apprised of the governor's orders, settlers began flocking into the Ohio country, and both the Iroquois and the western Indians had cause to realize that their ownership of these lands would not be respected by the Americans.

On November 1, returns were made for both battalions of Royal Yorkers. The first battalion, still around Montreal, showed 32 officers and 259 other ranks fit for duty, 29 sick in quarters, 1 in hospital, 271 on command, 4 on furlough and 26 as prisoners of the enemy. Thus this battalion numbered 542 rank and file, requiring 18 privates to complete the establishment. Of the second battalion 31 officers and 189 other ranks were fit for duty, 34 were sick in quarters, 1 sick in hospital, 212 rank and file on command, and 18 prisoners of the enemy. The total rank and file was 404, needing 156 privates to bring the battalion to full strength.

That autumn Allan Maclean assumed command of the upper posts from Watson Powell, who wanted to be relieved. Maclean reached Oswego in October, and after inspecting the garrison there and at Carleton Island the Highlander travelled on to Fort Niagara to take up residence. The Oswego garrison numbered 400 men, but, Maclean reported, there would soon be barracks sufficient for 600. Carleton Island he found undermanned, and must have a reinforcement of regulars before winter set in. Also, 74 of Butler's Rangers were to be moved there from Oswego, mainly to work as scouts.

On November 10, Ross informed Haldimand that his provincial troops had lost their sense of dedication to the war now that they were prohibited from taking the offensive in the cause they feared was lost:

They do not think the King will succeed, and from every quarter they have unpleasing tidings, their little propertys on the Mohawk River are taken possession of every day by the New Englanders; they conclude the best chance they have now is to make peace with the Rebels. Deserters they know are received and live quiet at Home. I'll venture to say that there are many men who would have suffered death rather than Desert some time ago, that nothing now but the fear of Death prevents them – in Short, their spirits are low, and I humbly beg leave to observe that the Troops raised from the Colonies are by no means so proper for this Garrison in the present situation of affairs as British Soldiers.

No wonder the regiment was disheartened. The men were, with a few exceptions, not professional soldiers. Having embraced the King's cause in order to preserve the way of life they cherished, they were reacting in the same manner as civilians indulging in guerrilla warfare have behaved before and since. Men who had won the war in the north, only to see Britain quit after the defeat of Yorktown, had little tolerance for the drudgery and boredom of garrison duty.

Winter arrived, to be enlivened briefly because of a rash and ill-conceived plan by the rebels to capture Oswego. If Colonel Marinius Willett was mystified that Major John Ross's fine body of troops caused so little harm in the Mohawk Valley the previous autumn, Ross had his opportunity to sneer when the biting winds of February whistled round his quarters.

Willett received permission from a somewhat deluded General Washington to make an attempt on the three forts at the mouth of the Onondaga River. On February 8, Willett gathered about 600 troops at Fort Herkimer, and they set off in sleighs towards Oswego. A warning that something was afoot spread quickly to the British outposts along Lake Champlain and among the neutral Vermont leaders.

Guiding Willett's expedition from Fort Herkimer was an Oneida scout, Captain John Oaawighton, who proved that he knew where he was going as far as Oneida Lake. Along the way the rebels stopped to make scaling ladders to use against the 30-foot-high walls of Fort Ontario, the strongest part of the Oswego complex. According to Willett, all went well until February 13, when the ice of the Onondaga River proved too thin to support the loaded sleighs. Oaawighton led the force into the woods, where the men wandered about until Colonel Willett decided their task was hopeless and suggested a withdrawal. The fate of the intended sneak attack on Oswego was sealed at dawn on the 15th, when scouts from Ross's garrison spotted Willett's expedition and fired towards the rebels from across the river. Willett's men responded by speeding up their retreat.[53]

Reporting his version of the episode to Haldimand, Ross maintained that he learned of Willett's presence from a deserter who found some of his wood-cutters. Ross immediately alerted his garrison and called in his work parties who had been getting firewood, some of whom were several miles up the Onondaga River. The troops were in high spirits as they prepared to defend the forts, and a second deserter from Willett's force arrived and informed Ross that the rebels had been misled by their Oneida guide. The major lamented the hasty departure of the rebels before he had the opportunity to cut them off.

Want of Snow Shoes was a motifying Circumstance and exceeding favourable to the Enemy on this occasion.

I cannot help observing to your Excellency that there never was a more ridiculous Expedition which may be explained as follows. Between five and six hundred men (most of them from Saratoga) came and laid down nine Scaling Ladders within two miles of this place and retreated with the upmost precipitation without so much as having seen the Fort or taking a single Prisoner. . . . I may add a professional Ignorance in whoever planned the expedition, to think of succeeding at any time, and particularly at the fullest time of the moon, when every object was as discernable as at noonday.

Governor Haldimand was delighted that Ross had been forewarned on the rebels' plan for Oswego, calling Willett's expedition a 'romantic and fruitless attempt to surprise the Post you Command.' In his account, Willett said that three Seneca Indians came upon his expedition, but they did nothing but offer friendship and pass by. Ross's version amplifies the rebel officer's account:

The Six Nation Indians covering our Wood Cutting Parties were with them on the morning of their Retreat, the Rebels bespoke them Friendship in which I think they were successful for on their arrival I found the rest more obstinate than ever, and was obliged to threaten them hard before I could get them to consent to join the Troops in pursuit of them. They were about ten in number, the rebels had only five Indians.

Haldimand admitted that he had half expected the rebels'objective was the posts along Lake Champlain or an attack on the Vermonters. Scouts returning to Captain Sherwood's blockhouse had reported 80 rebels in hospital at Albany with badly frostbitten feet, while others had drowned or frozen to death during the withdrawal through such bitter weather.[54] The rest of the winter passed quietly, and on April 26, Haldimand sent two letters to Major Ross, one for his eyes alone, the other for public consumption. In the first, the governor admitted that the terms of the preliminary articles of peace had reached him, but 'they are so unfavourable to this Province that I shall if possible avoid disclosing them in the Hope that some Provision will appear in the Particulars for the Six Nations and our other Indian Allies.'

Haldimand advised Ross to prevent the Indians surprising any small posts or detachments of troops he might send out, for they would be in a resentful mood if they discovered what was in those articles of Peace. In the public letter, Haldimand ordered Ross to discontinue work on Oswego's fortifications because they would not be needed. Ross replied that he had already obtained some of the news from an intriguing source:

> I have received His Majesty's Proclamation of a General Peace . . . it was transmitted to me by a Flag from Colonel Willett and a letter from that Gentleman dated Albany, the 15th Instant, announcing at the same time a Cessation of Arms on the Part of the United States. At first I had my doubts of its Authenticity on account of the Information so lately received from His Excellency Sir Guy Carleton, but upon deliberation I think it real.

For the men of both battalions there remained the atrophy of garrison duty, broken by the task of assisting refugees, who kept arriving at various posts. On June 1, 1783, the returns of the King's Royal Regiment of New York read as follows: for the first battalion, 1 lieutenant, 1 sergeant and 58 rank and file were at Sorel, St. Johns and Isle aux Noix; the remainder – 29 officers, 30 sergeants, 20 drummers, and 424 rank and file, including the sick – were in quarters at Terrebonne, Mascouche de Terrebonne, Ile Jesus, Lachine, Carillon and Côteau du Lac – all posts around Montreal. Of these, 17 officers and 238 other ranks were on duty in the city itself. The whole of the second battalion – 34 officers and 434 other ranks, except a few who were prisoners of the rebels – were at Oswego and Carleton Island.

That morale among the rank and file was low may be deduced from Major Gray's order to hold a Court Martial in Montreal on August 5th at which two enlisted men from the first battalion were sentenced to be flogged. The first was Private John Newton of Captain John Munro's company; the second, Private Michael Ferguson of Captain Archibald MacDonell's. The latter was the President of the Court, whose members were Lieutenants Peter Everett and William Coffin, and Ensigns Jacob Glen and Miles MacDonell. Private Newton was accused of being drunk, disobedient and impertinent. The Court found him guilty of the first count, a breach of Article 3 of the 20th section of the Articles of War, and sentenced him to 'One Hundred Lashes under the Usual Manner.' Private Ferguson got off more lightly. Charged with intent to desert, he said he was in the suburbs when he should have been in barracks, because he was looking for a 'Washer Woman' for two shirts, which he carried in a bundle under his arm. The Court found him innocent of suspicion to desert, but guilty of being outside the barracks too late at night, a breach of Article 3 of the 14th Section of the Articles of War, and sentenced him to fifty lashes 'after the Usual Manner.'[55]

By late autumn Governor Haldimand had received orders to disband all his provincial troops by the end of the year. Orders were sent for disbanding the first battalion by December 24, but could not be relayed to Cataraqui, where the second battalion was then on duty with Major Ross. On December 21, Mathews sent a letter to

Robert Leake, informing him that he had been appointed major in the second battalion, which would entitle him to more generous half pay. Mathews wished Leake well, because Haldimand had granted that officer leave to present his claim for compensation in England. The following day, the governor informed Sir John Johnson that John Ross would be appointed a brigade major as of December 24, a reward for his fine work that meant he would receive half pay for this rank. In the light of one of Ross's later letters, someone higher up than Haldimand may have disallowed the promotion after the regiment was reduced.

The men of the first battalion were expected to remain in their barracks throughout the winter, but some wanted to be in Montreal. Brigadier Barry St. Leger, then in charge of the district, recommended that Captain John Munro be in charge of them. Munro had children in school in the city – presumably the one kept by the Reverend John Stuart, who had received a grant from Haldimand to open his classical academy there.

On December 25, St. Leger informed Haldimand that he had disbanded the 'Royal Reg't of New York yesterday.' But he meant only the first battalion. The men's duties were assumed by five companies of the 53rd Regiment. The second battalion remained on duty throughout the winter. Writing to Ross on March 29, Haldimand ordered him to disband his men as soon as practicable, explaining that his instructions reached him too late the season before to be implemented.

With characteristic attention to economy, Haldimand hoped that most of the men disbanded near his upper posts would settle in the vicinity to save the cost of moving them elsewhere. Thus the second battalion was to be located on land close to Cataraqui, where Ross had been sent in July to establish a new post because the governor was afraid that both Oswego and Carleton Island might ultimately be inside United States territory.

Prior to disbandment, the second battalion was employed building new fortifications and a barracks at Cataraqui, and helping house refugee families that had fled to Fort Haldimand on Carleton Island. On May 7, Ross informed Mathews that he was sending a detachment of the 34th Regiment to replace the men of the King's Royal Regiment of New York at Oswego because the regulars were less prone to desertion. The governor's final order to disband the second battalion did not reach Major Ross until early in June 1784, and on the 14th, Ross replied that he would carry out his instructions, sending 20 of the 34th Regiment to replace the provincial troops at Carleton Island.

Ross's next letter raises some questions for which there may be no satisfactory answers. Since the first battalion had been disbanded earlier, Ross seemed to consider his battalion a provincial corps when he wrote:

> I have the honor to inform your Excellnncy that I disbanded the Regiment under my command on the day appointed, many of the Men were stopped at Long Saut, unavoidably on my part.

Apparently some of the men from his battalion, who may have been serving on bateaux, contrived to remain in the townships along the upper St. Lawrence that had been reserved for the first battalion, who were being moved there from Montreal in the spring of 1784. Ross declared:

> I am highly sensible of Your Excellency's kind intentions to serve me by the appointment of the command of a Provincial Corps which, with the confidence reposed in my many instances, shall never be effaced from my mind; yet I hope Your Excellency will not take it amiss, if I request, that you will consider that I am the oldest British Officer and perhaps the only one, in that predicament, who has reaped no solid advantage in military rank, by the same.

Ross seemed to imply that he was still a captain in the 34th Regiment, but the Army List of 1785 shows him as a major in the British army and a major in his own regiment. The date of his commission is June 7, 1782. Ross returned to England on leave in the spring of 1785, and later he served in Montreal.

Sir John Johnson continued living in Montreal, while Major James Gray settled among the men of his first battalion, later serving as a colonel in the militia and as the Lieutenant of Dundas County. Robert Leake, who succeeded Ross as the major in the second battalion, may have remained in England after his leave ended. Several of the officers from both battalions took a prominent part in the public affairs of their new communities, as justices of the peace and officers in the militia. William Redford Crawford, a lieutenant in the first battalion, a captain in the second, was the Sheriff of the District of Mecklenburg for many years.

As settlers, the disbanded King's Royal Regiment of New York made a good recovery, yet if this corps had been allowed to continue the start it made in 1777 at Oriskany, a decisive victory in northern New York might well have been a reality. The corps went on only three major expeditions subsequently. These men were capable of much more action than Governor Haldimand, conscious of his first responsibility to protect Canada, and handicapped by the problem of provisioning them, was able to permit.

Chapter 6: Butler's Rangers

The most active and most successful regiment operating in the Northern Department was Butler's Rangers. The name was appropriate; for the men did range over a vast area – from the Kentucky Valley where Virginians were encroaching on Indian land, to the boundary of New Jersey, along the frontiers of New York and Pennsylvania and westward into the Ohio Valley. Butler's Rangers was a provincial corps, the third to be attached to the Northern Department. It had special status owing to an arrangement which its astute commander, John Butler, made with Governor Sir Guy Carleton.

The tactics adopted by Butler were those that had been used with such devastating success in the Seven Years' War by the famous ranger hero, Robert Rogers. Both Butler and Rogers agreed that the first requirement for a ranger that he be able to endure severe hardship for long periods of time, miles from the comforts of civilization. Whereas regular troops and most provincials went into winter quarters when the weather turned biting, rangers were expected to operate all year round. In summer they marched or travelled in bateaux or canoes; in winter they used sleighs, skates or snowshoes.[1]

The key to success was mobility. Rangers travelled with a minimum of equipment to impede them, and their uniform consisted of whatever was comfortable and convenient. Armed with smoothbore muskets that fired buckshot or bullets, many rangers wore short jackets, carried tomahawks, powder horns and scalping knives, and leather bags dangling from their belts held shot. Some had small compasses as well fastened to the bottoms of their powder horns.[2] Other rangers had parade dress, but when operating in the woods they often wore long hunting shirts, leggings or overalls and moccasins. John Butler wanted his men to carry rifles, either their own, or government issue if available because of their greater accuracy.

In his 'Plan of Discipline' Robert Rogers had set down rules which all ranger corps followed. While on scouting missions rangers walked in single file with enough space between each to prevent more than one being a target for an enemy marksman. When crossing swampy ground, they marched abreast to confound trackers. Camp was made after dark, never before, and always in a spot where the sentries had a clear view and the enemy could not take them by surprise.

When a force of several hundred was out, the men split into

three columns, and each marched in single file, with the outer column at least twenty yards from the middle one, scouts forward, to the rear, and along the flanks, watching for indications of an ambush. Men so spread out were difficult to surround. This formation was the antithesis of regular tactics, where soldiers stood shoulder to shoulder and made fire power the important operation. Such concentrated formations could be disastrous in the forests and ranger technique was closely adapted in woodland conditions, where an enemy shooting from cover could slaughter a conventional column. Rangers would also advance from tree to tree, and if the enemy was very strong the front line of rangers would fire and drop, so that the rear line could advance through them, while the front one used the time to reload.

Rangers used darkness to effect. If they were encircled they formed a square and held out until nightfall afforded them the opportunity to steal away. Whenever the enemy came in pursuit, by night or day, rangers turned and circled back in the hope of setting up an ambush. Sentries went out in groups of six, two on duty at a time, the others sleeping. This avoided the normal procedure of sending out fresh sentries to relieve the old guard, which tended to inform spies lurking of the presence of an encampment.

The men were alert and armed by dawn, the choice time for an Indian attack on a ranger position. When returning from expeditions, rangers avoided fords, where the enemy was likely to try an ambush. When on the march they kept a safe distance between them and any stream, so that an attacking force could not pin them against the water.

In summer when rangers travelled by boat, they hid during the day and moved at night. Above all, surprise was the essence of attack. Hit and run were the rules, strike and escape to fight another day if a situation began to deteriorate. Robert Rogers' methods resembled those of modern commandos, and descriptions of Butler's Rangers in action show that they followed many of the rules for frontier warfare in dense forest and sparsely settled country.[3]

The records show that John Butler had less difficulty than other corps commanders in obtaining recruits to fill his ranks. Word spread quickly that the indefatigable rangers were attacking the rebels with devastating success, and were receiving more pay – both of which had great appeal to men willing to embrace the King's cause. During the war nearly 900 men served in Butler's Rangers, although full strength was one battalion. Losses in action, through disease and sheer overwork were higher than in the other corps.

For many provincials the defeat of Lord Cornwallis at Yorktown in the fall of 1781 spelled the end of their active participation in the war. The rangers remained in the field against the rebels even after Governor Haldimand had received orders to prevent all but defensive operations in June 1782 – the only provincial corps in the northern sphere not ordered to cease hostilities.

John Butler and his son, Walter

Colonel Daniel Claus, Colonel Guy Johnson's brother-in-law and deputy in the Indian Department, sneeringly called John Butler a devious fellow 'having been born and bred in New England.'[4] John was born in New London, Connecticut, in 1725, and received some education there, but this hardly made him a typical Yankee. John's father, Walter, was Irish, a lieutenant in the British regular army who had been sent to North America about the year 1711 and who saw considerable service along the frontiers of New York and Pennsylvania.[5] So far no one has identified his regiment because three Lieutenant Walter Butlers are shown on the army lists of that era.

In the course of his service Walter Butler acquired a knowledge of several Indian languages, and vast holdings in the Mohawk Valley. He was a close friend of Sir William Johnson, the Superintendent of Indian Affairs until his death in 1774. By 1733 the Butler family had moved to the Mohawk Valley. Later Walter received a grant of 60,000 acres of land on the north side of the Mohawk, near Johnstown, which he named Butlersbury. There, in 1760, he died, having been a lieutenant in the British army for seventy years, something of a record.

John Butler inherited Butlersbury, and with the land the knowledge of Indian languages and close relationship with Sir William Johnson that his father had enjoyed. The Butler house, built in 1742, is still standing, overlooking the Mohawk River from the heights above Fonda, New York. John devoted part of his energies to the militia and to Indian affairs, for which his patrimony and past performance had qualified him.

In 1753, he was on duty at Fort Hunter, and in July 1758 he was with General James Abercromby in his costly attempt to take Fort Ticonderoga from the French. From that calamity he joined Colonel John Bradstreet, 60th Regiment, on the successful expedition that captured Fort Frontenac from the French.

Then in July 1759, John Butler accompanied General John Prideaux on the expedition against Fort Niagara. Upon the death of Prideaux, Sir William Johnson seized command of the force, despite

John Butler, commander of Butler's Rangers. His coat is green with gold lace. Courtesy: Niagara District Historical Society; photograph by Mr. Shumilo.

the presence of a colonel in the 60th Regiment named Frederick Haldimand, who was the senior regular officer present. Sir William had been in charge of the Indian contingent with Butler as his second-in-command. When the former superseded Prideaux, Butler took over the leadership of the Indians.

Butler was on hand for the last heroic battle the French fought to retain New France, at Isle Royale, below the Thousand Islands of the upper St. Lawrence, in 1760. Colonel Frederick Haldimand was there with his battalion of the 60th Regiment, and Sir William Johnson was again in command of the Indians, with Butler as his second-in-command. After a delay of ten days caused by a few hundred French regulars, sailors and militia, Amherst's men rode on down the rapids of the river in whaleboats to the capitulation of Montreal, a city John Butler would see on several occasions before the American Revolution was over.

The war against the French concluded, John Butler returned to Butlersbury, but he was soon involved with the Pontiac conspiracy among the western tribes. He played a part in persuading the Iroquois not to join the Ottawa chief in his attempt to unite the Indians against grasping settlers wanting their lands.

Some years before the outbreak of the Seven Years' War, John had married Catherine Pollock, and they were destined to have seven children, of which two died in infancy: Walter born in 1753, Thomas, in 1755, Andrew born and died in 1759, William Johnson, in 1760, Andrew, in 1762, Deborah, in 1764, and John born and died in 1768.[6] Walter, the eldest, became notorious among the rebels for his role in setting the frontier aflame. Thomas and the surviving Andrew also served as officers in their father's regiment, but William Johnson, named for his father's benefactor, may have been a frail young man.

In 1772, Tryon County was established and named in honour of a newly arrived royal governor, Thomas Tryon, the last to receive the appointment. Until the revolution started, John Butler served as a county court judge, and lieutenant-colonel in a militia regiment raised by Guy Johnson, Sir William's nephew and son-in-law.

For reasons never specified, neither Guy Johnson nor Daniel Claus had any love for John Butler. He has been described as short, stocky, and inclined to repeat himself when he was excited, and a portrait owned by the Niagara District Historical Society reveals a man with rather heavy features, distinctive snub nose, and intense staring eyes. Governor Haldimand described him as 'deficient in Education and liberal sentiments.' and his son Walter as 'conceited and petulant.' Guy Johnson and Daniel Claus may have been jealous of Butler, a man more competent in his dealings with the Indians than they. Claus may have sided with Guy Johnson because his own situation within the family circle was far from secure. Guy was a blood relative, while Daniel, a German immigrant, was only married into the Johnson clan.

When rebel discontentment began to mount, the Johnsons and the Butlers, with their tenants, were the backbone of loyalism in Tryon County, whose inhabitants were described as contented by Governor Tryon when he visited the area in 1772. The first outward sign of revolutionary activity arose in May of 1775, when a Whig committee was formed at Cherry Valley, which complained to the Committee of Safety in Albany:

> This county had for a series of years been ruled by one family, the several branches of which are still strenuous in dissuading the people from coming into Congressional measures; and have even last week, at a numerous meeting of the Mohawk district, appeared with all their dependents armed to oppose the people considering of their grievances; their number being so great, and the people unarmed they struck terror into most of them and they dispersed.

A firm supporter of the Johnsons, despite their dislike of him, John Butler was one of the men against whom this complaint was lodged. Of great significance was the fact that most of the settlers in Cherry Valley were from democratic Connecticut, and viewed with dark suspicion by the New York frontiersmen. Guy Johnson observed that the committee meeting was called by an 'itinerent New England Leather-dresser' and conducted by people even more contemptible.

As an agent in the Indian Department, John Butler was concerned about unrest arising from the activities of unscrupulous men who were refusing to honour the boundary drawn in 1768, beyond which settlers were not to penetrate Indian lands. Known as the Fort Stanwix Treaty, it prohibited settlement west of a line drawn close to the fort, which stood at the carrying place between the Mohawk River and Wood Creek which drained ultimately to Lake Oneida and through the Onondaga River to Lake Ontario. Butler had also reported that French agents among the western tribes were assuring them that their father, the King of France, had not forgotten them, in the hope of fomenting an Indian war. From the Senecas, Butler observed, he had obtained an 'axe belt' presented to them by a man named Sang-blanc, one of these agents who posed as a trader. Butler knew that the Shawnees had also received belts from so-called traders.

Another threat to peace was the presence of settlers in Wyoming, on the Susquehanna River, and around Fort Pitt where the village of Pittsburgh had sprung up. Both areas were part of Pennsylvania, but at Wyoming the settlers were from Connecticut, which had an ancient claim to these lands. Those at Pittsburgh were Virginians who had seized blocks of land and were ready to defend them against Pennsylvania's claim to them. That Butler was very much aware of the Yankees at Wyoming and the Virginians at Pittsburgh as potential trouble-makers may be deduced by subsequent events. The Virginians captured Fort Pitt from its British garrison and held it throughout the revolution, while one of Butler's Rangers' earliest raids was against the Yankees at Wyoming.

As the year 1775 passed, the officers of the Indian Department were alarmed that the rebels in Massachusetts were intriguing to ensure Indian support for their cause. When news reached Guy Johnson from General Thomas Gage in Boston that the rebels were recruiting every available Indian, the superintendent felt compelled to absent himself. Guy marched up the Mohawk towards Oswego, and with him went Daniel Claus, Joseph Brant, Peter Johnson (Sir William's son by Molly Brant) as well as Gilbert Tice and John Butler and his son Walter. All were officers in the Indian Department.

They reached Oswego on July 17, and by the beginning of August were in Montreal, in time to be part of that city's defence force when the rebel expedition led by General Richard Montgomery moved down the Richelieu River in September.

Shortly before the rebels captured Montreal, Guy Johnson and Daniel Claus applied for leave of absence and went to England, accompanied by Joseph Brant and Gilbert Tice. Their motives for leaving at such a critical time were mixed. Guy was offended because Governor Carleton refused to allow him to turn large numbers of Indians loose against the rebels – in keeping with the governor's view that the rebels were merely misguided children who would soon see the error of their ways. Claus was offended because Carleton had allowed Major John Campbell to supersede him as the Superintendent of Indian Affairs at Montreal.[7] Joseph Brant went in quest of assurance from the highest authority that Britain would support the Six Nations against the rebels.

Carleton appointed John Butler to be Guy Johnson's deputy, with the rank of major in the Indian Department, and dispatched him to Fort Niagara with instructions to see that the Indians remained neutral until further orders. Butler did his best to persuade the Iroquois not to side with the rebels, and he sent able men among the more westerly tribes to fulfill the same mission. One of his most dependable agents was William Caldwell of Philadelphia, who had helped some British officers escape from prison there and guided them safely to Niagara. Another on whom Butler expected to depend was Alexander McKee, the Deputy Superintendent of Indian Affairs at Fort Pitt who exercised great influence over the Shawnees, and may have been part Indian. Then bad news arrived that McKee had been captured by Virginia frontiersmen who had overrun the fort, doing away with the formidable British presence there.

The setback at Pittsburgh was balanced by the steady stream of refugees coming to Fort Niagara. Butler found that he had many worthy men on whose services he could call, and most spoke one or more Indian languages. Because he was exerting such strong influence over the Iroquois, he soon learned that the rebels planned to have him kidnapped. Some refugees claimed that General Philip Schuyler, the rebel commander in Albany, was advertising a reward of $250 for Butler's scalp, while other informers claimed that the amount had been raised to $1,000.

In the spring of 1776, Guy Johnson returned to Canada, and was furious with Butler for not sending waves of Indians to ransack the homes of rebel frontiersmen, apparently unaware that Governor Carleton had not given any orders for such missions. Joseph Brant, who had returned with Guy, was touring the Indian settlements, drumming up support for Britain in contravention of Carleton's wish to keep the native people neutral. In Tryon County an army of rebels from New England was in occupation, and the situation for loyalists there had become precarious. The Yankees disarmed Butler's tenants, and those of the Johnson family. After Sir John Johnson fled from his home in May 1776, Lady Johnson and her son William were sent as hostages to Albany. Accompanying them into captivity were John Butler's wife, Catherine, with her three youngest children, William Johnson, Andrew and Deborah. The second son, Thomas, was spared because he had joined his father at Fort Niagara. Despite his fears for the safety of his closest relatives, there is no evidence that their situation softened Butler's approach to his duties, nor curbed his efforts to subdue the rebellion along the frontier.

With the coming of the spring of 1777, the rebels had succeeded in gaining the friendship of some of the Oneida tribe of the Six Nations, and Carleton's policy on Indian neutrality had shifted. Upon receiving instructions from London, the governor prepared to employ some Indians in Burgoyne's coming invasion of New York. Colonel Claus and Sir John Johnson both censured Butler for having kept the Indians inactive, pointing out that during the winter the rebels had taken possession of Fort Stanwix, strategically located to block the routes into the settled area from both Oswego and

Oswegatchie. Their wrath should have been directed at Carleton. Butler's duty was to follow orders, and there was nothing he could, with propriety, do to keep the rebels out of Fort Stanwix.

On June 5, Carleton sent Butler orders to collect as many Indians as possible, and join the expedition being organized by Colonel Barry St. Leger, 34th Regiment, that was to proceed through the Mohawk Valley from Oswego and meet Burgoyne's main force at Albany. Butler obeyed, and on his own initiative went a step further by enlisting 67 loyalist refugees who spoke Indian languages. Walter Butler held a commission as an ensign in the 8th (King's) Regiment, that had been on garrison duty at Fort Niagara. He went with the detachment of his regiment that accompanied St. Leger.

After St. Leger abandoned his attempt to reach Albany through the Mohawk Valley, John Butler led the men he had enlisted into the Indian Department back to Fort Niagara. From there he dispatched James Secord and a party of rangers towards the Susquehanna Valley to seize cattle to feed the garrison that winter. Soon after sending out Secord, Butler set out for Quebec City to confer with Carleton, who on September 15 signed a 'Beating order' or warrant to raise corps of rangers.

In the six years that followed, Butler was the tireless leader of his regiment, sometimes in the field, at others from Fort Niagara. From the autumn of 1778 until his death in October 1781, Walter Butler was his father's senior captain.

The first men who joined Butler's Rangers had been at the Cedars, or on the St. Leger expedition and had fought at the Battle of Oriskany with Sir John Johnson and Joseph Brant. On the payroll of the Indian Department Butler had placed 5 captains, at 10s. per day, 9 lieutenants at 4s.6d. per day sterling, and 67 ranks at 4s. New York currency per day – rates of pay that set a precedent for privates once he had permission to raise a regiment.[8] Carleton's beating order gave Butler the right to raise 'by beat of Drum or otherwise' a corps of eight companies of rangers, 'to serve with the Indians, as occasion shall require.' Each company was to consist of a captain, a lieutenant, 3 sergeants, 3 corporals and 50 privates. Two companies were to be of men speaking 'the Indian language and acquainted with their customs and manner of making war,' and these were to receive 4s. New York per day. The ranks in the other six companies were to be made up of men familiar with the forests and able to endure fatigue well, who would be paid 2s. New York per day. All were to clothe and arm themselves at their own expense.[9]

A subsistence account which Butler submitted in May, 1779, to headquarters in Quebec City for payment showed that the commis-

137

sioned officers were paid in sterling, all other ranks in New York currency. Butler also felt compelled to indicate the amounts due him in the other currencies circulating at the time, Halifax and dollars. Sterling had the highest value, Halifax the next, while New York was the lowest. The sum of £5 New York was worth £2.18s. 3¾ d. sterling, while £5 Halifax was valued at £4. 3s. 3¾ d. sterling. Butler noted that in calculating the account in sterling he used a value of 4s.8d. to the dollar.

The rates of pay in sterling for the commissioned officers were 15s. per day for the major-commandant; 10s. for each captain; 4s.8d. for each first lieutenant; 3s.8d. for each second lieutenant; 4s.8d. for the quartermaster and 4s. for the surgeon. Of the other ranks who received their pay in New York currency, a sergeant drew 5s. per day; a corporal, 4s.6d.; a drummer or a private conversant in Indian tongues, 4s.6d.; all other privates, 2s..[10] The rates of pay were not too disparate when compared to the 6d. sterling per day a regular soldier received. It was still more than twice the going rate for regiments of the British establishment but for whom deductions were smaller. At first John Butler had the rank he held in the Indian Department, but when his corps reached two-thirds strength he would be commissioned a lieutenant-colonel of provincials. On whose authority Butler divided his lieutenants into two categories is not clear, for such was not specified in his beating order.

The duties assigned Butler's Rangers fell into three phases. The first was from 1778 until 1779, when rangers and Indians raided settlements occupied mainly by New Englanders, to prevent them sending supplies to the Continental Army. The second phase followed the rebel expedition that destroyed the lands of the Iroquois Confederacy until the British surrender at Yorktown, Virginia, in the autumn of 1781. This was a period of vigorous retaliation against the rebels for the blow dealt Britain's Indian allies that almost emptied the frontier settlements. Many loyalists who had supplied the rangers earlier had fled to Canada or been imprisoned, and afterward small parties set out intending to be self-sufficient. The men were mounted, and they drove cattle before them, each beast loaded with a sack of flour, a bag of salt tied round its neck. These parties went in quest of intelligence, and where they were accompanied by Indians, to attack the hardy brave enough to remain in their fortified homes and villages.

During the third phase, after Yorktown, the rangers endeavoured to protect the western Indians – the Wyandots, Delawares, Shawnees and other groups such as the Mingos – from attack by frontiersmen from Virginia who were coveting their lands.

With his beating order in hand, Butler left Quebec City in September 1777, for the long journey back to Fort Niagara. In his absence the Indians had grown disheartened, for they thought they had been abandoned when St. Leger withdrew to Oswego, and they were being neglected at Niagara because many officers of the Indian Department were ill. General Philip Schuyler, the commander of the rebels' military department in Albany, took advantage of the Indian Department's temporary weakness by calling a council with some Iroquois chiefs at German Flatts, in the Mohawk Valley. Butler discovered that this meeting had taken place when he reached Carleton Island, where a letter from a trader informed him that the Oneidas, Onondagas and Tuscaroras had accepted a hatchet from Schuyler and had seized several loyalists fleeing through their lands. Even worse, his son Walter and two Indian Department officers had been captured near German Flatts and were lying in irons in Albany gaol.

Before he left Quebec City, Butler had been ordered by Carleton to gather together a large force and march to reinforce General Burgoyne. As soon as Butler reached Niagara, he began carrying out those instructions and hoped to march through the Indians' lands. Since so many of the Six Nations had turned hostile, he decided to go by the St. Lawrence. Before he was organized to depart, a dispatch arrived informing him that Burgoyne had surrendered at Saratoga, and Carleton had cancelled the orders. Soon afterward Joseph Brant came to Niagara after scouting among the Iroquois and reported that the Senecas and Cayugas were still friendly. Butler called a conference of the chiefs of the nations who had met with Schuyler. Willingly they surrendered the hatchet the rebel officer had given them and promised to remain loyal.

By mid December, the first company of rangers was completed, and James Secord's party returned from the Susquehanna Valley with 30 prisoners as well as cattle. Secord, then 45 years old, received a lieutenant's commission in the rangers, but within a year he returned to the Indian Department and took up the less demanding job of tavern keeper at Niagara. During the winter of 1777-78, Butler's agents were out in search of recruits. Many volunteers arrived from the east branch of the Susquehanna River in Pennsylvania, where Connecticut Yankee settlers were persecuting anyone suspected of loyalism. As spring approached, Butler decided to establish an advance post, and he chose Unadilla, on the east branch of the Susquehanna inside New York. There most of the residents were loyalists and had mills.

Butler's men could be provisioned locally, and the Connecticut settlers' homes were within comfortable striking distance. On May 2, 1778, Butler left Niagara with three nearly full companies of rangers for the march to Unadilla. From there he could menace the rebel frontiersmen and also march to join Sir Henry Clinton, should the commander-in-chief decide to move out of New York City. The advance post at Unadilla was 200 miles southeast of Niagara, and 120 miles from Clinton's headquarters.

Wyoming and Cherry Valley 1778

In April, Walter Butler escaped from Albany. He had been released from gaol in the custody of Richard Cartwright of Albany, a loyalist who was maintaining a low profile and whose son served for a while as John Butler's secretary at Fort Niagara. From the Cartwright house Walter made his getaway; travelling westward through the woods, he met his father at Kanadesaga, the Senecas' main village, where John Butler was holding a conference at the time.[11] Finding his son unfit for duty, he sent him on to Fort Niagara, with instructions to proceed to Quebec City to regain his health and to apply for arms and clothing for the rangers. Walter reached Fort Niagara on May 17 while his father returned to his base at Unadilla, planning to attack Wyoming, Cherry Valley and Schoharie – all heavily populated settlements wherein most of the inhabitants were Connecticut Yankees – the backbone of resistance in New York and Pennsylvania. That these settlements were hit first and hardest along with German Flatts, the focus of the Palatine alliance with the New Englanders was no coincidence.

His plans made, Butler sent a small party under Captains Barent Frey of the rangers and Joseph Brant of the Indian Department, to raid Schoharie and Cherry Valley, and he began preparations to lead a larger force against Wyoming. By the end of June, Frey and Brant reported that they had taken or killed 294 men and destroyed most of the farms in the Schoharie Valley, forcing the local rebels to seek shelter in Schenectady.

These rangers and Indians continued their tour of destruction, while Butler and 200 rangers, with 300 Indians, mainly Senecas and Cayugas led by the aging Seneca chief Sayenqueraghta (Old Smoke) floated on rafts down the Susquehanna towards Wyoming. Legend accuses Joseph Brant of being the monster of the Wyoming 'massacre', but he was near Schoharie and never did join Butler's expedition.[12] Although Brant was absent, many of his best-known contemporaries were with John Butler. Cornplanter was the second-in-command of the Indians. Also present were Sagwarithra, a

Butlersbury, built by John Butler's father, Fonda N.Y. Timbers are covered with siding to preserve them.

Private, Butler's Rangers, in field dress — deerskin breeches and green hunting shirt. Some rangers wore overalls (gaitered trousers). A belt or cartridge case plate was often pinned on the front of the cap.

Tuscarora sachem, Gahkoondenoiya of the Onondagas, Fish Carrier of the Cayugas, Little Beard, Blacksnake, and Hiadagoo – the latter the husband of Mary Jemison, who had been kidnapped by the Indians and wrote the famous account of her experiences. Another well-known participant was Ganiodaio, Cornplanter's half-brother, later to win renown as the religious leader, Handsome Lake. Lastly, a young warrior named Red Jacket was in attendance.[13]

Small groups of loyalists joined the flotilla as it passed downstream to take on the rebel garrisons at six different forts, wherein were stationed 60 Continentals and 800 men of the 24th Battalion, Wyoming Militia, commanded by a regular officer named Colonel Zebulon Butler (no relation to the ranger leader).

Butler landed his force at a place called Three Islands, then marched overland 100 miles towards Wyoming. By July 2, the expedition was encamped on a hill overlooking its prey. In the valley below lay three forts – Wintermute's and Jenkins' on the west bank of the river and Forty Fort on the east bank. Butler sent Lieutenant John Turney with a party to Wintermute's, while Captain William Caldwell led another against Jenkins'. Both forts surrendered without loss of lives, and the rangers burned them. Meanwhile, John Butler invested Forty Fort with the main body of his little army where Colonel Zebulon Butler refused to capitulate. On July 3, some 400 men sortied from the fort, and the battle commenced. Within about an hour the rangers and Indians had 227 scalps, and only five prisoners.[14] The following day Colonel Nathan Dennison, of the militia, came to Butler's camp, accompanied by a minister and four civilians, and asked for terms. Zebulon Butler had vanished during the night, leaving Dennison to face the humiliation.

John Butler agreed to leave the civilians in peace as long as they were disarmed, and all the Continental stores were to be delivered to him. He promised to restrain the Indians, again provided that Dennison and all who had borne arms would give their parole to take no further part in the hostilities during 'the present contest.'[15] Next, Butler's men destroyed three other small forts, which were all on the east bank of the Susquehanna, and the settlement of Lackawaxen, on the Delaware River. Writing to Colonel Mason Bolton, the commandant of Fort Niagara, Butler reported that civilians had been protected, and only those bearing arms had suffered. However, there may have been one death after Forty Fort surrendered. According to a local historian of Wyoming, Butler spotted a deserter from his rangers among the prisoners, and he exclaimed:

"Boyd! Go to that tree!"

"I hope, sir, that you will consider me a prisoner of war," Boyd cried.

"Go to that tree," Butler repeated sternly.

He intended to make an example of Boyd, to make certain the lesson was not lost on the rangers present. The petrified Boyd obeyed, and at Butler's command his firing party discharged their muskets.

Butler spared the houses, and ordered five of the forts burnt, leaving Forty Fort so that women and children could seek protection during future raids. As the rangers and Indians withdrew they left blackened fields devoid of livestock, the cattle removed to feed the expedition on its march towards other rebel villages. When his force reached Tioga, a loyalist settlement 70 miles up the Susquehanna, Butler succumbed to an attack of fever and ague. Leaving Captain Caldwell in command to continue harassing the rebels, Butler went to his base at Unadilla to recuperate, sending out scouting parties to bring back information on rebel activities. From Fort Haldimand, a new base on Carleton Island, a Mr. Adams of the Indian Department sent scouts towards Fort Stanwix, while a party of Senecas left Unadilla to keep watch over Fort Pitt.

Meanwhile, Sir John Johnson was in Quebec City making the acquaintance of Governor Haldimand who had arrived only a few days before, and as usual the Johnson family was doing its best to undermine John Butler. On July 16, Sir John wrote to Daniel Claus in Montreal that Haldimand:

asked me yesterday what Butler would be about all this time; that he thought he could have struck a blow ere now. I told him I thought I might venture to assure him that it was not his intention, that he would remain where he was or thereabouts till he could join the army from New York with safety, or till it was too late to do anything.

Johnson was being uncharitable, seeking to belittle Butler, who had just wiped out some 300 rebels at Wyoming and in the side trips Captain Caldwell had made after the major returned ill to Unadilla. Walter Butler may have been aware of Johnson's malice, for he was also in Quebec City from which he returned to Fort Niagara late in August. Accompanying Walter was Lieutenant John MacDonell of the Royal Highland Emigrants, who had transferred to the rangers because the corps offered more opportunities for action than his own regiment. News of Butler's foray into the Susquehanna Valley reached Haldimand soon after Sir John Johnson's unflattering comments, and the governor made a mental note that there was bad blood between the two refugees from the Mohawk Valley.

With the return of his son, Butler juggled his subordinates.

William Caldwell had been acting senior captain, but Butler arranged for Walter to transfer from the 8th Regiment to the rangers and take up his post. John MacDonell was given a captaincy, and Caldwell set off from Unadilla with 200 Rangers and 160 Indians for German Flatts. There the Palatine settlers had built two strongholds – Fort Dayton on the north side of the Mohawk River and Fort Herkimer on the south side – which were staffed by Continental soldiers. On the way Caldwell captured a party of Oneidas, and arriving at his destination in the pouring rain, found that the entire populace had taken refuge in the forts. Unopposed, Caldwell's men set to work, and he reported:

> We destroyed all the grain and buildings on the German Flats, from William Tygert's to Fort Herkimer on the south side of the river, and from Adam Starling's to Wydeck's beyond Canada Creek on the north side, except the church and Fort Dayton, and drove off a great many cows and oxen, horses and mares. The oxen were all large New England cattle, kept on the flats for the use of the Continental troops, and we took them out of the enclosure at Fort Dayton within pistol shot of the fort.

He released the Oneida captives; upon his return to Unadilla, he discovered that these Indians had attacked loyalist families near German Flatts and carried off some prisoners, among them two sick rangers whom Caldwell had left behind in the care of friends.

A rebel force 1,400 strong, part militia, part Continental, marched in pursuit of Caldwell, attacking some Scottish settlers who were loyal. By that time Walter Butler had left Niagara with 300 rangers and was at Kanadesaga. He marched towards German Flatts, joined Caldwell, and their combined force, supplemented by 800 newly arrived Indians, attacked the rebel rearguard and dispelled it. Caldwell and Butler separated, and the latter resolved on attacking Cherry Valley, where the rebels had stock-piled ammunition, corn and cattle for Continentals from Massachusetts, who garrisoned the forts in the neighbourhood.

Early in November, Walter moved on Cherry Valley with 200 Rangers, a detachment of the 8th Regiment, and 400 Senecas. Colonel Bolton reported to Governor Haldimand:

> Captain Butler's little army of Rangers & Indians amount to 800 & from his last letter intends to attack Cherry Valley where the enemy have a number of cattle & a large quantity of corn. Joseph [Brant] I have not heard from for a considerable time.

Although Bolton did not know where Brant was, the Mohawk leader had joined Walter with enough warriors to bring his strength to the 800 the colonel mentioned. On November 10, tramping through snow turning to rain, Butler's men reached the fringes of Cherry Valley village, and spent a miserable night, for they were without tents or blankets and afraid to light a fire.

Colonel Ichabod Alden, the rebel commander, prepared for the attack in a way that made the consequences inevitable. Officers were quartered in a house, the 300 Continentals and 150 militia in the fort, the elderly, the women and children in their houses unprotected. A detachment under MacDonell captured the officers, while Butler and the main body surrounded the fort. With Butler were Captains Joseph Brant, Jacob Lewis and Aaron Hill, all natives serving in the Indian Department, and Sir John Johnson's half-brother William of Canajoharie. While the rangers and a few Indians kept the garrison bottled up, the majority of the braves attacked the village and nearby farms, killing women and children, taking prisoners, setting buildings alight.

Throughout the carnage Butler waited, helpless, at the fort, unable to assist the civilians lest the garrison make a foray in superior numbers against his rangers and the Indians who had stood by him. While the attack on the civilians was reprehensible, the warriors who committed the atrocity deserve some sympathy. They were only repeating outrages committed against the women and children in their own villages by rebel frontiersmen. That Walter Butler was able to keep some of their leaders with him was something of a miracle.

American historians blame Butler for the massacre, but the rebel officers were also at fault for neglecting to place the women and children inside the fort where they would have been out of danger, leaving Butler to carry out his original plan to destroy only supplies. Furthermore, there is evidence that Cherry Valley had been forewarned, which made the rebel officers' oversight the more reprehensible. On November 12, Walter sent most of the Indians and a few rangers to drive the captured cattle and horses towards Niagara. He reported to Colonel Bolton:

> I have much to lament that notwithstanding my utmost precautions & endeavours to save the Women and Children, I could not prevent some of them falling unhappy Victims to the Fury of the Savages.

He said that Aaron Hill saved the elderly Reverend Samuel Dunlop, but could not prevent the deaths of his wife and daughter nor the capture of the families of John Moore and Samuel Campbell, absent on military duty. He rescued some prisoners and kept them close to the camp fires, surrounded by rangers, Walter's letter resumes:

> Tho' the second morning of our March, Captain Johnson (to whose knowledge and address in managing them I am much indebted), and I got them to permit twelve who were Loyalists and whom I had concealed the first day with the humane assistance of Mr. Joseph Brant and Captain Jacob . . . to return.

145

The Indian Department officer Walter praised was Captain John Johnston. All told, 31 people died, 38 prisoners were set free, and 33 were carried off by Indians. The fate of two families showed what could happen to loyalists caught in the middle. Living at Cherry Valley were James Ramsay and William McClellan, and both were captured by Indians and taken away. Ramsay had been warned, and had removed valuables from his house before the warriors burnt it, while McClellan was so discreet that his family was not molested by the rebels afterward, and his name was kept on a list of prisoners the rebels wanted exchanged.[16]

After the Cherry Valley raid, Walter and his rangers wintered at Fort Niagara, while the Indians returned to their villages. John Butler opened negotiations with General George Clinton; the rebel governor of New York State, for the exchange of his wife Catharine and three youngest children for prisoners taken at Cherry Valley. The governor agreed, but he charged the rangers with permitting outrages by the Indians. Walter Butler responded quickly and vehemently:

> We deny any cruelties to have been committed at Wyoming either by whites or Indians; so far to the contrary, that not a man, woman or child was hurt after the capitulation, or a woman or child before it, or taken into captivity. Though should you call it inhumanity, the killing of men in arms in the field, we in that case plead guilty. The inhabitants killed at Cherry Valley do not lay at my door, my conscience acquits me. If any are guilty (as accesories) it's yourselves; at least the conduct of some of your officers, first Col. Hartley, of your forces, sent to the Indians the enclosed, being a copy of his letter charging them with crimes they never committed, and threatening them and their villages with fire and sword, and no quarter.[17]

Walter mentioned other instances where the rebels had provoked the Indians. He maintained that the prisoners, when exchanged, would testify that he had acted correctly, adding: 'I must beg leave by the bye, to observe that I experienced no humanity or even common justice during my imprisonment among you.'

The negotiations for the exchange of the Butler family were protracted as letters passed back and forth and terms were arranged. Finally, Catherine, William Johnson, Andrew and Deborah were escorted to Skenesborough, and handed over under a flag of truce, early in the spring of 1780. For a time Catherine stayed in Montreal. Thomas, who had thus far served in the Indian Department, was commissioned a captain-lieutenant in the rangers on October 3, 1780.[18] Andrew, the fourth son, received a second lieutenant's commission in 1783, nine months before the corps was disbanded, when he was 21 years old.[19]

By December 1778, six full companies of Butler's Rangers mustered at Fort Niagara. Initially, they wore fringed hunting shirts of green linen, leggings or overalls of buckskin or linen, moccasins and forage caps that were probably cut down bicorne hats worn by battalion companies of other provincial corps. When they were issued with parade dress their coatees were of dark green cloth, faced with dark red, the officers' uniforms of better quality material. The forage caps may have been of leather, engraved with 'G.R.' encircled by 'Butler's Rangers.' Equally well, the caps may have been felt, cut down from bicornes, to which the men pinned cartridge case badges or brass belt plates. The officers wore gold lace, and the ranks' pewter buttons were stamped 'Butler's Rangers.'

Otherwise dress consisted of white small clothes, the same as worn by most provincials and regulars, although some of the waistcoats were green like the coatees. Overalls were of white linen, or the regiment wore white breeches of wool or linen, white woollen stockings, short canvas spatterdashes and low, black buckled shoes. Major Butler wanted his men equipped with rifles, their own or army issue. Many carried their hunting rifles, which made their marksmanship more effective, but some had old-fashioned muskets. Colonel Bolton lent Butler 100 firelocks, but he admitted to Haldimand that there was not one good flint for them at Fort Niagara.

Winter quarters were across the Niagara River, the site of the modern town of Niagara-on-the-Lake. The barracks were of logs, and cost £2,527.19s.2d. and distressed families were also accommodated there.[20] Although some time would pass before this was evident, Butler was founding one of the oldest communities in what became the Province of Ontario.

Sullivan's Punitive Expedition Against the Iroquois, 1779

During the winter the rangers were nearly as active as in summer. As the year 1778 was drawing to a close, Major Butler and Colonel Bolton had numerous small parties out scouting or in search of captives. James Secord was near Chemung, keeping watch on the rebels at Wyoming; Captain John Johnston was among the Senecas, reporting on happenings at Fort Pitt. Meanwhile, Governor Haldimand was asking for advice on how to make Niagara as self-sufficient as possible, owing to the difficulty of provisioning a large garrison and refugees so far from the lower St. Lawrence. In the midst of all this correspondence and the activities of parties of rangers, disastrous news reached Niagara from Detroit. Lieutenant-Colonel Henry Hamilton, the governor of the settlement there and commandant of the fort, had left his post on October

27 with a party of French residents and Indians and by December they had occupied Fort Sackville, at the small French settlement of Vincennes.[21]

Hamilton was known as 'the hair buyer' by the rebels, who accused him of arming the western Indians. A determined band of men from Fort Pitt, under the surveyor, Colonel George Rogers Clark, marched on Fort Sackville, which surrendered on February 24, 1779, and Governor Hamilton and the garrison were now Clark's prisoners. Major Arent De Peyster, Hamilton's deputy at Detroit, sent Colonel Mason Bolton an urgent appeal for reinforcements, and Major Butler dispatched Captain William Caldwell and 50 rangers to scout near the fort. At all costs, Clark must be kept from capturing this vital link in the defence of the upper country.

As the spring of 1779 advanced, ominous rumblings that something of importance was afoot along the Susquehanna River reached Niagara, although Butler's scouts could not discern the rebels' intentions. The garrison at Fort Pitt was building boats; an army was mustering at Wyoming; and there were 700 armed men at Canajoharie, in the Mohawk Valley. Then 600 men from Fort Stanwix marched westward and attacked the Onondaga Indians' villages, burning three. Two scouts, Caleb Clossen and John Walden Meyers, reached Fort St. Johns from Albany, and reported that 200 rebels had returned to that town with 35 Onondaga prisoners – a chief, three men, and the rest women and children.[22]

Meyers had come all the way from New York City with a misleading message from the British headquarters. According to Sir Henry Clinton, the rebels would make a feint up the Susquehanna to draw Major Butler's attention away from Detroit, the real target. The commander in-chief also warned Governor Haldimand to be wary, for the rebels planned to move up the Connecticut Valley and attack his stronghold of Quebec again. Major Butler was not to become alarmed by signs that the rebels planned an attack on Niagara.

The news of troop movements on the Susquehanna and the attack on the Onondaga villages had the Iroquois in a panic, and to calm them Colonel Bolton ordered John Butler to march to Kanadesaga with 400 men, the majority rangers. They were to take up a position, thereby reassuring the Indians of Britain's continuing support. Butler left Fort Niagara on May 2, and from Kanadesaga he found that he had to undertake gruelling forced marches, as reports from first one village then another reached him that a rebel attack was imminent.

Butler sent repeated appeals for assistance to Haldimand, but the governor remained convinced that Quebec City was in more danger. He was also waiting for the arrival of the spring fleet with provisions and other supplies, and felt he could do nothing for Butler until his 'victuallers' came. Nevertheless, he expected the ranger leader to hold his ground at all costs, and he dispatched him an order to this effect. Meanwhile, by order of George Washington, the rebels' commander-in-chief, an expedition ultimately more than 5,000 strong was converging on the Iroquois lands. The main body of 3,500 Continental soldiers and boatmen under General John Sullivan was advancing up the Susquehanna. General James Clinton was moving along the Mohawk River and southward to meet Sullivan at Tioga with 1,500 men, where 500 from Fort Pitt were expected to join them.

At this critical point, Major Donald McDonald, of the Royal Highland Emigrants, sent a letter to Captain John MacDonell informing him that unless he rejoined that corps soon he would be replaced. Butler wrote to Colonel Bolton on May 28, asking him to request Governor Haldimand to allow MacDonell to stay with the rangers over the summer, for 'The Indians are very fond of Captain McDonald & upon being told he was going down the Country have particularly requested that His Excellency would allow him to stay.'[23] MacDonell remained with the rangers, and he never did rejoin the Royal Highland Emigrants.

Although the governor granted Butler's request to retain MacDonell, he still refused to believe the rumours reaching him that an army of rebels was moving up the Susquehanna. There was disturbing troop activity in the Connecticut Valley too, and he was convinced that Quebec City and Detroit were in more danger than the Iroquois lands or Fort Niagara. For the protection of Detroit, he ordered his regulars shunted westward. Three companies of the 47th Regiment left Carleton Island for Niagara, to be replaced at Fort Haldimand by a detachment of Sir John Johnson's Royal Yorkers. When the men of the 47th Regiment reached Fort Niagara, some of the garrison set out for Detroit.[24]

While Butler marched and countermarched, bolstering Iroquois morale, small detachments of rangers and Indians continued their raids. On July 20, Joseph Brant and 60 Indians, with Captain Barent Frey and 50 rangers attacked the settlement of Minisink (ten miles west of the modern town of Goshen, New York) to obtain provisions. Four people were killed, one a lame schoolmaster named Jeremiah van Auken. He told his pupils to run, then left the schoolhouse to meet Brant and Frey on the road outside. Before he could reach the officers, a warrior tomahawked and scalped him. Brant put paint marks on the aprons of the little girls in the school, telling them that any Indian seeing that mark would leave them alone. The girls made their marks do double duty, by spreading their aprons over the boys' laps, which the Indians respected.[25]

Early in June, Butler discovered that Lieutenant Henry Hare, of the rangers, and Sergeant William Newberry, had been captured and executed as spies. Hare was hanged on a gallows erected before his house at Canajoharie, in full view of his wife and five children.[26] By the 19th, the land around Kanadesaga had been stripped of all provisions, and Butler moved to Genesee Falls, two days' march closer to Niagara, so that his men could be supplied by boats from the fort and fish from the river. MacDonell went foraging, and on August 5, he reached Tioga with cattle and halted to await news of General Sullivan, then at Wyoming. There the general was soon joined by James Clinton, and the detachment from Fort Pitt.

Washington's orders to Sullivan on the fate of the Iroquois were:

... the total destruction and devastation of their settlements, and the capture of as many prisoners of every age and sex as possible. It will be essential to ruin their crops now in the ground and prevent them planting more. Parties should be detached to lay waste all the settlements around, with instructions to do it in the most effectual manner, that the country not be merely over-run, but destroyed.

After you have very thoroughly completed the destruction of their settlements, if the Indians should show a disposition for peace I would have you encourage it, on condition that they will give some decisive evidence of their sincerity by delivering up some of the principal instigators of their past hostility into our hands; Butler, Brant, the most mischievous of the Tories that have joined them, or any others they may have in their power that we are interested to get in ours. They may possibly be engaged by address, secrecy, and stratagem to surprise the garrison at Niagara and the shipping upon the lakes, and put them in our possession.

Fortunately for Butler and Brant – and the present Canadian boundary – the depredations by Sullivan's army had the opposite effect on the Iroquois people. By August 15, Butler felt ready to move against Sullivan, and Richard Cartwright Jr. then his secretary, wrote from Kanadesaga to Francis Goring, a clerk at Niagara for some Montreal merchants: 'you need not send any of the Shirts at Present for as we are just going off to meet the Enemy the less we are encumbered with Baggage the better.'

Meanwhile, Sullivan was moving, ponderously – Continentals could be as slow as Burgoyne's regulars – with eleven regiments of infantry and riflemen, one of artillery, and the Wyoming Militia, driving 800 cattle and 1,200 packhorses, accompanied by 120 boats loaded with supplies, heavy baggage and nine field guns. On August 11th, he reached Tioga; two days later he ordered a detachment to make a night march to surprise the settlement at Chemung, but the men found the thirty houses there empty. Captain

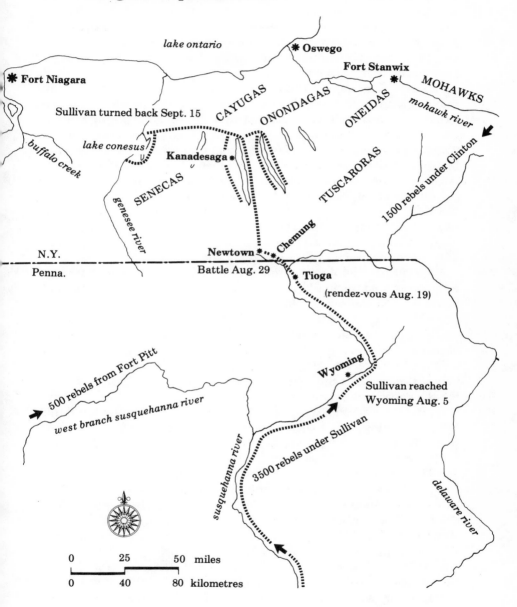

Sullivan's Expedition Against the Iroquois
August - September 1779

lake ontario

* Oswego

* Fort Niagara

Fort Stanwix

MOHAWKS

*

CAYUGAS

ONONDAGAS

ONEIDAS

mohawk river

Sullivan turned back Sept. 15

lake conesus

buffalo creek

Kanadesaga *

TUSCARORAS

1500 rebels under Clinton

SENECAS

genesee river

Chemung

Newtown *

N.Y.

Penna.

Battle Aug. 29

* Tioga

(rendez-vous Aug. 19)

500 rebels from Fort Pitt

west branch susquehanna river

Wyoming

*

Sullivan reached
Wyoming Aug. 5

susquehanna river

3500 rebels under Sullivan

delaware river

| 0 | 25 | 50 miles |
| 0 | 40 | 80 kilometres |

Rowland Montour of the Indian Department, who had forewarned the inhabitants, lay in wait with 40 men. In the ambush that followed, one Indian lost his life and 21 rebels were killed or wounded.

Meanwhile, General James Clinton's force, which had floated down the east branch of the Susquehanna, had joined Sullivan on August 9. At Kanadesaga, Butler waited with less than 300 Rangers, 14 of the 8th Regiment and, to his dismay, only 600 Indians. Fearful for their wives and children, many of the warriors he had counted on remained in their villages. Butler sought to deploy the Indians with him in small groups, to harry the rebels along the flanks in true guerrilla fashion, but they insisted on making a stand on a ridge near Newtown (now Elmira, New York.) There on the 27th, the rangers built a breastwork of logs and dug some rifle pits. MacDonell with Brant and 30 rangers and Indians held the right. Walter Butler and the remaining rangers were in the centre, while the main body of Indians, led by Sayenqueraghta were on the left at the foot of a steep incline. At night they camped nearby. None of the rangers had tents or blankets, and for two weeks they had had no meat, flour or salt. All had been subsisting on seven ears of corn per day, eaten raw because they dared not show any smoke.

Despite Butler's precautions, Sullivan had advance warning. His scouts had seen light from the Indians' campfires, and had heard axes in the woods. On the 29th, the rangers and Indians stationed themselves on the ridge. To Major Butler's disgust, the Indians did not like being pinned against the incline and changed their position, leaving the left flank unprotected. Rebel cannon began firing, and there was some skirmishing. Then a Cayuga chief came to warn Butler that Sullivan was sending a brigade of light infantry to take possession of the rangers' line of retreat. With Brant concurring, Butler ordered a withdrawal, but the Indians on the left flank refused to budge. This was unusual, for the Indian way of warfare was to disappear when the odds were not in their favour and await a better opportunity. As soon as hails of grape shot from Sullivan's artillery rained down on them they broke and fled into the forest. The rangers and Brant's party of Indians beat a more orderly but no less hasty retreat, in which Butler was very nearly captured. For the first time Butler's Rangers faced overwhelming odds, yet their losses were only 5 killed or missing and 3 wounded, while the Indians lost 5 killed and 9 wounded. Sullivan lost 42 soldiers and a Oneida scout, while 9 others were wounded. Even in defeat, John Butler took more of the enemy than he sacrificed.

Leaving Walter Butler with a small party to spy on Sullivan, John Butler led his rangers, half of them ill from malnutrition, fever and ague, back to Kanadesaga. From there he continued his withdrawal in slow stages back to Fort Niagara. Small parties of rangers fit for duty, and such Indians as were not totally demoralized and hiding out near their villages, kept worrying the flanks of Sullivan's expeditionary force. Slowly and systematically the Continentals advanced, destroying the Indians' homes and crops, driving off their cattle and horses, chopping down the orchards that were their owners' pride and joy. Although some Iroquois lived in longhouses and practised shifting agriculture, many had built homes as fine as their white neighbours of square timber or stone, with glass in the windows and had neat fields for their crops. On September 7, Sullivan's men reached Kanadesaga, by which time the Indians had recovered from the shock and were active along the flanks.

John Butler was soon on the march again, with 400 revitalized rangers and some Indians, and on the 13 September, he set up an ambush. Sullivan's vanguard was building a bridge over a swamp at the head of Lake Conesus. Butler intended to allow part of Sullivan's army to cross, then cut it off where it could not be strongly reinforced. The plot failed, because a rebel scout of 30 men stumbled into the midst of the rangers and Indians lying in wait, and the first volley from Butler's men killed 22 of them. The rest were captured, and the Indians tortured their officer, Lieutenant Boyd, to death.[27] From the other captives Butler discovered that Sullivan was not planning to cross the Genesee River, and had provisions for only one month when he left Tioga. Butler withdrew to the west bank of the Genesee, and on September 15, Sullivan's vanguard reached the east bank. Butler withdrew a few more miles and halted at Buffalo Creek – the site of the city of Buffalo, New York – hoping that Colonel Bolton could send reinforcements from Niagara.

In the meantime, suspecting that Niagara was Sullivan's objective, Bolton had recalled Captain William Caldwell and his company from Detroit, and at length even Governor Haldimand in Quebec City realized that the situation confronting Butler's Rangers and the Iroquois Indians was grave. His provision ships had finally arrived from Britain and he now had the means to mount a larger expedition than had been possible earlier in the summer. He ordered Sir John Johnson to take as many men as he thought sufficient and join Butler, and he sent 90 men of the 32nd Regiment and the Royal Highland Emigrants from Carleton Island to Niagara, to bolster the garrison while the loyalists and some detachments of regulars were in the field against Sullivan's army.[28]

Sir John left Montreal with instructions from Haldimand to take command of all the troops being sent into New York State. He reached Niagara on October 6, with his vanguard, where he paused for conferences with the Indians. By that time, everyone knew that Sullivan was withdrawing, followed by Captain William Caldwell and a party of rangers who were doing as much damage as possible to the rebel rearguard. Niagara was safe; but for the Iroquois, Haldimand had done too little, too late.

The rebels had burnt 40 Iroquois villages and 160,000 bushels of corn, and cut down all the orchards. Upon seeing the farms and villages, Sullivan expressed surprise that the Six Nations had reached such an elevated state of civilization. As soon as he was certain the rebels were retiring, Butler led his rangers back to Fort Niagara, where he met Sir John Johnson, who had a plan to use the troops he had brought from Montreal. At his conference with the Indians, he had persuaded them to assemble at Oswego for a raid against the Oneida villages, to punish them for aiding the rebels. On receiving Haldimand's approval, Johnson and Butler set out for Oswego in bateaux, with one company of rangers. Three companies were to follow. The governor informed the ranger leader:

His Majesty has been made acquainted with your services, and he has approved of them, and I hope the events of this campaign will recommend you still more to his Royal favor.

Whether Butler ever found out that Haldimand had planned to place his men under Sir John Johnson, had he arrived in time, is uncertain, but such an order would have been a slap in the face for the ranger, after the efforts he had expended in the service.

By October 15, Butler and his 200 Rangers had reached Oswego, and with Sir John Johnson he was preparing to set out towards the Oneida country. But when the two provincial officers discovered that a Cayuga who had been at Fort Niagara had alerted the Oneidas of the danger, they called off the raid. Johnson and his men sailed for Carleton Island, and Butler took his rangers back to Fort Niagara for the winter. At once he launched a vigorous recruiting drive to fill up the ranks of the regiment.

Sullivan's expedition failed to accomplish what Washington had hoped would be an end to Iroquois participation in the war. One rebel officer admitted 'the nests are destroyed, but the birds are still on the wing.' The remark was prophetic, for the desolation of their homeland stiffened the determination of the Six Nations to retaliate. The rebel settlements would feel the full weight of their revenge the following spring. What Washington had achieved was to align the Iroquois, most of the Oneidas excepted, firmly on the side of Britain. Yet in the long run Sullivan succeeded. The men of his expedition had viewed the rich farmlands of the Iroquois people, and would never rest until they belonged to them.

Governor Haldimand had learned a costly lesson. Writing to Lord Germain, the Colonial Secretary, he admitted that if he hoped to hold the upper country for the sake of the fur trade, some 1,000 to 1,500 regular troops must be relegated for that work in the spring. He also asked for permission to establish permanent settlements at the more important forts which lacked them:

> I have for many years regretted that measures were not adopted such as to prevent the safety of those posts depending upon supplies from home, so very distant, the transportation to extremely precarious, and attended with so heavy an expense to Government; all of which might be obviated, the troops infinitely better provided, and the different posts be in perfect security by raising grain and all kinds of stock at Detroit, which, from its central situation, could very well supply both Detroit and Michilmackinac.
> The same plan is very practicable at Niagara, and there is nothing wanting but a beginning.

Other evidence suggests that when Haldimand wrote that letter in September 1779, Detroit was fairly self-sufficient in food. The settlement left by the French after the Seven Years' War was a well-established farming community. In the fall of 1778, the governor had raised the matter of gardening and field crops at Niagara with Colonel Bolton, whose reply was cautious. The commandant warned him that encroaching on Seneca land might irritate the Six Nations, whom he was frequently reminding that the Great King George III had not taken so much as an acre from them since he had driven the French away. A more politic arrangement would be to plant crops on the west side of the Niagara River, in Mississauga territory.

Late in the autumn of 1779, Guy Johnson, long absent, arrived at Niagara to resume his duties as Superintendent of Indian Affairs, residing in the stone building within the compound which the Indians called the 'Castle.' The winter was long and severe, and the homeless people of the Six Nations fled to the fort to be cared for by Colonel Bolton. Huts had to be erected, or space found in the barracks, clothing and blankets shared, food rationed. Upon exploring, scouts found that Sullivan had missed some of the most westerly Seneca villages, and a few Indians were able to return there for the winter to hunt, which relieved the pressure at Niagara slightly. Some of the Cayugas and a few Delawares who lived among the Six Nations blamed John Butler for their plight, but the necessity of receiving provisions, and Butler's own powers of persuasion won most of them to his side. Despite the extreme cold, Butler had agents living secretly in the frontier settlements, gathering intelligence and seeking out recruits, and by the spring of 1780, his battalion of eight companies was at full strength. He soon received a promotion to lieutenant-colonel of provincials, and from then on even Governor Haldimand, who disliked high ranks for colonials and was inclined to address them as Mr., referred to the ranger leader as Colonel Butler.

While Butler had little difficulty filling his ranks, some of his methods were open to question. Prior to his departure from Montreal the previous September, Sir John Johnson asked Haldimand for permission to 'demand such men as I can make appear were entered for my Regiment and are now in Colonel Butler's Corps and with Joseph Brant.'[29] Replying, the governor begged Johnson not to rock the boat:

> When you have sufficiently reflected upon the disagreeable and even bad consequences that must arise from coming to difficulties with Major Butler at this interesting moment particularly on a subject in which Joseph is deeply concerned, I am sure you will for the present relinquish your desire of demanding the men inlisted for your Corps now serving with the Rangers, you may depend upon every Justice being done you when Times will permit.

He added a private letter repeating the need for forbearance:

> You are well acquainted with the Characters of Major Butler and his Son, the former deficient in Education and liberal sentiments, the latter conceited and petulent, Characters that require I confess much Patience to do business with. . . . Major Butler has certainly acquired a great share of Influence with the Five Nations, he had long studied their manners and dispositions, is possessed of those Qualities necessary to deal with them, and if nicely managed may be made a most useful Agent, a little attention wins his Heart. . . . Major Butler and his Son have by the success fallen in their way acquired great Credit at Home and I have the King's Orders to signify to them his Royal approbation of their Conduct.

In short, the governor was warning Johnson that he, not Butler, would be blamed should any disagreements surface.

Baron von Riedesel, the commander of the German troops, also complained that some of his regulars, captured with General Burgoyne, had escaped from prisoner-of-war camps and were serving with the rangers. Many Palatine settlers had joined the rebels, but there were enough German-speaking rangers for the regulars to be able to communicate with Butler's officers. Of all the bickering over recruits the most bizarre episode involved John Walden Meyers, attempting to raise an independent company at Fort St. Johns, and his sergeant, Joseph Smith.

In August 1781, couriers from Niagara reaching St. Johns informed Meyers that his sergeant was being detained, and some of his recruits were serving with the Rangers. Sergeant Smith was heading for Lake Champlain with these recruits when he met two of Butler's agents, Staats Springsteen and John Stoner, who also had some recruits. The two parties travelled together, the rangers sharing their provisions with Smith and his men. When their paths branched, Butler's agents insisted that since Smith's recruits had eaten rations intended for the rangers, the men were obliged to join that corps. After some fisticuffs, Springsteen and Stoner subdued Smith and marched the whole party to Chemung.

While one agent stood guard, the other went to Fort Niagara and returned with Colonel Butler's nephew, Captain Andrew Bladt. He struck Smith several times and escorted everyone to Niagara. Then Bradt, Springsteen and Stoner decided it would be wise to accuse Smith of being a rebel spy. They brought him before Brigadier Watson Powell, the commandant at the time, who tended to believe Andrew Bradt, the commissioned officer. Smith was a mere sergeant and completely unknown at Niagara. Poor Smith was thrown in the guardhouse, and Meyers' informant maintained that he was still imprisoned there. An irate Meyers appealed to Governor Haldimand, asking that his sergeant and recruits be returned to him. From his knowledge of all parties involved, Haldimand, who held Meyers in high esteem, knew where to lay the blame. He ordered Smith released, and the recruits sent to Fort St. Johns, and informed Brigadier Powell:

Enclosed is a representation of Captain Meyers, a most active and Zealous partisan, who on a former occasion had a number of Recruits taken away by the same gentleman of whose treatment he complains, and who was lately promoted to a Company in Lieut.Col. Butler's Rangers.

Please to issue such orders as will prevent anything of the kind in future and let Col. Butler represent to Mr. Brat the impropriety of his Conduct.[30]

This episode closed with a conciliatory letter from Bradt to Powell, in which he blamed the whole misunderstanding on Sergeant Smith who, he maintained, had been insolent. Yet there is no doubt that he would have kept the recruits had Meyers not made such a fuss, just as ranger officers had appropriated recruits promised to other companies and corps on previous occasions.[31]

Haldimand did not hesitate to intercede for Meyers, although he had refused to oblige Johnson and von Riedesel, because in the case of Sergeant Smith the infractions were so blatant and had so many witnesses that the governor felt on safe ground. Had Butler complained to Lord Germain, Haldimand knew he could justify his intervention.

Recruiting agents for Butler's Rangers did not need to resort to unfair practices, but they were rowdy fellows who enjoyed a good scrap. Living on the frontier among the Indians who were their friends, most were more at home around a council fire than in the drawing rooms of the east. Since the corps was constantly in action against the rebels, and receiving higher pay than other provincials, Butler could have filled his ranks without any of the sort of nonsense indulged in by Springsteen and Stoner. From the spring of

Actions by Butler's Rangers in New York and Pennsylvania 1778-82

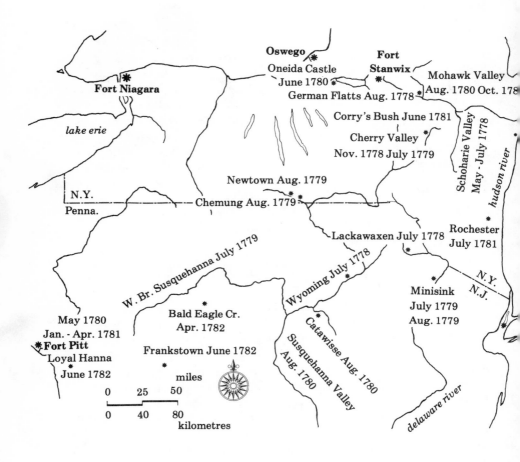

Oswego

Oneida Castle
June 1780

Fort Stanwix

German Flatts Aug. 1778

Mohawk Valley
Aug. 1780 Oct. 178

Fort Niagara

lake erie

Corry's Bush June 1781

Cherry Valley
Nov. 1778 July 1779

Schoharie Valley
May - July 1778

hudson river

Newtown Aug. 1779

N.Y.
Penna.

Chemung Aug. 1779

Lackawaxen July 1778

Rochester
July 1781

W. Br. Susquehanna July 1779

Wyoming July 1778

Minisink
July 1779
Aug. 1779

N.Y.
N.J.

May 1780
Jan. - Apr. 1781

Bald Eagle Cr.
Apr. 1782

Catawisse Aug. 1780

Fort Pitt
Loyal Hanna
June 1782

Frankstown June 1782

Susquehanna Valley
Aug. 1780

miles

0   25   50

0   40   80
kilometres

delaware river

158

1780 onwards, Butler was able to keep his corps at full strength, with new enlistments replacing men lost through death, wounds, sickness or retirement from the service.

Retaliation

That winter of 1780, the rangers were out in force. By February, despite cruel weather, a dozen parties accompanied by Indians had left Fort Niagara bound for German Flatts and other settlements along the Mohawk.[32] Early in April, Joseph Brant and Captain Hendrick William Nelles of the rangers appeared at the head of the Delaware River en route to Schoharie with 18 Rangers, 6 Mohawks and 4 Onondagas, and they received provisions from Thomas McMicking, who lived near Harpersfield.[33] About the same time, a company of Rangers under the command of Captain Gilbert Tice, was sent to Carleton Island, to serve as scouts for the garrison there.[34] Another company led by Captain Peter Hare of the Rangers left to undertake the same duties at Detroit.

In May, Sir John Johnson added the weight of his regiment to Butler's Rangers and the men of the Indian Department, when he led a relief expedition through the Mohawk Valley from Crown Point to Johnstown, demonstrating to Haldimand, who had once sneered at them, that the men of the King's Royal Regiment of New York were as capable with the firelock as with the axe. In June, the redoubtable Captain John MacDonell, with 40 rangers and Captain John Johnston with a party of Indians attacked the Oneida villages near the lake of the same name. On their way back to Fort Niagara, MacDonell was so ill with fever and ague that his men tied him on his horse.

Meanwhile, Lieutenant John Dockstader, with a party of rangers and Indians, had marched to blockade Fort Pitt, while Nelles and Brant were performing the same task at Fort Stanwix. In July, 300 Onondagas and Tuscaroras, formerly on the side of the rebels or trying to stay neutral, reached Fort Niagara as refugees. Back at Fort Stanwix, Nelles departed, leaving Lieutenant Joseph Clement in command of the rangers, where the force of Indians with Brant then numbered nearly 300. Clement and Brant turned their men to attack the Oneida villages again and marched westward. Finding the main village, Oneida Castle, deserted, the rangers and Indians burned it and turned back towards Fort Stanwix to resume their blockade. They stumbled upon Oneida warriors encamped and a few took to their heels, but 100 joined Brant and Clement. Then with Brant in command the men marched to Fort Plain, ten miles above

Canajoharie, where they found two small forts abandoned, several mills and some buildings containing grain, all of which they put to the torch. In the process they had taken 50 male prisoners, and some women and children. The latter they released before leaving the settlement with the other captives and 500 cattle and horses.

Then Brant and Clement divided their forces into five parts, each with a share of the livestock, and sent them against Schoharie, Cherry Valley and German Flatts where they took more prisoners and spread panic in their wake. More small parties of rangers and Indians were in the Susquehanna and Ohio valleys, doing relatively minor damage, but sufficient to cause the executive council of Pennsylvania – a rebel body – to offer $1,500 for each male prisoner, and $1,000 per scalp. Notification of these rewards was sent to all the county lieutenants – as in England the men responsible for raising militia units – and to Colonel Daniel Brodhead, in command at Fort Pitt.

While his rangers and the men of the Indian Department were thus employed, John Butler took advantage of the return of Guy Johnson to pay a visit to Quebec City to meet with Governor Haldimand. Just how the governor reached the conclusion that Butler was 'deficient in Education and liberal sentiments' is a mystery. At the time he wrote this comment he had never seen the ranger leader, unless the two men had known each other during the Seven Years' War. Much of the discussion in the Château St. Louis involved the production of food crops and domestic livestock at Niagara to reduce the garrison's dependence on provisions shipped from Sorel. The number of refugees and Indians was constantly increasing, and the governor was anxious that people so remote from the populated part of his domain should provide for themselves. When he left Quebec City, Butler was carrying several letters from Haldimand, and one was an order to Guy Johnson to open negotiations with the Mississauga Indians for the purchase of a strip of land along the west side of the Niagara River. Butler stopped in Montreal for his wife Catherine and three youngest children, and the family reached Niagara aboard the new sloop *Ontario* on August 8, 1780. [34]

On September 1, Bolton wrote to Haldimand, assuring him that Butler was offering him every assistance. The ranger officer had brought some loyalists with him from Montreal, and he had several good farmers in his corps who were 'advancing in years' and would be better employed on the land than for active duty.

At that time, rangers and Indians led by Captain Rowland Montour and Lieutenant William Johnson (a gunsmith, not William of Canajoharie, who joined the Indian Department that year) were on the Susquehanna below Wyoming marching to protect a settlement of loyalists in the Catawisse Valley, who had been provisioning their colleagues. A party of rebels set out from Wyoming to check Montour and Johnson, who invested two forts on September 5, then turned westward. On the 10th, they clashed with the rebels, killing their leader, Colonel Cairns, and 16 others, taking three prisoners. Montour was wounded in this skirmish and two weeks later he died.

Small parties of rangers and Indians continued worrying the rebels, but the main operation of the autumn was the expedition under the command of Sir John Johnson that entered the Mohawk Valley from Oswego. On September 30, Colonel Bolton at Niagara informed Haldimand that Sir John's expedition should have taken place a month earlier, at which time he could have sent more troops, and Colonel Guy Johnson more Indians. The number of men fit for duty had been much reduced by 'Fluxes, Fever & Ague' and Catherine Butler and most of her children were also ill.[35] Bolton's news is substantiated in the monthly report of the rangers dated October 6, 1780. Officers and non-commissioned officers included the lieutenant-colonel, 6 captains, 8 first lieutenants, 6 second lieutenants, a quartermaster, a surgeon, 24 sergeants and 16 drummers. The list shows 381 privates, of which 54 were fit for duty, 102 were sick in quarters, 2 were out recruiting, 3 were on furlough, 17 were prisoners of the rebels, 1 was a new recruit, and 202 were on command. Of the latter, 132 were with Colonel Butler on Sir John Johnson's expedition to the Mohawk Valley, 44 were at Detroit and 4 were somewhere in Indian country, 20 were on duty in 'Canada' and 2 were at Carleton Island.[36]

By taking every man who was even remotely fit, and ordering those who recovered to follow with all speed, Butler managed to scrape together four companies – 200 men – while Guy Johnson persuaded a goodly number of Indians to accompany Butler. In selecting his men, Butler was forced to interpret Haldimand's orders loosely, for the governor had instructed Bolton:

I would by no means have you send a single man who is not a good marcher and capable of bearing fatigue. The same must be observed in your choice of Officers; without paying attention to the rosters, as success will entirely depend upon your despatch and vigor; those whose personal abilities are not equal to these efforts would rather weaken than give strength to the detachment, for with every man that falls out one or two must be left behind.

In his letter to Haldimand of September 30, Colonel Bolton admitted that there were 2,600 Indians in the neighbourhood of Fort Niagara, but he would be imprudent to reduce his garrison too much lest they turn on him. Nor would Walter Butler be his father's the senior captain, for he was far from well and Bolton had given him leave to go to Montreal. (There Walter found the social life more strenuous than scouting, and he admitted that he had to resort to a hike on snowshoes around the mountain every other day to recover from excessive indulgence in food and strong spirits.)[37]

Apart from the difficulty in procuring enough healthy rangers, Bolton thought Johnson's expedition well timed. Many rebel militiamen from the Mohawk Valley had been called to serve with Washington's Continental Army, and here was a favourable opportunity for 'returning Mr. Sullivan's visit to the Six Nations.' Bolton had sent with Butler's Rangers and the regulars enough provisions to last 500 men six weeks, but flour was scarce at Niagara. Each ranger had been provided with a blanket, leggings and moccasins. Since Walter Butler was on leave, John MacDonell was the senior captain on the expedition. Thomas Butler may have been with his father, or among those too ill to march. He received his commission on October 3, but no records indicate that he was ever a party leader on the many forays the rangers made into rebel territory.[38]

On September 24, Colonel Butler embarked for Oswego with the regulars of the 8th and 34th Regiments, his rangers, and three guns which Bolton described as a grasshopper and two royals. Contrary winds on Lake Ontario prevented him joining Johnson until October 1. Not long after they set out, Joseph Brant, who had been at Schoharie, joined them and other famous warriors of the Six Nations rallied round Johnson. Sayenqueraghta (Old Smoke) of the Senecas was mounted on a horse, while Cornplanter, Blacksnake, Handsome Lake and Red Jacket had all come to help their white brother vanquish an enemy who had caused their people so much suffering the winter before.[39]

The sweep through the Mohawk Valley is described in detail in the history of the King's Royal Regiment of New York (pp97-109). By October 25, the men had returned to the boats they had left at the portage between Wood Creek and Lake Oneida, where they embarked and rowed for Oswego. All the horses had been butchered to feed the troops and Indians, and even Old Smoke was on foot. Upon reaching the forts on Lake Ontario, Butler found that 18 of his rangers, including Captain George Dame, were missing. He left some boats and provisions and embarked for the return journey to Fort Niagara. A few days later Dame and all the missing men reached their base safely.

Behind them the rangers, Royal Yorkers, and regulars and Indians had left a wide swath of desolation, and Washington informed the Congress in a letter written November 7:

> The destruction of the grain upon the western frontier of New York is likely to be attended with the most alarming consequences, in respect to the formation of magazines upon the North River. We had prospects of forming a very considerable magazine of flour in that quarter previous to the late incursion. The settlement of Schoharie alone would have delivered eighty thousand bushels of grain, but that fine district is now totally destroyed.

While Butler had been in the Mohawk Valley with his four companies, the rangers at Detroit had not been idle. Captain Peter Hare had marched with his company to take up a position at some Shawnee villages near the Ohio River. The rebels had made a surprise attack on these Indians, and having rangers stationed among them improved their morale. Hare withdrew as far as the Miami River, and built a blockhouse, but he kept his scouts operating along the Ohio River until the rebels withdrew to Fort Pitt and the Shawnees felt more secure.

Late in October, Brigadier Watson Powell arrived at Niagara to take up his duties as the commandant. Colonel Bolton was exhausted and had asked for a leave of absence in Montreal. On October 31, he set sail on the sloop *Ontario* accompanied by a lieutenant and 25 men of the 34th Regiment. A sudden storm struck and the sloop broke up and sank with a loss of all on board. A party of Butler's men searched for survivors in vain, finding only some clothing and parts of the vessel along the shore.

As usual the rangers spent the winter recruiting and scouting, keeping watch over the rebel settlements and strongholds. In January 1781, Haldimand gave Colonel Butler permission to raise two more companies, making up to full strength ten companies rather than the eight permitted by the warrant signed by Sir Guy Carleton. By that time, because of the widespread destruction, Butler's agents had to march farther afield in search of recruits and intelligence, carrying from three to four weeks' provisions with them. The loyalists who had provided such necessities had barely enough for themselves, or else they had fled from their settlements to Canada, the upper posts, or were in Schenectady posing as refugee rebels from the frontiers.

Captain Andrew Bradt returned from New Jersey, a journey of 300 miles each way, with 15 recruits, while other agents had spies brazenly recruiting in the streets of Albany. Here was one place the rangers might have been expected to avoid. That stockaded town was the headquarters of the rebels' northern military department. No references indicate that any rebel agents were behaving in like fashion in the narrow streets and stairways of Quebec City, even though some Canadians had gone to the rebelling colonies to enlist.

Bradt and the others gave no hint of how they travelled through the country. The colonel's nephew may have set out on snowshoes from Niagara, but some of his recruits probably provided a sleigh and horses for the return journey.

From February until the end of May 1781, Joseph Brant and Lieutenant John Bradt, also Butler's nephew, blockaded Fort Stanwix. Then the rebels abandoned the fort, because it was badly in need of repair and had not proved of any value in keeping loyalists and Indians out of the Mohawk Valley. Temporarily the rebels took shelter in Fort Herkimer and Brant and Bradt withdrew. The rebels reoccupied Fort Stanwix for another year before moving their headquarters to Canajoharie. All winter the men from the Indian Department blockaded Fort Pitt, and in April 1781, a party of 50 Rangers led by Lieutenant William Bowen of the Indian Department and the Mohawk Chief David burned a deserted fort at Cherry Valley, destroying the nearby settlement of Bowman's Creek.[40] Another party marched as far as Sussex County, New Jersey, burning mills and alarming the local people for weeks. When the men returned to Fort Niagara they brought prisoners and loyalists who wanted sanctuary.

Five scouting parties were in the Mohawk Valley, and single rangers were hiding with friends who still had homes. In June, Lieutenant Robert Nelles, of the Indian Department, on the western margin of Pennsylvania with 40 men, skirmished with about the same number of rebel militia three miles from Frankstown, in Bedford County. One of Nelles' men was killed and two were wounded, but the rebel losses were 13 killed, 7 captured, and 5 wounded, and the lieutenant of the county was known to be asking the state authorities for assistance.

New York was also taking steps to protect her frontiers from the depredations of the loyalists and Indians. The Congress of the state appointed Colonel Marinius Willett to command all the troops stationed along the Mohawk. Willett had been with the garrison of Fort Stanwix when St. Leger's expedition tried to capture it, and now he made his headquarters at Canajoharie, almost as strategically located as the old fort. He had two regiments of Continentals stationed there, and he reported that his militia had been reduced from 2,500 to 800. One third of the missing men had been killed or taken prisoner, another third had deserted to the British, and some 560 were in safer territory. Between Schenectady and German Flatts – a distance of 63 miles – were twenty-four forts, each able to shelter from 10 to 50 families. To protect those brave enough to stay in their homes, Willett kept small parties of soldiers constantly marching, changing their routes regularly to avoid walking into ambushes.

On May 9, 1781, after nearly a year of bargaining, Colonel Guy Johnson reported to Haldimand that the Mississauga Indians had agreed to sell a strip of land on the west side of the Niagara River for 'Three Hundred Suits of Clothing.' By the 20th, Brigadier Powell informed the governor that the Royal Engineers had finished surveying the boundary of this tract. Although several refugee farmers and off-duty rangers set to work clearing and planting, Haldimand told Sir Henry Clinton that the difficulties of provisioning his upper posts were so serious that ever since the war began, the rangers had been within a few days of evacuating Fort Niagara for want of a food supply. Provisions had to be stored for 2,000 men to last twelve months, and for presents to the Indians, of which three quarters of those around the fort were women and children. At Niagara alone, the garrison and refugees needed 4,000 rations a day and nearly everything had to be brought by bateau 200 miles up rapids, over carrying places then along Lake Ontario to Niagara.

On June 1, Lieutenant John Dockstader of the Indian Department left the fort with 70 men, and on the 7th, they skirmished with some rebel militia near Corrystown, on the west branch of the Schoharie Creek. Two days later, Dockstader's rangers and Indians were 11 miles from Canajoharie, where they burnt 20 houses and removed 120 cattle and horses. Colonel Willett smelled the smoke at his headquarters, and set out in pursuit of Dockstader and his men. By nightfall another 170 rebels followed, and Willett's advance party of 70 men got in front of Dockstader and lay in wait. A scout warned Dockstader of the ambush, and that officer ordered his men to disperse and attack the ambush site. After a lengthy skirmish, Dockstader suspected he was outnumbered and called a retreat. He got his men clear and took 6 prisoners, but he had to abandon the livestock captured earlier.

In July, Captain William Caldwell left Niagara bound for Schenectady, and on August 3, he joined forces with Lieutenant John Hare and a small party. Together the two ranger officers advanced with their combined force that numbered 87 rangers and 250 Indians. Boldly they planned to raid into Ulster County, miles inside the zone firmly controlled by the rebels. They swung southward and eastward, and by the night of August 10, they were passing a fort on the Lackawaxen River, 260 miles from Fort Niagara. They burned two mills at Niperack, and destroyed Rochester, which was scarcely 12 miles from the temporary capital of New York State, at Esopus, on the Hudson River (now Kingston, New York.) Upon hearing that two regiments of militia were massing to follow them, Hare and Caldwell began a leisurely retreat, driving cattle, hoping to lure the rebels into the woods where the rangers and Indians would have the edge. The warriors insisted on killing cattle for their amusement, before the animals were needed for food, and as a consequence the men were living on horsemeat by the time they regained Fort Niagara.

On September 8, Lieutenant Joseph Clement of the Indian Department with 74 rangers and Indians, went to German Flatts and ambushed some rebels who had been sent to capture him, while far to the west, rangers were operating from Detroit. That post was being threatened by Colonel George Rogers Clark from his base at Fort Pitt, and he hoped to capture the fort for the security of his own people. To distract the rebels by striking close to their homes, Captain Mathew Elliot of the Indian Department made a raid into the Kentucky Valley, his men floating down the Ohio River on rafts, and marching 60 miles across country to the neighbourhood of Bryan's Station, where they burned a magazine of provisions, and reported that settlers were leaving their farms and moving into the station for safety.

Next, Captain Andrew Thompson of the rangers left for the blockhouse on the Miami River, while Joseph Brant headed for Detroit with a party of warriors. Colonel Brodhead, the commandant of Fort Pitt, was advancing with a force of rebels towards the Delaware villages in the Ohio country, while Clark was known to be moving with a force of rebels from Fort Pitt and Wheeling, Virginia, to attack the Wyandot villages at Lower Sandusky. A party of rangers hurried to the Sandusky River, and marched forward to intercept Clark before he reached the Wyandot settlement. The rangers remained in the vicinity of Sandusky keeping watch over Clark's movements, and by mid August the rebel officer's expedition was moving down the Ohio on rafts. Captain Thompson marched to cut off Clark's vanguard, but he arrived too late.

Then an advance party of Indians under Joseph Brant, guided by George Girty, ambushed 100 rebel-rangers and militia and not one escaped. George Girty and his brothers, Simon and James, had grown up among the western tribes, for their family had been taken captive and held for many years. Hated and vilified by the rebels – a tradition kept alive by American historians since – the Girtys frequently acted as interpreters and scouts for rangers operating in the Ohio country. Joseph Brant and George Girty staged their ambush on August 26, and the rebel troops were commanded by Colonel Archibald Lochry, of Clark's advance party. Lochry, 6 other officers, and 30 privates were killed, and the rest captured.[41]

Andrew Thompson and his company of rangers, accompanied by several hundred Indians, caught up with Brant and Girty and they planned to attack Clark at the Falls of the Ohio (the site of Louisville, Kentucky) where the rebels had built a fort. A scout went forward, but only 200 of the Indians decided they would continue. The scout returned and reported that Clark was withdrawing and had abandoned his plan to attack Detroit. The rangers had been marching without food for four days, and Thompson, Brant and Girty decided their numbers were insufficient to assail Clark. Thompson turned towards the Shawnee villages in quest of provisions, and his men shot two bears to sustain them on their march.

Joseph Brant, accompanied by Alexander McKee, the Deputy Superintendent of Indian Affairs at Detroit since his escape from the rebels holding him at Fort Pitt, with the 200 remaining Indians, marched through the woods into the Kentucky Valley (then part of the state of Virginia). Early in September they were moving towards the fort at Boonesborough, the home of the American folk hero, Daniel Boone, when they encountered some horsemen whom they attacked and routed. The Indians remained in the neighbourhood following this skirmish, and the next day a larger mounted party returned to bury their dead. They rode into an ambush wherein most were killed by Brant and McKee's marksmen. This was the final action of the season, although Thompson and his company of rangers stayed in the country of the Shawnees, Wyandots and Delawares until the danger of attacks by Clark and Brodhead seemed past. For weeks they had subsisted on green corn given them by the Indians, and when they marched into Fort Detroit their shoes, hunting shirts and leggings were in tatters, their bodies emaciated after the rigorous months in the wilderness.

At Fort Niagara, Colonel John Butler completed his last two companies by mid September, and the corps stood at 590 all ranks. In Quebec City, Governor Haldimand had authorized another sweep of the Mohawk Valley, and this time it would be commanded by Major John Ross, because Sir John Johnson had gone to England on leave.[42] From Fort Niagara, some regulars, 169 rangers under Captain Walter Butler, and 109 Indians under Captain Gilbert Tice, set out for Oswego to meet Major Ross with part of his second battalion of Royal Yorkers and detachment of regulars. (pp 109 – 128)

On this expedition Lieutenant John Dockstader of the rangers died of wounds on October 7, 1781. Walter Butler was killed by a rebel sharpshooter while leading the rearguard action at West Canada Creek on the 30th. American and British sources are at odds on how Walter met his end. American legend had him mounted on a horse – most improbable because the rangers were consuming them at that stage – and shot through the thigh. Walter called for quarter, but was set upon by an Oneida who tomahawked him and scalped him.[43] British sources contend that Walter was shot through the head, mortally wounded, or was mercifully dead before the Indian used his scalping knife. Colonel Willett, the rebel commander, said that Walter was not killed by a shot through his head but that he was despatched by an Oneida.[44]

No one knows what became of Walter's body, although the rebels found it after the battle. Colonel Willett said that Walter's pocket book, taken from his corpse, had a list of the various corps participating in the Ross expedition, together with the numerical strength of each. One popular myth claims that Walter's bones lie beneath the floor of a church in Schenectady. More likely it was given a hasty burial near West Canada Creek, or rotted away in some secluded spot. At Fort Niagara, John Butler went about his work with a heavy heart, sorrowing for the first born whose body had been obscenely mutilated by a member of the race he had served most of his adult life.

During Ross's withdrawal towards Carleton Island, his men were subsisting on a ration of half a pound of horsemeat per man per day as they jogged non-stop to escape their pursuers. When the men reached Carleton Island, Ross found that 13 rangers were missing, but all turned up later. After they sailed back to Niagara, Captain William Caldwell set out to relieve Captain Andrew Thompson at Detroit, but Thompson never reached Niagara for a well-earned rest after weeks among the Shawnees. He drowned while on his way to that base.

The Battle of Johnstown is often called the last of the American Revolution, and it took place on October 25, six days after Lord Cornwallis surrendered with some 8,000 regulars and provincials at Yorktown. For the British and German regulars, the fighting was more or less over, but not for Butler's Rangers, nor certain provincials in the south who continued foraying along the coast. The rangers were destined to fight their last battle on September 21, 1782. Many loyalists were gloomy when they heard the news from Yorktown, but there is no evidence that morale slumped among the rangers, not after their successful summer of 1781. The situation in the north looked promising. In Albany, New York leaders were meeting to discuss a separate peace with Britain. Vermont was neutral, and there were riots in New Hampshire over the prospect of sharing the Continental Congress's war debts. In the northern states Britain had won her war, largely through the efforts of Butler's Rangers, Sir John Johnson's Royal Yorkers, the regulars who supported them, and the Indians who shared the expeditions and went on many raids of their own, accompanied by Indian Department officers.

The disaster of Yorktown did not render the rangers inactive. As winter set in more recruits came to Niagara, allowing older men to retire in order to perform necessary civilian duties, and in the Ohio country a ranger presence was required to protect the Indians from Virginia frontiersmen.

On December 7, 1781, Colonel Butler informed Haldimand:

I flatter myself that in a short time the farmers will be found to be of essential use in this post. They have maintained themselves since September, and were only allowed half-rations from the first.

The settlement on the west side of the Niagara River had made real progress and Butler requested blacksmith's tools, for he had a suitable man in his corps to work iron. At that time Haldimand had begun refusing requests from rebel prisoners in Montreal to be free on parole, because of breaches of the rules of war. A horrifying report reached him on the treatment meted out to some of Butler's Rangers who were captured during Ross's raid. The prisoners' hands were chopped off at the wrists, then their arms at the shoulders, after which they were tomahawked and scalped.[45]

As the spring of 1782 approached, the rangers were busy as ever. Haldimand wanted the forts at Oswego occupied, and he ordered Ross to move there, leaving Carleton Island under the command of Captain William Ancrum, 53rd Regiment. In April, 200 Rangers left Niagara to reinforce Carleton Island, replacing some of the men who had gone to Oswego. From Fort Haldimand, a party of rangers led by James Secord – temporarily absent from his more serious duties as tavern keeper at Niagara – served as scouts for Ross at Oswego.

Far to the west, the rangers continued the kind of operations they had been conducting since the autumn of 1778. They were there to assist the Indians of the Ohio country against the frontiersmen who cast envious eyes on their lands. Little did the rangers realize that their efforts were to be in vain, and they were helping delude these poor souls. Britain was able to offer sanctuary to the Iroquois Indians, by granting the loyal members a tract of land in Canada, but the Shawnees, Wyandots and Delawares, and several smaller groups, would be abandoned in the final boundary settlement, their claim to the lands they occupied brushed aside.

Aiding the Western Tribes

Most of the actions of the year 1782 occurred in the Ohio country and the Kentucky Valley, but the hunting season on rebels opened with two small excursions into Pennsylvania. The first, on April 15, was a raid on the settlements along Bald Eagle Creek, a tributary emptying into the west branch of the Susquehanna River. A party of rangers and Indians led by Lieutenant Robert Nelles of the Indian Department captured a blockhouse from the rebel militia garrison and destroyed it. Although many parties of rangers and Indians were out scouting, keeping track of rebel movements, the next strike took place in June, against a blockhouse on the main road to Philadelphia with the deceptive name of Loyal Hanna, 25 miles east of Fort Pitt. The attackers were led by Captain John Powell of the Indian Department, and Sayenqueraghta – Old Smoke – the Seneca chief. The local Indians had asked for protection, fearful their villages were about to be molested.

In April, about the same time as the raid on Bald Eagle Creek, word reached Detroit and Niagara of the massacre of some Delaware Indians at their village, Gnadenhutten. Known as Moravian Indians as they had been converted to Christianity by German-speaking missionaries, these Delawares had taken no part in the conflict. Their determination to remain uninvolved was so firm that some of their Indian neighbours had forced them to move three of their villages – Gnadenhutten, Schonbrunn and Salem – from their original sites on the Muskingum River to the upper Sandusky River. On March 7, a party of Moravians returned to their deserted villages on the Muskingum to fetch some corn which they had left behind.

A few days earlier, the wife and children of William Wallace, whose home was at Racoon Creek a few miles to the south, had been killed by Indians. Colonel David Williamson of the Pennsylvania rebel militia, accompanied by the irate father and husband, rode north at the head of a body of men hell bent on avenging the massacre of the Wallace family. In their black mood, and with William Wallace calling for blood, any scapegoat would suffice. To these frontiersmen, the only good Indian was a dead one, and after finding a white settler's clothing among the possessions of the innocent Moravians at Gnadenhutten, the infuriated settlers fell upon them, beating and tomahawking 96 people to death, two thirds of them women and children. Simon Girty, dressed in Indian clothing, spying in the vicinity, sent the report of this outrage to Major Arent De Peyster, the commandant of Fort Detroit, saying that after the

Operations of Butler's Rangers in the Ohio Country 1782

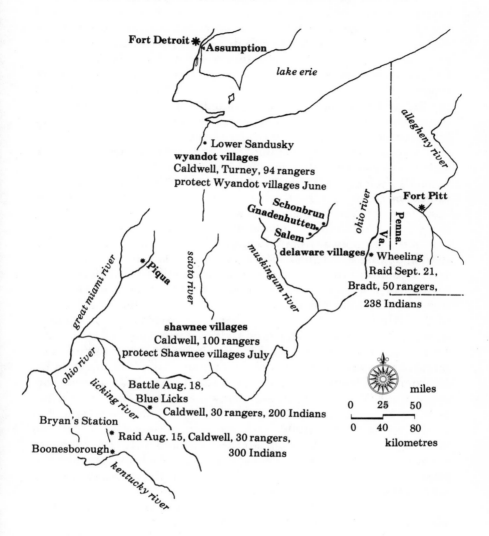

Fort Detroit ✴ • Assumption

lake erie

allegheny river

• Lower Sandusky
wyandot villages
Caldwell, Turney, 94 rangers
protect Wyandot villages June

Schonbrun
Gnadenhutten •
Salem •
delaware villages ✴ Wheeling

ohio river

Fort Pitt ✴

Penna.

Va.

Raid Sept. 21,
Bradt, 50 rangers,
238 Indians

✴ **Piqua**

scioto river

muskingum river

great miami river

shawnee villages
Caldwell, 100 rangers
protect Shawnee villages July

ohio river

licking river

Battle Aug. 18,
Blue Licks
✴ Caldwell, 30 rangers, 200 Indians

Bryan's Station
✴ Raid Aug. 15, Caldwell, 30 rangers,
300 Indians

Boonesborough ✴

kentucky river

miles
0   25   50

0   40   80
kilometres

171

slaughter the Pennsylvanians burned all three Moravian villages.[46]

Afterward the Pennsylvanians made no secret of their plans to march against more Delaware villages, located on the west side of the Ohio River. In May, when scouts brought this information to De Peyster, he dispatched Captain William Caldwell with his company of rangers and a party of Indians to assist the Delawares. With Caldwell's party marched Alexander McKee, the Deputy Superintendent of Indian Affairs at Detroit, and Captain Mathew Elliot of the Indian Department as the commander of the Indian component. About the same time, 24 rangers under Lieutenant John Turney left Niagara, planning to join Caldwell and McKee.

A rebel expedition moving from Fort Pitt was led by Colonel William Crawford, with the rebel leader David Williamson as his second in-command. With Crawford rode 500 mounted militia, an indication that with hostilities easing elsewhere, the rebels had more men available to attack the western tribes.

On June 4, Caldwell advanced towards a crossroads on the far side of the Ohio River from Wheeling, Virginia, on the rebels' line of march, hoping to cut them off before they could penetrate the Delawares' country, and trying to guess which village Crawford would try to attack first. Caldwell wanted to stall for time, because Alexander McKee was on his way from the Shawnee villages, southwest of the Delawares', with reinforcements. Crawford's rebel vanguard appeared, and in the skirmishing Caldwell was wounded by a bullet that passed through both thighs. Lieutenant Turney assumed command of the rangers, assisted by Lieutenant Ralfe Clench, while Elliot continued leading the Indians. A small party left the scene carrying Caldwell to the nearest Delaware village and dressed his wounds. Meanwhile at the crossroads, the Indians and rangers hid in the woods for the night, and the skirmishing resumed on the morning of June 5. At noon, McKee appeared with 160 Shawnee warriors and encircled the Pennsylvanians, who broke through the Shawnee position and fled towards the Ohio River, pursued every step on the way by rangers and Indians.

In the course of this mêlée, Crawford and several other rebels were captured and carried to a Delaware village. There, despite the presence of an unidentified officer of the Indian Department, Crawford was scalped, red hot ashes were poured on his head, and he was roasted to death. Before darkness fell, all the prisoners had suffered the same fate.[47] American secondary sources claim that Simon Girty was on hand, unmoved by the spectacle, which may be true. Both De Peyster at Detroit, and Brigadier Powell at Niagara expressed horror over these atrocities, although Powell admitted that he was not surprised. In his report he reminded Governor Haldi-mand that the Indians in the Ohio country had been exercising re-straint for a year, until the rebels' utter barbarity against the unde-serving Moravians.

On his part De Peyster threatened to withdraw the rangers if any more grisly incidents occurred. To Alexander McKee he wrote:

I must therefore, reiterate my injunctions to you, of representing to the chiefs that such a mode of war will by no means be countenanced by their English fa-ther, who is ever ready to assist them against the common enemy, provided they avoid cruelties. Tell them I shall be under the necessity of recalling the troops, (who must be tired of such scenes of cruelty) provided they persist.

By modern standards, Powell showed appropriate sympathy for the Indians, while De Peyster was being a racist. The white settlers were the aggressors, helping themselves to land the Indians be-lieved was theirs, punishing them when they dared to resist. Since the Royal Proclamation of 1763, it had been British policy to pro-hibit settlement west of the Allegheny Mountains, but for years the frontiersmen had been ignoring that ruling, while the small British garrisons at the upper posts were powerless to stem the tide. Then, too, most British officers applied a double standard. It was wrong for Indians to torture their captives, yet those same British officers could stand and watch with equanimity a wretched soldier, tied to the halberts for a trivial offence, suffering the torture of hundreds of strokes of the lash. Drums beating, this was a civilized ritual, quite unlike a whooping, savage display of cruelty.

On June 6 and 7, the skirmishing between the rebels, rangers and Indians continued, before the former began to withdraw across the Ohio River. One ranger had been killed, and two in addition to Captain Caldwell were wounded. The Indians had an interpreter and four warriors killed and eight wounded. Despite the atrocities, Lieutenant Turney wrote that he had nothing but praise for the conduct of the Officers, rangers and Indians. 'No people could be-have better. Capt. Elliot and Lieut. Clench in particular signalized themselves.'

Next, rumours reached the rangers that Colonel George Rogers Clark, then at Fort Pitt, was planning to move against the Shaw-nees, much as he had attempted to attack the Wyandots the year before, when the rangers and Indians foiled him. On July 12, Cald-well, who had retired to the Wyandot country until his wounds healed, returned and took command of the rangers. With his com-pany and a party of Indians he marched towards Wheeling, Virgin-ia, from the upper Sandusky country, intending to attack that rebel settlement. Reaching the Scioto River, he heard from a runner that the Shawnees at the village of Piqua, on a tributary of the Miami

River, were expecting Colonel Clark to attack them. Caldwell swung westward, while McKee pushed ahead and rounded up a force of 1,000 Shawnees, but the report was false, and the Indians began to disperse.

In haste, Caldwell formulated a plan before all his native allies vanished. With McKee, Simon Girty, 30 rangers and 300 Indians, Caldwell led a march towards Bryan's Station, the strongest fortified village in the Kentucky Valley. The remaining rangers of Caldwell's company stayed behind as scouts, while their officer and his force descended the Ohio River until they were close to the point where the Kentucky River enters it. Colonel Clark maintained a large row galley, heavily armed, which patrolled the Ohio to prevent Indians crossing into the territory that later became the state of Kentucky.[48] The boat was ineffective; all Caldwell's force had to do was lie in wait until it passed by, then make their move. On August 13, they crossed the Ohio and began their march 60 miles overland to reach their objective.

Bryan's Station was a village of 40 houses, enclosed by a stockade 12 feet high. It lay 20 miles north of Boonesborough, where Daniel Boone lived with his wife and family. According to local mythology, Caldwell and the Indians – no rangers are implicated – began their siege on August 15 before the people of Bryan's Station had had time to fetch water. The villagers chose 35 wives and daughters to take bottles and jugs to the spring, 60 yards outside the stockade, on the accurate assumption that Caldwell would be chivalrous and refuse to allow them to be attacked. The women got back inside the stockade with the precious water, and when the men declined all exhortations to come out and do battle, Caldwell regretted not taking a few hostages.

This story hardly rings true. The settlers would have built their stockade and village around the spring, or dug a well, so that their water supply could not be in jeopardy. Also, according to Caldwell's report, not a soul ventured outside those walls, and unopposed the rangers and Indians wrought havoc on crops and all buildings in the neighbourhood that were not protected by the stockade.

For two days Caldwell continued his journey of destruction; then, finding that the men in Bryan's Station could not be lured outside, the visitors went off to see what other damage they could do. Caldwell left the neighbourhood along what he called the 'Great Buffalo Trail,' which grazing animals used to reach the Ohio River.

Before Caldwell's force had gone far, 100 Indians departed, leaving the captain with only his 30 rangers and 200 warriors. He turned northeastward towards the Licking River and the village of

174

Blue Licks, so named because of salt deposits nearby. Surmising he would be pursued, Caldwell selected a good ambush site at a ford over the Licking River and he positioned his men in a hollow on the right bank. There the rangers and Indians lay concealed by tall grass and trees.

Meanwhile, the men of Bryan's Station and Boonesborough were raising a force to go after Caldwell's party, just as the captain predicted. By August 18, 200 mounted riflemen led by three colonels of militia – John Todd, Stephen Trigg and Daniel Boone – were on their trail. Boone, wise in the ways of Indians, was puzzled. The trail Caldwell and his men had made was too easy to discern, and Boone knew that Indians usually dispersed and left few signs of their line of retreat. He was reckoning without the presence of the rangers. When the Kentuckians reached the ford over the Licking River, Boone hesitated, wary. Todd, Trigg and their subordinates urged him on, hinting they thought him a poltroon. What transpired next is remembered differently in rebel and loyalist sources. According to the rebel version, the pursuers crossed the ford, dismounted, climbed a rise and descended on foot into a treed ravine where the ambush occurred.[49] According to Caldwell's report, his rangers and Indians had a good view of the river, and when all the riflemen had dismounted to cross the ford, his force opened fire. The discrepancy arose because some of the rebels retreated by circling around Caldwell's position and climbing the ridge above the rangers and Indians. Some of Caldwell's men followed them, keeping up a running battle. Both accounts agree on the casualties – 146 rebels killed or captured – and a survivor admitted, 'he that could mount a horse was well off; he that could not had not time for delay.' In the battle no ranger was even scratched, although 6 Indians were killed and 10 wounded, while an interpreter from Detroit named Labute also died. Caldwell wrote that he met his end: 'like a warrior, fighting arm to arm. The Indians behaved extremely well, and no people could behave better than both officers and men in general.'

Daniel Boone was among the 54 who escaped the ambush unscathed, but his son Israel, shot while fighting in the rearguard, died in his father's arms a short time afterward. Caldwell began his retreat towards the Shawnee country to the north, leaving behind him the carnage at the ford over the Licking River.

Meanwhile, Captain Andrew Bradt, Colonel Butler's nephew, was marching from Fort Niagara at the head of his company of rangers. They reached the Delaware villages early in September, hoping to overtake Caldwell. Finding that the latter had departed for Bryan's Station, Bradt collected a party of 238 Indians and threaded his way through steep mountains towards Wheeling, Virginia. On the 11th, Bradt's force put that settlement to the torch, and drove off enough cattle to sustain them on their return march towards the Shawnee country where they joined Caldwell on September 21.

Andrew Bradt's raid on Wheeling was the last action fought by Butler's Rangers during the American Revolution, and probably the last in which any loyal provincials were involved. In May, Sir Guy Carleton arrived at New York City as commander-in-chief, with instructions to bring the conflict to an end in preparation for the final cessation of hostilities. Carleton had begun withdrawing all his units from the coastline to New York City; and he had already issued orders to Governor Haldimand that only defensive actions were to be permitted.

Caldwell, Bradt and their rangers stayed in the Shawnee country for another month, in case the rebels had any other plans for terrorizing the Indians and burning their villages. Then, as winter was upon them, they turned their steps towards Fort Detroit, 150 miles to the north, and at least a week's march away by their standards. When they arrived at his post, Major De Peyster declared in his report that the rangers were 'walking spectres' so weakened were they by hunger, exposure and disease.

Either that autumn or early the following spring, Captain Bradt and his company boarded vessels of the Provincial Marine for their return journey to Fort Niagara. There Brigadier Allan Maclean had replaced Brigadier Watson Powell as the commandant in November 1782. Caldwell remained on duty at Detroit with his company lest the rebels make a last ditch attack to wrest that stronghold before the peace treaty was signed. At Niagara, Colonel John Butler had been ill for some weeks. On January 28, 1783, Maclean informed Haldimand that the ranger leader was sufficiently recovered to resume his duties as Deputy Superintendent of Indian Affairs, and he was in the Highlander's opinion, 'the only person here equal to the business.'

Maclean also reported sending two strings of wampum to the Shawnees to hearten them and show that the King had not forgotten them. Another item in Maclean's letter must have cheered the thrifty governor. Upon assuming the command of Fort Niagara, the brigadier discovered that Colonel Butler was allowing artificers employed by the Indian Department 5s. New York a day, and labourers 3s., whereas artificers working for the Royal Engineers were only permitted 15d. and labourers 10d. Maclean pointed out the discrepency and Butler conceded that he had been extravagant. In future, all artificers and labourers he employed would receive the same pay as those working for the engineers.

The proclamation on the cessation of hostilities was made public at Quebec City on April 27, 1783. Scouts coming to Niagara carried American newspapers whose editorial columns exuded threats of continued persecution of loyalists. A few rangers who had ventured to return to their homes had been treated savagely. While some who had fled to Niagara had returned and were living quietly at home, others were ordered to quit the country on pain of severe measures for 'their crimes and nefarious defection.' In May, Maclean wrote to Haldimand:

> Col. Butler says that none of his people will ever think of going to attend Courts of Law in the colonies, where they could not expect the shadow of justice, and that to re-purchase their estates is what they are not able to do; that for much smaller sum the Mississaugas will part with twelve miles more along the lake, and that they would rather go to Japan than go among the Americans, where they could never live in peace.

That summer, Major William Potts, of the 8th Regiment, inspected Butler's battalion, except for Caldwell's company, still at Detroit and the detachments serving at Carleton Island and Oswego. In May, with Governor Haldimand's approval, Potts had been assigned to the rangers. Colonel Butler was finding his duties too heavy. After complimenting the rangers as a fine body of troops, Potts wrote:

> 'The late views of the great part of the corps was to return to their former homes as soon as reduction would take place. . . . but from the late publications of the colonists and the disposition they seem to have avowed to abide by, had much abated the ardour and anxiety of the men on the purpose to return home, and the promises of Col. Butler to obtain some general settlement upon the neighbouring lands of this lake and river seems to have taken up and engaged both their consideration, hope, wishes, and expectations, that they may succeed in grants of land to that end, which I believe most of them at present are disposed to settle upon.'

A return of Butler's Rangers at Niagara showed 469 men, 111 women and 257 children, and many had begun providing for themselves, for 713 acres of land had been cleared. At the time the regiment was at full strength, and this return did not include the rangers at Detroit, Carleton Island and Oswego. Captain William Caldwell and his company returned to Fort Niagara for the winter of 1783-84, as did the detachments of rangers that had been serving at other posts.

Two months after the peace treaty was signed in September 1783, Governor Haldimand received his orders to disband the provincial corps by the end of the Year.[50] That autumn Brigadier Maclean went to England on leave and Major Robert Hoyes, 34th Regiment, was temporarily in command of Fort Niagara. Butler's Rangers remained on duty there throughout the winter and spring of 1784, because the order to disband them came too late to be carried out by the end of 1783. In June, De Peyster, promoted to lieutenant-colonel of the 8th Regiment, arrived from Detroit to succeed Brigadier Maclean, and he carried out the disbanding of the rangers. At that time 46 farmers were at work on the more than 700 acres of cleared land, and they were soon joined by reduced rangers, who settled across the Niagara River from the fort with their families.

Chapter 7:The King's Loyal Americans

When the revolution ended, five provincial corps of the British Army were attached to the Northern Department, and the fourth to be formed was the Loyal Rangers, led by Major Edward Jessup. Established in November 1781, this corps was an amalgamation of two earlier units which had accompanied General John Burgoyne on his expedition into New York State by way of Lake Champlain in the summer and autumn of 1777. The first of these older units was the King's Loyal Americans, commanded by Ebenezer Jessup, whose brothers Edward and Joseph were officers under him. The second corps, the Queen's Loyal Rangers, was led by John Peters. Following Burgoyne's campaign, which culminated in his surrender at Saratoga on October 17, 1777, both these units were well below strength. Jessup had had difficulty obtaining enough recruits, while Peters' men had suffered grievous losses at the Battle of Bennington, two months prior to the capitulation of Burgoyne's army.

Permission to raise both these corps was given by Governor Carleton, to fulfill a commitment made by Governor William Tryon of New York. The two regiments were immediately handed over to General Burgoyne. Apparently Carleton intended these corps to be temporary, and since Tryon was at New York City, the two units could be considered part of the Central Department.

The King's Loyal Americans and Queen's Loyal Rangers were not the only small units that had joined Burgoyne and had returned to Canada after that campaign. Others were led by Francis Pfister, Daniel McAlpin, Dr. Samuel Adams and Samuel McKay. The latter, a half-pay lieutenant from the 60th Regiment during the Seven Years' War, had settled near Fort St. Johns afterward, and had declined the command of a company of Canadians in order to be with Burgoyne.[1] Of these, only Pfister's had a name, and it was known as the Loyal Volunteers.

All the leaders, except Dr. Adams, had served as officers, either regular or militia in the earlier war. Pfister, whose home was near Bennington, was killed in the battle there in August 1777. Temporarily Robert Leake, one of Pfister's captains, assumed the leadership of this group. Then Samuel McKay took command of Pfister's men, although he had a few recruits of his own prior to the other's death. Robert Leake and Daniel McAlpin, also half pay lieutenants from the 60th Regiment, were given responsibilities by Haldimand earlier than Jessup and Peters. One list identifies Leake's and McKay's provincials as the 'Corps of Loyal Volunteers' and is entitled a 'Subsistence Account for Captain Leake's Corps from 3d September to 24th December 1777, being – 52 days.' On it, Samuel McKay is shown as the first captain, Leake the second, and Samuel Anderson (who later received a captaincy in the first battalion, Royal Yorkers) as the third.[2]

Because the history of all these small units is bound together with the King's Loyal Americans and Queen's Loyal Rangers, the information on them had been recounted as it unfolded in the annals of these two regiments, and occasionally on the second battalion, King's Royal Regiment of New York, for some were eventually taken into the latter.

Until a shortage of reinforcements for Haldimand's regular regiments caused him to attempt enlarging his provincial units, the officers and men of the below-strength bits and pieces suffered a lengthy period of uncertainty, leading a precarious existence, paid for whatever work they did, provisioned and sheltered when they were not employed, shunted about to build a blockhouse here, a sawmill there, or to forage for hay. They suffered the most during the revolution, for their losses were substantial when they served with Burgoyne, and they were under-used by Governor Haldimand. Yet among the different leaders, John Peters was the only one who allowed bitterness to surface in his writings. The conservative Swiss governor's treatment of these small groups of provincials shows how his policies restrained and frustrated them.

Some of the officers undoubtedly had delusions of grandeur, and might have been guilty of self-interest, but by and large their only desire was to defeat the rebels and see their homes and properties restored to them.

The Jessup Brothers

The three Jessup brothers were born in Stamford, Connecticut, but they were not typical New Englanders. Their great-grandfather, Edward Jessup, had emigrated from England in the 1640s and settled in Westchester County, New York. His son, also Edward, moved to Connecticut, where Joseph, the father of Edward, Joseph and Ebenezer, was born in 1669. Joseph Jessup Sr. and his three sons were destined to become loyalists.

In 1743, Joseph's wife died, and the following year the widower took his three young sons to Dutchess County, New York, where their grandfather Edward was then living. The county records show that Joseph Jessup bought Lot No.32 in the Upper Nine Partners Patent – so named because it was originally granted to nine proprietors in 1706 – for £300. Later the elder Jessup bought 360 acres, part of Lot No.34 for £440 on January 18, 1760.[3]

Thus Edward, Joseph and Ebenezer Jessup had a dual background, part Yankee, part Yorker, which had interesting implications. They possessed the drive and ambition of New Englanders and the acceptance of a landed gentry that prevailed in New York. These traits guaranteed that nothing would stand in the way of their pursuit of wealth; and until the revolution, nothing did.

In 1759, during the Seven Years' War, Edward served as a captain in command of a company of militia.[4] Little is known about the early life, or even the later life of Joseph, beyond the fact that he stayed in Dutchess County with his father, until 1771. Edward and Ebenezer caught the frontier spirit earlier, but before they departed domestic needs intervened. In 1760, the two brothers journeyed back to Stamford, Connecticut, their birthplace, and wed two daughters of Jonathan Dibble. Edward chose Abigail, while Ebenezer settled upon Elizabeth. Back in Dutchess County, the bridegrooms joined their father in a number of real estate transactions, all profitable. Then in 1764, they both decided to move to Albany, where the opportunities for business ventures were almost unlimited.

Edward and Abigail were the parents of a daughter, also Abigail, born in Dutchess County in 1761, and a son Edward, born in Albany in 1766. Ebenezer and Elizabeth were more prolific, having one son; Henry James, born in 1762 and five daughters, Leah, Sarah, Elizabeth, Deborah and Mary-Ann-Clarenden. Prior to the move to Albany, Edward and Ebenezer mortgaged their lands in the Upper Nine Partners Patent, which yielded each of them £300, and they used the capital to finance their fresh start.

The two Jessups prospered in their new surroundings, and with success came respectability. They soon turned their attention to the north, where land along the upper Hudson River had become available to speculators after Seven Years' War, an area established as Charlotte County in 1772.[5] Some men were buying the land directly from the Indians, others from the government, which had declared certain portions Crown land, available for purchase. Edward and Ebenezer set about acquiring vast acreages, some to establish themselves as landed gentry, most for trading. At times they acted as agents for non-residents interested in becoming landowners. On other occasions the Jessups acted in concert with partners – from fifteen to thirty-seven at a time. This method was used to circumvent a law limiting grants to any individual to 1,000 acres.[6] Characteristic of their time, some of the Jessups' business practices were suspect.

Their last homes in New York State were about ten miles north of the present village of Glen's Falls. Jessup's Landing, a name that was later changed to Corinth, was situated where the Schroon and Sacandaga rivers join the Hudson. There logs were landed above a waterfall on the Hudson known at that time as Jessup's Falls, and both brothers owned saw and grist mills in the neighbourhood, and large houses of logs. The exteriors were rustic, belying the extent of luxury within, for the interiors were lavishly appointed with fine linens, silver plate, the best of furniture, glass and even paintings. Ebenezer was famous for his hospitality, whether at home or at the nearby tavern kept by Abraham Wing. Like the Jessups, the proprieter had moved north from Dutchess County.[7] The two brothers also operated a ferry across the Hudson above the falls.[8]

Typical of most prosperous men along the frontier, the Jessups were well acquainted with Sir William Johnson, and through him they negotiated their largest land transaction – 305,000 acres – for £8,693, on behalf of two shipwrights named Joseph Totten and Stephen Crossfield.[9] By 1775, Edward and Ebenezer were among the wealthiest men on the upper Hudson, and while their surroundings were primitive and their houses not the baronial mansions of the Johnson family, their Yankee ambitions were admirably fulfilled. They were also on friendly terms with Governor William Tryon of New York, and in January 1776, Ebenezer visited him and applied for permission to raise men in support of His Majesty's government in America.

Events of 1776

After the Declaration of Independence on July 4, 1776, loyal residents of Charlotte County were the recipients of considerable abuse from their rebel neighbours. In the autumn, Edward and Ebenezer decided to lead a band of the faithful to join General Sir Guy Carleton's army, then at Crown Point on Lake Champlain. Their party numbered some 80 men, and with them went their father, aged 77, and brother Joseph. One American source claims that Edward Jessup did not fly until April or May 1777, while Ebenezer left earlier, and this is incorrect. The memorials of both brothers state that they met Carleton's force in November 1776, but a story related by a Dr. Holden is worth repeating. He said that Edward escaped from a band of irate rebels by leaping across the Hudson River at Little Falls, racing through the town of Queensbury and on to Skenesborough.[10] Holden may have been telling the truth, but the incident occurred when Edward was back in the vicinity of his home in the spring of 1777, trying to get recruits for the King's Loyal Americans, not when he first fled to join the royal standard in November 1776.

Sir Guy Carleton was anything but pleased to discover that groups of loyalists persisted in joining him at Crown Point. From his perspective they should have remained in their homes, awaiting the arrival of his army of liberation.[11] According to Ebenezer, the Jessups and their friends had come 'to conquer our enemies and re-establish civil government for the honour of the Crown and the true interest of the Colonies.'[12]

The Jessups went aboard the armed schooner *Maria* where Carleton had his headquarters, and announced that they had come to join the King's troops, in response to word from Governor William Tryon of New York that important commands awaited men of standing in their communities. Men of influence the Jessups were, although only Edward had served as a militia officer, and only a captain at that, which hardly qualified any of them to expect senior appointments.

For his part Carleton had no firm orders on what to do with loyal colonials beyond a vague directive that they were to be encouraged to oppose the rebels. Besides, he was about to withdraw his army to Canada for the winter, and would not need the help of loyalists until the following spring. To his chagrin, the small groups who had come to Crown Point would have to be provisioned and given clothing and shelter at government expense. For the time being he ordered the Jessups to take their men to Chateauguay to be billeted until he could decide how to make use of them. On November 29, Carleton wrote to Brigadier William Phillips, then the commandant of Fort St. Johns, to inform him of the arrangements he had made for the new arrivals from the rebelling colonies:

The plan approved by Governor Tryon as Mr. Jessup reports seems to me to be very judicious; it is to be wished this Gentleman and his followers had remained at their homes till it remained practicable; it cannot now take place before next summer; in the meantime I should recommend it to them to join Sir John Johnson's regiment and enclosed is an order to Major Gray to take them under his command, to pay three of those destined by Governor Tryon to be officers as Captains, half the remainder as Lieutenants, the other half as Ensigns, three of the remainder as Sergeants, three Corporals, and the rest as privates.

Carleton referred to Edward. Neil Robertson, who served with the Jessups for a time, later wrote that he came with more than 80 men through the woods to 'this Province 1776 with Major Jessup as our chief guide.'[13] When Carleton authorized the Jessups to raise a provincial corps Ebenezer was the lieutenant-colonel, with Edward as his second-in-command. For the first few months, however, Edward was regarded as the leader of his party. With respect to pay for

183

the officers and men, and provisions, Carleton's instructions to Phillips continued:

> Mr. Jessup will declare upon his honour who are destined as officers and rank them according to merit. Major Gray will pay them at the rate from the day they joined the King's forces, and may either cloath them as the Royal Reg't of New York, or buy them some cheap uniform cloathing to keep them from the severity of the weather as you shall be pleased to direct.
>
> This is not intended to interfere with any project of Mr. Tryon's to advance them higher but merely as an asylum, till they can do better for themselves; they will then be at liberty both men and officers, if, on reflection they do not think it more advisable to be incorporated with that corps.

Edward and Ebenezer stuck stubbornly to their expectation of raising their own regiment, and refused to join the King's Royal Regiment of New York. On November 11, Carleton issued orders to Major James Gray, Sir John Johnson's second-in-command, that these refugees were not to be regarded as soldiers, and only if they agreed should Gray form them into companies. The governor sent more instructions to Gray on December 1, with respect to the Jessups and their party, then at Chateauguay. Edward and Ebenezer might be given captaincies and placed in command of companies, but Carleton had no intention of establishing a provincial corps from among their followers.

The King's Royal Regiment of New York was at Pointe Claire, and the Jessups were expected to join it there for the winter. On January 12, 1777, Major Gray informed Carleton that 'Mr. Jessup' could not muster his men because some were still at Chateauguay, ill with smallpox and an ailment resembling yellow fever. The Jessups and their men had been issued with uniforms, which Gray said were red coats faced with dark green. The cost of provisions and uniforms would be deducted from the men's pay, which Gray said was the same as for regulars. Each private was entitled to 6d. per day Halifax currency, less rations, clothing and hospital expenses, but since Halifax was worth less than the sterling used for the regulars, they were not as well paid as Gray maintained.[14]

From the outset the Jessups' men behaved in a manner characteristic of colonials who enlisted in the King's service, by demanding that they serve under officers of their own choosing. In the colonies they had left, it was customary for militiamen to elect their officers, and they expected to continue this method of displaying confidence in their leaders. Carleton would have no such nonsense in his service, and he issued orders to this effect to Gray on January 13, 1777. The following day Carleton instructed Gray to administer oaths of allegiance to the Jessups and their men, and any who refused were to be imprisoned.

All signed these oaths, for loyalty was not the issue. Apparently Gray was confused at having men under his command who were not to be treated as soldiers. In March, Carleton again informed him that the Jessups' party was not part of the King's Royal Regiment of New York, and had only been assigned to Gray for convenience. The men kept referring to themselves as Jessup's Corps, and after several letters had reached Carleton in Quebec City, he grew exasperated. On April 3, he wrote to Brigadier Phillips:

I know of no such thing as Jessup's Corps, mentioned by Major Gray, nor did I direct that Adams' party should be compelled to join Mr. Jessup and his followers; they are at liberty to follow what plan of life they please except that they must be obliged to continue in a fixed residence, and not move from it but by permission from you or Major Gray, as it is improper for many reasons that they should straggle about the country.

The Jessups persisted in their mission to establish a separate regiment, and they had tried to include a party of men who had come to Canada with Dr. Samuel Adams, whose home was near Arlington, in the Green Mountains. A muster of Jessups' men at Pointe Claire on January 24, 1777, showed that they had been formed into three below-strength companies, led by Captains Edward and Ebenezer Jessup and Jonathan Jones, with 4 lieutenants, 4 ensigns, 3 sergeants, 3 corporals, Dr. Solomon Jones as the surgeon's mate, and 62 privates. Joseph Jessup was serving as Ebenezer's lieutenant.[15]

With Burgoyne, 1777

As June of 1777 drew near, Carleton relented and allowed the Jessups to have their provincial corps, although the warrant he signed has not been preserved. Plans for an expedition into New York State were well advanced; by June 7, the first officers had been appointed by the governor, and the men were uniformed in red coats that had dark green facings. The new corps was known as the King's Loyal Americans. Ebenezer Jessup was the lieutenant-colonel and Edward the major. The payroll list for the regiment, dated from June 25 to October 24, 1777, makes no mention of Edward at all, but shows six companies, led by Lieutenant-Colonel Ebenezer Jessup, Captains Joseph Jessup, James Robins, Jonathan Jones, Christian Wehr and Hugh Munro. This latter company, of 14 men, is shown as on bateau service. James Robins may have been in command of Edward Jessup's company temporarily when the payroll was made up, for a subsequent list drops his name and includes Edward's.[16]

Major Gray had found the loyalists attached to his battalion but not part of it a trial, for on April 20, he admitted that he had been a soldier for thirty years, but never had he dealt with a more contentious group of fellows.[17] Gray had been an officer in the 42nd Regiment during the Seven Years' War, who settled in New York when his corps was reduced. He did not elaborate, but part of the problem may have been that there were too many aspiring officers and too few willing to fill the ranks.

The King's Loyal Americans, with John Peters' Queen's Loyal Rangers, and smaller groups led by Samuel McKay, Daniel McAlpin, Samuel Adams and Francis Pfister, were assigned to Burgoyne's expedition, which was forming at Fort St. Johns in June. Of these, the only group that had a name at that time was Pfister's, tentatively called the Loyal Volunteers. On June 16, the King's Loyal Americans left Pointe Claire for Fort St. Johns to take their place beside the British and German regulars and other provincials. The main body of troops was to invade New York State by way of Lake Champlain, while Colonel Barry St. Leger led a smaller force, including Sir John Johnson's Royal Yorkers, to Oswego and from there meet Burgoyne in Albany.(see pp. 74 – 81)

Many secondary accounts maintain that Burgoyne was to meet an army Sir William Howe would send north from New York City when he reached Albany, but recent research has refuted this. Supposedly Lord Germain neglected to inform Howe that he was to effect a junction with Burgoyne, but the colonial secretary was never ordered to relay such instructions. Earlier, Howe had raised a matter of protocol. Both he and Carleton were of equal rank, but Sir Guy was senior to Howe. If an expedition from Canada entered New York it should be led by a junior officer, to avoid embarrassing Howe.[18] In fact, Howe had informed Carleton that he would be going to Pennsylvania before Burgoyne set out. Burgoyne knew that he might not receive assistance from the south. His only orders were that he was to reach Albany and place himself under Howe's command.[19]

Burgoyne's army began embarking on June 17, an impressive flotilla a mile long moving up the Richelieu River, the frigate *Royal George* carrying the commanding officer and his staff – and, so rumour went, his mistress. The troops travelled in bateaux, protected by gunboats, canoes of painted Indians preceding them. Some 9,000 people sailed into Lake Champlain, including 300 women to care for the men, and a few children. The invading army made a colourful spectacle, set against the backdrop of Green Mountains to the east and the Adirondacks to the west. The British regulars and provincials were in red coats, the artillerymen in blue, as were most of the Germans. Strains of martial music floated over the sea of boats – the brass bands of the German regiments, fifes and drums of the English and provincials, bagpipes of the Scots Highlanders.

By June 27 the vanguard had reached Crown Point, and the entire armada arrived there three days later. Four miles on, Burgoyne began landing his troops, the Germans on the left under their commander, Baron Friedrich von Riedesel; the British on the right. A plan of this line of battle in Burgoyne's orderly book shows Jessup's and Peters' corps as the advance party on the left, followed by the German vanguard under Lieutenant-Colonel Heinrich von Breymann, consisting of his light troops and some artillery.

Burgoyne may have placed these provincials with the Germans initially because both Peters and Jessup had German-speaking men in their corps who could communicate with what the commander-in-chief called his foreign troops. However, the orderly book contains many references to provincials serving under General Simon Fraser, who led the British vanguard. Burgoyne moved them around as the army proceeded southward. Evidence suggests that Peters' corps spent most of its time with Fraser, but exactly what Jessup's men did is more obscure. Both corps were intended as foragers, to bring in food, horses, wagons and cattle from the surrounding countryside. Small parties of King's Loyal Americans may have been sent out on such missions.[20]

Burgoyne made very few references to Jessup's men in his orderly book or in his work, *A State of the Expedition from Canada, as laid before the House of Commons* which he published in London in 1780. There is evidence that the Queen's Loyal Rangers were in the thick of the fighting, but the information on Jessup's men is found mainly in the petitions and memorials written later by members of the corps. No record on the strength of the King's Loyal Americans when it left Fort St. Johns has survived, but it must have numbered some 100 all ranks. Reporting to Lord Germain on July 11, Burgoyne wrote:

Mr. Peters and Mr. Jessup, who came over to Canada last autumn, and proposed to raise battalions, one from the neighbourhood of Albany, the other from Charlotte County, are confident of success as the army advances. Their battalions are now in embryo but very promising; they have fought with spirit.[21]

Sir Guy Carleton had given Burgoyne blank commissions, to sign when each of these battalions reached two-thirds strength. Jessup was having difficulty getting recruits, because most of his men were leaving Albany County, which was an armed camp as the rebels awaited Burgoyne's arrival, and recruiting was hazardous.

The provincials were mustered for the first time on July 27 at Skenesborough, and the King's Loyal Americans numbered 172 officers and men. On October 7, this figure was 175, after some casualties.[22] Later, Ebenezer Jessup wrote that a considerable number joined him as the expedition proceeded, but not as many as he hoped. Some went to New York City, while others were taken prisoners, and he lacked 63 men to qualify for his commission.[23] Assuming that a full company under the terms of Carleton's warrant was 50 men, two-thirds strength implied 333 ranks, and Ebenezer Jessup recruited about 270 men. A payroll stretching from June 25 to October 24 shows a total of 228 rank and file, 6 captains, 8 lieutenants, 5 ensigns, 12 sergeants, 4 corporals, 1 drummer and the surgeon's mate.[24] A list entitled 'Strength of the King's Loyal Americans on Burgoyne's Campaign' reveals that men moved from one corps to another. It was compiled for Governor Haldimand, Carleton's successor, in the summer of 1780:

Lieutenant-Colonel Ebenezer Jessup had 57 men in his company.
Major Edward Jessup had 49 men in 1777. 16 joined McAlpin, 4 joined McKay.
Captain Jonathan Jones had 31 men on July 17, 1777. 6 joined McAlpin. Captain Jones had joined in 1776.
Captain Joseph Jessup had 60 men. 22 joined McAlpin. 13 were taken prisoners. 1 was killed, 12 deserted, 7 were discharged to do carpentering. 5 are in Canada.
Hugh Munro was appointed a Captain July 13, 1777. Had 14 men. Joined McAlpin in August 1777. Now wants to come back.
Christian Wehr joined August 27, 1777. He had 40 men.
Lieutenant David Jones came in 1776.
Lieutenant William Lamson came in 1776. Was Ensign then.
Lieutenant James O'Neal, appointed August 21, 1777.
Lieutenant Hendrick Simmons, appointed August 27, 1777
Lieutenant Guisbert Sharp, appointed September 22, 1777.
Ensign William Snyder, appointed in 1776.
Ensign Thomas Man, appointed June 25, 1777.
Ensign John Dusenbury, appointed August 21, 1777.
Ensign Christian Haver, appointed August 27, 1777.
Ensign Neal Robertson. Joined MaAlpin's as a Lieutenant.
Quartermaster John Man. Appointed September 7, 1777. Up to this time Jessup's Corps had no quartermaster to see to their provisions.
Surgeon's Mate Solomon Jones, appointed in 1776.[25]

The list shows a total of 251 ranks, short of Jessup's claim of about 270 ranks. The foregoing tends to confirm that Burgoyne's provincials fought with spirit. If Ebenezer Jessup had only 175 men on October 7, he had lost between 75 and 100 of the men he recruited during Burgoyne's campaign. These figures compare unfavourably with the casualties sustained by Butler's Rangers and the King's Royal Regiment of New York. Although detachments of regulars attended Sir John Johnson's expeditions, and some of Butler's, they used hit and run tactics – loyalists' natural style of warfare. Where they were part of a ponderous expedition of regulars, moving slowly, encumbered by heavy artillery, they were more vulnerable. Burgoyne was a humane and popular commander, dubbed 'Gentleman Johnny' by the regulars, but he had no idea of how to conduct a wilderness campaign, nor did most of the British and German regulars, who were accustomed to the open fields of Europe. Nor were concentrated musket volleys a match for frontier riflemen who preferred to shoot from cover, aiming at the silver and gold gorgets flashing on the officers' chests.

The capture of Fort Ticonderoga was Burgoyne's one brilliant stroke during an otherwise lacklustre campaign. Under the direction of Lieutenant William Twiss, Royal Engineers, the troops dragged two 12-pounder guns to the summit of a hill overlooking the fort which the rebels had failed to fortify, and when these cannon began firing on July 5, the rebel general in command, Arthur St. Clair, decided to evacuate Ticonderoga. At dawn the next day, the British army marched into the fort. The credit for this success was given to Twiss in all the official reports, but two provincial officers may have helped in the operation. Samuel McKay, on hand with a small company, and Justus Sherwood, who commanded Peters' third company, had both reconnoitered the fort for Governor Carleton before the expedition set out.[26]

Of the two, Sherwood was the man more likely to have been on the spot with Twiss. McKay's men were on bateau duty in the rear, bringing up supplies, while Sherwood and his company were with the Germans who advanced on the rebel post, Mount Independence, across the lake from Ticonderoga. Since Twiss found the right path up the hill, which the soldiers soon christened Mount Defiance, and had his guns mounted in less than a week, he had help from some local man. The country is mountainous and still heavily forested. Nothing is found in the public record but Twiss had Sherwood by his side, or at least a copy of either his report or McKay's when he selected the place where the axemen hacked their trail up the side of Mount Defiance. Otherwise the guns would not have been ready to fire by July 5.

Leaving Brigadier Watson Powell in command of the fort with a garrison of his battalion companies and some detachments of Germans – in all 900 men – Burgoyne pushed on after the fleeing rebels. He sent a detachment under General Fraser into the New Hampshire Grants to follow the rebel army, and as soon as the guns of the *Royal George* had smashed a log boom the rebels had strung across the lake, Burgoyne sailed on after their fleet, up the narrow arm of Lake Champlain towards Skenesborough. Exactly where the King's Loyal Americans were during these operations is obscure, although the Queen's Loyal Rangers were with General Simon Fraser and his vanguard.[27]

Gentleman Johnny's attempt to reach Albany, as ordered, was doomed to fail. One historian blames Carleton, who might have

Burgoyne's Campaign June — October 1777

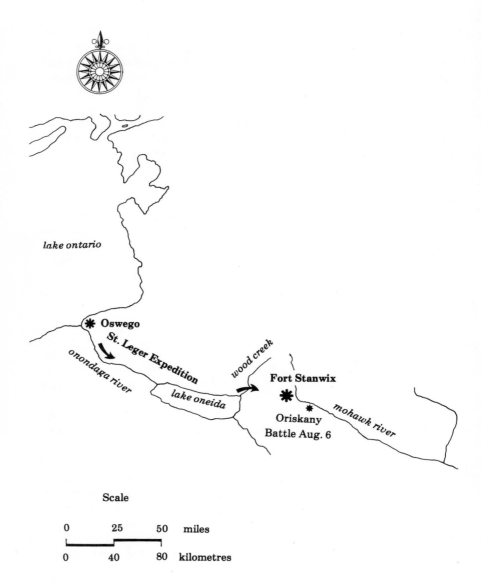

lake ontario

Oswego

St. Leger Expedition

onondaga river

lake oneida

wood creek

Fort Stanwix

mohawk river

Oriskany
Battle Aug. 6

Scale

| 0 | 25 | 50 | miles |

| 0 | 40 | 80 | kilometres |

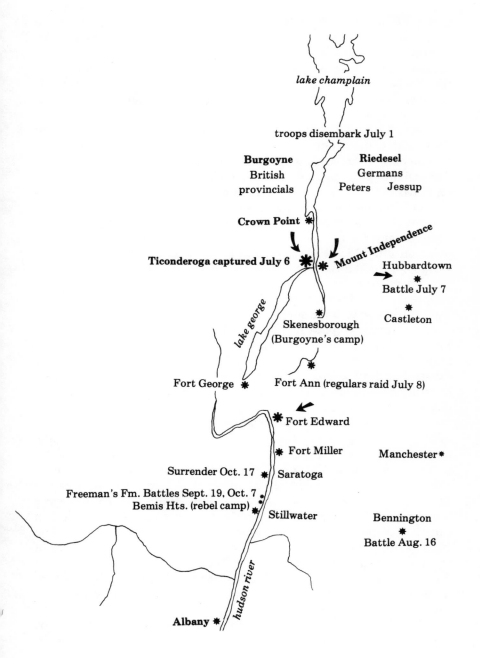

lake champlain

troops disembark July 1

Burgoyne   **Riedesel**
British   Germans
provincials   Peters   Jessup

Crown Point ✳

Ticonderoga captured July 6 ✳ ✳ Mount Independence

Ticonderoga captured July 6

Hubbardtown
✳
Battle July 7

✳
Castleton

lake george

✳
Skenesborough
(Burgoyne's camp)

✳
Fort George ✳   Fort Ann (regulars raid July 8)

✳ Fort Edward

✳ Fort Miller   Manchester ✳

Surrender Oct. 17 ✳   Saratoga

Freeman's Fm. Battles Sept. 19, Oct. 7 ✳
Bemis Hts. (rebel camp) ✳   Stillwater

Bennington
✳
Battle Aug. 16

hudson river

Albany ✳

191

achieved that goal had he pushed forward the year before when the rebels were less prepared, but Burgoyne was equally inept. The best way to travel through the forests was by water, and he should have returned to Ticonderoga, and sent a strong vanguard along Lake George to take possession of Fort Edward, the first rebel post on the Hudson River, with all speed. A passable road linked this lake with the Hudson. The rebel army fled over the longer, more difficult route to the east of Lake Champlain, because British and provincial troops were blocking the entrance to Lake George.

Instead, Burgoyne sailed past the charred remains of the rebel fleet, which they had scuttled, and settled himself comfortably in the fieldstone house belonging to Philip Skene, the proprietor of Skenesborough, who had come from Canada as Burgoyne's adviser on matters local – a poor choice. There, possibly on the recommendation of his host who wanted his property improved, Burgoyne had his men build a road to the Hudson, which was time wasting and unnecessary. In the ensuing delay, the rebel army reached Fort Edward on July 12, its lines of supply back to Albany intact, when Burgoyne could have taken that post before the enemy reached it.[28]

Burgoyne's decision to linger was a bad blunder. His lines of supply stretched back to Fort St. Johns, while the rebels were moving ever closer to their supply base at Albany, and the army of ragged frontiersmen opposing the British expedition was daily growing larger. General Philip Schuyler, who was removed from the command of the army in the field and replaced by General Horatio Gates, had laid waste to the countryside before his demotion, and evacuated all known loyalist families whose homes were on Burgoyne's line of march.

Belatedly, Burgoyne admitted he could not bring all the heavy artillery and baggage by his road, for he was short of draft animals, and he sent some of it back to Ticonderoga to be brought on bateaux along Lake George. Not until July 30 did the main army reach Fort Edward, which the rebels had abandoned. While the army was encamped there, the famous tragedy of Jane McRae occurred. Jane's home was a few miles away, and with her aunt, Mrs. McNeil, a cousin of Brigadier-General Simon Fraser, she set out towards the British camp, hoping to join her fiancé, Lieutenant David Jones of the King's Loyal Americans. Some Indians scouting for Burgoyne found the two women. Mrs. McNeil escaped, but poor Jane was tomahawked and scalped. Her attackers came into Fort Edward bearing her long blonde tresses.[29]

This incident, although not an isolated case in a bloody war, was used to great advantage by the rebels, so much so that Burgoyne was called to account for it before the House of Commons. The rebel newspapers were full of lurid descriptions, overlooking the fact that the lass was a loyalist, engaged to a hated Tory officer. British officers, too, embellished the tale, claiming that David Jones recognised Jane's scalp and asked to be relieved of his duties. When his commanding officer – presumably Ebenezer Jessup – refused, Jones deserted and fled to Canada, never to smile again. Such was far from the truth. David Jones stayed at his post and in 1780 did yeoman service in a raid on Fort Edward.

Following the capture of Fort Ticonderoga, each encounter with the rebels was a costly one for Burgoyne. He lost 1,200 Germans and Queen's Loyal Rangers at the Battle of Bennington in August. At that time the main British and German force was at Fort Miller, a few miles below Fort Edward. While the army was in that neighbourhood, there occured an action which Ebenezer Jessup recalled in a letter he wrote when Burgoyne was back in England in 1778:

I had the honour to command the Party that retook the 18 Batteaux and scows of provisions etc from the enemy near Saratoga Crick and ordered Major [Edward] Jessup with a part of the Corps to ford the River to the Island under whose cover they were brought up the Crick, with the remainder of the Corps I brought up the Rear covering the Whole; & was ordered to the Barracks from whence we were ordered to take post on the High Ground.. . . . Captain McAlpin left the ground between us and the Germans that afternoon & the 47th Reg't being recalled that night there was not a man but ourselves above the German lines Which you thought proper to order us into the Camp as soon as it came to your knowledge.

The reference to the barracks shows that the rescue of boatloads of supplies took place in August, for the camp to which Jessup returned was Fort Miller. Saratoga Creek is a short distance to the south, and although the rebels had not made any improvements to the fort, some of Burgoyne's troops were able to use the barracks they found there.

About the same time, Burgoyne ordered 120 provincials incorporated into his regular regiments for the duration of the campaign. After the losses his troops had sustained, the commander thought this measure necessary, although the limited numbers of local men with him would have been better employed operating as irregulars along his flanks.

On August 28, Captain Samuel McKay led some scouts of his company to Stillwater, farther down the Hudson Valley, and returned with 100 sheep. Here was one example of how provincials foraged to help feed the British army. Other provincials brought supplies from Ticonderoga, through Lake George, where Brigadier Watson Powell had established an advance post on Diamond Island to assist bateaux of provisions moving towards the portage to the Hudson.

193

On September 19, Burgoyne's troops fought the Battle of Freeman's Farm against the rebels under General Horatio Gates. Some loyalists were with General Simon Fraser's force of light infantrymen that served on the right flank, but whether any King's Loyal Americans were included is doubtful. Soon word reached Burgoyne that a detachment of rebels led by Colonel John Brown had tried to attack Fort Ticonderoga. The rebels occupied the carrying place around the rapids between Lake Champlain and Lake George for four days, until Powell's garrison drove them away. In the course of the actions, nearly four companies of Powell's 53rd Regiment were captured, and the rebels released 100 of their own prisoners of war. Although Brown's men only cut Burgoyne's supply lines for a short time, any interference with the movement of provisions at that critical time was serious.[30]

Finally, after more heavy losses at the second Battle of Freeman's Farm on October 7, Burgoyne ordered a retreat up the Hudson, hoping to reach Fort Ticonderoga where Powell waited with his garrison. The weather was appalling. Rain teemed down, turning the road to a quagmire as the vanguard set out. Emaciated horses and oxen drew the heavy guns, trailed by men with hardly the strength to put one foot ahead of the other. Provisions had been short for days, and the much-reduced army struggled onward. Near the village of Saratoga, seven miles north of Freeman's Farm, Burgoyne decided the men could go no farther, and he ordered them to encamp. During this period the Jessups and some of their men were running bateaux of supplies past the rebels stationed up the Hudson, who were planning to cut off Burgoyne's line of retreat. A certificate signed by Captain John Schanck, of the Provincial Marine, signifies that Major Edward Jessup

. . .was attacht to the Naval Department on the Hudson's river by Order of His Excellency General Burgoyne for the purpose of Guarding and Navigating the Batteaux and during that service he shew'd great Zeal and attention to the orders given him for the preservation of the Provision etc.[31]

Here was valuable work for an army desperately short of food and all other necessities. Burgoyne's once-proud force now made a miserable spectacle, the men as wretched as they looked. Gentleman Johnny had planned a short summer campaign, and his troops had no winter clothing. By October 14, Burgoyne knew he would have to capitulate, and he gave his provincials permission to escape in small groups to Canada. Many did, fearful the rebel commander, General Gates, would regard them as traitors to his superiors in the Continental Congress.

The three Jessup brothers elected to stay with Burgoyne, and Ebenezer kept a small detachment of King's Loyal Americans behind. They still had work to do, running supplies past the rebel blockade. The following year Ebenezer wrote to Burgoyne:

Desert you we did not and you were pleased to tell me after all the others had gone, that it was the determination of all the generals and officers, to fall a sacrifice themselves before you would yield up the few Provincials that stuck by you, to the will of the enemy.

Also known to have remained with Burgoyne were Captain Justus Sherwood, Queen's Loyal Rangers, Captain Samuel Adams, and others not named. In all, 9 captains, 8 lieutenants, 5 ensigns, 3 staff officers, 15 sergeants and 172 ranks of provincials were captured at Saratoga. As well, 303 other provincials were captured earlier on the campaign.[32]

Under the surrender terms Burgoyne was able to protect his provincials. Article 8 of the Saratoga Convention stipulated that all captured persons were British subjects, rather than subjects of the Continental Congress. Horatio Gates, a former regular who had once served under Burgoyne, made his men abide by the rules of war, and honour the convention he had signed with Burgoyne.[33]

The Jessups, and all the other captured loyalists, signed paroles to take no further part in hostilities, and were sent to Brigadier Powell at Ticonderoga. The British and German regulars set out under escort for Boston, to be sent to England when transport vessels were available. On subsequent muster rolls, the three Jessups and the others are shown as 'under convention,' indicating that they could not perform military duties. The officers might have had to wait until they were exchanged for rebels of like rank. However, Burgoyne had never signed their commissions; officially they were privates, eligible to be paroled without a prisoner exchange. Writing to Burgoyne later, Ebenezer Jessup observed that he had promised 24,000 acres of his own land, to be distributed among his troops when the war ended. He had expended £700 of his private funds over a period of four months, and implied that he had been ill used.[34]

One estimate of the number of provincials that escaped to Canada, or were sent as paroled prisoners of war was 562.[35] Burgoyne's orderly book gives a higher figure that included most of the women and children, and some refugees who had sought his protection:

```
Prisoners Surrendered by Capitulation 16th Oct 1777

    British prisoners ───────────────────────────── 2,442
    Foreign      "    ───────────────────────────── 2,198
    Gen. Burgoyne & Staff Officers, incl. 6 members
                                      of Parl't ────      12
    Sent to Canada ──────────────────────────────── 1,110

    Sick & Wounded ──────────────────────────────      598
                                                     ─────
                                                     6,350 [36]
```

195

At Fort Ticonderoga, Brigadier Powell received orders from Brigadier Maclean, the commander at Montreal who was then at Chimney Point on Lake Champlain, to withdraw after destroying anything that might be of value to the rebels. Maclean had been ordered forward with some of his Royal Highland Emigrants to keep in communication with Powell on October 19, which was two days after Burgoyne handed his sword to Gates at Saratoga.

When Powell withdrew from Fort Ticonderoga, with him went such provincials as had not already been sent on to Fort St. Johns. Britain's last attempt to conquer her rebelling colobies from Canadian bases was over.

From Pillar to Post

From the day of their return to Canada following Burgoyne's surrender until the autumn of 1780, the King's Loyal Americans lived a precarious and demoralizing existence – stepchildren denied a place in the sun by governors who wished they would go away and stop bothering them. Little information has survived on how the corps passed the succeeding months, but the men went into winter quarters at Lachine, and once again Governor Carleton placed them under the command of Sir John Johnson, to the satisfaction of no one. The records the governor kept on Burgoyne's provincials was referred to as the temporary list, implying still that these were Governor Tryon's men. At Lachine the corps was mustered on January 12, 1778, and those under the Saratoga Convention were marked as not available for duty. The others seemed to have been employed on bateau service, transporting supplies, or as workmen on various building projects. On February 1, Ebenezer Jessup wrote to Carleton requesting payment for the private funds he had expended on the corps, but any reimbursement was to be slow in coming.

A report on the several detachments of 'Royalists' who had returned from Saratoga yielded this information: Captain Daniel McAlpin had 2 lieutenants, 3 sergeants, and 26 rank and file on duty in Canada, while 1 lieutenant, 2 ensigns, 1 surgeon, 4 sergeants and 38 rank and file were under the Saratoga Convention.

Serving with Captain Samuel McKay were 1 other captain, 8 lieutenants, 4 ensigns, 1 adjutant, 1 quartermaster, 15 sergeants and 88 rank and file. Under Convention were 2 of McKay's captains, 1 sergeant and 20 rank and file.

'Captain' Ebenezer Jessup had 1 captain, 1 lieutenant, 1 ensign, 2 sergeants and 25 rank and file, with 16 others shown as prisoners of the rebels. Under Convention were 4 captains, 5 lieutenants, 2 ensigns, 1 adjutant, 1 quartermaster, 10 sergeants and 60 rank and file. Another 16 privates were shown as remaining with General Burgoyne, although what that meant is a mystery.

'Captain' John Peters had 5 captains, 4 lieutenants, 3 ensigns, 1 adjutant, 1 quartermaster, 1 surgeon's mate and 9 sergeants, with 53 rank and file available for duty. Under Convention were Captain Justus Sherwood, and 10 privates, while 79 others were prisoners of the rebels.

Dr. Samuel Adams, also ranked as a captain, had no active officers and only 13 privates ready for duty. Under Convention were Adams and another captain, 2 lieutenants and 1 ensign, with 28 rank and file. All told the list showed 9 captains, 15 lieutenants, 9 ensigns, 5 staff officers, 29 sergeants, and 205 rank and file able to be active. Under the Saratoga Convention were 9 captains, 8 lieutenants, 5 ensigns, 3 staff officers, 15 sergeants, and 156 rank and file. Another 16 were with Burgoyne, and 303 privates and 9 commissioned officers were prisoners of the rebels. The remnants of Burgoyne's provincial force – all ranks – was 796 men; of these 468 were safe in Canada, and 196 of them were under Saratoga Convention.[37]

Captain Robert Leake, who had served under Francis Pfister prior to his death, and then with Captain McKay, had attached himself and his company to the King's Royal Regiment of New York shortly after Burgoyne's surrender and his return to Canada.

In the spring of 1778, orders went out from headquarters to Lieutenant-Colonel Ebenezer Jessup to bring his entire corps to Quebec City, including the men who were still prisoners of war on parole. Another order, dated June 1, was sent to all post commanders informing them that the King's soldiers were to disregard the Saratoga Convention, because the Continental Congress had broken its terms. That body had refused to abide by General Horatio Gates' agreement that all captured British and German regulars would be sent to England. Although these men had signed paroles and were not eligible for service in America, they could be used to relieve soldiers on duty elsewhere, and these could be sent against the rebels. The only men allowed to return home on parole were Burgoyne himself and certain of his staff officers. The rest of his army had been marched to prison camps in the southern colonies where food was more plentiful. When the spring fleet brought dispatches from Britain informing Carleton, he revoked all the provincials' paroles.

The King's Loyal Americans remained on duty in Quebec City, working on fortifications until September, when the new governor,

General Frederick Haldimand, ordered them to Sorel. From that time until August 1780, the regiment was quartered there. Haldimand established Sorel as the main base for all his provincial troops, with the exception of Butler's Rangers and part of the King's Royal Regiment of New York. Edward Jessup's receipt book, which he kept from November 1778 until August 1780, shows that all entries were made at that post. On October 19, 1778, Haldimand, who had been toying with the notion of placing all the below-strength corps from Burgoyne's army in a second battalion, King's Royal Regiment of New York, wrote to Sir John Johnson informing him that he had changed his mind. Fearing too much dissent, he had decided to leave them on the temporary list, and he apologized to Sir John for the trouble these men were causing him, promising to make some other arrangements soon, or find some means of attaching them to the Royal Yorkers.

The leaders of some below-strength corps at Sorel knew that Haldimand had been contemplating placing them in the King's Royal Regiment of New York, for on November 12 they forwarded a memorial stating their willingness to join Sir John Johnson, as long as they could have the same terms as officers of provincial corps that were in the southern army. They meant that their commissions would be signed once each officer had recruited the required number of men. The memorial was signed by Robert Leake, John Peters, and Ebenezer and Edward Jessup. The governor declined on the grounds that recruiting for a second battalion would interfere with completing the first battalion and Maclean's Royal Highland Emigrants.

On December 9, the same leaders wrore again to Haldimand, complaining that their men had been issued with blue coats trimmed with white, the very colours worn by many regiments of the enemy's Continental Line, and asking to be issued with red coats. They feared many heavy casualties should their men be expected to go on a campaign dressed in such ridiculous garb. Haldimand ignored their petition, for he had no intention of undertaking an expedition into the rebelling colonies, and for men doing garrison duty, miles from the rebel army, the blue and white was sufficient – it was clothing that must have been in the quartermaster's stores at Sorel since the Seven Years' War.

A winter of discontent followed. Then, on May 17, 1779, Haldimand informed Sir John Johnson that he had come to a decision about the below-strength corps. He was removing them from the baronet's command:

I have thought proper to appoint Captain McAlpin to have the command and direction of the several Corps of Loyalists including both those who are paid and those who are not, and in a few days Captn. McAlpin will wait upon you to receive all instructions, Lists, or any other Papers in your Possession which may assist him in arranging these irregular Corps and I request you will give Captain McAlpin every private information in your Power relative to that part of the Service.

Haldimand had some faith in Daniel McAlpin, because that officer had served as a lieutenant in the 60th Regiment – the governor's own – during the Seven Years' War. All the small corps, including the King's Loyal Americans, were placed under McAlpin at Sorel, but the leaders were determined to preserve their separate identities. That spring, the loyalist officers asked several times for back pay due them, and a warrant dated July 19, at Quebec, authorized the payment of £1,634. 8s. 10d. sterling,

being the allowance made for the present relief of several Corps of Royalists belonging to General Burgoyne's army, and sundry other persons who have taken refuge in this province from the Rebellious Colonies between the 25th June and 24th August, 1779 Inclusive.

The subsistence return accompanying this warrant indicated that the money was for these officers and men:

Capt. Daniel McAlpine. 78
Mr. Peters 61
Part of Capt. Leake's 30
Part of Mr. Adam's 34
Unattached to parties 36
337

Thus Haldimand still maintained that these units – unflatteringly called parties – were Burgoyne's responsibility and not part of his Northern Department, except as refugees, entitled to provisions unless they could be employed as workmen in his service.

Writing to Lord Germain on November 1, 1779, Haldimand showed that he was having a change of heart. When Peters and Jessup had first requested having their corps re-established, he had deferred the question. Now, however, he had agreed to allow them to raise two battalions. The first battalion, Royal Highland Emigrants was completed, and he had authorized enlarging these companies, while the first battalion, King's Royal Regiment of New York, was also nearly at strength. The commissions for Peters' and Jessups' officers, Haldimand maintained, would not be approved until the ranks were raised.[38] Once he had authorized more recruiting, the governor had to take action on the quarrelling over the few who had so far been brought to Canada, as well as those who would be coming in the future. The bickering was aggravated by the arrival of Major James Rogers in quest of recruits for the recently authorized King's Rangers, a provincial corps that was part of Sir Henry Clinton's Central Department.

On January 29, 1780, Haldimand issued instructions for the

establishment of a Board of Officers to mediate disputes. It would convene at Fort St. Johns on February 8, and meet at regular intervals to hear claims. Some of the complaints in the governor's records dated from 1777, and the officers would decide where the various recruits should be assigned. Initially, the members were Lieutenant-Colonel Barry St. Leger and Brigadier Allan Maclean; Majors Christopher Carleton and John Adolphus Harris; Captains Alexander Fraser, 32nd Regiment, and Thomas Scott, 53rd Regiment; and lieutenants of provincials, James Parrot, Edward Carscallan, Abraham Stiles, James O'Neil and Jonathan Philips.[39]

Haldimand thought he had solved all his problems over the below-strength provincial units. But, on July 22, 1780, Daniel McAlpin died; once again Haldimand had to put the units under the command of Sir John Johnson. The governor called them McAlpin's battalion, but the individual parts still insisted on retaining separate identities. On July 26, Ebenezer Jessup wrote to Haldimand asking that 68 of his men who had been drafted for bateau service, and then into McAlpin's corps, be returned to him now that McAlpin was dead. Neil Robertson, formerly of the King's Loyal Americans, serving with McAlpin's corps, replied to Colonel Jessup from Montreal on August 6, at Haldimand's request. Of the 68 men Ebenezer wanted returned, Robertson stated, 25 were with the rebels, 22 were dead, and the other 21 were with McAlpin's men. The records show that Jessup received 11 of the men he claimed from McAlpin, but he had to surrender Private David Scott Senior, who was serving with the King's Loyal Americans and who had been recruited by McAlpin.[40]

By the autumn of 1780, Haldimand was finally taking appropriate steps to assist the recruiting agents, granting incentives that had been British policy since the beginning of 1779. On September 4, from his headquarters in Quebec City, the governor issued a general order informing the various commanders that officers of provincial corps were subordinate to regulars of the same rank, but they would receive the same wages. Those whose regiments were completed to ten companies of 56 rank and file, and 3 'Contingent Men' would have their ranks made permanent in America, entitling them to half pay when their corps were reduced. At the same time Haldimand authorized a bounty of 22s. 6d. for each new recruit.

At long last, here were the badly needed inducements for both officers and men. As of August, the lists for the below-strength corps showed even fewer names than the year before, as men retired to seek civilian employment, deserted, died or joined other corps:

200

Operations along Lake Champlain Autumn 1780

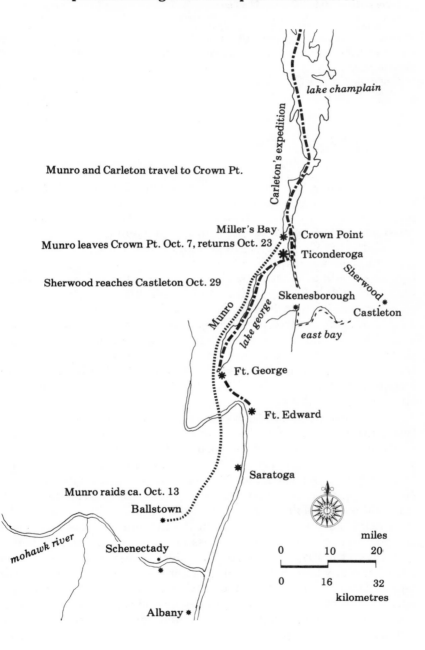

lake champlain

Carleton's expedition

Munro and Carleton travel to Crown Pt.

Miller's Bay

Crown Point

Munro leaves Crown Pt. Oct. 7, returns Oct. 23

Ticonderoga

Sherwood

Sherwood reaches Castleton Oct. 29

Skenesborough

Castleton

Munro

lake george

east bay

Ft. George

Ft. Edward

Saratoga

Munro raids ca. Oct. 13

Ballstown

mohawk river

Schenectady

miles

0   10   20

0   16   32

kilometres

Albany

Jessups 6 Sergeants 6 Corporals 71 men.
Peters 4 Sergeants 4 Corporals 46 men.
Late Major McAlpin 6 Sergeants 4 Corporals 72 men.
Mr. Adams 3 Sergeants 0 Corporals 23 men.
Captain Leake's 3 Sergeants 3 Corporals 14 men.

Yet officers were available in over-abundance, both active and pensioned:

Captains 8
Lieutenants 26
Ensigns 10
Assistant Adjutant 1
Quartermaster 1
Assistant Surgeon 1
Pensioned Officers 47

94[41]

In summary, 94 officers and 39 non-commissioned officers were in charge of only 226 men – about 5 privates for every active commissioned officer. Captain Leake had more men than this list indicated, for he had begun forming an independent company that was attached to the King's Royal Regiment of New York.

In December, Haldimand issued orders that the several corps of loyalists would be looked upon as one regiment, and commanded by Major John Nairne, Royal Highland Emigrants. Dr. Samuel Adams was assigned to lead McAlpin's corps. To his immense relief, Sir John Johnson was free of the responsibility for these small units, and able to concentrate on raising his second battalion, King's Royal Regiment of New York from among other recruits. At the same time, Captains Peter Drummond and William Fraser were empowered to raise independent companies for service wherever Haldimand posted them.

The autumn of 1780 provided the first opportunity since the Burgoyne campaign for the King's Loyal Americans to do some fighting. A detachment of the corps, led by Major Edward Jessup, accompanied an expedition of King's Rangers and regulars under Major Christopher Carleton that went up Lake Champlain to destroy all the outposts belonging to New York State. The purpose of this raid was twofold: to make the lake safer for the vessels of the Provincial Marine; and as a cog in the machinery Haldimand was building to persuade Vermont to assume a neutral stance or, better still, rejoin the British Empire. The raiders invested Fort Ann and Fort George, where both rebel garrisons surrendered. Then Lieutenant David Jones led part of the detachment to Fort Edward, where he procured a supply of provisions and captured several prisoners. Captain John Chipman, the commandant of Fort George and the most important prize, was returned a few weeks later by Captain Justus Sherwood through a prisoner exchange.[42]

Writing to Haldimand on November 2, Ebenezer Jessup reported receiving a letter from his brother Edward, who was at Crown Point, asking for permission to have some prisoners taken during the raid join the King's Loyal Americans. To this request Haldimand gave his approval. About the same time, 34 rangers accompanied Captain John Munro, of the King's Royal Regiment of New York, who raided Ballstown, a village north of the Mohawk River opposite Schenectady.

Now that Haldimand was actively encouraging recruitment, and admitting that the small units were part of his Northern Department, both Ebenezer and Edward Jessup were trying to complete their battalion. On October 11, Ebenezer wrote to the governor requesting that the Reverend John Bryon be appointed chaplain for his corps, but no chaplain was shown on any of his lists of officers. Edward was working harder than Ebenezer, by seeking to demonstrate that his men had fine fighting qualities. As the winter of 1781 progressed, he proposed raids on Fort Edward or towards the Connecticut Valley but the governor refused to sanction them. That season the headquarters of the King's Loyal Americans was transferred from Sorel to Verchères, close to Montreal. Not all the men were stationed there, for some were on duty at other places. After Major John Nairne received command of all the below-strength provincial units, Neil Robertson served as his adjutant, Titus Simmons as quartermaster, and Ephriam Jones as commissary.[43]

Soon after Haldimand made known his plans for improving the strength and quality of the small provincial corps, he decided to uniform all of them in green coats with dark red facings. On January 24, he issued an order that 'all Royalists' who had received clothing were to parade before Major Nairne on February 8, then march to relieve the garrison stationed in one of the blockhouses at Yamaska, on the south shore of the St. Lawrence a few miles east of Sorel. Then the tailors were to concentrate on clothing for Captain William Fraser's independent company. On April 8, a payment of £1,028. 13s. 8½d. was authorized to Ebenezer Jessup for the support of his corps. That same day the Board of Officers meeting at Fort St. Johns agreed that a further payment of about the same amount be made on June 28, 1782, and Haldimand approved the sum.

In October 1781, when Major John Ross was leading an expedition of detachments of regulars, Royal Yorkers, and Butler's Rangers through the Mohawk Valley, Captain Robert Mathews, the governor's secretary, wrote to Major John Adolphus Harris, Royal

Highland Emigrants then at Fort St. Johns, ordering Major Edward Jessup to take all the men Harris could spare and make a feint towards Saratoga. Jessup was to prevent General John Stark, there with a detachment of rebels, from attempting to join the Continental troops and rebel militiamen in the Mohawk Valley who were trying to intercept Ross. Jessup obeyed, and on November 2, Colonel St. Leger, temporarily occupying Crown Point with a force of regulars and provincials, informed Mathews that Jessup had returned the day before, and General Stark, convinced that his position would be attacked, had remained at Saratoga.

By that time Governor Haldimand had decided to establish a new regiment, absorbing Jessup's and Peters' corps. Edward Jessup, who had been showing his mettle of late, would be the major-commandant. The governor had never been impressed by Ebenezer, who spent too much time complaining about money, and he placed more confidence in the elder brother. As of November 12, the King's Loyal Americans and Queen's Loyal Rangers were no more, and the new provincial corps was known as the Loyal Rangers.

Edward was an admirable choice for a corps that combined Yankees and Yorkers. His background, Connecticut birth and life in feudal New York gave him a foot in each camp. Initially, the new corps had six active companies, taking in Drummond's and Fraser's hitherto independent companies. The others were the major's own company, Captain Justus Sherwood's, John and Jonathan Jones' . Ebenezer was placed in command of a company of pensioners, while John Peters, to his disgust, was given a company of invalids.[44]

Of the remaining below-strength units, when Samuel McKay died in 1781, Robert Leake took charge of his men. Leake's expanded company and Samuel Adams' small one ultimately joined the second battalion King's Royal Regiment of New York. Adams, whose name does not appear on the last list of officers for that corps, must have retired from the service.

Chapter 8: The Queen's Loyal Rangers

The Queen's Loyal Rangers, raised from the spring of 1777 onward, was the largest provincial corps that served with Burgoyne. It also suffered the heaviest casualties because the officers and men were with the vanguard of Burgoyne's army, whereas most of the other provincials were employed part of the time bringing supplies from behind the army over the long route back to Lake George.

John Peters

Typical of many officers and men who served in provincial corps, John Peters came from a family seriously divided over the issue of rebellion, and he suffered accordingly. His father, a well-to-do farmer and a colonel in the militia, was an ardent rebel, while his uncle, the Reverend Samuel Peters, was a loyalist who exerted considerable influence over his nephew.

Born in Hebron, Connecticut, in 1740, John Peters was educated at Yale College, where he studied law, receiving his Bachelor of Arts degree in 1759. It was there he formed a lifelong friendship with Edmund Fanning, who would become the lieutenant-governor, first of Nova Scotia and later of Prince Edward Island.

In 1761, John married Ann Barnett, whose father was a merchant of Windsor, Connecticut, and two years later they moved to Piermont, New Hampshire, on the east bank of the Connecticut River. There John built a house, sawmill and barn. Governor Benning Wentworth, the man who established the controversial New Hampshire Grants in the Green Mountains, appointed Peters a captain commandant of militia, and Deputy Surveyor of the King's Woods.[1] The latter job involved laying out townships, and reserving the tallest, straightest pines to provide masts and spars for the Royal Navy when required. By 1770, John and Ann had moved to Moortown, on the west side of the Connecticut River, which was in Gloucester County, New Hampshire Grants, Province of New York.

At Moortown John acquired large holdings, under New York title, and he erected a house, barn, saw and grist mills, in addition to farming part of his land. When Governor Tryon came to rule the province in 1772, he appointed Peters a colonel of militia, justice of the peace, Judge of Probates, Registrar of the County, Clerk of the Court, and Judge of the Court of Common Pleas, for which his degree in law made him well qualified.

Writing a narrative of his life many years later to 'a Friend in London,' Peters described how his world began to crumble when 'the spirit of discord and rebellion so far prevailed as to occasion me much trouble.'

The counties of Cumberland and Gloucester (since called Vermont) desired me to attend the Congress to meet at Philadelphia in 1774, which appointment I accepted of, and passing through Hebron on my way to Philadelphia I was mobbed with my uncles, the Rev. Samuel Peters, Mr. Jonathan and Mr. Benjamin Peters, by Governor Trumbull's Liberty Boys, because we were accused of loyalty. I was liberated after suffering much ill language from the mob.

Earlier, the Reverend Peters had advised John to accept the appointment to the Congress, if only to find out what the members aimed to accomplish. After attending a session in Philadelphia, John came away convinced that nothing short of independence would satisfy most of the delegates. He refused to take the oath of secrecy to the Congress, and wrote to this effect to his uncle Samuel, who had fled to England for safety. When John set out to return to his family in Moortown, he was 'seized by three mobs, ill treated and dismissed, at Weatherfield, Hartford and Springfield.'

John reached home in April 1775, where another mob seized him and threatened to execute him as an enemy of the Congress. They carried him before the Committee of Safety, where Deacon Jacob Bailey, a neighbour and former friend, was the president. Peters was accused of corresponding with Governor Carleton of Canada, but Bailey, later a general in the rebel militia, discharged him at midnight for lack of evidence. Once again Peters was seized by a mob, demanding that he sign a covenant to oppose the King and the British army with his life and property. This time he stalled by promising to think about the matter.

When the news of the shooting at Concord and Lexington reached Moortown, the mob ordered Peters to prepare the militia to march on an hour's notice. He obeyed, thus buying himself more time. Then the mob, suspicious again, attacked Peters' house, ate and drank their fill, taking whatever papers they found and many of the family's personal effects before departing. To add to John's discomfiture, his father 'wrote against me and urged on the mobs, assigning for reason 'that his uncle Peters, the clergyman who had taught him bad principles, was driven out of the country, and that he soon would become a friend of America if severity was used'.'

By January 1776, John had resolved to escape his tormentors by whatever means came his way. He applied to a rebel, Timothy Bedel, who was about to depart for Canada with reinforcements to aid the expedition that in 1776 was trying to capture the province. Bedel agreed to let Peters accompany him, obtained the consent of the Committee of Safety, and promised John that he would not be obliged to bear arms.

206

They left Moortown in March, and when they reached the Cedars, above Montreal, Peters prevailed upon Bedel not to burn the village. Peters contrived to send a messenger to Captain George Forster, who had left Fort Oswegatchie with some regular soldiers, loyalists and Indians and travelled down the St. Lawrence to attack the Cedars. Forster sent word to Peters that he would attack Bedel's position – a small fort the rebels occupied – advising him to keep out of the way. Near the appointed time, Peters asked permission of Bedel to go into Montreal for provisions, which the other granted. Thus John was absent when Forster's men captured the fort.

In Montreal, Peters showed the same bravado he was to demonstrate as the commander of the Queen's Loyal Rangers. He dined with 'Dr. Franklin and the other Commissioners from Congress, also General Wooster and Col. Arnold.' Little did Benedict Arnold suspect that one of his guests was a cuckoo in the rebel nest, for he bragged that a force of 700 men was about to attack Captain Forster. Peters passed this information to a friend in the city, who saw that Forster was warned in time to escape across the St. Lawrence. Later, when Arnold was about to evacuate Montreal knowing that Sir Guy Carleton was approaching with a large army, Peters discovered that the rebels intended to burn the city. This news he passed to a Mr. Wheatly who alerted the inhabitants. Then, as Peters asserted, the residents set a watch until Arnold's men had left.

For a reason not explained, Peters was unable to slip away from the rebels and he made his way to Sorel. There General John Sullivan, the rebel commander in that village arrested him on the not invalid suspicion that he had been in communication with Captain Forster. Peters remained with the rebels during their retreat as far as Isle La Motte, on Lake Champlain, where he was set free, because the only evidence Sullivan had against him was a letter from Deacon Jacob Bailey inferring that Peters had loyalist sympathies. When the army evacuated the island for the next stage of their withdrawal, Peters and a Dr. Skinner hid in the woods. On June 28, they sneaked into the rebel campsite and found it deserted, the enemy having moved on to Crown Point. Peters discovered a canoe, and the two escapees paddled the nearly 40 miles back to Fort St. Johns. There, on June 29, they found a British force and met the commanding officer, 'General Simon Fraser.'

That officer received Peters kindly and conducted him to Fort Chambly, where Governor Sir Guy Carleton had arrived from Montreal. Satisfied that Peters and Skinner were loyal, the governor gave them permission to travel to that city. The people of Montreal gave Peters a warm welcome, aware that his timely warning had prevented destruction of their property – or so he maintained. He stayed in the city, and met another old friend in August, Mr. Peter Livius, who escorted Peters to Fort Chambly and introduced him to Governor Carleton (who apparently did not recall Fraser's earlier presentation), recommending him as a dependable person. In consequence, Peters went as a volunteer on Carleton's expedition up Lake Champlain, serving as one of the pilots in Fraser's vanguard. Following the defeat of Benedict Arnold's fleet in October 1776, the British army withdrew to Fort St. Johns and went into winter quarters. Peters and several other loyalists found billets around Montreal.

Back in Moortown, Ann Peters and their eight children remained in their home until January 1777. At that time the Committee of Safety confiscated John's property, and General Jacob Bailey ordered the family out of the house and sent,in a sleigh with only one bed, towards Fort Ticonderoga. There a rebel garrison commanded by General 'Mad Anthony' Wayne was in residence. Two deserters from the rebel army who reached Montreal in March informed Peters that Ann and his children travelled nearly 140 miles through the woods in dead of winter, a nightmare of foul weather and bad roads. John described his wife as 'a small delicate woman' although Ann had presented him with seven sons and one daughter, all of whom grew to maturity, and she outlived her husband by many years. In April Wayne sent the family 30 miles forward, where their escort of rebel guides left them with three weeks provisions in a deserted house 'near fifty miles from any inhabitants between them and Canada.' This rings true, for such escorts were inclined to turn back out of fear that a British patrol might capture them. Peters' narrative resumes:

Here she stayed eighteen days with her children only (the Eldest being fourteen years) her servant having been detained by Deacon Bailey (for which Gen. Wayne said he ought to be damned.) At length a British boat discovered and carried them to a vessel, and thence to St. Johns, where they all arrived on the 4th. of May, 1777, well but naked and dirty.

About this time, Carleton gave Peters permission to raise a regiment, and he was to have the provisional rank of lieutenant-colonel commandant. On June 14, Burgoyne instructed him to bring the men he had raised and join the army that was about to invade the northern colonies. With Peters on the Burgoyne campaign went his eldest son, John Jr. Although scarcely 15 years old, he was one of the ensigns. Ann Peters and the other seven children stayed in Montreal, and were befriended by Allan Maclean, the commandant of the city's garrison.

Hubbardtown, Bennington, Escape from Saratoga

Peters had been in the Montreal area for more than a year when, in May 1777, he received permission from Governor Carleton to raise a battalion of loyalists, to be called the Queen's Loyal Rangers. Like Ebenezer Jessup's warrant for his King's Loyal Americans, the warrant Peters received has not been found. Both corps of loyalists were to accompany General John Burgoyne's expedition into New York State. Writing to the Colonial Secretary, Lord George Germain, Burgoyne implied that Peters would be recruiting in the Albany area when he meant Charlotte County.[2] (Burgoyne's knowledge of the geography of that corner of the world was as hazy as George Bernard Shaw's when he wrote his play *The Devil's Disciple*.) Peters was from Gloucester County, then the northern half of the New Hampshire Grants that later became the State of Vermont. Most of Peters' recruits would come from the Green Mountain area, which included Cumberland County, to the south of Gloucester, and the eastern slice of Charlotte County.

A certificate signed by Justus Sherwood in October 1777, shows that the commander-in-chief, Sir William Howe, had a hand in establishing the corps – the reason why Carleton and Haldimand regarded Peters' men as only temporarily in Canada. The first officers appointed were Captain Francis Hogel and Lieutenant Gershom French, who were chosen by Howe on October 26, 1776, at his base in New York City, long before Carleton gave his permission for the formation of the Queen's Loyal Rangers. Peters' own appointment as the lieutenant-colonel commandant is dated June 27, 1777, at which time Justus Sherwood was made the corps' senior captain. Others were, in order, Captain Jeremiah French (Gershom's brother), Ensign John Peters Jr., Major Zadock Wright, Lieutenant James Parrot, Lieutenant John Dulmage, Lieutenant Philo Hurlburt, and Quartermaster Titus Simons. All but Francis Hogel and Gershom French received their appointments from General John Burgoyne.[3] (Omitted were two officers who had transferred to another corps, and several who were killed in action or prisoners of the rebels when Sherwood compiled the list).

About the time Peters was sending agents into the Green Mountains to recruit for his corps, the local people were proclaiming the New Hampshire Grants the independent Republic of Vermont. Legally it was part of New York, but most of the settlers, like Peters himself, were from Connecticut, and the instigators of secession considered the sins of New York and its governor, William Tryon, much more heinous than those of Britain. Most of the supporters of the republic lived in Charlotte County on the west side of the Green Mountains, where, from Bennington, Ethan Allen, his brothers and friends, had spearheaded the revolt against New York. Peters had scant sympathy for the lawless ways of the Green Mountain Boys, but he was a Yankee himself, who had never crossed swords with the Allens. He was congenial enough to make an acceptable leader to loyalists from Ethan Allen's band of rowdy frontiersmen, and he was to demonstrate his ability to act with characteristic Green Mountain Boy bluff.

Aware of the situation in the Green Mountains, Sir Guy Carleton was too astute to attempt placing loyalists from that neighbourhood in the same corps as New Yorkers. At the start of Burgoyne's expedition, Ebenezer Jessup and John Peters had scarcely enough men for one fledgling battalion, but Carleton knew where the fighting would take place if he tried to mix Yankees and Yorkers under one command. The Queen's Loyal Rangers were destined to be the largest group of provincials with Burgoyne, and to play the most important part in the campaign.

Many of Peters' men were recruited individually, either from among refugees in the Montreal area, or by agents travelling into the Green Mountains, but one group had come to Crown Point to meet Governor Carleton in October 1776. Numbering about 40, they were piloted by Justus Sherwood, of New Haven, in the New Hampshire Grants, but half of them were Yorkers from the Camden Valley who had set out under the leadership of Edward Carscallan. This latter group had become lost, and Sherwood, leading a party of Yankees, found them and led them the rest of the way. Carscallan and his followers had come to join Francis Pfister's Loyal Volunteers, but General Phillips, Burgoyne's second-in-command, assigned all the men who had come with Sherwood to the Queen's Loyal Rangers. John Peters formed them into a company with Sherwood as the captain, Carscallan as the lieutenant, and John Wilson, also from the Camden Valley, as the ensign.

Immediately the men with whom Carscallan had set out objected and asked to be allowed to join Pfister, the officer of their choice. Peters refused, and after some argument the men decided to remain with Sherwood for the time being. As John Wilson explained in a memorial, 'your Petitioners agreed to be under the command of Colonel Peters on condition of leaving him if they thought proper.'[4] Some of the dissent arose because Justus Sherwood was a former Green Mountain Boy, and the Yorkers with Carscallan wanted no part of him.

210

At first the Queen's Loyal Rangers were quartered on the south shore of the St. Lawrence near Longueil, opposite Montreal. Early in June, Burgoyne landed at Montreal from Quebec City, and on the 11, left for Fort St. Johns in a carriage. The following day Peters received orders to march his corps there. By that time the King's Loyal Americans and the Queen's Loyal Rangers had been uniformed in red coats with dark green facings.[5] Details of the part played by the corps in the Burgoyne campaign are sketchy, but it appears that Peters' men spent most of their time serving under General Fraser, who led Burgoyne's vanguard.

After capturing Fort Ticonderoga, Burgoyne ordered General Fraser to pursue the rebel army that was escaping through Vermont, and with him went 300 of Peters' Queen's Loyal Rangers, local men who knew the country.[6] Meanwhile, Burgoyne left a garrison at Ticonderoga, and sailed on to Skenesborough with the bulk of his army. Marching after the rebels, General Fraser asked Peters to recommend an officer to lead a scouting party in search of the enemy's rearguard. Peters chose Captain Justus Sherwood, who took some former Green Mountain Boys from his company and a few Indian scouts.

Sherwood returned and reported that Colonel Seth Warner and his Green Mountain Boys, then a rebel regiment, were at Hubbardtown after covering the retreat of General St. Clair's army. The Queen's Loyal Rangers officer also brought in four prisoners who had crossed his path, whom he could not risk leaving behind lest they notify Warner that he was being pursued. On July 7, Fraser surprised some New Hampshire militiamen who had bivouacked without posting guards and was routing them when Seth Warner and his Green Nountain Boys appeared. The skirmish turned into a full-scale battle, and Warner almost had Fraser outflanked when, amidst all the firing, his men heard voices lustily singing a Lutheran hymn; it was Baron von Riedesel arriving at the head of a column of Germans. When the blue coats hove into view, the Green Mountain Boys, in true guerilla fashion, took to their heels.

The battle of Hubbardtown was a minor encounter, but the casualities were heavy. Of Seth Warner's force of 730 strong, 41 were killed, 96 wounded and 234 captured. With von Riedesel's reinforcements, 1,030 British, Germans and provincials were engaged, and of these 60 were killed and 148 wounded.[7] Among the wounded were 6 Queen's Loyal Rangers, but Peters' men had fared better than the regulars. Once the rebels fled, Fraser arranged to have the prisoners escorted to Ticonderoga, where Brigadier Powell sent them on to Montreal. Then the combined force marched back to the shore of Lake Champlain and turned south to rejoin Burgoyne, encamped at Skenesborough. Fraser and von Riedesel did not think they had sufficient supplies with them to continue their pursuit of the rebel army.

Burgoyne was staying in the fine fieldstone home of Philip Skene, the proprietor of Skenesborough, a half pay officer from the Seven Years' War. Skene was Burgoyne's chief adviser on local matters, and it was Skene who was thought to have persuaded Burgoyne to build a road to the Hudson, instead of using the superior, existing route through Lake George.

During the delay necessitated by road building, Peters took the opportunity to have his agents bring in recruits from the nearby frontiers. When his corps was mustered for the first time on July 23, he had 262 men, but agents were still out in search of more. Later, Peters was to write: 'I had mustered 262 men only, but I raised in all 643 though as my situation was generally in the advance party, my men were killed off not quite as fast as I enlisted them.'

He also said he was present at every skirmish with the rebels; except 'Hulestown,' by which he may have meant Hubbardtown. On that occasion he was on hand if not actually leading his men. Captain Sherwood missed this battle because Peters had sent him foraging, and after the action he returned with a goodly supply of flour, some cattle, horses and wagons. Peters may have been foraging with a small party during the battle.

At the muster on July 23 Peters had 14 non-commissioned officers. In addition to Justus Sherwood, the other captains were Jeremiah French, David McFall and Francis Hogel. Peters distributed funds to the officers to be disbursed to their men, and the pay list is dated July 28, 1777.[8] On August 25, Burgoyne announced that provincials would receive the same pay as the King's troops, for the period from June 25, to August 24, and the lump sums allotted show that each captain received 10s. per day, but whether in sterling, Halifax or New York currency was not specified.

By the 26th, the road to the Hudson was finally open, and the vanguard marched. Once the entire army had reached Fort Edward, Burgoyne settled himself in the home of Patrick Smyth, a lawyer suspected of loyalism who had been taken to gaol in Albany as the British army approached. While the army was encamped, many refugee wives and children made their way to Fort Edward for safety. One such was Barbara Heck, driving a wagon with five small children and a grandfather clock.[9] Her husband Paul had come from the Camden Valley with Edward Carscallan to join Francis Pfister, but at that time he was in Justus Sherwood's company of the Queen's

Loyal Rangers.

Soon after reaching Fort Edward, Burgoyne formulated his plan for a force to go across Vermont towards the Connecticut Valley. This expedition was to be led by Colonel Friedrich Baum, with 500 German troops, escorted by the Queen's Loyal Rangers and Francis Pfister's Loyal Volunteers, to obtain horses for the thus far unmounted Brunswick Dragoons, to forage for provisions to feed the army, and to complete Peters' corps.[10]

So much conflicting information exists over exactly what occurred when the Germans and loyalists tangled with superior numbers of rebels near Bennington that only the consequences are not open to question. In his 1976 account, Joseph W.R. Parke was skeptical about Peters' claim to have been there at all, and concluded that Francis Pfister merely gathered together a group of his Tory friends and went to help the Germans.[11] Parke was describing the battle using only rebel materials, but a 1973 version by Philip Katcher, sympathetic to loyalists, states that Jessup's corps accompanied the Germans to Bennington.[12] Burgoyne's orders to Baum, and Peters' own account leave no doubts. The Queen's Loyal Rangers and the men Pfister had raised marched from Fort Edward with Baum and fought the Battle of Bennington.

Any thought that foraging and taking horses might be incompatible with inducing recruits to join Peters did not enter Burgoyne's head. After all, his trusted adviser, Philip Skene, who would accompany Baum had assured Gentleman Johnny that the country was occupied almost solely by loyal colonials. He seemed to think they would welcome an invasion by foreign troops helping themselves to precious horses and the food they were storing to feed their families through the coming winter. After all, the provincials travelling with the Germans would explain why Burgoyne's army had need of their possessions.

Apparently Burgoyne's decision to give this mission to the Germans rested on a question of etiquette. The Germans were encamped to the east of the British, and Burgoyne would not offend von Riedesel by leap-frogging his redcoats over the German position. However, the commander could with propriety send the Queen's Loyal Rangers, Pfister's men, and one company of British riflemen, because von Riedesel had asked for them. The loyalists knew the country, and the baron wanted a few marksmen on hand. This expedition set out on August 11; it was about 1,000 strong, including the 500 Germans, the loyalists and riflemen. With Baum went the Brunswick Dragoons, in their heavy leather boots and plumed hats, quite unsuitable for a march through a hot, humid forest, each carrying a halter in case he found a horse. Leading the riflemen was Captain Alexander Fraser, the general's nephew. Burgoyne also assigned some Indians to act as scouts.

Captain Justus Sherwood had been sent ahead with a small party to gather intelligence, while his lieutenant, Edward Carscallan, was making for Fort Edward with 20 recruits for the Queen's Loyal Rangers. Sherwood discovered that Seth Warner and his Green Mountain Boys were encamped at Manchester, while at Bennington, 20 miles to the south, he found that the rebels had a huge stock-pile of supplies guarded by only 400 militiamen. He sent a message to inform Burgoyne that if he wanted supplies he should stage a quick raid on Bennington without delay.[13]

Upon receiving Sherwood's communications, Burgoyne, who had told Baum to march towards Manchester, ordered him to make for Arlington and 'take post there until the detachment of Provincials under the command of Captain Sherwood shall join you from the southward.' As soon as Sherwood reached Baum, the German commander sent him foraging with 80 men, and on August 13, he returned to the column with some cattle; horses, carts, wagons, and five prisoners.[14] He also reported that 1,000 militia from New Hampshire had marched into Bennington with rebel General John Stark, a onetime captain in Rogers' Rangers who was about to put his Seven Years' War training to great effect.

The rebels were reinforcing Bennington because Baum's approach was hardly furtive, and allowed ample warning. The German regulars were marching at scarcely one mile an hour, ranks meticulously dressed, a brass band playing, dragging two 3-pounder brass cannon. (Today these guns grace the steps of the Vermont Legislature.) Butler's Rangers or possibly the Queen's Loyal Rangers on their own, might have been in and out of Bennington before the rebels knew what had hit them, but Baum's ponderous approach gave plenty of time to prepare a hot reception. The army of militiamen at Bennington was increasing. Seth Warner was marching from Manchester with a small detachment of his regiment, and the main body of Green Mountain Boys was to follow as soon as possible.

From Cambridge, inside New York, the column advanced southward and Baum dispatched a rider to inform Burgoyne that he would need reinforcements before taking on the Bennington rebels. Then, without warning a party of men in frontier dress, white paper in their hats, appeared on the road ahead of the column. Skene assumed these must be loyalists coming to join them, for other friends had come in earlier on the march. To his astonishment, the newcomers opened fire. One casualty was Skene's horse, and when the smoke cleared the rebels had vanished.[15]

By the afternoon Baum's force had reached White Creek, where the rebels had destroyed a bridge the expedition had to cross. After repairing it the Germans and provincials moved on as far as the Walloomsac River, four miles from Bennington, and found the bridge across this stream intact. Here Baum decided to dig in and await his reinforcements, and he made the fatal mistake of scattering his force into five parts and placing some in spots he could not see from his own position.

The setting was a hill, the Walloomsac winding round it, the bridge on the road to Bennington at the base. Francis Pfister and his men, and Justus Sherwood's company of Queen's Loyal Rangers, were sent to the east side of the Walloomsac to build a redoubt. Regulars were stationed on the west side of the river to hold the bridge. Behind them on the hill Baum placed his German troops, with an outpost of Brunswick Grenadiers and Captain Fraser's marksmen partway down slope. Colonel Peters was on the road to the rear with some 230 Queen's Loyal Rangers. The provincials were divided into approximately two equal parts, for Pfister had about 200 men in his Loyal Volunteers. Peters chose Sherwood's company to join Pfister because many of the men in it wanted to serve with that officer. At all five positions the men dug in, making barricades of logs and covering them with earth.

During the night of August 14, heavy rain fell, and the downpour continued all the following day, sending the earth slithering off the barricades. The party of Indians who had come on the expedition vanished, and some American writers claim that Baum had lost the eyes and ears of his army, an overstatement because many skilled woodsmen were serving in the Queen's Loyal Rangers.

August 16 dawned sunny but moist, and at nine o'clock the rebel attack commenced from three sides. New Hampshire militia came towards the German position on the hill from the northwest. General Stark with the main body of New Hampshiremen moved in from the east towards the redoubt where Francis Pfister was in command, and his men were soon escaping over the bridge to join the regulars on the west side of the Walloomsac River. Their leader lay mortally wounded in what today is still called the Tory Redoubt, and Justus Sherwood took command of them. Meanwhile, a large force of Bennington militia crossed the river on a ford farther downstream and circled round to attack Baum's Germans on the hill, out of sight of Fraser's riflemen and the Brunswick Grenadiers. Peters takes up the story:

215

Battle of Bennington August 16 1777

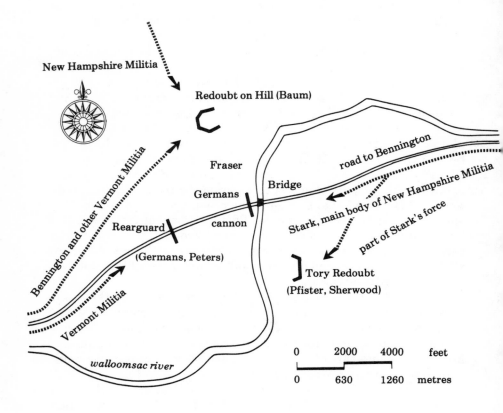

New Hampshire Militia

Redoubt on Hill (Baum)

Fraser

road to Bennington

Bridge

Germans

Bennington and other Vermont Militia

Rearguard

cannon

Stark, main body of New Hampshire Militia

(Germans, Peters)

part of Stark's force

Vermont Militia

Tory Redoubt
(Pfister, Sherwood)

walloomsac river

0	2000	4000	feet
0	630	1260	metres

> I commanded the Loyalists at Bennington, when I had 291 men of my regiment with me, and I lost above half of them in that engagement. The action commenced at 9 o'clock in the morning and continued until near 4 o'clock in the afternoon when we retired in much confusion . . . I observed a man fire at me, which I returned. He loaded again as he came up, and discharged again at me, crying out 'Peters, you damned Tory, I have got you.' He rushed on me with his bayonet, which entered just below my left breast, but was turned by the bones. By this time I was loaded, and I saw it was a rebel Captain Jeremiah Post by name, an old schoolmate and playfellow and a cousin of my wife. Though his bayonet was in my body I felt regret at being obliged to destroy him.

The air was soon filled with blue smoke that obscured the appalling slaughter. While Baum prayed for his reinforcements to arrive, the rebels were attacking his positions separately. Had his men been closer together they might have fought off the onslaught. In the midst of the carnage Philip Skene cut the traces of a horse hitched to a supply wagon and rode off in search of desperately needed fresh troops, hoping to speed them on their way. Suddenly, an ear splitting explosion shattered the air above the popping of musketry. The rebels had fired into a tumbrel carrying Baum's powder. Except for what each man still carried in his cartridge case, his force was out of ammunition, and the commanding officer himself lay dying on the hill surrounded by dead and maimed German troops. Peters' account resumes:

> We retreated from Bennington to the reinforcement that was coming up, which was soon attacked and obliged to retreat to the bridge at the mills in Cambridge, which I broke up after the troops had retreated towards the camp, which we reached the next day. General Fraser received me very kindly and as I was wounded in the breast and was also lame with a hurt I had received in a skirmish the day before the action by a ball grazing my foot, and was much fatigued, and for some time had been harassed with the fever and ague, he generously gave me up his bed for the night, and he laid himself in his cloak on a bench. I received his and Gen. Burgoyne's approbation for my conduct in this action.

The reinforcements led by Colonel Heinrich von Breymann had been trudging slowly through the rain along the muddy road, dragging their feet because von Breymann had no love for Baum. Two miles from the battlefield the column was set upon by Seth Warner's Green Mountain Boys, who had just arrived from Manchester. As Peters said, von Breymann's men were dispersed before they came in sight of the slaughter that had taken place beside the Walloomsac River.

Not all the able-bodied Queen's Loyal Rangers left the field with Peters. Justus Sherwood took command of Pfister's loyalists after their leader's death. With him was Captain Robert Leake of Pfister's Corps, and evidence suggests that these two officers had the good sense to find some cover. Before the battle, Sherwood's company was completed to 60 men, and he succeeded in saving 46 despite the heavy fire rained upon them.

217

Most secondary accounts of the Battle of Bennington record that the Tory-loyalists were all at Pfister's redoubt, but a map prepared by Lieutenant Durnford, Royal Engineers, also shows a position about 1,000 yards back from the river, in a rearguard location. Peters left the field earlier than Sherwood, after his men had taken a terrible beating. All told the casualties were staggering.

Colonel Baum had no notion of how to conduct himself and deploy his men under forest conditions. That nearly half the loyalists escaped shows either their better grasp of what was happening, or merely that many were new recruits who had no red uniforms. In drab clothing they were less easy to spot through the smoke of battle. By the night of August 16, the remnants were hurrying up the road towards Cambridge. Between them Baum and von Breymann had commanded some 1,500 men; after these two encounters with the rebels on the road to Bennington, Burgoyne reported his losses as 1,220 killed, wounded or captured.[16] The rebel attacking force led by John Stark and Seth Warner numbered nearly 2,500 men, and their casualties were scarcely 30 killed and 50 wounded.[17]

An oft-repeated myth about the affair near Bennington maintains that Colonel Baum had no means of communication with the provincials, nor with the rebels. Serving in Justus Sherwood's company were several men whose mother tongue was German. If Peters wanted to talk with Baum, or the German officer needed a parlay with the rebels, they had no shortage of interpreters.[18]

The survivors straggled back to Burgoyne's army, now at Fort Miller, 35 miles from Bennington. There, on August 20, Peters found trouble brewing in the ranks of Sherwood's company. Lieutenant Edward Carscallan, Ensign John Wilson, and 23 men were asking for permission to transfer out of the Queen's Loyal Rangers and serve under Captain Samuel McKay, who had added Francis Pfister's men to his own command. If these dissidents departed Sherwood would be left with only 19 men on his muster roll, of which four were prisoners of war, and one had deserted, while one was in public employ.

Peters gave the dissidents the choice of serving with him or going to the guardhouse in the fort. To Sherwood's dismay all chose the latter, and were led away to be locked up.

Burgoyne found the imprisoned men adamant, and he ordered them sent to Samuel McKay as the most expedient way of returning them to duty. With rations short, he could not afford to leave men confined, drawing food when they were not doing any work. Burgoyne allowed Sherwood his full pay, because he was aware of the man's bravery and devotion to the cause. In his *State of the Expedi-*

218

First Battle of Freeman's Farm September 19 1777

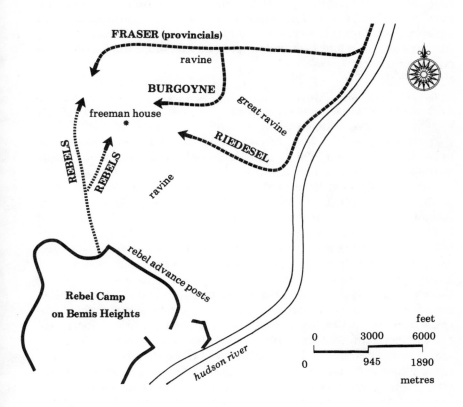

FRASER (provincials)

ravine

BURGOYNE

great ravine

freeman house
*

RIEDESEL

REBELS

REBELS

ravine

rebel advance posts

Rebel Camp
on Bemis Heights

hudson river

feet

0	3000	6000
0	945	1890

metres

tion from Canada, the general observed: 'Capt. Sherwood was forward in every service of danger to the end of the campaign.'

In the meantime reports on the defeat near Bennington had reached Montreal. Allan Maclean paid a visit to Mrs. Peters to prepare her for bad news. He broached the matter by warning her that casualties had been heavy, then admitted hearing rumours that her husband and son had been wounded, and had since died. John's account continues:

> Mrs. Peters said 'My calamities are very great, but thank God they died doing their duty to their King and country. I have six sons left who as soon as they shall be able to bear arms, I will send against the rebels while I and my daughter will mourn for the dead and pray for the living.'

Fortunately, Maclean was misinformed. True to her pledge, three of Ann Peters' boys served before the end of hostilities. Andrew, the second son, was a midshipman of Lake Champlain, while Samuel, the third, became a volunteer.

At the Battle of Freeman's Farm on September 19, when Burgoyne chose 3,000 troops to attack the rebels, some Queen's Loyal Rangers were with General Fraser's force that was on the right flank, while Burgoyne was in the centre and von Riedesel on the left. Fraser led his men up to the high ground away from the Hudson, skirted a deep ravine, and called a halt south and west of Burgoyne. Below they heard shots and some puffs of smoke rose above the trees. The right wing advanced aimlessly, looking for the enemy's flank. Then Fraser received orders to reinforce Burgoyne's centre, where casualties had been heavy. General Horatio Gates's rebels advanced into the clearing. Cannon boomed, spewing out grape and cannister shot, muskets popped, and the entire battlefield vanished beneath a blanket of blue smoke. When it cleared, the rebels were running towards the trees at the far side of Freeman's field.

Darkness fell, and the British army lay on the field through the night, the men clutching their arms. At dawn, when the rebels did not return, Burgoyne declared a victory. In the battle, rebel losses were 65 killed, some 200 wounded, while Burgoyne lost 600 killed, wounded or captured; 57 Queen's Royal Rangers were among the dead.[19]

On October 1, Colonel Peters took stock of his situation, in a report entitled 'A State of the Queen's Loyal Rangers at 1777 Sundry Times':

```
Augt. 10 — 1 Lt Col. 1 Majr. 4 Captains 2 Liets 2 Ensigns &
           Rank & File, Non Commissioned Officers & Privates — 311

       15 — Killed and Missing in the Defeat at Bennington ——— 111
            Remained                                            200

       16 — Mr French joined with 3 officers ———————————————     94
            Total                                               294
```

Second Battle of Freeman's Farm (Battle of Bemis Heights)

October 7 1777

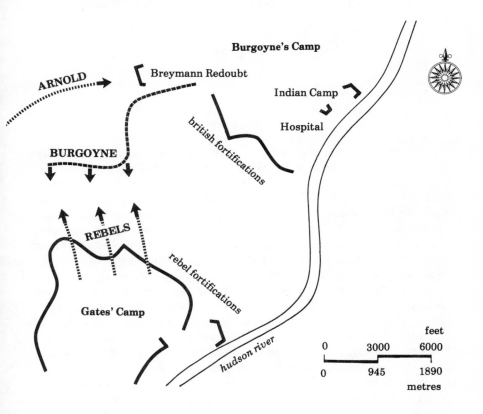

Burgoyne's Camp

Breymann Redoubt

ARNOLD

Indian Camp

british fortifications

Hospital

BURGOYNE

REBELS

rebel fortifications

Gates' Camp

hudson river

		feet
0	3000	6000
0	945	1890
		metres

```
22 Sent to McKay's Corps and other Imployment ──────── 122
                                                        ───
                                                        172

   Discharged at Several Times by the Board of
   Regulations between the 22 of Augt and 1 of Oct ──  24

   Deserted ─────────────────────────────────────────   2

   Deceased ─────────────────────────────────────────   4
                                                        ──
                                                        30

   Effective Oct. 1 ───────────────────────────────── 142
   Missing Since the Defeat at Stillwater ──────────    80
                                                        ──
                                                        62

   Joined since ─────────────────────────────────────   3
                                                        ──
                                                        65

   (indecipherable signature)

   John Peters Lt. Cole⟨20⟩
```

By Stillwater Peters must have meant Freeman's Farm, which was not far from the village. While Burgoyne had declared a victory, Peters knew the score. On October 7, Gentleman Johnny undertook a large reconnaissance of the rebel position. With 1,500 men and two 12-pounder guns, he advanced on the rebel camp at Bemis Heights, less than four miles away from his own camp. General Fraser, with companies of light infantry and most of the surviving provincials moved by secret paths through the woods behind the rebel position, hoping to engage them from the rear and prevent too much strength being hurled against Burgoyne in command in the centre. Fraser's men never reached the rear of the rebel encampment. The enemy broke through Burgoyne's line, and the men of the 24th Regiment – Fraser's own – were keeping a path open for their commanding officer and the men with him to reach the safety of the British camp. In the headlong dash General Fraser was mortally wounded in the stomach, held on his horse by his friends.

Towards dusk the rebels, led by Benedict Arnold and Daniel Morgan, overwhelmed a redoubt northwest of the British camp that was held by von Breymann's Germans and some provincials. The Battle of Bemis Heights – sometimes called the Second Battle of Freeman's Farm, or the Second Battle of Saratoga – was over. With the loss of von Breymann's redoubt, Burgoyne's position had become untenable. On the morning of October 8, his vanguard began the retreat towards Ticonderoga. The more severely wounded men were left behind, and at the village of Saratoga the ragged army halted. By October 14, Peters knew that surrender was imminent and he feared for the safety of his remaining Queen's Loyal Rangers.

News of the fate of the loyalists captured at Bennington had filtered through to the rest of Burgoyne's army. One dying provincial whose eye had been hit by a musket ball was thrown over a horse that had a similar eye injury and paraded before the guffawing rebels. Others were tied in pairs to the traces of horses, and to add to the insult the horses were ridden by black slaves. Still others were sent to tramp down roads where snow had made them impassable, whether they possessed shoes or not.[21] Peters approached General Phillips, the second-in-command, and informed him that although Burgoyne had ordered loyalists to escape and make for Canada, he would not leave without written permission. Should Peters or any of his men do so they might be branded deserters by British officers they would encounter later. Phillips nodded his agreement, entered Burgoyne's tent, and emerged with the desired paper. Soon afterward Peters set out with 34 men, among them John Jr. and Major Zadock Wright. They walked in single file and with considerable bravado bluffed the rebels:

When we had travelled two or three miles from the Royal camp we were challenged by a party of rebels, I replied 'from General Gates, and we're in pursuit of some Tories who have fled from Burgoyne's Camp.' The rebels demanded the countersign, and who commanded. The answer was Colonel Peters and eighteen hundred men, and they might fire as soon as they pleased was the countersign; The darkness and the surprise caused the rebels to take prudent care of themselves that night but next morning they pursued us with about one hundred men whom we saw at a distance from a hill but whether they saw us I cannot say.

Later on, a loyalist with a canoe ferried the party across the Hudson River above Fort Edward, and helped Peters obtain provisions – bear meat and dried moose, and Indian corn. Peters soon found that he had been wise in demanding written permission before leaving Burgoyne's army for on the 19th of October:

Near sunset when we were almost famished, we struck Lake George where Major Irwin of the 47th commanded. He received us very uncivilly till I produced my written order. He then treated us with great kindness and Humanity, giving us food and ordered boats to carry us to Diamond Island, about five miles, where Major Aubery, of the 47th, commanded, and had done good service. He treated us with all possible kindness, and as I was in a fever and ague, with which I quitted the camp, and much fatigued, he was so good as to make me sleep in his bed, while he went somewhere else for the night. Next day he gave us boats which carried us across the lake, from whence we marched to Ticonderoga, where we remained under the command of General Powel till the fort was evacuated when we returned to Montreal.

When Burgoyne surrendered on October 17, the only Queen's Loyal Rangers captured with him were Captain Justus Sherwood, wounded in one of the last encounters with the rebels, and 10 privates. Safe with Peters were 5 captains, 4 lieutenants, 3 ensigns, 1 adjutant, 1 quartermaster, 1 surgeon's mate, 9 sergeants and 53 rank and file.[21] Major Wright's name was not on the record, which was compiled in May, 1778, for by that time he had been captured while scouting in rebel territory. During Burgoyne's disastrous attempt to penetrate New York State, some 500 Queen's Loyal Rangers lost their lives, or were prisoners of the rebels. The stragglers who reached safety that autumn amounted to scarcely 80 eligible for duty, and 11 on parole.

Years in Limbo

The Queen's Loyal Rangers that had escaped from Saratoga were eligible for military duties, and only the 11 on parole were not permitted any service. After accompanying Brigadier Powell from Fort Ticonderoga to Fort St. Johns, where Powell became the commandant, now that Brigadier William Phillips was a prisoner in rebel hands, Colonel John Peters and his men continued on to Montreal. Soon afterward the colonel made his way to Quebec City,

> where General Carleton received me with approbation, but could not pay me till he had official accounts from Gen. Burgoyne. Hitherto I had received no pay from the King for my services. Gen. Carleton had put me on the subsistence list at 30 pounds per muster, and had behaved with great attention and humanity to my family.

The officers and men of the Queen's Loyal Rangers were posted to Fort St. Johns for the winter, although with all the other below-strength corps that had been with Burgoyne, Carleton had placed them under the command of Sir John Johnson. As the spring of 1778 approached, some of the men were sent on scouting missions along Lake Champlain, and into the Green Mountains area as far as the Connecticut Valley. They gathered intelligence on rebel activities and brought in a few recruits to fill the badly depleted ranks. On June 1, the governor ordered all troops bound by the Saratoga Convention to return to duty, as the rebels had broken the surrender terms.

In June Peters journeyed to Quebec City to be introduced to the new governor, General Frederick Haldimand. In the course of their meeting Haldimand ordered Peters to lead a party of

> 200 white men and 100 Indians, and to march to Cohos, on the Connecticut River, and to destroy the settlement there. Having arrived at Lake Champlain on my way to Cohos General Haldimand's letter overtook me, which gave leave to all my party to return that chose to go, but permitted me to pay a visit to Onion River. He also directed me to leave my orders. We all went on by water one day, which some got discouraged and returned with all the Indians, and all the white men except thirty-four, with whom I proceeded to the head of Onion River; and following it down we destroyed the Block-house and all the buildings on it for about thirty miles, as I was ordered, after which I returned with my thirty-four men to St. Johns the 23rd of August, 1778.

Peters did not explain why Haldimand changed his mind over the mission to Cohos, but he may have feared the loss of the entire force if he let the expedition continue deep into rebel territory.

In September, Peters received orders to march his corps to Sorel, where the governor had decided to establish a base for all his
provincial troops except Butler's Rangers. Haldimand ordered the
Queen's Loyal Rangers and other below-strength corps to remain at
Sorel, working on fortifications for the winter. On November 12,
John Peters joined Robert Leake, and Ebenezer and Edward Jessup,
in petitioning Haldimand to have their small corps formed into a
second battalion of Sir John Johnson's regiment, but Haldimand refused.

As the season progressed, Peters asked Haldimand to pay him
for his services under General Burgoyne in 1777, but according to
Peters, the governor informed him 'that the matter had been trans-
acted before he took command, and he could do nothing in it till he
should have official returns; but he continued me on the subsistence
list, where Gen. Carleton had placed me.'

One subsistence list is dated July 19, 1779, which authorized a
payment of £1,634. 8s. 10d. sterling to cover the period from June
25 to August 24, 1779, the money to be divided among the various
small units.[22]

Peters' personal share was £30. Carleton had permitted 9s. per
day for the support of himself and his family and for work assigned
to him while directing his men at building fortifications and other
tasks.[23] The above-mentioned return showed that Peters had 61
men, and his share was £299. 7s. 8d. for them as well as the £30 for
himself. Captains Francis Hogel and Justus Sherwood were also allowed £30. which confirms Peters' later observations that he was
never recompensed with a lieutenant-colonel's pay for the time
when he carried the full responsibility for his regiment. At the time
this return was made, Major Zadock Wright was still a prisoner of
the rebels.

Haldimand placed great confidence in Justus Sherwood, and
soon after the governor arrived he gave him responsibilities that
caused tension between the junior officer and Colonel Peters. As
senior captain, Sherwood should have assumed Major Wright's
duties, but he was of little use to the Queen's Loyal Rangers because Haldimand kept him at Fort St. Johns, interrogating prisoners and refugees and helping organize parties of scouts going into
the northern states in quest of intelligence. While Peters' star was
falling Sherwood's was rising. The captain was displaying competence but Peters continued complaining that he had not been paid
what he deserved, and he had gone over the governor's head. He
wrote to his uncle, the Reverend Samuel Peters, who was still in

London,
> . . .who applied to Lord George Germain on my behalf, and his lordship wrote to Gen. Haldimand to settle my accounts and others in a like situation. Gen. Haldimand seemed to be offended, and accused me of complaining home against him, which, in truth, I had not done. . . . He appointed a Board of officers to examine my claims, but ordered the Commissioners not to allow pay for any men that were killed or taken in the year 1777, or lot and forage, or any money advanced by me or my officers to the men in the campaign of 1777 who had not returned to Canada. The Commissioners obeyed his orders, although I produced Gen. Burgoyne's General Orders, given out at Battenkill, August 20th, 1777, that all Provincial Troops should be paid the same as the British troops. By this injustice I lost what was due me on British pay from the 1st of August to the 24th of December, 1783, when we were disbanded.

Exactly what Peters hoped to achieve is not clear, unless he thought he should have been paid as a lieutenant-colonel until the end of hostilities. Such a demand would have been unreasonable, but he did deserve the pay of a battalion commander for his services while with Burgoyne. The records indicate that his captains got their full pay, but these do not show that Peters ever drew the pay of a lieutenant-colonel.

The Board of Officers met several times, and on February 19, 1781, writing to Haldimand's secretary, Robert Mathews, Justus Sherwood added this postscript: 'I understand that I have lost some men that I claimed in Rogers' Corps by not being there to support my claim, or rather to state it, as it seems Col. Peters has left them out of his List.' Peters may have overlooked Sherwood's men out of spite, because his inferior officer was fully occupied with prisoners and refugees, and gradually assuming the running of Haldimand's secret service.

Sherwood was at Fort St. Johns by order of Colonel Peters, to give evidence before the Board of Officers against Captain Jeremiah French and his brother Lieutenant Gershom. Peters charged the two officers with selling to civilians flour they had drawn from the commissariat for their men. Sherwood had witnessed one such transaction, and the French brothers were relieved of their duties. Later; Jeremiah received a lieutenant's commission in the second battalion, King's Royal Regiment of New York. Gershom became a lieutenant in the Loyal Rangers when that corps was formed.

By the autumn of 1780 Haldimand had established real incentives for bringing the small units to strength. All Regiments completed to ten companies, each of 56 rank and file, and three 'Contingent Men' would have their Officers' commissions made permanent. These inducements were sorely needed, for a list of the below-strength corps made that August showed that Peters had 4 sergeants, 4 corporals and 46 men, as well as an unspecified number of temporary commissioned officers.[24] Captain Jeremiah French, captured during the Battle of Bennington, had been returned to duty through a prisoner exchange arranged by Captain Sherwood some time in 1779.[25]

On December 5, 1780, Haldimand issued orders that the several corps of loyalists would be regarded as one regiment, under Major John Nairne of the Royal Highland Emigrants. The arrangement was to be temporary until the officers could complete their battalions.

A muster roll dated July 14, 1781, at Verchères, shows how the few men Peters had were employed at various posts. Including himself, the colonel listed 11 officers, but one, Lieutenant Philo Hurlburt, had detached himself and was recruiting for the King's Royal Regiment of New York. Major Zadock Wright was still a prisoner of the rebels; Captain Justus Sherwood was on command – running the secret service and building his Loyal Blockhouse on North Hero Island in Lake Champlain. Lieutenant James Parrot was with Sherwood, while Lieutenant Gershom French was with the Engineering Department. Of 6 sergeants, 3 were with Sherwood, 2 with the Engineers, 1 on loan. Of 6 corporals, 2 were with the Engineers, 3 with Sherwood, and 1 was on duty at Verchères with Peters. The only drummer Elisha Mallory, was also at the Loyal Blockhouse. Of 7 volunteers – recruiting agents hoping to qualify for commissions – 3 were with Sherwood, 2 were at Verchères, 1 was on his way from Quebec City, and the last, the colonel's second son Andrew, was serving with the fleet on Lake Champlain.

Of 83 private men, 27 were with the Engineering Department, 18 were with Sherwood, 12 were on duty at a blockhouse at Yamaska, 4 had been discharged, 7 were seamen on the lakes, 2 were working in the King's woods, 2 were on duty at Carleton Island, and 2 were prisoners of the rebels. Of the remaining 9 men, 1 was on leave, 1 sick in quarters, 1 sick in hospital, 1 in Quebec City by order of Governor Haldimand, 1 was on the way back from the same place, 1 had transferred to Rogers's corps, and 1 had joined Robert Leake's independent company, while the last 2 were at Verchères.[26]

As the year 1781 was drawing to a close, Governor Haldimand amalgamated the King's Loyal Americans and Queen's Loyal Rangers to form a new regiment, the Loyal Rangers. The other below-strength units – Leake's that then included Adams', and the men commanded by Samuel McKay, who had died, were all absorbed into the second battalion, King's Royal Regiment of New York. On November 12, when Haldimand issued his instruction for the establishment of the Loyal Rangers, he named Edward Jessup as the major-commandant of the new corps.[27] Ebenezer Jessup, the provincial lieutenant-colonel of the King's Loyal Americans, was made a captain in command of a company of pensioners. The item pertaining to John Peters reads:

Invalids Lieut.-Col. Peters as Captain Nov. 17
Gerhsom French as Lieutenant Dec. 1
Thomas Sherwood as Ensign Nov. 25

Haldimand had dealt Peters a shattering blow. The invalids were those who had retired because of illness or injury, commissioned officers excepted, for both Gershom French and Thomas Sherwood were in the best of health. For Peters, Haldimand's demotion was the last straw:

This cruel degrading change was worked while I was at Skenesborough, where I had been sent by Gen. Haldimand with a flag and rebel prisoners, with a view to gain intelligence from the Southern Army, which I performed and reported to him.

This statement is suspect. Peters may have been romancing, for Sherwood was in charge of prisoner exchanges and gathering intelligence through Skenesborough. The records show other officers acting in Sherwood's stead, and other post commanders sending Haldimand intelligence, but no mention was ever made to indicate John Peters in these roles. His own account continues:

On my return to Quebec I complained to the General of the hard measures he had dealt out to me by degrading me below those who had been under my command in 1777; nor did I understand why I was invalided. Mr. Mathews, a secretary to Gen. Haldimand, gave me for answer I had a wife and eight children and I might starve if refused captain's pay; besides I should not be allowed rations if I refused. My subsistence money being stopped, I was obliged to accept the pay of a captain till Dec. 24th, 1783, or perish with my family.

The subsistence money was ended because Haldimand had dispensed with his temporary list when he placed all the men on it into permanent regiments. For most of them this was a blessing, but Peters had more to say about some of the officers assigned to the Loyal Rangers.

My son John, the oldest ensign in the Queen's Loyal Rangers, was neglected by Gen. Haldimand when he drafted the Provincial corps in Canada, and a son of Major Jessup's quite a boy, who had never done any service, was appointed lieutenant over my son and all the ensigns who had served during the war.

Again Peters was not painting an accurate picture. By the oldest ensign in the Queen's Loyal Rangers he meant that John Jr. had been the first ensign appointed, for all the other ensigns selected in 1777 were mature men and his son was 15 years old at most. Edward Jessup Jr. was shown as a lieutenant on a later list of officers, which states that he served six and one half years.[28] This length of service may have been exaggerated, for Edward Jessup Jr. was 15 years old when the Loyal Rangers was established. Several of the other ensigns may have been disgruntled over his appointment as a lieutenant. Thomas Sherwood, for example, was 36 years old when he became Peters' ensign for the company of invalids.

Peters, who had been an effective lieutenant-colonel during Burgoyne's campaign, was an embittered man, ready to make mischief after the Loyal Rangers was disbanded. The subjugation of the Queen's Loyal Rangers and the humiliation of their commanding officer was a sad conclusion to the history of a corps that began with some promise in the early days of the campaign of 1777. The regiment was sacrificed on the Bennington battlefield, and never recovered from that blow. Had Haldimand felt able to embark on a more positive recruiting policy the Queen's Loyal Rangers might have become, if not a full battalion, certainly a more substantial corps. Instead Haldimand felt helpless as the numbers dwindled to a pitiful handful before his provisions were increased and he changed his approach late in 1780.

John Peters was not entirely ethical in some of his dealings with Haldimand, but he had suffered a great deal on Burgoyne's campaign and subsequent to it, with his family in exile, and the subsistence of 9s. per day hardly adequate for people accustomed to the comforts he had been able to provide before the war disrupted their lives. Haldimand's action in giving Peters the command of invalids, virtually placing him in retirement seems unjustified.

Chapter 9: The Loyal Rangers

By the time the Loyal Rangers was formed in November 1781, rumours reaching Quebec City hinted that the British expeditionary force in the southern states might be in trouble. Cornwallis had surrendered his army at Yorktown on October 19, nearly a month before Haldimand authorized the establishment of the Loyal Rangers, but the reports were not confirmed until the end of the year. Haldimand's motive for tidying up his below-strength corps at that time was twofold. First, if Cornwallis were to fail, the governor wanted to have his provincial troops organized more effectively in case George Washington decided to turn his victorious Continental Army and his French allies towards Canada. Second, if Haldimand had a proliferation of small units in his records, his returns for the Northern Department would compare unfavourably with those of the Central and Southern Departments. Once the corps of Loyal Rangers was completed to ten companies the governor would have four full-strength provincial corps to his credit.

A time of uncertainty followed the confirmation of Cornwallis's surrender at Yorktown. In the meantime, Governor Haldimand looked to Canada's defences. The Loyal Rangers spent their time on fatigue or garrison duty, guarding border access points, and assisting refugees who arrived in search of protection. Loyal Rangers were on duty at the two blockhouses on the Yamaska River, at Rivière du Chene, Isle aux Noix, and the Loyal Blockhouse on North Hero Island in Lake Champlain.

Pay rates for officers are rarely spelled out in records, but a subsistence return dated October 25, 1783, to December 24, 1783, for the Loyal Rangers and signed by Major Edward Jessup yields this information:

Major	15s.	per day	
Captain	9s.	" "	
Lieutenant	4s:8d.	" "	
Ensign	3s:8d.	" "	
Adjutant	4s.	" "	
Quartermaster	4s:8d	" "	
Surgeon	4s.	" "	
Mate	3s:8d.	" "	①

Thus the rates permitted this corps by Governor Haldimand were lower than the wages allowed during Burgoyne's campaign, when captains received 10s. per day. The currency was not specified, and unless this schedule was in sterling and Burgoyne's rates in

Halifax or New York currency, Haldimand was indulging in his usual economy, guarding the public purse. From the same motives he had decided that the Loyal Rangers did not require a lieutenant-colonel. Major Edward Jessup would continue holding his former rank.

On January 2, 1782, Jessup wrote to Haldimand requesting that his men be uniformed in green coats with red facings. The governor approved, for he had decided that all provincial corps in the Northern Department whose names did not include Royal should be so garbed, the officers' lace and accoutrements of silver.

During the winter some of the Loyal Rangers were posted to Verchères, and as spring approached, the regiment consisted of eight companies – seven battalion companies and one company of artificers.[2]

Recruiting for the companies needed to complete the battalion was going well. On May 17, Jessup wrote to Haldimand's secretary, now Major Mathews, that he had 66 men more than were needed to complete his existing companies, and asked that one be formed taking in Captain John Walden Meyer's independent company, which had only 19 men. Jessup recommended John Ruiter as the lieutenant and Hermanus Best as the ensign. Haldimand approved, and put his instructions to Jessup in a militia order dated May 30, 1782. Meyers' commission, which was typical, reads:

To John Walter Meyers Esq.

By virtue of the power and authority in me vested I do hereby constitute and appoint you to be captain in the corps of Loyal Rangers whereof Edward Jessup Esq., is Major-Commandant. You are therefore carefully and diligently to discharge the duty of captain by exercising and well disciplining both the inferior officers and soldiers of the corps, and I hereby command them to obey you as their captain, and you are to observe and follow such orders and directions as you shall from time to time receive from me, your Major Commandant, or any other of your superior officers, according to the rules and disciplines of war, in pursuance of the trust hereby reposed in you.

Given under my Hand and Seal at Arms, at the Castle of St. Lewis at Quebec this thirtieth day of May, one thousand seven hundred and eighty-two and in the twenty-second year of the Reign of our Sovereign Lord, George the Third, by the Grace of God, of Great Britain, France and Ireland, King.

Fred Haldimand.

By His Excellency's Command.

R. Mathews.[3]

Meyers' was the ninth company. On June 22, the officers of the tenth and final company were appointed. Lieutenant Thomas Fraser was the captain, James Robins the lieutenant, and William Lamson the Ensign. Then on October 4, Sergeant-Major John Ferguson, 29th Regiment, was appointed the quartermaster of the Loyal Rangers.[4] Two days later Major Jessup informed Mathews that the regiment had reached full strength. An undated list, but

Back view, provincials's uniform, showing cartridge case and plate with royal cypher. Also pictured are Canadian chasseurs, and canvas sacks for provisions.

one made not long afterward, shows 9 captains. The first company was the major's own, and after him were Captains Ebenezer Jessup, John Peters, Justus Sherwood, Jonathan Jones, William Fraser, John Jones, Peter Drummond, John Walden Meyers and Thomas Fraser. The adjutant was Mathew Thompson, a sergeant-major from the 31st Regiment, the quartermaster John Ferguson. Solomon Jones, a medical student from Albany, was the surgeon's mate, and Dr. George Smyth, Justus Sherwood's deputy in dealing with prisoners and refugees and the secret service, was the regimental surgeon. No chaplain was mentioned.[5]

The most complete muster roll for the corps was made on January 1, 1783, at Rivière du Chene, but enlistments were accepted afterward, and at least one officer was appointed.[6] Samuel, Captain Justus Sherwood's brother, was made a lieutenant, a rank to which he had aspired for many months.[7] Where Samuel Sherwood succeeded, John Walden Meyers' eldest son, George, failed. Writing to Governor Haldimand in April 1783, the captain requested permission for George, then 18, to recruit for an ensign's commission, to which Major Jessup had given his consent. Soon afterward Haldimand stopped all recruiting, because he had received the Preliminary Articles of Peace. George Meyers was unable to raise the required number of recruits to qualify for his commission.

Earlier, Major Edward Jessup and James Rogers had discussed amalgamating the Loyal Rangers and King's Rangers, and on January 2, 1783, Rogers informed Haldimand that the union would be acceptable to him. The governor disapproved; although he had decided to admit the King's Rangers to the Northern Department, he wanted to limit further enlistments to men who came into Canada voluntarily. Mathews explained to Edward Jessup that the privilege of recruiting had been so abused that the governor did not want agents going into the revolted colonies.

Late in the summer of 1782, Jessup was in command of a haying foray along Lake Champlain to feed the army's livestock at Fort St. Johns, Isle aux Noix, Pointe au Fer, the Loyal Blockhouse, and other posts. Jessup was to receive 20s. per ton, and his Loyal Rangers were protected by 50 riflemen. On July 18, his party was at the Loyal Blockhouse, and by August 7, near Crown Point. Jessup reported that they were making good progress, but finding the grass thin – an indication that the summer had been dry.

At that time Baron von Riedesel, the commander of the German troops in Canada, expressed concern for the safety of Jessup's men. The baron had been taken prisoner at Saratoga when Burgoyne surrendered, and after a period in various prison camps, followed by some months at New York City as a prisoner of war on parole, he had been exchanged and returned to duty. Now he was in command of the Sorel military district, with authority over several outposts. Von Riedesel ordered Commodore Chambers of the Provincial Marine on Lake Champlain to send an armed vessel to keep watch over Jessup's party.

From Crown Point, Edward Jessup sent out a party of scouts to observe enemy activities around Saratoga, and at Castleton, Vermont, for rumours circulated that a large rebel force was in the neighbourhood.[8] By August 30, Jessup and his men, who found these rumours false, had reached Pointe au Fer, and the major sent a report on his mission to von Riedesel before he retired to Verchères for the winter.

That autumn, desertion had been a problem with the garrison at the two blockhouses along the Yamaska River, where detachments of Loyal Rangers were stationed. Men sent out on scouting missions were inclined not to return, and a portion of a letter to von Riedesel, dated December 19, 1782, suggested that if some Indians were kept in the woods nearby with instructions to bring in deserters' scalps, the men would be more conscientious in their duties. The letter has no signature, but the proposal sounds very like others made by Barry St. Leger, at that time in command of the district of Montreal.

On January 12, 1783, von Riedesel informed Haldimand that he had discovered artificers of Jessup's corps employed by the Engineers cutting timber along Lake Champlain, who had no arms or accountrements, and he asked that they should not be sent out unprotected. Then on February 26, an order sent out from headquarters in Quebec City stated that Major Rogers' men and Captain Meyers' company of the Loyal Rangers should be issued with black carbines. All others in the Loyal Rangers were to receive the carbines if they had no better weapons. At that time Meyers' company was at Fort St. Johns, and the rest of the corps was on duty at the various posts under von Riedesel's command.

Governor Haldimand realized there were tasks which provincials could perform more satisfactorily than regulars, for in February he ordered some of Major Jessup's best woodsmen to escort a party of British troops into the woods. The Loyalists were to instruct them in the methods of 'hutting' and living in the forests so that they would be less helpless on wilderness campaigns.

Over the years, the King's Loyal Americans, and later the Loyal Rangers, did a lot of work for the Engineering Department. From London on March 23, 1782, Captain William Twiss, who had been 'Commanding Engineer in Canada between 1777 & 1783' wrote a certificate for Major Jessup stating that his men:

> . . .ware of infinite service in constructing the several posts erected for the defence of the Province and ware more particularly usefull in providing Timber for the new works at Quebec and that the men of this corps did their duty with great cheerfulness from the zeal which Major Jessup and his brother Lt. Col. Jessup and Captain Jessup always shewed to forward the King's service upon all ocations.[9]

Such praise was gratifying, and revealed that most of the soldiers who served under the Jessups were frontiersmen who had pioneered in the forests, gaining experience in the art of survival there, and in clearing land to develop their farms. Men of such stock were to have little difficulty adjusting to life in the Canadian wilderness when the time came.

On April 27, 1783, the *Quebec Gazette* published the Proclamation on the Cessation of Hostilities, but the troops continued their garrison duties. Then on August 1, a list showed that 132 Loyal Rangers were at Isle aux Noix, where Major John Nairne was the commandant. Another 46 were at the Loyal Blockhouse, where Ensign John Dusenbury was temporarily in command. Captain Sherwood was about to undertake a journey of exploration for Governor Haldimand, to see whether loyalists could be resettled around Gaspé Bay and along the east coast. Lieutenant John Dulmage, normally in charge of Sherwood's garrison, must have been ill or called away by family matters. Captain William Fraser was at the upper Yamaska blockhouse with 30 Loyal Rangers, which accounts for 208 of the rank and file.[10] The others were on leave, or doing duty at Verchères, their main base.

During the course of the summer, Major Jessup enlisted a few German soldiers whose regiments had been disbanded in Canada, and who had no desire to return to their own country. Haldimand did not approve, for on July 7 Major Richard B. Lernoult, the adjutant-general, wrote to Jessup ordering him to cease recruiting discharged Germans until further notice. Even though the peace treaty had not yet been signed, the war was over, and Jessup, whose regiment was at full strength, had no further need of recruits. Conversely, while some Germans were willing to enlist in the Loyal Rangers, many of Jessup's men stationed at Isle aux Noix were asking to be discharged from the service. Jessup visited them and informed them that their demands were premature.

In November, Haldimand received orders from the British government to disband all his provincial troops by the end of the year. Although these instructions arrived too late to be implemented for the men at the upper posts, Haldimand resolved to execute them for the provincials at his lower posts. On December 25, Brigadier St. Leger wrote from Montreal: 'I disbanded the Royal Reg't of New York yesterday . . . Major Jessup has received the same Order for disbanding and for regulating the Men's Conduct during the Winter.'

Jessup was to settle his accounts without delay, and all provincials were to surrender their arms and ammunition, but those who settled on lands the governor had chosen for them would have their weapons returned. The disbanded men were to be removed from the outposts and billeted 'in the country' as long as none had smallpox or other dangerous diseases. On December 24, Ensign Thomas Sherwood marched a detachment of Loyal Rangers from the Loyal Blockhouse to Fort St. Johns, and a detachment of regulars replaced the provincials at that outpost.[11] About the same time Captain William Fraser evacuated the upper blockhouse at Yamaska and brought his garrison of Loyal Rangers to Verchères, where they spent the winter.

When the regiment was disbanded, the number of people attached to it was 1,289. These were described as 3 field officers, 7 captains, 24 subalterns, 60 non-commissioned officers, 449 privates and drummers, 56 gentlemen on pensions, and 690 women and children. Their numbers also included 20 black slaves who were not put on any list.[12] The corps appeared to be short by some 100 rank and file, but many of these may have been in Montreal, or in the United States bringing out their dependants, for the regiment was considered to be at full strength.[13] The officers received their half pay, which implied that the corps met Haldimand's stipulations for ten full companies.[14]

Chapter 10: The King's Rangers

The King's Rangers, raised commencing in 1779, never amounted to much, and for nearly four years it was not part of the Northern Department. Sad to relate, its history destroys the image of the once great commander, Robert Rogers, the folk hero of the Seven Years' War in the forests of the northern colonies. Some who served in its ranks and certain of the officers were men of good character and conscientious, but this small unit harboured more than its fair share of scamps and ne'er-do-wells. As went the commander, so followed too many troops. By the time the regiment was being recruited, Robert Rogers was addicted to alcohol, and probably senile as well – an embarrassment to his elder brother James, and a laughing stock in three military departments. The King's Rangers make an unfitting ending to what had hitherto been a very distinguished career, followed by misfortunes not entirely of Robert's making.

As the leader of all the rangers in the Seven Years' War, Robert Rogers perfected techniques similar to the tactics used by commandos in World War Two. While training his men, Robert prepared some officers for the parts they played during the American Revolution. Notable were Moses Hazen, John Stark and James Rogers, all of whom were captains in Robert Rogers' corps of rangers.

Robert and James Rogers.

Too much is known about Robert Rogers' later years, too little about the life of his brother James. Robert stood on the pinnacle of success at the close of the Seven Years' War, and the rest of his life was a series of disasters. James, the elder, steadier brother, seems to have led an exemplary life by the standards of the day, and to have coped effectively with civilian life in times of peace.

The most reliable date for Robert's birth is November 7, 1731, the place, Methuen, Massachusetts.[1] One reference gives James' date of birth in Ireland, tentatively, as 1726, making him five years Robert's senior.[2] The parents of these brothers, James and Mary Rogers, were of Scottish descent and had emigrated from Ireland some time before Robert's birth. Another son, Richard, was born in 1733, nearly three years after Robert. The Rogers family moved to Merrymack County, New Hampshire, about the year of 1746. Robert and James grew up able to roam the wilderness, learning how to survive at any time of year, making themselves familiar with the vast territory that lay between the British and French frontier set-

*Line engraving of Robert Rogers, dated October 1, 1776, in the
uniform he wore during the Seven Years' War.
Courtesy: Metropolitan Toronto Library.*

tlements.[3]

A print thought to be Robert Rogers, dated 1776, but probably from an earlier painting, implies a rugged countenance, a shade pugnacious, sturdy rather than handsome, with a glint in the eye that says here is a man who will not step aside for any living being. The print captures the essence of the man, who was first and foremost, very strong, able to endure incredible hardship, every inch a leader in battle. He had the right education for the most significant role he played. He wrote well, apparently knew some French, and had acquired several Indian languages by the time he came of age. His other asset was the insatiable urge to explore that led to an intimate knowledge of the area on both sides of Lake Champlain. This was the territory where he operated most often during the Seven Years' War.

In his history of Rogers' Rangers, H.M. Jackson concluded that Robert generally treated his men as equals, and had no difficulty maintaining discipline. A different image emerges from the pages of a narrative by Stephen Jarvis, who wanted to transfer from his regiment to the Queen's Rangers in 1777. At the time Robert was raising this corps on Long Island, and Stephen's cousins, Munson and William Jarvis, had joined him. Robert raised the Queen's Rangers before he received his warrant for the King's Rangers, and Stephen wrote:

I set off to apply to Mr. Jarvis to procure an exchange; when to my great surprise I saw the Lt. Col. of this Regt., who was mounted, attack the Sentinel, at his Marquee, and beat him most unmercifully with his cane, over the head and shoulders. After viewing this transaction I wheeled about; took my knapsack, and marched off with my Regt., without even taking leave of my relations.[4]

A personality change between the two wars might explain Robert's brutality. However, one War Office record paints an equally disconcerting portrait of brother James:

Mr. Simons was forbid doing duty as an Officer by Major McAlpin in 1779, the other officers of the corps having refused to do duty with him as he had in the most patient submissive and good natured manner received a decent cudgelling from Major Rogers.[5]

James' victim was Henry Simons, who later served as a lieutenant in the Loyal Rangers. Putting these pieces of evidence together, it is difficult to avoid concluding that both the Rogers brothers made casual use of severe correction. Stephen Jarvis' astonishment may have arisen because he was from Danbury, Connecticut, an old, more staid community. Rough and ready frontier style justice, or injustice, was new to Jarvis' experience in 1777.

By whatever means Robert Rogers commanded respect, he perfected hit and run tactics. He did not invent the concept of ranger companies operating with greater mobility than conventional infantry. These had been used earlier along the frontiers, but he evolved the techniques to a fine art, in part imitating the Indians' way of making war, in part using his imagination, improving his methods as he gained experience. The first record of Rogers in action was 1755, when Indians foraying from the French fortress at Crown Point, on Lake Champlain, were terrorizing the British frontier settlements.

Sir William Johnson was preparing to lead an expedition of Indians, New York and New England frontiersmen to march against the French position. Volunteers gathered in Albany, and Robert Rogers was there with a company of New Hampshiremen. They were employed scouting in advance of the main armed force and Rogers proved himself so valuable in that first encounter that in the spring of 1756, General William Shirley, then commander-in-chief of all British forces in the colonies, placed him at the head of a company of rangers. His brother Richard was his first lieutenant and John Stark was his second lieutenant. In July, a second company was formed with Richard Rogers as the captain.[6] Before the spring of 1757, there were seven companies, and others were added as time passed. Robert named his corps the Queen's Rangers, and detachments served in all the theatres of the war – Louisbourg, Quebec, and the final expedition from Oswego to the capture of Montreal in 1760. The companies were large, usually 100 men or more, and the corps became known far and wide as Rogers' Rangers.

James Rogers began his service as an ensign in Captain Thomas Speakman's Company of rangers.[7] In January of 1757, James and Robert were on an expedition that tangled with the French and their Indian allies on the shore of Lake Champlain, half way between the enemy occupied forts at Crown Point and Ticonderoga. The French ambushed the entire force in a small valley while the rangers were making their way in single file towards Lake George. The rangers traded fire with the French, during which Robert Rogers was shot in the wrist. Night fell, and he ordered a withdrawal under cover of darkness.

Late in March, while Robert was recovering from smallpox, four companies of rangers were ordered to Halifax to take part in a planned attack on Louisbourg. Three companies remained at Fort William Henry and Fort Edward. On July 23, while Robert was scouting towards Louisbourg, Richard died of smallpox at Fort William Henry and was buried there. A month later, taking advantage of the absence of the troops bound for Louisbourg, the French commander-in-chief, the Marquis de Montcalm, ordered an attack on the fort. It fell and immediately the Indians butchered 50 members of the garrison. Then they dug up the corpses in the cemetery and scalped them, including Richard Roger's.[8]

Following the disaster at Fort William Henry, the planned attack on Louisbourg was postponed, and Robert Rogers and three companies of Rangers returned to Albany. Robert sent agents to recruit in New Hampshire and Massachusetts, to fill his depleted ranks. At the same time he received 50 regular soldiers to be trained in his tactics.[9] In January, he was authorized to raise five more companies, of which four were to be sent to Louisbourg to accompany an expedition for another attempt to capture the French coastal stronghold. The instructions specified that each ranger company was to consist of 1 captain, 2 lieutenants, 1 ensign, 4 sergeants and 100 privates. Robert received a commission as major of rangers in His Majesty's Service, dated April 6, 1758.[10]

Robert's commission gave him the command of all the rangers – those about to leave for Louisbourg with his brother James, and the rangers who later accompanied General Wolfe to Quebec, as well as two companies of Indians. Louisbourg surrendered to Wolfe on July 26, 1758, and afterward the rangers were used in minor actions. Some were in the Saint John Valley, where Captain John McCurdy was killed, and the command of his company devolved on Moses Hazen, the man destined to lead his regiment of disenchanted Canadians in the service of the rebels during the American Revolution.

That summer of 1758, General Abercromby, the commander-in-chief, set out from Albany for Fort Ticonderoga with more than 15,000 men, including 600 rangers led by Robert Rogers. His men did the scouting and were the vanguard for the march to Ticonderoga. When Abercromby decided to withdraw after heavy losses, Rogers' Queen's Rangers covered the retreat.

The fall of Louisbourg marked the beginning of the end for France in Canada. On June 5, 1759, Wolfe left Louisbourg bound for Quebec, and with his expedition went four companies of rangers, with James Rogers as the senior captain. During the summer the rangers staged raids into the countryside to destroy villages, capture food and gather intelligence. After Quebec capitulated, Moses Hazen's company stayed behind as part of the British garrison, augmented by 25 men from the other three companies. James and the remainder sailed for Boston, and were discharged in November 1759. The officers remained on the pay roll, for General Amherst, the new commander-in-chief, knew he would need them soon. Meanwhile, the four companies of rangers under Robert Rogers were on duty along Lake Champlain.

241

The last task facing Amherst was the capture of Montreal. By the spring of 1760, he had decided on a three-pronged thrust, and accompanying each arm was a detachment of rangers. The city capitulated on September 8, and Robert Rogers received a new assignment before he could catch his breath. Taking 198 men, he embarked in whaleboats bound for Detroit and Michilimackinac to accept the surrender of the French garrisons at these and other outposts.

Apart from an encounter with Pontiac, the mission went smoothly. Small detachments of rangers were assigned to several frontier posts, and the main body wintered at Fort Niagara. In the spring, some marched to Albany and those wanting to leave the service were mustered out. Others volunteered for duty in the West Indies, where the war was not over.[11]

The two Rogers brothers then had time for their private lives. Robert used it to form Major Rogers and Associates (a land company from which he expected to make his fortune), and to take a wife. On June 30, 1761, he married Elizabeth Browne, the daughter of a New England minister.[12] He received a grant of land on the west side of Lake George in July – an acquisition that spelt trouble. The local Indians claimed that the land belonged to them, and Sir William Johnson, their Superintendent, agreed with them. He protested to the New York Legislature, and the governor's council, but the Indians' claim was disallowed, thus gaining for Rogers an unflagging dislike on the part of the powerful and influential Baronet of the Mohawk Valley.[13]

That same month, Robert took part in an expedition against the Cherokee Indians – a forewarning of events to come, as Pontiac sought to unite the tribes in the Ohio Valley against the British post commanders who had replaced the French, and the encroaching settlers. By May 1763, Pontiac and his warriors were laying siege to Detroit. Some rangers were in the garrison there, as well as at Niagara, and others had been captured or slaughtered at small outposts the Indians had taken. Alarmed for the safety of his men, Robert returned from the Cherokee country. Assisted by James, he gathered around him an expedition of 220 men, and in July, broke through a cordon of Indians surrounding Fort Detroit. Casualties were heavy, but enough of Robert's party reached the fort to reinforce it until 60 men arrived by schooner. These were sufficient to hold out until the Indians wearied of the game and withdrew.[14]

After Pontiac's war, the rangers were disbanded. Robert received a captaincy in the regulars, which assured him of 5s. per day in half pay.[15] Soon afterward he sailed for England, and in London found that he was the man of the hour. Word of his exploits and those of his rangers had preceded him, and he received considerable adulation. He took time from the social whirl to have his journals published. It has also been suggested that he had a hand in the creation of *Ponteach; or the Savages of America*, a verse drama on the Indian war. Robert also tried to find backers for an expedition to search for the Northwest Passage. He failed, but he did receive the command of Fort Michilimackinac, under strict orders that no funds were to be expended on travel or exploration. The government had expended too much on a costly war, and was trying to curb expenditures.[16]

The taboo on exploration was Rogers' undoing. Placing the ranger leader in the wilderness and expecting him to refrain from satisfying his curiosity was akin to putting meat before a starving dog in the expectation that he would ignore it. All unwitting, he played into the hands of Sir William Johnson.

In his dealings with Indians, Rogers was Sir William's subordinate, while as commandant of a fort he was also subordinate to General Thomas Gage, the commander-in-chief.[17] Neither superior was happy that Robert had been selected for Michilimackinac. Johnson sent Captain Benjamin Roberts to the fort as his agent to oversee the fur trade, an officer whose duties overlapped those of the commandant. In the summer of 1766, Rogers arrived at Michilimackinac, accompanied by his wife Elizabeth. Soon afterward he sent out expeditions to explore, on the assumption that profits from trade would more than cover the cost of these journeys.[18]

Rogers was disobeying orders, but he justified himself on the grounds that other Europeans would reach the Indians of the interior and cut off trade if Britain's servants did not push westward.[19] Meanwhile, Rogers had Roberts, Sir William's watchdog, arrested for locking rum in the store and refusing him the keys. In retaliation Roberts accused Rogers of being in communication with the French, intending to help them regain their lost empire.

Accusations flew back and forth, and finally in January 1768, Captain Frederick Spiesmacher, in command of two companies of the 60th Regiment on duty at the fort, received orders from General Gage to arrest Major Rogers on a charge of treason. Suspecting that Rogers was planning to escape, Spiesmacher clapped him in tight leg irons.[20] On June 6, Gage relayed instructions to have Rogers sent to Niagara, and on to Montreal. The journey was completed, but not without hazard. The Indians were on Rogers' side, and Spiesmacher had to send an armed escort with the brigade of boats conveying the prisoner.[21]

Governor Carleton ordered a court martial. Conducting his own defence, Rogers pointed out the stupidity of suggesting he was planning to escape. In dead of winter no man in his right mind would attempt such folly from Michilimackinac, set in the howling wilderness. He was acquitted on the charge of treason, but he lost the command of Michilimackinac.[22] As the summer of 1769 approached, Rogers shook the dust of Canada from his boots and sailed to England, leaving his family behind in New Hampshire.

Meanwhile, brother James had married Margaret, a daughter of the Reverend David McGregor of Londonderry, New Hampshire, and acquired a large tract of land in the New Hampshire Grants.[23] As land-hungry as most New Englanders, James was, nevertheless, living an obscure but respectable existence, as though compensating for the excesses of his flamboyant younger brother.

In London Robert was feted for a time, and demanding compensation for his services and suffering – a baronetcy and a pension of £600 per annum. When he ran out of money he was sent to the Fleet prison for debt. There he lay until October 1772, when James had settled his accounts. When rumblings of rebellion reached him in 1775 he sailed for home.

On arrival in North America he was beset by indecision over which side to join. As a British officer on half pay, he owed allegiance to the Crown, but as an American he was under pressure to take the oaths required by Congress, the Committee of Public Safety, and the state legislatures that supported independence. The rebels viewed him with dark suspicion, and in August 1776, after being arrested several times in the course of seeing his family in New Hampshire and brother James, Robert decided he had had enough. He headed for New York City to see Governor William Tryon, who sent him on to meet Sir William Howe, in command of an invasion force that had recently occupied Staten Island. On August 6, he received a commission as lieutenant-colonel commandant of a new battalion of rangers to be raised among loyalists in the neighbourhood.[24] The regiment was to be a reincarnation of Rogers' former corps with the same name, the Queen's Rangers. For loyalists around New York City the very sound of Rogers' name was magic. Recruits arrived, slipping past rebel patrols. Few realized they were joining a broken man with a mind clouded by alcohol who no longer faced reality.

The first recruits were New Yorkers, but at the end of August 1777, the regiment was brought to full strength when it absorbed the Queen's Loyal Virginia Regiment, which had come to New York City with Lord Dunmore, the governor of Virginia, who had fled for safety.[25]

Some American sources maintain that Robert mismanaged his corps, was careless over funds, and unscrupulous in his recruiting methods.[26] These allegations may be true, especially with respect to money, the sound management of which had never been one of Rogers' strong points. Equally well, he may have been disenchanted with the role assigned this second regiment of Queen's Rangers. Part of Sir William Howe's army for some months, the corps was on garrison duty in New York City, work that had scant appeal for a man of action like Robert Rogers. Lacking a taste for mundane employment, during the winter of 1776-77, he either relinquished or was relieved of his command and was superseded, first, by Major Christopher French, and later by Major James Wemyss, who led the corps at the Battle of Germantown in October 1777. Ultimately, the command passed to Captain John Graves Simcoe of the 40th Regiment, who received the provincial rank of major.[27]

Soon after Rogers lost the command of the Queen's Rangers, he set about finding the means of raising another regiment.

Robert's Machinations.

In October 1778, Robert Rogers paid a visit to Canada, and asked Governor Haldimand to allow him to raise 'a Corps of Royalists upon the Frontiers of this Province.' Haldimand declined, because recruiting for such a corps would interfere with completing provincial regiments for which beating warrants had already been signed. Robert had better luck with General Sir Henry Clinton, the commander-in-chief at New York City, who, on May 1, 1779, signed the following warrant for Rogers to raise a new regiment of provincial troops:

Lieutenant Colonel Robert Rogers
Sir
Your are hereby authorized and empowered to raise for His Majesty's Service Two Battalions of able bodied Rangers, each Battalion to be composed of one Major, Nine Captains, one Captain Lieutenant, Nine Lieutenants, Ten Ensigns, one Adjutant, one Quarter Master, One Surgeon, Thirty Serjeants, Thirty Corporals, ten Drummers and Five Hundred and thirty Privates, to be divided into Ten Companies, each to consist of one Captain, one Lieutenant, one Ensign, Three Serjeants, Three Corporals, one Drummer, and fifty three Privates, who will engage to carry arms under my Orders, or the Orders of the Commander in Chief of His Majesty's Forces for the time being, for Two years, or if required, during the continuance of the present Rebellion in North America, to receive the same Pay, and be under the same Discipline as His Majesty's Regular Troops.
The Officers to be approved of by me, and as their Appointments by Commission will depend upon their Success in Recruiting, They are to be instructed to raise the following Numbers to entitle them hereto – vis. a Captain Thirty-two Men, a Lieutenant Sixteen Men, and an Ensign, Twelve Men and is to be made known to them that their Pay will not commence untill half the above Number raised and

approved.

In like manner when Men raised in either Battalion sufficient to compleat four Companies, a Major will be commissioned to such Battalion, and a Commission as Lieutenant Colonel Commandant of both Battalions will be given you Six Hundred Men being raised.

The same Bounty will be allowed to each Man Inlisted and approved as is given to the Provincial Corps.

All Officers Civil and Military and others His Majesty's liege Subjects, are hereby required to be aiding and assisting unto you and all Concerned in the Execution of the above Service, for which this shall be to you and them a sufficient warrant and Authority.

To be known as the King's Rangers, the corps was part of the Central Department, and under the patronage of Sir Henry Clinton. Robert Rogers promptly issued a warrant of his own, to Captain Daniel Bissonet, to raise both battalions, and when ready their lieutenant-colonel commandant would inspect them! The wildly optimistic instructions to Bissonet are a fine example of how Robert Rogers had lost touch with reality. Raising two battalions was an enormous task, and a responsibility that required the constant attention of the commandant personally. Another piece of correspondence hints that the British officers at New York City were hoping to rid themselves of the old ranger's services. On May 23, Lord Rawden, Sir Henry Clinton's adjutant-general wrote to Haldimand, recommending that His Excellency give Colonel Rogers his protection, should the ranger leader feel compelled to take refuge in Canada.

On his part, Robert Rogers took Rawden's suggestion literally, for to his astonishment Governor Haldimand discovered that some officers of the King's Rangers were on their way to his province with or without his approval. Writing from New York City on July 17, Rogers informed Haldimand that in order to fulfill the terms of his warrant from Clinton, he had to send officers to Canada, where they would receive recruits more conveniently than at the headquarters of the Central Department. He also asked, boldly, that his officers be assigned to Colonel John Butler until he could join them, and that they be allowed passports, provisions, and permission to recruit in Canada.

This letter must have made Haldimand fume. Having turned down the old war horse once, now he was being presented with an accomplished fact. Yet Rogers was not being totally irrational, for his friends were living on the frontiers of New Hampshire, Vermont and New York, a long and difficult journey from the Central Department's headquarters. Robert hoped to slip recruits into Canada, or, better still, find them among refugees already there – an activity guaranteed to upset officers of provincial corps that belonged to the Northern Department.

The offending officers were commanded by James Rogers, who was to become the major of the new corps. With him came Captains John Longstreet, John Hatfield, Daniel Bissonet, Charles Babington and Patrick Welsh; Lieutenants John Throgmorton, Michael Smith and John Whitworth; Ensigns John Robins, Joseph Bears and Eleazor Taylor. John Walsh was a volunteer, and the group included two sergeants. Officers listed as 'gone through the country from New York' were Captain John Stinson, Lieutenant John Leydon and Ensign Anderson.[28]

Stinson, Leydon and Anderson were recruiting. James and the other officers left New York City with provisions to last until July 24, travelling up the Hudson towards Lake Champlain – a dangerous journey where they must have been incognito. When his party reached Fort St. Johns, James discovered that no provision had been made for them, and they soon petitioned Haldimand for relief.[29] Haldimand was being unco-operative; he felt that James could not possibly raise many men along Canada's frontiers because the governor had authorized new levies for the Northern Department that were not complete.

On the same day as James prepared his petition, Haldimand wrote to Robert ordering him to recall his officers from Canada without delay. James, he explained, was wasting his time in Canada, for most loyalists preferred the King's Royal Regiment of New York, Butler's Rangers, or the corps being raised by Ebenezer Jessup and John Peters. Furthermore, Haldimand had no authority to supply James Rogers and his officers with money. He agreed to allow them half pay until further orders, but he was determined to have them look for their recruits elsewhere.

A week later, Daniel Bissonet wrote to the governor, complaining that he was 'distressed' and asking permission to return to New York City. Instead of obeying and withdrawing his officers, Robert Rogers wrote from Fort Howe, on the Saint John River, on September 26, to inform Haldimand that he had sailed from New York City on the H.M. S. *Bland* to Penobscot. Again he asked Haldimand to assist brother James, and said he would be in Quebec City that winter. This letter was carried by Paul and Joseph Duyer, and Robert asked Haldimand to pay them £20 for their expenses, or take the money from the contingency funds of the King's Rangers. Again Haldimand fumed. Where was he to find £20 for the Duyers, or contingency funds for the King's Rangers? The latter question was too trivial for the lofty Robert to consider.

Meanwhile, poor James struggled to fulfill his obligations to get recruits. On October 29, he wrote to the governor to say he

247

hoped to meet some men at British frontier posts, asking for provisions, and enquired which posts His Excellency wanted the officers to use in receiving their men. About the same time John Longstreet enquired when the King's Rangers might receive subsistence and winter clothing. While the officers' activities distressed the governor, they infuriated the officers of other provincial corps, struggling to fill their own ranks. Competition for recruits was keen, especially among agents working for Ebenezer Jessup and John Peters. Neither could tolerate the additional strain placed on the skimpy supply of recruits by the aspirations of the King's Rangers' officers.

Furthermore, Rogers' agents were competing for recruits among loyalist refugees in Montreal, who were already on government rations. When James and his officers arrived, Haldimand thought they should get their recruits along the frontiers, and that refugee loyalists already under his protection should be assigned to regiments in the Northern Department. Mathews, the governor's secretary, informed James that he was to confine recruiting to rebel territory, avoiding Montreal, and to refrain from accepting men who reached border posts after pledging to join other corps. Replying, James then ill in Montreal, protested that recruits who had promised to join the King's Rangers had been bribed to join Joseph Brant's 'rangers' by offers of half a dollar a day.

In the midst of all this confusion, Robert Rogers arrived in Quebec City, triumphantly announcing thad he had raised 700 men in Nova Scotia. For a fleeting moment Haldimand thought he had solved his problem; on February 10, Mathews ordered Robert to take his officers and join the 700 men he had left in the Saint John Valley. The tone of this letter implies that neither His Excellency nor the secretary were taken in by Robert. However, Rogers had given them the excuse to suggest that so many men required the supervision of their officers immediately.

Besides, Robert could draw funds from the Paymaster of Nova Scotia for the King's Rangers' subsistence, relieving Haldimand of that responsibility, to his great satisfaction. Robert had been petitioning Haldimand to pay the King's Rangers' debts. He professed that he had delivered a statement to the Provincial Paymaster at Halifax for his new levy of rangers, but had not received his letter of credit, which he was expecting soon. On February 25, 1780, Robert again wrote to Haldimand, stating that he must have £469. 3s. 3d. in Halifax currency to pay his officers.

Haldimand refused the request and Mathews expressed surprise that Robert was still in Quebec City, since the governor had advanced him money to travel to Halifax ten days before. Robert took this hint, for three days later, Captain Longstreet wrote to Mathews complaining that he was destitute. Rogers had promised him £25., but had left without paying him after giving orders that Longstreet and five other officers should follow after him. The governor obliged, dipping into public funds, if only to be rid of these troublesome officers. Soon afterward Haldimand received a letter from Robert, written at 'Lake over Ye Grand Portage' apparently the Chiputneticook Lakes in the St. Croix River, close to the upper waters of the Penobscot River. He reported that Captains Hatfield and Walsh and one sergeant were sick, but these men were not to give His Excellency any more trouble, and Robert apologized for offending him.

In Robert's wake, James Rogers continued his efforts to raise recruits, amidst considerable resentment. In February 1780, by Haldimand's order, a Board of Officers convened at Fort St. Johns to hear complaints and rule on which men would be assigned to the various provincial corps.[30] Soon after Robert's departure, James asked for permission to send out a party to Gloucester County, Vermont, and he wanted to be allowed to go aboard a vessel at Crown Point to meet some men he expected to arrive there. Also, one of his agents, a Mr. Church, wanted to go to Otter Creek and Split Rock in quest of other recruits. Haldimand approved, and as well he allowed Lieutenant Michael Smith, King's Rangers, to draw half pay.

The meetings of the Board of Officers did not end the quarrelling, for on April 26, Mathews sent James new instructions. All recruits were to be taken to the commanding officer of whatever post they reached, and were to declare whether they had promised to join any corps. Thus all the men engaged for the King's Rangers would be sent to Major Rogers – or so Haldimand fervently prayed. The corps was to be attached temporarily to Sir John Johnson, and James was to receive his half pay regularly from Mr. Jordan, the paymaster at Fort St. Johns. Mathews assured James that brother Robert's 'extraordinary behavior shall not be turned to Your Prejudice.' This must have relieved James' anxieties, for in a letter that crossed Mathews' he admitted, 'The Conduct of my Brother of late has almost unmann'd me.' By May 10, James was asking to resign from the King's Rangers and to be wholly under Haldimand's protection within the Northern Department.

In his reply, Mathews explained that Haldimand could not accept James' resignation, because his appointment was made by Sir Henry Clinton. The major must be patient in the hope that his brother Robert would succeed in raising a battalion. Sad to relate, James had not heard the end of Robert's extraordinary behaviour.

The 700 men he bragged of enlisting in Nova Scotia were, in fact, scarcely 40, and his debts were something alarming. Mathews forwarded a bill on July 15 which Haldimand expected James to pay out of his personal funds, if he had any. James replied that he could not pay this debt, and he was unhappy about having his accounts confused by requests from Halifax. Robert had written from there on April 2, airily expecting money to be forthcoming from Canada.

James sent other requests for permission to send out recruiting agents, but these were rejected, because Haldimand did not want too much activity until the expedition Sir John Johnson was leading through the Mohawk Valley had returned. Consent was finally forthcoming on July 6, and Mathews reiterated that all disputes would be settled by the Board of Officers. In spite of himself, Governor Haldimand was gradually coming to accept the presence of the King's Rangers in his midst, and he admitted that since his department had to pay subsistence at least, the fledgling corps might be employed in useful work. Although James Rogers, his officers and recruits, were officially part of the Central Department, Haldimand ceased suggesting that they return to New York City where they belonged. Slowly but surely, James was winning his battle to separate himself and the officers who had remained in Canada with him from his erratic and dissembling brother Robert.

In 1780, Robert went to England again, and James assumed the debts his brother had amassed. Robert's wife Elizabeth divorced him and remarried a New Hampshire man, but little is known of the ranger leader afterwards, beyond the fact that he died on May 18, 1795, in a rooming house in London, and was buried in the churchyard of St. Mary, Newington.

James at the Helm

Although the ranks of the King's Rangers remained thin, Governor Haldimand found a valuable service for many to perform. These were sent to Captain Justus Sherwood, the Commissioner of Prisoners and Refugees, and commander of scouts working from Fort St. Johns and Isle aux Noix. Several officers worked as secret agents, going into rebel territory singly or in charge of small scouting parties in which enlisted men served. Names on the muster rolls frequently show 'on secret service' in the duty column, and the names of officers, both commissioned and non-commissioned, appear regularly in Sherwood's letters to Governor Haldimand and Robert Mathews.[31]

Because of the King's Rangers' involvement in scouting, the

corps continued to be quartered at Fort St.Johns, rather than at Sorel, the main base for provincial troops. On September 4, Mathews authorized James to complete two companies, held out hope for a third one, and assured the major that all would be employed in Canada. Rogers was to receive James Breakenridge and his brother David, the first to be captain-lieutenant, the second an ensign. Both men were from Bennington, Vermont, but somehow, in the course of his ramblings it had been Robert, not James, who had promised them commissions. Mathews also ordered James to prepare a detachment of King's Rangers to accompany regulars and Indians for a scout along Lake Champlain.

Four days later James sent Mathews a muster roll showing himself as the major, Azariah Pritchard of Connecticut as a captain, 5 lieutenants, 2 sergeants, 4 volunteers, and 36 enlisted men.[32] In a covering letter he explained that his men had only the arms they had brought from their homes, and some of these were not dependable. He also noted that men going to New York City were allowed $8. if their weapons became King's property, and asked for permission to make payments for sound firearms. In his next letter, James enquired whether he would have captain's pay once he had a full company, which should be soon. The men still lacked arms, and he hoped to be allowed the same clothing as other provincials. Certain of the new arrivals were 'almost naked' and he needed provisions for women and children as well.

On September 18, Mathews informed James that he should apply to Brigadier Watson Powell, the commandant of Fort St. Johns, for arms, clothing and provisions. Three days later the secretary wrote that Haldimand would approve a captaincy for James when the first company was completed, and that the women and children would be cared for in the same manner as those at Machiche, provided the men were actively engaged in recruiting.

A detachment of King's Rangers accompanied Major Christopher Carleton's raid on the New York outposts along Lake Champlain, in which a contingent of King's Loyal Americans and Royal Highland Emigrants also took part. Writing from Fort St. Johns on October 26, Ensign David Breakenridge asked that prisoners captured at Forts Edward and George be permitted to join the corps. All were young, and had never taken up arms as 'Contenettal' soldiers, although they had been drafted into the 'Milisha.'

By November 22, James reported that he had chosen 15 of the prisoners and he now had 133 men in his corps, but most still needed clothing. They were naked except for the ones who had gone with Major Carleton. These had drawn clothing, a blanket each, 'overawls and 1 pr. mogasons.' He had also drawn 42 'Indian pieces' for the expedition, but he was in debt to some Montreal merchants and he wanted bounty money for his recruits.

A new barracks at Fort St. Johns housed his men, and some were able to cut wood, which the fires consumed rapidly, but many men were unable to go outside because of a shortage of warm clothing. Also, Haldimand had authorized payment of an account for Richard Ferguson, one of James' agents, but he did not know 'who to or whair he may apply, beg You will inform Him how he may receive the Money.' Mathews forwarded an order from the quartermaster-general to Mr. Dysart, the quartermaster at Fort St. Johns, to furnish every corps with clothing, for which receipts showing all names were to be submitted. No more arms were available at present, and Captain Campbell, the Deputy Muster Master, would soon muster all the new levies. Rolls prepared by the commanders of corps must show the date of enlistment of each man, and Major Rogers should send all his accounts to Colonel Barry St. Leger, who had replaced Brigadier Powell as the fort's commandant. If the colonel was reluctant, Rogers was to send his accounts to headquarters, and a separate warrant would be issued. The King's Rangers was too small a unit to require a quartermaster or surgeon, but Rogers could use a surgeon of regulars when necessary.

The governor had received complaints over the extreme youth of certain of James' men. Writing from Montreal, one George Law observed that such lads should be billeted in homes there. As King's Rangers they had to be accoutred and paid by government, although they were not fit for duty as soldiers.[33] James was quick to retort. He had three nearly completed companies, and some of his men had been on duty in Montreal. All could pass muster; for the youngest was in his 'Early 17th Year, Fine likely boys.' While not personally acquainted with all the prisoners, James had sent officers to interview them in Montreal, and all but two had worked out well. These, 'I have found had been Guilty of words unbecoming A Loyalist I ordered them confined.'[34]

In December 1780, Major John Nairne, in command of all the below-strength provincial corps, conducted an inspection; and reported that James Rogers had the bearing of an old soldier, but some of the officers in his corps were of doubtful character. Despite this mildly favourable comment, the quarrels over certain recruits assigned to the King's Rangers continued. Both Ebenezer Jessup and John Peters were up in arms, but James had many complaints of his own. To Mathews he insisted that the disputes were caused by officers in other regiments. Mr. Sharp and Mr. Lamson, of Jessup's

Corps, had been at Crown Point on a vessel, claiming men who had promised to join the King's Rangers. Ever since His Excellency's orders of April 24, James affirmed, he had not spoken to any man before he declared which corps he had chosen. Rogers was also unhappy about James Breakenridge. Robert had promised him a captain-lieutenantcy, but Breakenbridge had not brought in a single recruit.

Replying, Mathews said that the Board of Officers would soon convene to settle disputes, and Captain Breakenbridge was to remain on the subsistence list for the time being. By an express lately arrived from Halifax, Mathews discovered that the officers of Colonel Robert Rogers' corps there had not been allowed subsistence, and therefore, 'those who are & have come into this Province have no reason to Complain.' Furthermore, since Major Rogers had not said he had been refused clothing, Mathews assumed that he had not demanded any of Quartermaster Dysart.

On February 19, 1781, Justus Sherwood informed Mathews that he had lost some of the men he had recruited for his company, the Queen's Loyal Rangers, to Rogers, because he had not been at Fort St. Johns to state his case when the Board of Officers held a hearing. The following September, the Board recommended that since the King's rangers belonged to the Central Department, and came under Sir Henry Clinton's command, they should be treated differently than other provincials in Canada. Nevertheless, now that three companies were complete, His Excellency Governor Haldimand should approve officers for the corps.[35] The governor agreed, and appointed these officers: to the first company, Major James Rogers, Captain-Lieutenant James Breakenbridge, Lieutenant Israel Ferguson, and Ensign William Buell; to the second, Captain Azariah Pritchard, Lieutenant Solomon Johns and Ensign Joseph Bettys; to the third, Captain Henry Ruiter, Lieutenant William Tyler and Ensign David Breakenbridge.[36]

By late November 1781, all provincial troops except those designated as Royal were being uniformed in green coats with dark red facings, and throughout the year the tailors were busy sewing. Previously such uniforms as the King's Rangers received had been the despised blue coats with white facings that resembled uniforms worn by some Continental regiments.

James Rogers' letters were filled with requests for subsistence and clothing for his men and their families, and with repudiations of charges levelled at his King's Rangers by other provincial officers. According to James, a memorial sent to Haldimand by Messrs. Jessup, Peters and Fraser denouncing recruiting agent Richard

Ferguson's misconduct at Kingsbury, northern New York, was without foundation, and Major Christopher Carleton could verify the fact that Ferguson had not been offering half a dollar a day to men who joined Rogers' Corps. Nor was there a shred of truth in the rumour that men who enlisted in the King's Rangers would be sent to Halifax. Moreover James' officers were not saying that other loyalist officers could give no bounties, while his could offer half a dollar per day.

However, James did refer to Robert's original warrant to raise the regiment which allowed bounties to recruits. Also, Sir Henry Clinton had promised that each recruit was to be allowed $5, and three guineas when the corps was half-completed, although James may have known that these provisions might not apply to Canada. Rogers further denied that his agents were spreading gossip that women and children of the men in his corps were receiving full rations, or that the men enlisted with Sir John Johnson were in that regiment for life. Nor was it true that King's Rangers were never employed on active duty. In fact, 70 were on fatigue duty, while others were guarding the barracks. Had he been aware of any unfair practices, James assured Mathews, he would have curbed them.[37]

Meanwhile, brother Robert then in New York City, had issued a warrant to John Walden Meyers, a native of Albany County, to raise a company of King's Rangers. Meyers reached Fort St. Johns on November 24, 1780, with five recruits, and with promises enough to fill his company when he could lead the men to Canada. Meyers never did succeed in piloting out most of the others, and James lost his services the following spring. After a daring raid on Ballstown, where he captured four rebel militia officers and freed all the loyalists imprisoned there, Meyers carried a dispatch to headquarters in Quebec City. While interviewing him, Haldimand allowed Meyers to recruit for an independent company to operate along the frontiers of Canada.[38]

For the final two years of the war, the King's Rangers were employed mainly in scouting and recruiting, or on fatigue duty at Fort St. Johns. On June 16, 1781, James wrote to Haldimand to say that since His Excellency was so unwilling to allow him to bring in recruits, he wanted to send a messenger to New York City to ask Sir Henry Clinton for permission to remain in Canada, wholly under Haldimand's protection. Robert had gone to England and James was anxious to sever all connections with his brother, now a great embarrassment. Again Haldimand refused to take the King's Rangers in his Northern Department, but after the British defeat at

Yorktown in October, he showed more willingness over recruiting. As winter drew near, some King's Rangers were detailed for duty at the Loyal Blockhouse, where, since July, Captain Justus Sherwood had commanded the Secret Service, Northern Department.

Known to have been employed as secret agents were Captains Azariah Pritchard and James Breakenridge, Ensigns Joseph Bettys and William Buell, Corporals Thomas Welch and Moses Hurlburt, and Roger Stevens (called an ensign although his name was not on any list of officers). Pritchard was a Yankee, who escaped from the rebels in Connecticut when his father bribed the court and had him acquitted of charges that he had carried dispatches for the British. Azariah was also devious, involved in passing counterfeit money and selling forged passes for rebels travelling on Lake Champlain.[39]

James Breakenbridge made at least one journey to consult his father at his farm near Bennington, on whether Vermont could be persuaded to rejoin the British Empire. Roger Stevens also scouted in Vermont, and he was reprimanded for being indiscreet while in Quebec City with a dispatch he had carried from the Loyal Blockhouse.[40] Ensign Joseph Bettys was what eighteenth-century writers would have described as born to be hanged, a fate that later befell him.

Corporal Moses Hurlburt, sent into Vermont with a dispatch, attended a public dance in Arlington, where, inebriated, he was reported openly recruiting.[41] Worse, three King's Rangers went into Vermont in quest of recruits after stealing money while in Livingston's Manor, New York. They were pursued by local men who wounded one and captured the others. The latter two would be sent to Captain Sherwood in a prisoner exchange, but the wounded ranger was destined for Albany to stand trial for robbery.[42]

In October of 1781, a detachment of King's Rangers joined St. Leger's expedition that occupied Crown Point in a show of force Governor Haldimand hoped would induce the people of Vermont to accept his terms for becoming a British province. Also on the foray was Major Edward Jessup and some of the King's Loyal Americans. In a letter dated December 13, 1781, James referred to a recent visit he had made to Quebec City, and noted that his officers had been entitled to full pay since August 25. His own pay was 15s. per day, but he had not included this amount on his bill because he had not discussed the matter with Governor Haldimand. Replying on December 31, Mathews said he could not tell James when his officers would receive full pay, and he should send in a bill only for subsistence.

The correspondence over bills and how and when they would be paid, and whether the King's Rangers could receive bounty money preoccupied James Rogers constantly. Mathews was critical of items included in the bills he submitted, and challenged him over certain men for whom he claimed subsistence. The monthly return of officers and men rarely matched the subsistence list, and Mathews was continually sending the accounts back to James for corrections before they could be paid. On January 17 1782, Mathews promised to make out a warrant for part payment of a bill, and told James that Major Nairne should remove from the pension list all King's Rangers who had been put on his last muster roll. Officers of three companies, now almost complete, were to be allowed 'Batt and Forage Money for the last 165 days of the Campaign of 1781.' Four days later he took James to task for enlisting William Dods, an indentured servant. This was illegal, for apprentices and other bonded persons were not eligible for service.

By April 1782, James had a private worry. He asked Mathews for permission to send someone to the Connecticut River for his eldest son, James Jr.:

> He is now in his Seventeenth Year and I am afraid he will be pressed into the Rebel Service before I can get him from them. . . Mrs. Rogers will be sent on here Next Summer, but my oldest Boy will not have the Liberty to come with her which makes me wish to have him stolen away before she comes.

Replying on April 28, Mathews asked James to postpone any attempt to rescue his son because Haldimand had a special assignment for him. He was to proceed to the Loyal Blockhouse with two trusty men, and not to reveal to anyone but the commandant, St. Leger, that he was leaving Fort St. Johns. At the headquarters of the secret service, James would receive sealed orders.

The letter which Rogers opened at the Loyal Blockhouse pertained to a plan prepared by a resident agent in the Connecticut Valley – 'Colonel Beadle' – the Timothy Bedel who had joined the rebel invasion of Canada early in 1776, and who had allowed John Peters to travel to Montreal with him. Sherwood described Bedel as 'one of the most subtle Cunning geniuses in that part of the Country.' Captain Pritchard had been in communication with Bedel, who specified that a field officer be sent to visit him. Haldimand felt that Bedel's plan was 'very Romantick' but James was to give his full attention to the mission and refrain from recruiting during his journey. After conferring with Sherwood and his deputy, Dr. George Smyth, James was to set out with Pritchard and 'you could perhaps have a man in the country to discover what steps Beadle may take after your interview.' Rogers was to establish a channel to keep Haldimand informed on enemy intentions, and enclosed with these orders was a small slip of paper which he could show to Bedel if he thought it safe, but which he was not to trust in the agent's possession lest it be used for blackmail or fall into the hands of the Congress.

What Bedel proposed was never revealed, and on April 28, Mathews wrote to inform James that the mission was too dangerous and had been cancelled. Instead, he was to go into the country to gather intelligence, and to consider some way to retrieve his son.

By June 11, Rogers was back at Fort St. Johns and probably had his son James with him. He enquired how long Ensign Joseph Bettys, hanged in Albany in May, should remain on the muster roll. Replying, Mathews said that Bettys' widow should receive her husband's pay until June 24, and afterward a pension of £20 per year. James soon informed Mathews that he had more than enough men for his three companies and was returning three contingent men. Then there occurred an episode that brought Haldimand's wrath down on James' head, one caused – as might be expected – by dear brother Robert.

Captain John Stinson, who had gone to New York City with Robert three years before, arrived at Fort St. Johns carrying a parole from the rebels, in return for which he had promised that rebel Captain Simeon Smyth would be exchanged. In a covering letter, James explained that Stinson had left New York City in March 1781, for Penobscot, to 'Distribute some Manifestoes,' and was captured on his return journey and taken to Newberry Port. He got the parole after promising that Captain Smyth would be sent home. To compound the felony, James asked that Captain Stinson receive back pay due him! Mathews' reply was testy. Stinson had no right to promise anyone in exchange, and he was to be sent to Halifax, allowed no subsistence, and given only enough money for his journey. Because of the rebels' infractions of the rules of war, Haldimand would not treat them generously.

Late in November James asked for permission to form a fourth company, claiming that now he was better able to pick out the deserving men. He also wanted the right to choose his own officers, rather than abide by Haldimand's decisions. The last such appointment had been 'disagreeable to us and laughed at by Officers of the British troops.' Again Mathews' reply was testy. James must not nominate officers. He was not even the commander of the corps – only a detachment – and should not take liberties. As for the appointment that had been a laughing stock, if James had been referring to Ensign Bettys, 'whatever his Private Character might formerly have been, he had rendered many Services to Government and fell an honourable Victim to his Duty.' Furthermore, James had had no complaints about Bettys when he was bringing in recruits for the King's Rangers. Officers in the more recently formed Loyal Rangers under Major Edward Jessup were appointed solely on the basis of the number of men recruited, and the same applied to the King's Rangers.

In his next letter James began by retorting that the officer he mentioned was not Bettys, adding that Captain Pritchard had brought good news from New York City. Sir Guy Carleton, who had succeeded Sir Henry Clinton as commander-in-chief, and under the impression that Major Rogers had a full battalion in Canada, had recommended placing the King's Rangers under the patronage of General Haldimand. Pritchard would soon come to Quebec City to give His Excellency a full report. Colonel Robert Rogers, now in England, had no objections to James' being commissioned in the Northern Department, and the major had held a conversation with Major Edward Jessup, the commander of the Loyal Rangers, on the prospects of having the King's Rangers taken into his battalion. James wanted the governor to know that he had no objections to such an amalgamation.

In reply, Mathews said that uniting the Loyal Rangers and King's Rangers could not be effected at present, because too many arrangements would be required. In any case, recruiting had done more harm than good for the King's service, and in future it would be confined to men coming into the Province.

Although nothing in the correspondence passing between headquarters in Quebec City and James Rogers at Fort St. Johns indicates when the corps was accepted into the Northern Department, it must obviously have taken place about the beginning of 1783. Since the summer of 1782, Haldimand's supply of provisions had improved, but he still feared a rebel attack and therefore accepted Carleton's suggestion. By March 24, Mathews was again pointing out disparities between James' subsistence accounts and the numbers of men shown on his monthly return. This time he criticized Rogers for drawing pay for two sergeants that were prisoners of the rebels. No regiment, 'not even of the Establishment' charged for prisoners and the major was ordered to deduct the wages for the two sergeants.

Not one to take anything lying down, James defended himself. It had been the custom during the Seven Years' War to keep prisoners on returns and allow them pay! Besides, the pay due Sergeant Lemuel Casswell, one of the prisoners, was going to his wife for her support, and he asked to be allowed to list this man as a private, so that some assistance could be continued to Mrs. Casswell. Mathews reiterated that no prisoners were to receive pay, and told James that he had corrected the accounts himself to save time.

Having been refused permission to unite his corps with the Loyal Rangers, in May James sent a petition to Sir John Johnson asking to be taken into his second battalion. It was signed also by Lieutenants Israel Ferguson and Solomon Johns, and Ensign William Buell. Clearly James was aware that officers of regiments not completed to ten companies would not be entitled to half pay when such were reduced. Backed by his junior officers, Rogers was willing to submerge the King's Rangers in order to secure the future.

Mathews again complained about James' accounts, this time because the Major had claimed pay for a man who had died, and was still on the monthly return, although he had been dropped from the subsistence list. The secretary was clearly annoyed at the time he had to spend on the King's Rangers' accounts. To this James replied that the man had drowned, and if Mathews had looked more closely he would have found that pay was listed only to the day before. The bickering over accounts, and James' many requests for bounty money, continued until November, when Governor Haldimand received instructions from London to disband the provincial corps by the end of the year.

Haldimand informed James that disbandment would take place on December 24, and he was to draw provisions to this date. Again the accounts for the King's Rangers were in disarray and the governor's long-suffering secretary redid them himself to save time in paying the men. On this occasion James had claimed bounty money due his non-commissioned officers for two years, but Mathews discovered that they had received it until June 24, 1783. Mathews also begged Rogers to submit his hospital and contingency accounts which he had not received. The following was finally made up and sent to Quebec City:

A contingency bill for the King's Rangers.					
Hospital	25 pounds				
Nurse	4 "	10 shillings			
Stationary	15 "				
Hospital charges (earlier)	76 "	10	"		
Nurse	13 "	10	"		
Postage		15	"	7	pence
Total C. Bill	139 "	5	"	11	

Lieut. Ferguson to act as Quartermaster to the disbanded King's Rangers. Given 7 days provisions, awaiting His Excellency's orders.

James had not added the account correctly, for it shows 4d. too much. He also requested passports for himself and Lieutenant

Henry Ruiter to go to Vermont to settle business. He reported that he had paid a surgeon himself, since no provision had been made for one by the government.

Despite the fact that his corps was disbanded, James made one futile attempt to have Haldimand appoint officers to a fourth company. On January 23, 1784, he asked that half pay be granted to the men who would have commanded this company had he received permission to incorporate it. As with many other of James' brainwaves, Haldimand gave this one the cold shoulder.

While winter drew to a close, James made his journey to Vermont, to fetch his family. On his return he informed Mathews that he was surprised, after all the assurances he had received from the leaders of that republic, to be met with gross insults; nonetheless he found that many people wanted to remove to Canada. On March 28, James suggested that he send some men from his corps to Cataraqui to find a good landing place for boats and to build huts, because the majority of his people wanted to settle there. Haldimand had no objections, but Mathews warned James that enough information could be obtained from Deputy Surveyor-General John Collins, Captain Sherwood and others who had explored the area. James' request was odd, for Lieutenant Solomon Johns, of his corps, had been one of those who accompanied Sherwood, and was in a position to give such information.[43]

The men of the King's Rangers and their families wintered at Fort St. Johns, some in the barracks where they had been quartered soon after James Rogers arrived to raise the corps. The last return showed three companies, with 10 commissioned officers, 18 non-commissioned officers, 6 volunteers, 1 drummer, and 178 rank and file.[44] A list of disbanded troops and loyalists settled upon the King's lands in 1784 showed that 120 men, 47 women, 118 girls and boys under 21, and 14 servants, or a total of 299 people, were in Township Number 3, Cataraqui which was assigned to the regiment.[45] Most of Rogers' men and their families eventually joined their commanding officer although some stragglers remained at Fort St. Johns for an extra winter. A few King's Rangers went to Mississquoi Bay, while the Breakenbridge brothers, Solomon Johns and William Buell elected to settle among the Loyal Rangers beside the upper St. Lawrence. The commissioned officers for the three companies received half pay, despite Haldimand's ruling that only officers in completed regiments were eligible.[46]

There remained other mysteries to boggle the mind of a reader of primary sources. Robert Rogers went to England and never returned, but the following is a partial list of Guides and Pioneers of

260

the Central Department:

```
Lt. Col. Robert Rogers.
                                        Age
Captains ─────── John Longstreet ─────── 37 ─────── American
                 John Hatfield ───────── 43 ─────── English

Lieutenants ──── Thomas Okronson ─────── 34 ─────── American
                 Joseph Miller ───────── 35 ─────── Ireland

Ensigns ──────── Charles Stockton ────── 34
                 Eleazor Taylor ──────── 32 ─────── American(47)
```

A further peculiarity is a 'Return of Officers from New York under the Command of Major James Rogers' which was found among Governor Haldimand's papers:

John Longstreet Capt. lst Battn. Genl. Skinners Brigd.
John Hatfield Capt. 3rd Battn. Genl. Skinners Brigd.
Daniel Bessonett Capt. 4th Battn. Genl. Skinners Brigd.
John Throckmorton Liet. 1st Battn. Genl. Skinners Brigd.
Richard Smith Lieut. 4th Battn. Genl. Skinners Brigd.
John Robins Ensn. 1st Battn. genl. Skinners Brigd.
Joseph Biere Ensn. 5th Battn. Genl. Skinners Brigd.
Eleazor Taylor Ensn. New Hampshire Volunteers.
Charles Babington Capt. 2nd Battn. Genl. Skinners Brigd.
Patrick Welch Capt. Formerly in The Queens Rangers.
John D. Whitworth Lieut. Formerly in The Queens Rangers.
John Welch Volunteer.[48]

Thus two of the officers had left the Queen's Rangers to serve with Robert after he lost that regiment. Brigadier Cortlandt Skinner's brigade was the New Jersey Volunteers, and with five battalions it was the largest provincial corps raised for any department. Most settled in New Brunswick after gathering at New York City in 1783. Of these officers, only Ensign Charles Stockton is shown in the loyalist records of that province, where he is described as an officer in 'Rogers' Rangers.'[49] None are found on other lists of officers in the King's Rangers, and none are on lists of refugees being provisioned in Canada. Presumably, the officers were on a list sent to James Rogers, because he was the senior member of the corps at the close of the war. Since the land records do not show that any of these officers received grants, they vanished into the wilderness parts of Nova Scotia or Canada, no doubt indulging in some illicit business to survive.

As well, there are numerous references in loyalist claims to men having been officers and non-commissioned officers in the King's Rangers who are not on the last return James Rogers sent Governor Haldimand. One man of mystery was Jacob Miller, described as a sergeant in the corps and an adjutant of the Associated Loyalists.[50] This latter group formed at New York City, and some of the party that sailed to Canada in the spring of 1783 could have been from the detachment of King's Rangers which Robert Rogers raised. Likewise, Roger Stevens was called an ensign, but his name was not on James' return for the corps. John Dafoe, referred to as a captain, died sometime in 1783.

The King's Rangers, consisting of only three companies and rejected by Haldimand until after the preliminary cessation of hostilities of June, 1782, had an insignificant yet confusing history. Its only actions were two forays along Lake Champlain, one in the autumn of 1780, the other at the same time of year in 1781. Its most valuable contribution was scouting and the secret service, and part of the interest lies in the correspondence that passed between headquarters in Quebec City and Fort St. Johns, as Robert Mathews tried to follow Haldimand's instructions to bring James Rogers into line and make him keep the rules laid down. Other corps commanders had their troubles as they strove to have their own way, but James Rogers was the most awkward of any of them. His regiment was a disappointment to all concerned.

Chapter 11: Special Services

Officers of provincials were inferior to regulars of like rank, yet even the governors-in-chief agreed that certain tasks were performed better by loyalists than by professionals. The most important of these was providing intelligence. Loyalists knew the country, and while they spoke English with a miscellany of accents – German, Dutch, Irish, Scots, Yankee and so on – they could pass as locals everywhere. In relative safety they were able to visit 'Friends of Government' still in their homes who were willing to operate as resident agents. The fate that overtook the most famous British spy, John André, showed his unsuitability for clandestine operations. André was a captain of regulars serving as the major of the Queen's Rangers, of the Central Department. Caught while attempting to reach New York City in September 1780 with a dispatch concealed in the toe of his stocking that implicated him in Benedict Arnold's defection, André was hanged.

Another unlucky regular was Lieutenant Daniel Taylor, 9th Regiment. In the autumn of 1777, Taylor set out from New York City bound for Saratoga with a message from Sir Henry Clinton informing Burgoyne that he had carried out a raid against two forts on the lower Hudson River. Taylor carried a thin scrap of paper in a tiny silver ball concealed in the queue of his hair. Near New Windsor some men in red coats found him and agreed to lead him to an encampment where General Clinton was staying. Assuming they meant Sir Henry, Taylor went with them and found himself in the presence of Sir Henry's American cousin, General George Clinton, the rebel governor of the state. Taylor swallowed the silver ball, but a physician administered an ametic and the rebels found the message. Taylor was court martialed, and like Major André, hanged.[1]

At least three loyalists working as secret agents for the Northern Department were captured and executed, but for the numbers involved they fared better than regulars. The agents used two lines of communication to reach New York City. One led from Fort St. Johns southward to the Hudson or through Ballstown, and the men selected the way least heavily patrolled. Another was from Quebec City through the Saint John Valley and the St. Croix River. As well, scouts coming to Niagara reported on the western end of the Mohawk Valley, Pennsylvania, including Philadelphia, and even the southern states. The first news that Cornwallis might surrender at Yorktown, in the autumn of 1781, was brought by scouts to Niagara.[2] The most frequently used route was by Lake Champlain and the Hudson River.

A key person to emerge for the secret service was Captain Justus Sherwood; another his cranky but garrulous deputy, Dr. George Smyth. Sherwood and Smyth had led somewhat different early lives than the corps commanders, and each suffered more violence at the hands of the rebels. Their stories expose a variant on what it meant to be a loyalist in the Thirteen Colonies at a tempestuous time.

Justus Sherwood

In the autumn of 1776, Justus Sherwood, 29 years old, tall and spare, wearing frontier leggings and a hunting shirt, appeared at Crown Point at the head of 40 loyalists. There, Governor Sir Guy Carleton was encamped with his British expeditionary force. Sherwood's arrival marked the end of a period of persecution by rebels in the Green Mountains, at that time the New Hampshire Grants, and an unwilling part of New York State. For Sherwood and the men with him, their only recourse was to seek safety in Canada, which was firmly in the hands of the British army following the rebel invasion of the year before.

Justus Sherwood was born in Newtown, Connecticut, on March 7, 1747. From his actions, the New England character emerges with clarity not found in the backgrounds of other Yankee loyalist leaders. The strict Calvinists who founded Connecticut preached diligence for its own sake, while cautioning against avarice. Most of the land was held in common until King Charles II suggested giving part of the province to one of his brothers as a dukedom. When it was rumoured that land not owned by individuals would be considered crown land, the Puritan leaders responded by introducing private property on a wider scale. Overnight freehold tenure became the goal of every freeborn man.[3] By the time Sherwood was born, ambition for material gain had become respectable, freeholding a right; yet concern for the 'Publick Good' remained a strong force in his community.

Like all New Englanders, Sherwood believed in limited democracy, and he was fascinated by politics. Local government was by town meetings, and Connecticut had an elected govermor as well as a legislative assembly. Any freeman who met the property qualification could vote and share in government. His background made Sherwood an ambitious, politically active man, yet one whose drive was often tempered by a Puritan conscience. Justus had some education; and he expressed himself well in the journals and reports that have survived, although his writings have an oral flavour and lack the classical allusions typical of scholarly authors of his day. He became a licensed surveyor, and with the money he earned he purchased three small farms around Newtown, in all 22 acres of land.[4]

Justus soon realized that if he wanted to progress rapidly, he should look towards the frontier where land was cheap, opportunities almost unlimited. Connecticut was overcrowded, her soils stony at best. By 1772, he had sold his holdings in that province and moved to the New Hampshire Grants, purchasing a hill farm of 100 acres in Sunderland Township. Later he bought more land and made money in the lumber and potash trade as well as by surveying. Two years after he settled in the Green Mountains, he married Sarah Bothum, whose father, Elijah, was a pioneer in Shaftesbury Township, immediately to the south of Sunderland. That year the Sherwoods moved 90 miles north to a farm in New Haven Township – a much better piece of land, gently rolling, with good, deep soil.[5]

Soon after he reached the New Hampshire Grants, Sherwood found he had come to a land in turmoil. He had become acquainted with two shrewd land speculators in brothers Ethan and Ira Allen, a friendship that had a far-reaching effect. Even before his marriage he was embroiled in the land war raging between settlers from New England and those from New York. The Green Mountains were claimed by both New York and New Hampshire, and the governor of New Hampshire awarded the first grants of land. In 1764, the British government ruled that the New Hampshire Grants were the property of New York – a decision that caused consternation among the New Englanders settlers.

They barely tolerated being in New Hampshire, subject to an appointed governor, but being a part of feudal New York was a disaster. The settled areas of New York were laid out in estates, and most of the farmers were tenants – a situation unacceptable to freehold-loving Yankees. The governor of New York refused to recognize the validity of the New Hampshire land titles unless the claimants paid him a quit rent. Most declined, and the governor awarded patents without regard to whether the land was already occupied by settlers. At this the New Englanders took action.

Led by Ethan Allen they raised the Green Mountain Boys – vigilantes to keep New York settlers from taking possession of their land. Justus Sherwood, whose title to his own land was from the Governor of New Hampshire, became one of Allen's followers, riding with the Boys when they clashed with the New Yorkers. They intimidated surveyors trying to lay out estates for New York landlords, and to their more stubborn victims they administered

265

floggings – which they called 'chastisement by twigs of the wilderness' or 'impressment with the beech seal.' Blood-letting was rarely necessary. The rowdy Boys usually managed to achieve their ends by bluster and dire threats.[6]

In 1772, the new governor of New York, William Tryon, determined to restore order and he issued a writ for the arrest of Ethan Allen, Remember Baker, Justus Sherwood, and other ringleaders in what New Yorkers called the Bennington Mob, and ordered rewards of £50 for their capture.[7] Baker was caught and while the posse led by the New York magistrate, John Munro, was en route to Albany gaol, a band of men, including Justus Sherwood, swooped down and rescued him. Munro was the man destined to be a captain in the first battalion, King's Royal Regiment of New York. He was also a man who carried a grudge, as Sherwood learned to his cost.

As the time of open rebellion approached, Justus was an outlaw in the eyes of the British, but he and the other Green Mountain Boys eluded all attempts to capture them. They knew the trails through the forests. But despite the chaos in the New Hampshire Grants Justus and Sarah were becoming wealthy; in 1774 they had a son they named Samuel. Sherwood continued his involvement in local politics, and as late as 1775, his allegiance was still with the rebels. When the Green Mountain Boys captured Fort Ticonderoga from its small British garrison, one of the first acts of war, Sherwood supported them. Ethan Allen's motive was the security of his vast holdings near Lake Champlain, and Sherwood, who by that time owned about 2,000 acres under New Hampshire title, shared Allen's fear that the British might reinforce the fort, bringing more law and order – New York law. The landowners of New York would have their titles secured, to the detriment of holders of New Hampshire titles. (No documentation supports Sherwood's presence at Ticonderoga, but he also owned 1,000 acres in that other Connecticut inspired trouble spot, the Susquehanna Valley.)[8] Ethan's suspicions were correct, for the wealthy New York landowner, Philip Skene, was sailing home from London with a commission as commandant of Ticonderoga.

Sherwood was not with the Green Mountain Boys who joined the rebel expedition to capture Montreal in the autumn of 1775. In the interval he had had second thoughts about where his loyalties lay. Since 1774, when the rebels set up the Continental Congress, the people of the New Hampshire Grants had been asking to be admitted as a separate state. The voice of New York was strong in the Congress, and nothing happened, since that large state's support was necessary to the success of the rebellion. From Sherwood's point

266

of view, and that of certain neighbours, their future security was the issue. Could Congress, who refused to grant them separate status, defeat the British? If not, would a victorious Britain, in return for their aid, grant them a separate government when the rebellion had been put down?

In New Haven, where Sherwood was the proprietor's clerk – the leading politician – his opinion was respected for a time.[9] In the spring of 1776, while on business in Bennington, a hotbed of rebellion, he found that advocating loyalty landed him in an embarrassing predicament. A gang of irate rebels subdued him and took him before Judge Charles Lynch, who ordered 20 lashes, a sentence which was duly executed with a beech rod on the village green.[10] This humiliation did ot deter Sherwood, who soon began supplying information to Sir Guy Carleton. Primary sources do not reveal how Sherwood became an informer, but secondary ones claim that he sent a message to Governor Tryon – the very man who had made him an outlaw – offering his services, the usual way of joining the 'Friends of Government.'

In August 1776, Sherwood's activities became known to the rebels. He was dragged before the Committee of Safety and condemned to life imprisonment in Simsbury Mines. This was a dungeon built into an abandoned mineshaft at Simsbury, Connecticut, but, as Sherwood explained, 'before they could Execute this shocking Sentence (worse than Death) Your Memorialt had the good Fortune to break away from his Keepers and fly to the Mountains.'[11]

Once free he went to his father-in-law's farm in Shaftesbury, where Sarah, seven months pregnant, had been staying since his arrest. He put the title to his New Haven farm in Elijah Bothum's name in the hope that it would not be confiscated, and headed towards Lake Champlain, leading some 20 loyalists. Along the way he found Edward Carscallan, leading a party of New Yorkers from the Camden Valley who were lost. Thus Justus' party was 40 strong by the time he reached Crown Point.

All went with the British army when it returned to Canada, and in March 1777, aware that Sherwood had provided reliable information in the past, Sir Guy Carleton sent him in command of five men to reconnoitre Fort Ticonderoga. Before they had completed their investigations a rebel patrol captured two of the men. Sherwood and the others escaped by snatching the rebels' boats and making off down Lake Champlain. This mission took five weeks, and in the course of it Justus visited Sarah at the farm in New Haven and saw his daughter Diana, born the previous December, for the first time.

In June 1777, Sherwood was commissioned a captain in Colonel John Peters' Queen's Loyal Rangers. In the memorial he wrote after the revolution he claimed:

> Your Memorialist commanded the Loyalists after Col. Festers Death at the Battle of Bennington and was employed in various Scouts and services under Genl Burgoyne and was in every Action and Skirmish thro' that Campaign at the unfortunate Conclusion of which your Memorialist became a prisoner at the Saratoga Convention and suffered many Insults and abuses by the Rebels who happened to know him.[12]

According to his descendants, Justus was wounded, the reason why he was captured when most of his regiment escaped from Saratoga.

In November, Sarah Sherwood reached Ticonderoga with Samuel and Diana, accompanied by a young slave named Caesar Congo, travelling under a safe conduct given by the rebels at Bennington.[13] At Fort St. Johns on December 12, she gave birth to a son, Levius Peters Sherwood, conceived when Justus made his furtive visit to the Green Mountains during his investigation of the defences of Fort Ticonderoga.[14] The following year Justus learned that the rebels had confiscated his property, except for 400 acres in New Haven, 50 of which were in his father-in-law's name. At the same time, the Vermont Legislature passed an order banishing him forever from the Green Mountains.[15]

Governor Carleton allowed the family a pension of £30 per year, because Sherwood's pay had been suspended while he was a prisoner of war on parole. For some months Justus was not permitted military duties, until June 1, 1778, when Carleton revoked all paroles after he learned that the rebels had broken the terms they signed at Saratoga.[16]

In the period while his regiment was more or less in limbo, and Sherwood was an officer on the temporary list, he made himself useful gathering intelligence, interrogating refugees and prisoners brought to Fort St. Johns and gaining the confidence of the British commanders who dealt with him. By the spring of 1779, Justus had been appointed Commissioner of Prisoners and Refugees by Governor Haldimand. He was responsible for arranging exchanges of prisoners with rebel emissaries from New York, and Vermont. Since 1777, the latter had been maintaining a precarious stance as an independent republic. Sherwood was also charged with arranging safe conducts for refugees, or in some cases exchanges of loyalists the rebels were holding for Americans held in Montreal. When Sir Henry Clinton asked Haldimand to investigate the possibility that Vermont might become a British province, the Canadian governor appointed Sherwood as his commissioner for the negotiations.

By 1781, Haldimand had made Sherwood head of the secret service, Northern Department, responsible for all scouting and gathering of intelligence. For complete privacy, Sherwood established his own headquarters, the Loyal Blockhouse on North Hero Island, Lake Champlain.[17] Agents from New York disliked serving under a Green Mountain Boy, and to sweeten his choice, Haldimand appointed Dr. George Smyth as Sherwood's deputy. The relationship was not an easy one, for Smyth resented working for a younger man.

Dr. George Smyth ('Hudibras')

Little is known about the background of George Smyth, a physician who loved intrigue, and who, after his escape from Albany became Justus Sherwood's deputy. Smyth had emigrated from Ireland with his wife and sons Terence and Thomas, in 1770. The family lived in Albany for a time, then moved to Fort Edward. The doctor's brother, Patrick, was a lawyer who had resided there for some years.[18] As the time of open rebellion approached, both brothers supplied information to Governor Carleton in Canada. On April 7, 1777, George wrote a report entitled 'A true description of the situation of Ticonderoga with an exact account of its fortifications & the Number of forces therein &c., &c' for Carleton and signed it 'Hudibras.' As his chosen code name suggests, Smyth was something of an intellectual. He was given to lacing his reports with Shakespearean allusions, to the bewilderment of the Swiss governor, Frederick Haldimand.

When Burgoyne's army began to move southward towards Lake Champlain in June, George and Patrick, long suspected of loyalism, were arrested and taken to Albany gaol. As far as is known, both were living at Fort Edward, on Burgoyne's line of march. However, the doctor also had a house in Albany, and another at Claverack, some 25 miles south of that town. According to the minutes of the Board of Commissioners for Detecting and Defeating Conspiracies of the State of New York, Dr. Smyth was apprehended and brought before the members at Fishkill, on the lower Hudson River, on March 27, 1777. At that time George was permitted to return to Claverack, but he was ordered to appear before the Board in two weeks' time.[19] Following their second arrest in June 1777, the brothers were confined eighteen months, and when released on parole in January 1779, were ordered to remain within the confines of Albany. Afterwards Patrick made several clandestine journeys to New York City with dispatches for Sir Henry Clinton, while George was employed as a surgeon in the rebels' military hospital, keeping an ear to the ground.[20]

Despite the fact that the rebels were watching him, Hudibras kept on supplying information to the British in Canada and at New York City, expanding his spy network and passing messages. Both his sons worked as couriers, and his wife operated the network while George was in gaol. An early reference to Hudibras in Haldimand's correspondence is found in a letter the governor wrote to Sir John Johnson on April 3, 1780. The doctor had written to Johnson, using his code name, and Haldimand enquired whether the spy could be trusted, asking what the baronet thought of 'his character in General and His political Conduct hitherto.' Since Hudibras was employed by the rebels he might be a double agent. [21]

Johnson's reply was reassuring. Dr. Smyth did work 'as a Surgeon in the Rebel Hospital' but he was nevertheless a friend. The rebels were not suspicious of him, and he would make an excellent source of information. Johnson did not realize that the paroled Hudibras was under surveillance, a situation that was not deterring him. Satisfied, Haldimand ordered Johnson to 'establish a Correspondence with Mr. Smith and provided he could communicate to us early and authentic intelligence I would certainly reward him very handsomely.'

By August, Smyth was arrested once again and confined, this time in irons. From Albany gaol, he succeeded in sending a letter to Sir John, begging that his son Terence, code name 'Young Hudibras,' not be allowed to return from Canada lest he be captured.[21] By early October, the doctor's health was failing, and he was released on bail put up by his brother Patrick.

Hudibras slipped off to Fort Edward, and when this news was brought to the Board of Commissioners for Detecting and Defeating Conspiraces in Albany, he was escorted back and placed under house arrest. About the same time, Terence was captured in the vicinity and lodged in Albany gaol. The Commissioners ordered the doctor 'to remain within the limits of his dwelling House and Yard and not to depart from the same.'[22] He was also instructed to refrain from being in correspondence, or having conversations with anyone on political subjects.

Smyth soon asked that his family be exchanged for prisoners held in Canada, or be allowed to go to New York City. The Board of Commissioners agreed to let him leave with his wife, son Thomas and a black servant, provided that two prisoners would be sent from Canada. No arrangement was made, but for the next few months, and in spite of Smyth's delicate situation, the spy network continued providing Haldimand with information. Hudibras extended his contacts as far as the Fays in Bennington, and James Ellice of Schenectady, who signed his letters 'Z. L.' for zealous loyalist. In his letters the doctor made suggestions for the reduction of Albany, should either Haldimand or Sir Henry Clinton decide to send an army to the vicinity. This message was carried to New York City by Patrick Smith, in the hollow handle of a hunting knife, and he also took a packet of dispatches from Canada that had been brought by another courier to Albany. Sir Henry Clinton allowed Patrick a pension of £170 per year, and later, when the lawyer's wife and family joined him, a house as well.[23]

At an unspecified time Terence Smyth was released, for in April 1781, Young Hudibras reached Fort St. Johns and travelled on to see the governor in Quebec City. To Sir John Johnson Haldimand wrote:

Mr. Smyth lately returned from the neighbourhood of Albany, informed me that he found means from his concealment to acquaint Hudibras of his arrival, but that the messenger, his brother-in-law, returned immediately and informed him that Hudibras had only time to tell him that a warrant was issued to apprehend him & that he was just setting out for Vermont to take refuge with a Major Fay – That one Hewson, a volunteer with Joseph Brant, had deserted to Fort Stanwix and from thence was sent to Albany to give information against Hudibras and some other matters of intelligence he had collected for that purpose.

The rebels had also issued a warrant against Terence, and he was caught on his next journey to Albany. Meanwhile, the doctor was in hiding and planning to go to Bennington, in Vermont, and the house of Major Joseph Fay, one of the conspirators seeking reunion of that republic with Britain.

Hudibras was unlucky. He set out in a hired wagon with Abraham Lansingh, and his two sons, Jacob and Levinius. Smyth reached Bennington, but some rebel supporters turned him over to a party of New Yorkers, who resolved to return him to Albany. The three Lansinghs were arrested for 'conveying away' Hudibras but after they insisted they were innocent they were released for lack of evidence.[24] Smyth's guards escorted him back inside New York to the neighbourhood of Hoosic. At some point a scout working for Justus Sherwood named Mathew Howard discovered Hudibras' whereabouts and rescued him.[25]

Just how Howard executed his rescue operation is not clear. Some sources have concluded that Smyth was lodged in Albany gaol, where Howard was also a prisoner, and the two broke out together. No evidence in Howard's memorial, nor in a letter Smyth wrote to Haldimand supports this. More plausibly, Howard spirited Smyth away while the party was somewhere on the road to Albany, or sneaked into a house where the doctor was being held for the night and found the guards napping.

Howard hurried the far from robust Hudibras over forest trails, stopping for breath only when they reached the safety of the British post at Pointe au Fer, on Lake Champlain. From there the doctor travelled by boat to Fort St. Johns, arriving on June 14, 1781. The following day, he wrote to inform Haldimand of his escape, apologizing for not coming on to Quebec City immediately:

> Yesterday I arrived at this post, much indisposed. The Climbing of Mountains & Rocks & travelling thro' Swamps & Thickets renders me incapable, at present to pay my personal respects to your Excellency, but when my Health is restor'd will do myself the Honor of waiting on you when I shall inform you of the Cause of my flight &c.

Early in July, somewhat refreshed, the doctor set out to meet the governor. By the time he had reached the Chateau St. Louis and met Haldimand, Captain Sherwood was on North Hero Island, building his Loyal Blockhouse, the new headquarters for the secret service. The governor had appointed Major Richard Lermoult, his adjutant-general, to assist Sherwood in the negotiations with Vermont. Lernoult had fallen ill, and Haldimand needed a substitute. After interviewing Smyth, he decided to make him Sherwood's deputy in all his offices – the secret service, prisoners and refugees, and the discussions with commissioners appointed by the Vermont leaders. On the surface, Haldimand had made a wise choice. Smyth was well acquainted with many loyalists around Albany, had corresponded with Sir Henry Clinton, and knew many of the Vermont plotters personally. Unfortunately, Smyth tried to pretend that Sherwood was his assistant, which led to friction.

Before he left Fort St. Johns to meet Haldimand, Hudibras wrote to his wife to let her know he had reached safety. On June 29, she replied from Albany:

> This moment I received your kind letter dated the 18th June at St. Johns. It is a great comfort to me to hear of your safe arrival altho' the difficulties you had to struggle with on your way & my apprehension of your being attacked by your old disorder gave me much concern. Terry is yet in prison – all my endeavours to have him released are in vain. . . there is a penknife on the way – pray Enquire for it when you receive this. My Dear I could write. . . but am fear'd as I am Drowned in trouble alredy.

The reference to the penknife alerted her spouse, and concealed in it was a message for the governor. From Quebec City, Smyth hurried to join Justus Sherwood at the Loyal Blockhouse, which was nearing completion.

Hudibras' indifferent state of health was a source of unpleasantness. While Sherwood operated from the blockhouse, Smyth was often at Fort St. Johns, which was more comfortable. He insisted on asserting his right to send agents directly in New York state, despite Sherwood's wish to have all agents sent by him. Sherwood was in the right, for he wanted to know where each man was going; to prevent a manhunt for one whom the rebels discovered endangering the safety of others. When he sent out his scouting parties he tried to make sure each was operating at a safe distance from other parties. As a result Sherwood had many complaints which he relayed to the governor's secretary, Robert Mathews.

While Sherwood was not charmed by his deputy, Smyth's correspondence makes most amusing reading. Showing off the spy's ingenious use of slang, Smyth once informed Mathews, 'Blackbirds Pearch on my branches to the South,' meaning the rebels were watching him. An irked Mathews retorted:

I am totally at a loss to understand the last Paragraph of your letter. Oriental Intelligence is of no weight and Black Birds Spray upon my Branches to the South – In all matters of Business excuse my Requesting that you would be explicit – I am more particular in this as I lay my Letters before His Excellency and feel awkward if not able to explain every Circumstance they relate to.

Early in September 1781, Mrs. Smyth decided that Albany had become too dangerous, and she left for Bennington, accompanied by a black woman servant whom the doctor described as a 'Negro wench.' They were more successful than Hudibras, for in Bennington Major Joseph Fay received them and refused to allow Mrs. Smyth to be searched – a blessing, for she carried a dispatch from Sir Henry Clinton for Haldimand. The Fays sent her to Skenesborough, where she met her son Thomas, a lieutenant in the King's Loyal Regiment of New York, who had come with a flag of truce to represent his father and Captain Sherwood at a prisoner exchange. She reported that Terry was still in Albany gaol. Young Hudibras was to have been paroled, but after an abortive attempt by John Walden Meyers to kidnap General Philip Schuyler, Terry was questioned; when he refused to divulge where Meyers might be hiding, or what route he would use to leave the area, he was returned to gaol, all hope of a parole lost.[26]

Smyth's letter to Haldimand, written September 25, is a mixture of elation and sorrow: 'Fay had behav'd well. . . & thro' his means I am possessed of my Rib again! but Alas; my poor boy: what will become of him?'

Fortunately, Terence took care of himself by escaping from gaol and making for Bennington, where Joseph Fay sheltered him. Once he had recovered from his confinement, Ethan and Ira Allen had him spirited away to join a party of Sherwood's scouts whom they knew to be in the neighbourhood.[27] Thus the family was reunited at Fort St. Johns, although the doctor observed that the only house available was no bigger than a racoon box. It stood a mile from the garrison, near the military hospital that was housed in the same barracks as the King's Rangers.

One evening in May 1782, while the doctor was seated at his door, some of Major James Rogers' men noticed a sinister looking man lurking near 'the necessary house, not ten yards from where I was sitting. As I am conscious the rebels will spare no pains nor cost to either take or Deprive me of my life, this circumstance gives me some suspicion of the intent.'

Living so far from the main body of troops, the doctor feared the rebels could kidnap him at any time. Thereafter, he reported to Mathews, Major Rogers had posted a 'Centinel' near his house.

Because he spent so much time imprisoned, Terence Smyth did not have enough time to recruit men to earn a commission. In January 1784, Major Rogers made his futile attempt to appoint officers for a fourth company, King's Rangers, with Terence as the lieutenant. Thus Young Hudibras, who had carried many dispatches, remained a civilian, while Thomas, the younger son, qualified for a lieutenantcy under Sir John Johnson. When the Loyal Rangers were formed in November 1781, Hudibras was appointed the surgeon of the battalion. However, the men received little care from him for he was rarely on hand. Prisoners and refugees, the secret service, and the Vermont horse trading took up most of Smyth's time when he was well enough to be on duty.

The Secret Service

The organization that Sherwood and Smyth were to operate had evolved gradually. Under Sir Guy Carleton the secret service was haphazard, with various post commanders choosing loyalists they thought dependable to carry their dispatches and bring back intelligence. Burgoyne consulted Daniel McAlpin, who commanded a party of loyalists, when he needed a courier to carry dispatches on his impending surrender to Sir Henry Clinton's headquarters. McAlpin selected Joseph Bettys, who slipped away from the British encampment near Saratoga and reached New York City safely.[28]

Carleton also depended on informers still in their homes to supply intelligence to couriers when they passed by. After Haldimand succeeded Carleton, the British Secret Service, Northern Department, began to evolve. Haldimand depended on several people to keep him informed, from the time of his arrival in Quebec City in 1778 until on into 1781. At first he relied heavily on Sir John Johnson.[29]

Agents working for Haldimand were usually officers or noncommissioned officers from the below-strength corps on his temporary list. Undoubtedly this sidetracked many and impeded the work of getting recruits in rebel-held areas to complete these units. For example, John Walden Meyers tried to raise a company for DeLancey's Brigade, of the Central Department, before he switched to recruiting for the King's Rangers. In May 1779, Meyers came to Fort St. Johns with a dispatch from Sir Henry Clinton. Brigadier Watson Powell, then the commandant of the fort, sent Meyers on to Quebec City to repeat his story to the governor. Meyers returned to Fort St. Johns under orders to wait until Haldimand had dispatches for New York City. The courier kicked his heels at the fort or in Montreal until mid October, before dispatches finally reached Fort St. Johns.[30] The governor had kept Meyers idle for nearly five months, time he might have spent leading recruits to New York City.

By January 1781, the secret service was being placed in the hands of Justus Sherwood, through an arrangement he made with Haldimand while visiting Quebec City to report on a mission he had made into Vermont. Beforehand, Sherwood had demonstrated his ability at carrying dispatches and analysing information brought to Canada by refugees and prisoners. Because of his past associations with the Green Mountain Boys he was destined to become Haldimand's chief negotiator in an attempt to persuade Vermont to rejoin the British Empire. Sherwood's journey to Vermont was his first important undertaking for Haldimand's secret service.

Vermont's behaviour from 1777 until after the peace treaty is a fascinating subplot in the revolution. American secondary sources leave out elements that give the tale a fresh twist. The missing ingredients are found in the correspondence of Haldimand and his officers. Some of this information has been explored by Vermont historians, but they tend to overlook the geography of the Green Mountains, and certain intercepted letters intended for the Continental Congress that found their way to the Chateau St. Louis.

On the eve of the revolution Vermont was disputed territory, occupied mainly by New Englanders, legally part of New York. By 1773, after three decades of land granting there were 127 townships in the Green Mountains. These had three types of land tenure: grantees under New Hampshire title (hence the name New Hampshire Grants), patentees under New York, and townships where settlers covered themselves by holding their titles from both provinces.[31]

New Hampshire titles were usually farm lots and freehold, while in New York it was customary to grant large acreages to owners who divided them into farm lots which they leased to tenants. The efforts of Ethan Allen and his Green Mountain Boys, who held their titles from New Hampshire and refused to pay quit rents to New York, were directed at keeping settlers holding leases from landlords of that province out of the district.

The capture of Fort Ticonderoga and Crown Point, and the occupation of Skenesborough in May 1775 were acts of war. The question often left up in the air is, against whom? Sir William Howe regarded Allen's action as rebellion, but the move was also aimed against New York. Allen feared that the forts would be reinforced and he was justified. Philip Skene, the proprietor of Skenesborough and a typical New York landlord, was then sailing from England with a commission to take command of Ticonderoga and Crown Point.[32] Allen's men seized Skenesborough because it had a shipyard and was a potential naval base for the control of Lake Champlain. Names on muster rolls of provincial corps indicate that Sherwood was not the only former Green Mountain Boy to become a loyalist when the time came to be counted.

Today the Breakenridge farm near Bennington is touted as the place where Vermont was born. In October 1771 the sheriff of Albany County, with 150 supporters, attempted to evict James Breakenridge, whose land was under New Hampshire title, so that a New York owner could take possession of it. When the sheriff arrived, Jim had an inordinate number of armed guests lounging about, and the Yorkers withdrew.[33] No one whispers that Breakenridge's two sons; James Jr. and David, were officers in the King's Rangers who dared not return home after the revolution.

The outbreak of the rebellion gave the people in the Green Mountains the opportunity they sought. Since the Congress would not admit the New Hampshire Grants as a state, owing to New Yorks' objections, on January 15, 1777, the ringleaders proclaimed their area the independent Republic of Vermont. Thomas Chittenden, one-eyed and illiterate, was the governor, with a council and a legislature that met at various places, most often the Green Mountain Tavern in Bennington. Preoccupied with the war, the Congress could do little to coerce Vermont. Ethan Allen, captured near Montreal in 1775 and exchanged in 1778, became a general in the republic's army, and from that time onward, separation from New York took precedence over the rebellion against Britain.

As the year 1780 opened, Sir Henry Clinton and Governor Haldimand agreed to some probing to see whether the situation in Vermont could be exploited to the advantage of Britain. Intrigue that would send Justus Sherwood on a bizarre journey, began at headquarters in New York City. Colonel Beverley Robinson, from West Point on the Hudson, was the commander of the Loyal American

Regiment, and Sir Henry Clinton's adviser. On March 30, with the approbation of Lord George Germain, the Colonial Secretary, Robinson wrote to Ethan Allen, stating that he knew the other was not in sympathy with the rebels. Robinson proposed, through letters or trusted emissaries, that they discuss the benefits to be accrued through Vermont's reunion with the mother country.[34]

Robinson noted that the Allens, Chittenden and the Fays were conspiring to ensure Vermont's continued independence from New York. The Congress refused to admit Vermont because France objected. The French had made their alliance with thirteen states and were balking at extending it to include a fourteenth, especially one that bordered on Canada, where Haldimand might send troops to occupy it.[35] British propaganda had been successful. The rebels were convinced that the governor had 10,000 crack regulars poised to invade Vermont. In fact, Haldimand had some 7,000 regulars scattered from the Gaspé to Michilimackinac. A neutral state on Canada's border would be a blessing for Haldimand.

For Vermont, Robinson's suggestion had two advantages. It would impede Congress – because of the danger of tangling with Haldimand's mythical army – and it would assure that this same mythical army did not descend from Canada, with fire and sword, to end the rebellion in Vermont. Robinson's letter was sent to Albany and forwarded to Arlington by Dr. George Smyth, where his messenger, dressed as a farmer, slipped it to Ethan Allen in the village street.

After much furtive shuffling, because a faction in Vermont favoured continuing the war, the leaders sent a letter to the Congress, pointing out that the republic had never waged war against Britain – overlooking the contribution of the Vermont militia at the Battle of Bennington – nor joined the Congress by confederation. If the Congress would not admit Vermont, she was free to make her own terms with Britain, with whom she was at peace.

On duty at Fort St. Johns, Sherwood knew that something was brewing, for Brigadier Powell, the commandant, asked him what he knew of Ethan Allen. Sherwood replied that he was well acquainted with Mr. Allen, and was certain the Vermonters would accept any proposal rather than give up their lands to New York, adding:

I should be extremely happy to be in some measure instrumental in bringing deluded people to their right senses and the allegiance they owe their Sovereign which I think may be done by buying their leaders.[36]

In August, Captain Samuel Wright, a loyalist held in Bennington, was released to carry a message from Chittenden to Haldimand. On the 24th, Sherwood sent a message to a friend named

Hawkins telling him that reunion with Britain could be effected because the Vermonters were disenchanted with the Congress. He did not realize that the plot was hatching on the west side of the Green Mountains, where most of the people were Yankees. To the east were pockets of Yorkers and more conservative Yankees who wanted to continue the rebellion. The clique at Bennington and Arlington who planned to open negotiations with Haldimand had to keep their plan secret from many people in Vermont.

Chittenden's letter, which Captain Wright carried to Quebec City, proposed a truce. Towards the end of September, with Lord Germain's approval, Haldimand accepted Chittenden's offer, and suggested talks under a flag of truce. While these talks, disguised as prisoner exchanges, were taking place, Chittenden promised that Vermont would be neutral. As commissioners to represent the republic, Chittenden chose Colonel Ira Allen and Major Joseph Fay. Haldimand selected Captain Justus Sherwood as his commissioner, assisted by Major Alexander Dundas, the commandant of Isle aux Noix. The Green Mountain plotters assured Haldimand that Sherwood would be in no danger.

Early in October, Haldimand sent Majors Christopher Carleton, James Rogers and Edward Jessup with a combined force of regulars and provincials to attack the outposts belonging to New York. The governor used this raid to put the folk in Vermont in a receptive mood. While this expedition was still marauding, Sherwood received orders to leave for Castleton, where Ethan Allen had his headquarters, and he left Isle aux Noix with five privates and a drummer – in full regimentals, a British officer and his escort on an official mission.[37]

After camping at Miller's Bay Sherwood and his escort made their way in a cutter to East Bay, a long creek running from Lake Champlain towards Castleton. Leaving two men to guard the cutter Sherwood marched inland with three privates and the drummer. At Fort Vengeance, four miles from Castleton, a party of men stopped him. Sherwood was blindfolded and led into the presence of Colonel Samuel Herrick, where he handed over his official dispatches – those pertaining to a prisoner exchange – keeping others which he was to disclose only if Ethan Allen agreed. The following day Sherwood had a private chat with Allen, and attended a meeting of the Vermont Council – all old acquaintances amused at the sight of Sherwood dressed up as a redcoat. At Allen's insistence, only prisoner exchanges were discussed, for he claimed he needed time to prepare the council to accept reunion.

The council agreed to a cartel for exchanging prisoners, and promised that during the negotiations Vermont would be neutral. Sherwood sent a message to Major Carleton, still at Miller's Bay on Lake Champlain, informing him of the truce, and Allen wrote to his post commanders to the same effect. Then Ethan, the chieftain of the Green Mountains, left for Bennington to address the legislature, and the fun began. Ethan's cousin, Major Ebenezer Allen, who had attended the meeting, wanted no part of the British. Once Ethan was out of the way Ebenezer ordered two sentries to guard Sherwood, and they threatened his life. By order of Ebenezer, Sherwood and his men were put in charge of a captain and 20 soldiers and marched 28 miles to Pawlet.

Everywhere Sherwood found the populace alarmed, for Ebenezer had spread rumours that Major Carleton and a party of Indians were nearby, in the hope that someone with an itchy finger on his firelock would dispatch Sherwood. If Allen could demonstrate that British officers were not safe under their flags, Haldimand would refuse to send any more of them. From November 1, Sherwood's journal read:

Marched 10 Miles in a tedious Snow Storm. 2nd. Marched 20 miles to Arlington. This morning received a Message from Gov. Chittington expressing his disapprobation of Maj. Allen's Conduct, and his orders. . . that I should be treated in a manner that an officer of a Flag had the right to expect, and by no means to keep me any longer under the least restraint.[38]

On November 7, after five days of name-calling by Ebenezer Allen and the governor, Sherwood's party was given horses and escorted to Castleton. More delays followed, caused by Ethan's obnoxious cousin, and it was the 11th before Justus, with Ira Allen and Joseph Fay, who were to go to Canada with him, reached East Bay. They found the cutter frozen in two inches of ice. For three days they broke ice, and on the 14th, Sherwood recorded:

Allen and Fay turned back and said they would come to St. Johns by ice as soon as possible – I had the day before shown them the General's proposals, after perusing them and discoursing largely on the subject – we burned them.

Sherwood referred to the papers he was to disclose if Ethan agreed. He did not, but he decided that Ira and Joseph should read them in Canada. In desperation Sherwood showed them to the two commissioners when he realized they would not be continuing with him. Ira insisted that if Congress admitted Vermont, the negotiations were to remain a secret, lest the plotters be charged with treason. This demand hints that the conspirators were only talking reunion to force the Congress to grant statehood. Sherwood was undaunted because Ethan had assured him that the terms Vermont intended to ask would be unacceptable to the Congress. Ira shared Ethan's sentiments, but the brothers were not certain they could carry the whole republic with them.

Meanwhile, in Quebec City, Haldimand had received a report that Major John André had been hanged, and he was alarmed for Sherwood's safety. He cautioned Major Carleton to stand by to withdraw the commissioner as soon as possible, since the fate of André showed 'the fatal consequences of being frustrated.'[39]

After Ira Allen and Joseph Fay returned to Castleton, Sherwood's men continued breaking ice, and it was November 19 before they reached open water on Lake Champlain. By that time, convinced that he would never see Sherwood alive, the weather piercingly cold, Major Carleton had withdrawn his force, which reached Isle aux Noix on November 14. By the time Sherwood's party gained the lake he was short of provisions, and he set out for Skenesborough with one man to obtain food, appropriating a skiff because their loads – pork and Indian corn – were heavy. They rejoined the cutter and the others near Ticonderoga. By the time they reached Pointe au Fer, they were on half rations, for 'Captain McDonald's Family' had joined them at Skenesborough, and they had picked up two men, four women and four children who had been four days without food. Sherwood's enlarged party reached Fort St. Johns on November 26. On the 28th, with Major Carleton, he set out in a sleigh for Quebec City, a journey that took three days.

After discussing the results of his mission with the governor, Sherwood returned to Fort St. Johns with orders to take charge of scouting parties, and in an optimistic mood. Haldimand, however, soon smelled a rat. Writing to Sir Henry Clinton on February 28, he warned him that he had received a letter from Dr. George Smyth, soon to be Sherwood's deputy but at that time still sending information from Albany:

I have been put on my guard by an intelligent and Staunch friend in Albany against the People of Vermont, with whom I have been sometime in Treaty, who seek to deceive both the Congress and the Royal Army. I shall spare nothing to work upon that people, and, if I succeed, I shall not fail to tell you, but I have great doubts.

Whatever the fate of the talks on reunion, Haldimand resolved to maintain the truce, so that he would not be 'deprived of intelligence' and subject to 'mistakes & losses of reputation.'

Back at Fort St. Johns, Sherwood informed the governor's secretary, Mathews, that he could easily find three trusty guides to accompany two agents whenever Colonel St. Leger, who had recently assumed the command of the fort from Brigadier Powell, gave the order. By January 28, 1781, Sherwood was in hot water with St. Leger, and writing to Mathews requesting clarification as to which post commander was his superior officer. Major Dundas, at Isle aux Noix, Major Carleton at Pointe au Fer, and St. Leger, were all asking for scouts to bring them information. When he left Quebec City, Sherwood understood that he was to take his orders from Dundas, at whose post he was dispatching his scouts for greater secrecy than was possible at Fort St. Johns. St. Leger assumed that all scouting parties required his permission before entering rebel territory, and he ordered Sherwood to provide six men to accompany Lieutenant William Twiss, Royal Engineers, who wanted to explore for defence sites along Lake Champlain.

Sherwood had six men at Isle aux Noix, all assigned and about to depart. Two parties were already out, one near Albany, the other bound for the Connecticut Valley. Replying to Sherwood's letter, Mathews assured him that Haldimand was pleased with his work, but he mentioned nothing about straightening out which officer was his superior. In the interval St. Leger had given Sherwood a nasty dressing down because he had no scouts to send with Lieutenant Twiss.

Haldimand also made use of resident agents who gave information to scouts who called on them, or sent letters directly to the Chateau St. Louis. Two of these were Elnathan Merwin of Arlington, Vermont, code name 'Plain Truth,' and Colonel Samuel Wells of Brattleboro, on the east side of the Green Mountains. One who may have been a double agent was Thomas Johnson, kidnapped from his home near Newbury, Vermont, by Captain Azariah Pritchard, King's Rangers.[40] Johnson was a lieutenant-colonel in the rebel militia, and St. Leger entertained him at his house, inviting Major James Rogers to join them. As befit a man of such rank, St. Leger gave Johnson the freedom of Fort St. Johns, but he asked Sherwood to talk with him. Johnson was offering to become a resident agent if he were allowed to return home, and if Sherwood thought him dependable he could be useful.

From Verchères, Colonel Peters, Sherwood's commanding officer in the Queen's Loyal Rangers, heard of Johnson's arrival, and sent a note of caution. Johnson was a friend of General Jacob Bailey, a devoted rebel.[41] Since Bailey was the man who had driven Peters' wife and children from their home and sent them to Ticonderoga in dead of winter, Sherwood suspected that Peters was prejudiced. He informed Haldimand to this effect, admitting that he thought Johnson was plausible and might be trusted. In due course he was sent back to Newbury.

As the weeks of winter slipped by, Sherwood waited for some indication that the Vermont commissioners were coming. The ice remained soft, the weather mild, and not until May 8, 1781, did Ira Allen, without Joseph Fay, reach Isle aux Noix for a conference.[42]

The meeting was utterly unsatisfactory. Ira insisted that the time was not ripe to talk of reunion, while Sherwood wanted to discuss little else.

Among the letters intercepted by Sherwood's agents was a packet brought in in April that was intended for the Continental Congress. One was from Micah Townsend, a son-in-law of Colonel Samuel Wells, the resident agent at Brattleboro. Townsend's letter revealed the precarious state of the war in the north. Writing to the Congress he pointed out that General Philip Schuyler was willing to grant Vermont statehood, lest she make a separate peace with Britain, to the detriment of the war effort. If Vermont returned to the British fold, her territory, extending into the heart of the northern states, could be used to attack her neighbours. Since Vermont had become neutral all kinds of people were flocking there – loyalists, deserters from the Continental Army, the disenchanted of all hues. Vermont had annexed the New Hampshire counties of Cheshire and Grafton because the residents wanted out of the war. Townsend urged the Congress to admit Vermont before the war in the north collapsed completely.[43]

That June Haldimand solved the problem over who was Sherwood's superior officer in matters involving the gathering of intelligence and Vermont. On the 18th, Mathews informed Sherwood that he was the head of the British Secret Service, Northern Department, in charge of all scouts, except those working from western posts. Even after Haldimand placed Sherwood in command, the governor played his cards close to his chest. In 1782, Baron von Riedesel, in command of the military district of Sorel, which included the Lake Champlain outposts, sent a party of men to search for the Bailey-Hazen Road. This was a line of corduroy that ran from the vicinity of Newbury, in the Connecticut Valley, towards the Canadian border. First proposed to the Congress in 1776 as a supply route for an invasion of Canada, General Bailey had been chosen to oversee the project. The man in charge of construction was Moses Hazen. His battalion of Canadians worked on the road for $10 per month, plus food and a daily ration of half a pint of rum.[44]

Haldimand had known where the road ran for two years before von Riedesel sent his men to look for it. On May 17, 1780, Major Carleton, at Pointe au Fer, had sent Haldimand a report, stating that there were magazines of provisions cached along it. Then in September 1781, a scout reported that Hazen's men had built blockhouses every five miles, information the governor chose not to pass on to von Riedesel. Hazen and his Canadians abandoned their efforts some ten miles short of their objective, but all told they built

Summer cottage on the site of Sherwood's Loyal Blockhouse, North Hero Island, built by Oscar Bredenberg, an authority on the history of Lake Champlain.

Monument to the Green Mountain Tavern in Bennington. The tavern is called the Catamount, a name used some years later.

50 miles of what has been called the only lasting memorial to the revolution in Vermont.

Soon after his appointment as head of the secret service, with Haldimand's consent Sherwood began building his Loyal Blockhouse on North Hero Island, the name chosen to emphasize that this was a loyalist operation. By July 1 he was at Dutchman's Point, on the island, reporting to Mathews:

I arriv'd here yesterday with 23 men including old men, Boys and unincorporated Loyalists. I am now Building an Oven & Hutting the men, shall tomorrow begin felling timber for the block house. Timber is not so plentiful here as I expect'd & we must draw it a mile at least.

Later, Sherwood reported that he had employed some 70 men – officers, pensioners and privates – and commencing July 1, 1781, he had paid them at a muster every two months, as follows:

Captains £30 Sterling
Lieutenants £14 Sterling
Ensigns £11 Sterling
Pensioners £14. 15s. 0d Sterling

All officers had 2½ d. per day deducted for rations. Sergeants were paid £3 per muster, with 2d. per week deducted for surgeon's fees; corporals £2 with 1½ d. deducted for the surgeon, and privates at 10s. with a penny a week deducted for the surgeon. All had 2½ d. per day taken from their wages for rations.[45]

On July 29 Sherwood reported to Mathews that his men had built a very good and large blockhouse, and there was 'not so proper a place on the Frontier as this for the residence and departure of secret scouts.' Prior to joining Sherwood as his deputy, Dr. Smyth had visited Quebec City. When he reached Dutchman's Point he had permission to carry out a plan mooted for some weeks. Small parties of loyalists were to kidnap important New York rebels, whose removal would have a devastating effect on morale – as well as provide valuable prisoners for exchange.[46]

Eight parties would go into New York State, each to consist of from four to six loyalists and, at Haldimand's insistence, two British regulars in civilian clothing, on the excuse that these were better marchers, but more likely because the governor did not trust loyalists.[47] Sherwood and Smyth were to choose the loyalists, St. Leger the regulars. All were to be close to their quarry by July 31. None were to strike earlier, so that parties with farther to travel could be in position before anyone gave the game away. In some cases Indian guides were provided. All were to depart from the Loyal Blockhouse after Sherwood briefed them, to avoid misunderstandings.

Sherwood had confidence in three of the parties, those led by Joseph Bettys, John Walden Meyers and Mathew Howard. All had proved themselves reliable in the past. In the others he had misgivings, but Meyers' intended captive was the most important – General Philip Schuyler, the commander of the rebels' military department in Albany. Bettys was to abduct Samuel Stringer from his home near Ballstown, while Mathew Howard was to take John Bleecker near Hoosic. By July 26 all the parties were on their way, with orders to memorize their instructions from Sherwood and destroy them.

The Loyal Blockhouse was almost complete, and Sherwood had a small garrison to run the place while his agents came and went. At times he had as many as 50 provincials whose duties were to guard the site, cut firewood, plough and plant, so that the headquarters would be as self sufficient as possible. About 50 men worked as scouts and couriers, or as escorts. Many were secret agents, but some were members of the blockhouse garrison. There Sherwood and Smyth waited for news of the parties of kidnappers.

Their attention was soon distracted by the arrival of Major Joseph Fay, officially to discuss a prisoner exchange with Vermont. At a stormy session aboard the *Royal George*, Fay had nothing to offer on the subject of reunion with Britain beyond assurances that the conspirators needed more time. An exasperated Sherwood reported to Captain Mathews that the Vermonters were seeking 'Two strings to their bow.' Scouts returning from Vermont reported that the leaders wanted reunion but the public was opposed. Soon after Fay left for home, news of the kidnap parties began to come in, none of it encouraging.

Joseph Bettys' men returned to the Loyal Blockhouse minus Samuel Stringer and their leader. Bettys had left his men to carry out the kidnapping and gone off to visit a girl at Norman's Kill, close to Albany, and the men panicked when their leader failed them. Next, Bettys persuaded the lass he visited to run off with him – scandalous for he was a married man with a family at Ballstown. Bettys turned up at Fort St. Johns, where St. Leger confined him to the garrison, for 'refusing to deliver up his Desdemona,' Smyth wrote after he hurried from the Loyal Blockhouse to question the miscreant. Bettys declined to say where he had hidden the girl. An irate Smyth called her Bettys' 'female recruit.' Eventually she was found, and Smyth was loath to send her home, 'for I think he would not be long after her which would ruin many of His Majesty's loyal subjects.'

Five other parties returned, all without their captives, and there was no news of Meyers or Howard. The latter succeeded in capturing John Bleecker, but then his entire party was taken – 18 men, for he thought the six loyalists and two British regulars he brought from Canada insufficient. Now all 19 were in gaol at Bennington.[48]

On August 17, an irate Meyers stormed into Fort St. Johns. On July 31 he had been ready, with a party of 12 men, for like Howard, Meyers thought the loyalists and British regulars in his party inadequate and had co-opted some local friends. Meyers dared not strike on that day, because scouts informed him of a manhunt for Joseph Bettys, who was supposed to be 25 miles away at Ballstown, kidnapping Samuel Stringer. By August 7, Meyers thought all was clear, but he did not know that the rebels had found Sherwood's written orders when they caught Howard, nor that Schuyler had been forewarned. When Meyers' men broke into the Schuyler mansion, two miles south of Albany, they found armed men waiting. After a short skirmish, in which both his British regulars were wounded, Meyers ordered a withdrawal. His men carried off two of Schuyler's as they fled into the forest. St. Leger's report on Meyers' failure reached Quebec City two days later, carried by James Breakenbridge, riding express, which meant changing horses at inns and cat napping by the roadside.

The battle in the Schuyler mansion took place in the wide central hallway, but someone made a side trip into the dining room for some silver, to the mortification of Haldimand. The governor ordered the booty returned, but Meyers could find only a few spoons. The valuable part, tankards and plates, had been looted by local loyalists, who had long since sold it.[49] The matter of the silver cropped up over and over until Haldimand finally admitted that it could never be recovered. The entire kidnapping caper was an embarrassment to the governor. No one was seriously hurt, and the loyalists with Mathew Howard were exchanged at Skenesborough in September. Their leader lay in Bennington under sentence of death. Three times a halter was put round his neck and he was drawn up in an effort to make him reveal information on the strength of Haldimand's garrison.[50]

After delicate negotiations by Sherwood and Smyth, Howard was exchanged, along with the two regulars from the 34th Regiment who were with his party. An undated report by St. Leger is headed 'Return of Exchanged Prisoners of His Majesty's Regular Regiments and Provincial Corps by last Cartel from Vermont.' It shows 19 names – Lieutenant Howard and Cadet Daniel Carr, of Colonel Ebenezer Jessup's regiment, Private Charles McArthur of Major Rogers', and Ensign Harleton Spencer, no regiment named. The men from the 34th Regiment, captured 'near Bennington' on

August 6 with Howard were Corporal Andrew Temple and Private William Slone. The others were regulars from the 9th, 53rd and 47th Regiments, captured during Burgoyne's campaign.[51]

That autumn of 1781, Vermont annexed another slice of territory, by extending her western boundary to the Hudson, because people in that area were war weary.[52] This made Skenesborough, where Sherwood conducted prisoner exchanges and received refugees, neutral ground and safer for his missions. In September, while exchanging prisoners, Sherwood and Smyth met Ira Allen at Skenesborough. Allen recommended that if Haldimand would send a proclamation offering his terms on reunion, he would greatly aid the work of the conspirators. The governor agreed, and on October 10, the proclamation reached Fort St. Johns. Colonel St. Leger was ordered to occupy Crown Point with 1,000 regulars and provincials, with the same purpose as Major Carleton's foray of the year before – to put the Vermonters in a co-operative frame of mind. Major John Ross was to lead an expedition from Carleton Island, and instructions for raids were sent to Colonel John Butler at Niagara. All these measures were, in part, intended to demonstrate how much better off were the inhabitants of the neutral zone than those living in New York State.[53]

Sherwood and Smyth journeyed to Crown Point, where Ira Allen had told them he would send a messenger to pick up the proclamation. When, after several days, no one had come from Ira, Smyth suggested that a patrol be sent to kidnap a Vermont scouting party, which could be released to take the proclamation to Castleton. St. Leger agreed, and he sent out an officer and 12 men to the vicinity of Mount Independence, opposite Fort Ticonderoga, where they encountered a patrol of a sergeant and five men. When ordered to surrender the Vermonters raised their firelocks, whereupon one of the British opened fire, killing the sergeant, one Archelus Tupper.[54]

To Sherwood's dismay, the patrol returned with five prisoners and one corpse – an act of hostility that might spell trouble for the truce – and led St. Leger to overplay his hand. He released the survivors, carrying Haldimand's proclamation, the dead sergeant's clothing, and a letter of apology to Governor Chittenden, as well as an invitation to the deceased's friends to come under a safe conduct to attend the funeral.[55] Soon after this ceremony, Sherwood received a letter from Ira Allen describing the blockade of Lord Cornwallis at Yorktown by the French fleet. He asked Sherwood to refrain from sending the proclamation, but requested that he and Dr. Smyth come to Castleton for a meeting. The two commissioners accepted, and found that the Vermont Council was still willing to keep the truce, but all talk on reunion was to be postponed. If Cornwallis surrendered, George Washington would be free to turn his army against Canada or Vermont.

After Sergeant Tupper's death, Ira explained, some of the militia had been called out, but when St. Leger's letter of apology reached Vermont, the men returned home, Nevertheless, the rebel faction was aroused, and people wondered why a high and mighty British colonel with his two gold epaulettes should apologize for the death of a mere sergeant of militia. Ira replied, deadpan, 'Good men are sorry when good men are killed.'[56] Sherwood heaved a sigh of relief when he found that no one at Castleton suspected that he and Smyth had had a hand in the capture of the patrol. He dared not raise the question of whether the proclamation had arrived, nor which Vermont leader had it in his possession. Thus ended another round in the sparring.

Back at the Loyal Blockhouse, Sherwood and Smyth were called upon to conduct some counter intelligence, and they investigated a resident of Montreal, one Mrs. Cheshire, whom Sir John Johnson suspected of passing information to Albany and aiding rebels on parole seeking to escape. On November 7, 1781, Smyth reported that they had sent three counterspies to visit 'Madam Cheshire' in her home. The agents carried Yankee firelocks, some paper money from Vermont and Connecticut, and a forged letter from General Jacob Bailey. Dressed in shabby clothing they set out, and confirmed Johnson's misgivings. The lady was a spy.[57] What Brigadier Allan Maclean, then the commandant of the district, did was not recorded. He may have left Mrs. Cheshire alone, and put a watch on her house so that her visitors could be whisked away to an internment compound near the city.

The winter of 1781-1782 was a busy one for the secret service. After Cornwallis' surrender at Yorktown, Haldimand sought to discover whether George Washington would turn his army against Canada. Writing to Mathews on February 7, Sherwood declared that the Yorktown defeat was a 'Whiggish plot.' Soon his scouts were bringing in reports of a troop buildup at Albany, cannon stockpiled at Hartford, Connecticut, and a supply of uniforms at Poughkeepsie. Haldimand ordered him to redouble his efforts to find out Washington's intentions.

As with the corps commanders, money was a problem for Sherwood. He had to send his accounts to Quebec City, where Haldimand scrutinized them, criticizing many of his expenditures. As a consequence, Sherwood's men's pay was often in arrears, and he was chronically short of supplies. He paid his agents 2s. 6d. a day when they were on missions, which Haldimand thought excessive. On May 14, 1782, Mathews informed Sherwood that His Excellency was displeased at 'the vast expense you have incurred on that service by paying such high wages to persons regularly subsisted and provisioned by Government.' When Sherwood tried to reduce these wages the men refused to risk their lives. He resorted to supplementing what Haldimand allowed from his own slender funds.

Another difficulty was the innate garrulousness of the scouts. On February 14, 1782, Mathews wrote complaining that Ensign Roger Stevens, King's Rangers, had arrived in Quebec City with Sherwood's dispatches, but the news of his presence – and the content of much of his packet – was known all over the place. To Dr. Smyth, then at Fort St. Johns, Sherwood admitted:

It is easy to trace the source of this unpardonable conduct – Messengers arrive, and the inquisitive and impertenent flock around them for news. They sit down together to pass the evening, and over their glasses make the Business they have been upon the topic of conversation – From there they retire to their Homes and renew the Subject with their wives & families – By the first post or express, it is conveyed all over the Country, no matter by Friends or Enemies, the effect is the same.

By the spring, the news that Cornwallis had surrendered was widely known, and refugees were flocking to the British outposts. Sherwood received many at the Loyal Blockhouse. Soon people were aware that the prime minister, Lord Rockingham, had representatives in Paris discussing peace terms. Prior to these events many loyalists had remained in their homes hoping that Britain would yet succeed in quelling the rebellion. Now they were packing and making their way to Canada. A mood of bleak despair permeated the several outposts, not helped in Sherwood's case by the behaviour of his deputy, Smyth.

The doctor had retired to Fort St. Johns because he was exhausted, but he persisted in acting without informing his superior, sending out scouts on his own initiative. After Sherwood lodged several complaints, Mathews suggested that although he was indeed Smyth's superior, he should be less touchy.[58] A month later Sherwood admitted that he was forwarding all his reports to Smyth before sending them on to Haldimand, to avoid 'uneasiness.'

At the time Sherwood was worried about the safety of three agents, Joseph Bettys, John Parker and Jonathan Miller, who had left the Loyal Blockhouse together in March. Bettys was bound for New York City with a dispatch, while the other two were to remain around Albany gathering information. A scout returning reported that Bettys and Parker had been captured. They were confined in the basement of the town hall in Albany because the gaol was overflowing. Gloomily Dr. Smyth informed Mathews that the agents would undoubtedly be hanged. When this letter reached the Chateau St. Louis, Haldimand ordered Sherwood to have these agents exchanged, and to state that Bettys was entitled to be treated as a British officer. Furthermore, the governor threatened to retaliate if the rebels executed either man.

'The war,' Mathews wrote, 'has not furnished *a single instance* where a Prisoner has suffered Death in this Province.' In vain Sherwood sent a scout towards Albany. Bettys and Parker mounted the scaffold before the messenger reached the town. Bettys was a scamp, but a lovable one, whose widow brought his children to Canada, where they could grow up among people who did not call their father a traitor.[59]

In May, Sherwood sent Azariah Pritchard and seven men to kidnap General Jacob Bailey, ordering them to visit Thomas Johnson, released to return to his home as a resident agent. Johnson would advise them on the best way of catching Bailey. When Pritchard's party reached Bailey's house the bird had flown across the Connecticut River into New Hampshire. Pritchard had to be content with abducting Bailey's son, and Sherwood was suspicious that Johnson had warned the general. Dr. Smyth was convinced that Johnson, unwell at the time, was not to blame for Bailey's escape.[60]

As the summer of 1782 approached the garrison at the Loyal Blockhouse was poised against a rebel attack, for the post was on the front line for the defence of Canada. In July, at Haldimand's request, Sherwood sent agents William Amesbury and John Lindsay (both privates in his company) to see whether they could blow up Captain John Paul Jones' ship *America*, a vessel of 63 guns under construction at Portsmouth, New Hampshire, their home state. On August 17 the two were back at the Loyal Blockhouse, and Lindsay reported that the ship was being paid for by France, to serve in that country's line. Pretending to be privateers, Lindsay and Amesbury were hired to work eight weeks – until the vessel was to be launched – at 4s. a day. Lindsay described Jones as 'a middling sized man of dark complexion, dressed very grant with two gold aupelets very like Col. St. Leger's.' Sherwood's men worked on the ship, and helped guard her! Captain Jones feared a raid from the sea. Lindsay continued:

> We could at any time have put fire in many places on her, but as her inside work was not done & she would not burn well we thought it best to come in with our report, and to go again when the General should think proper. When we came away I told Capt. Jones we must go to Boston to git some wages we had due, and we promised to return in Augt. or September and if possible to bring some ship carpenters with us from Boston.[61]

In saying the ship would not burn well, Lindsay referred to her oak planking. The pine to be used for her upper decking would be more suitable for arson, once it was in place. Lindsay and Amesbury did not have a second chance, for the cessation of hostilities intervened. Otherwise Sherwood might have collected together a party of carpenters 'from Boston' and sent them to put a torch to the famous captain's vessel.

Throughout the year 1782, Sherwood received many reassuring messages from Vermont, although Ethan Allen's were vague and confusing. Reunion was still an issue because many people in the Green Mountain republic did not like what was happening in other states. Haldimand never held out much hope that Vermont would rejoin the British Empire, but he encouraged Sherwood. The governor wanted to maintain the truce, for the sake of his sources of intelligence, as well as for loyalists seeking refuge there. For many loyalists Vermont was the escape hatch, mercifully closer than the British posts.

Those who reached Vermont were often sent on to Canada, or allowed to resettle in peace. As for Sherwood, he prayed for reunion so that he might be welcomed home to resume his former life. He did have cause for optimism. People rioted in many states when the Congress ordered legislators to levy taxes to pay war debts. Since the issue of taxes had started the rebellion many felt betrayed. Paper money was valueless, and farmers who could not pay taxes in hard cash saw their properties auctioned off. Mobs gathered to hinder the bidding and tax collecting was nearly impossible.

Vermont had none of these problems, for she had been financing herself on the proceeds of departed loyalists' property. Although the republic stopped confiscation when the truce began, the legislature had passed the Absentee Act, wherein the property of any owner not there to pay a small tax was forfeited. Sherwood wrote that Vermont abolished confiscations so as not to appear hostile to Britain, which was a pretence.[62] However, Sherwood took heart from the riots over the Continental debt, another reason why Vermont must prefer reunion with Britain over the Congress.

A further hopeful matter was Vermont's trade patterns. All goods moved by water, and Vermont's rivers north of the Battenkill at Arlington drained to Lake Champlain, thence to the St. Lawrence. If the Green Mountain people could not retain their traditional lines of trade the economy would suffer. The republic's source of wealth was timber, and logs did not float upstream.

The Vermonters' need for trade was amply demonstrated after Cornwallis surrendered in the autumn of 1781. Although Chittenden and Haldimand agreed to prohibit trade, since Washington might seize on dealing with the enemy as a reason for invading Vermont, an incident occurred in November, 1782, that disturbed Sherwood lest it upset the delicate balance he was maintaining with his former countrymen. Corporal Thomas Welch, of the blockhouse garrison, arrived aboard a British vessel escorting two men from Vermont with three tons of beef to sell.[63] Sherwood arrested all three, and appealed to Major John Nairne at Isle aux Noix for advice. Nairne ordered him to hold a court martial. Corporal Welch was exonerated, for Azariah Pritchard had ordered him to take the two traders to the British ship.[64] Sherwood dismissed Pritchard and returned him to duty with the King's Rangers, where Major Rogers would deal with him.

The ban on trade did not prevent a stream of hopefuls coming to the blockhouse with wares, eager to proceed to Montreal. One who came was Ebenezer Allen, Ethan's cousin who had marched Sherwood through Vermont those snowy days of November 1780. Sherwood told Mathews that it was so painful to see Allen that 'I can barely treat him with common civility.'

In February 1783, the Loyal Blockhouse garrison endured a moment of panic, for scouts reported that 600 rebels in sleighs had left Albany with Colonel Marinius Willett, and when last seen they were making for Saratoga. Sherwood prepared to withstand a seige, but the crisis passed when his scouts discovered that the sleighs were destined for Oswego. They were unsuccessful in their attempt to capture that stronghold from Major John Ross and his garrison of regulars and the second battalion, King's Royal Regiment of New York.

With the formal proclamation that the war had ended, in April 1783, the work of the secret service wound down, but Sherwood's men remained on duty and many visitors flocked to the blockhouse. Some were refugees, but others were rebels, smelling success and very arrogant. The latter claimed that Sherwood's headquarters was on New York territory and he should be evicted forthwith. Hostile men came to demand the discharge of friends and brothers serving in provincial corps, or prisoners around Montreal. Rude though they were, Sherwood felt obliged to protect them. He admitted to Mathews that his men would certainly cut such visitors to pieces if he did not keep a sharp lookout.[65]

In May, Mathews ordered Sherwood to come to Quebec City with seven or eight men, and to apply for a whaleboat at Isle aux Noix. His time as head of the secret service in his blockhouse was over, but Dr. Smyth stayed there, carrying on until the autumn.

Sherwood was sent to explore for land on which displaced loyalists could be resettled. For the secret service there remained only the settling of accounts, which Sherwood and Smyth accomplished later in the year.

The secret service had some successes, some failures. Of three agents Smyth complained 'the first is a simpleton, the second proves himself a knave, & the last I believe unfit for anything Except weaving Lindsey Woolsey.'[66] Describing the secret service of the Southern Department, John Bakeless decided that both sides were equally served by their intelligence, 'and quite as badly served by their counter intelligence.'[67] The same could be said of the contestants in the Northern Department.

The Vermont negotiations that kept the republic neutral served to hold a sensitive part of the Canadian border safe for the final three years of the war. American historians maintain that the machinations of the Allens, Fays and Chittenden were calculated to prevent Vermont being coerced by either side, and that Sherwood was their pawn. This view would be more valid had all negotiations ceased with the end of the revolution but they did not. In 1786, representatives from Vermont visited Canada asking for free trade.[68] This they were granted, but what might have happened had the Canadian border been closed to the people of the Green Mountains? For the sake of the economy the little republic might have decided that the future looked more rosy as part of British North America.

Prisoners and Refugees

As in every war, particularly a civil one, the American Revolution caused an upheaval in the lives of many people. Both sides took prisoners, while loyalists were forced to flee their homes to escape persecution by their rebel neighbours. Most of the men who enlisted in provincial corps came into Canada as refugees; and the records of the corps show that some who had been captured chose to enlist rather than remain in Canada as prisoners of war. Again, as in all wars, the refugees whose plight was the saddest were the women, children and the elderly. Some accompanied their men – sons, husbands and fathers – but many came on their own through the wilds, after being ordered out of their homes. Often these were pursued. Others were piloted to Canada by couriers who carried dispatches, by agents in quest of recruits, or agents dispatched specifically to rescue families in distress.

On the other hand, around Montreal and to some extent Quebec City, were American businessmen and their families who had come into Canada searching for opportunities after the Seven Years' War. Many supported the rebellion and were deemed a security risk. Carleton, and later Haldimand, had some of them interned. Others were allowed to be free as long as they promised to remain within certain confines, for example the limits of Montreal. Then, too, prisoners captured during encounters with the rebels were brought to the Montreal area and held in a compound, in private houses, or on Prison Island, at the head of the Cedars Rapids, from which escape was difficult.

Governor Haldimand was anxious to return many of the rebel sympathizers to avoid having to provision them. In some instances he allowed them to go to the United States as long as they signed paroles to do nothing to foster the rebel cause. On their part the rebel Committees of Safety, or in the case of New York, the Boards of Commissioners for Detecting and Defeating Conspiracies, were happy to send loyalist families into British-controlled territory so that they would not have to be cared for at public expense. The arrangements for returning people to either side were complex. Some loyalists were held hostage to ensure the good behaviour of their relatives serving in provincial corps, and elaborate horse trading was required before they could be released or exchanged.

Following the rebel attack on Quebec, Governor Carleton deemed prisoner exchanges necessary. On August 10, 1776, captured Americans were sent on ships to New York City. When these vessels arrived that city had been occupied by the British. General Sir William Howe allowed the ships to be unloaded, and the prisoners were free to make their way home. A like number of British prisoners was later traded for them.[69] By the time Governor Haldimand assumed command in Canada, the problem of prisoners held there, and loyalists asking for sanctuary or merely arriving, had become acute. Upon meeting Captain Justus Sherwood in the autumn of 1778, Haldimand appointed him Commissioner of Prisoners and Refguees.

The bargaining was a challenge, even for a businessman like Sherwood. Officers were exchanged rank for rank, but civilians held in Montreal might be acceptable for enlisted men the rebels were holding. In some instances, the rebels insisted on the exchange of loyalists. One such was the Reverend John Stuart, Anglican missionary to the Mohawk Indians at Fort Hunter. He was placed under house arrest in Schenectady; and some thought was given to exchanging him for a colonel.[70] Late in the autumn of 1780, Sir John Johnson recommended that Colonel James Gordon, captured when Captain Munro raided Ballstown, be exchanged for the Reverend

Stuart. Governor Haldimand rejected the suggestion because Gordon had helped foment a revolt among the prisoners at Montreal and had been removed to Quebec City.[71] In October 1781, the clergyman was allowed to leave with 50 other refugees, mostly women and children, and with his family and slaves, journeyed to Montreal.

In the spring of 1780, Catherine Butler and her younger children were exchanged at Skenesborough after a series of negotiations between Brigadier Watson Powell and rebel General van Schaik. Captain Sherwood arranged several exchanges that year, escorting his prisoners aboard an armed vessel after having them searched from the skin out. Skenesborough was the usual place where he met the rebels under his flag of truce, and thus far he had dealt with emissaries from New York who were sent on behalf of General John Stark, then on duty in Albany or at Saratoga.

In August, Justus's younger brother Samuel, with his wife and year-old daughter, and a slave arrived from Kingsbury, in Charlotte County. He had moved from Connecticut to pioneer where land could be leased cheaply.[72] About the same time a large group arrived from Vermont. Governor Thomas Chittenden, of the self-proclaimed republic, had given passports to loyalists who wished to join the King's troops in Canada, a prelude to Vermont's becoming neutral ground.[73]

In July 1781, Justus Sherwood was joined by his new deputy, Dr. George Smyth. They conducted exchanges sometimes together, sometimes separately at Skenesborough. On other occasions, Sherwood's brother-in-law, Ensign Elijah Bothum, or Smyth's son Thomas acted on their behalf.

The men exchanged were not necessarily captured in battle or on raids by regulars and provincials. Small parties went out deliberately in quest of men whom they kidnapped and marched to the British posts. One who suffered this fate was Seth Sherwood, the father of Ensign Thomas Sherwood, and Justus's uncle. Seth was an ardent rebel, and when Dr. Smyth discovered that Sir John Johnson had allowed him free on parole in Montreal, and was contemplating having him sent home, the doctor protested to Haldimand:

the Indulgence given Prisoners to return on Parole has been detrimental to our Friends. Adam Fonda. . . Seth Sherwood snr, Moses Harris and a certain Mr. Abel have not a little Contributed to the afflictions of many worthy Inhabitants.[74]

Despite Smyth's objections, Seth Sherwood was allowed to return to his home in Kingsbury, near Fort Edward. The whole episode must have caused his nephew and son considerable embarrassment.

Early in August 1781, Major Joseph Fay met Sherwood and Smyth and conducted the first prisoner exchange with the Vermonters. On the 7th, Fay came to the Loyal Blockhouse after leaving 34 prisoners on the east shore of Lake Champlain. Fay joined the two British commissioners aboard the frigate *Royal George* where Sherwood had the men he wanted to exchange. Fay complained that the men returned to him were in poor condition, but Sherwood was quick to retort. The next day he wrote to Robert Mathews and reported that Major Zadock Wright, of the Queen's Loyal Rangers, was displaying the 'incipid enthusiasm of a Shuffling Quaker.'[75] Religious tolerance was not one of the commissioner's virtues.

By October, aboard the row galley *Trumbull* near Crown Point, another exchange took place, this time with New York emissaries sent by General John Stark. Often the work of prisoner exchanges could not be separated from Sherwood's role as head of the secret service, and on the 18th, he reported to Haldimand an atrocity that had raised his blood pressure. One of his agents was Ensign Thomas Lovelace, of the King's Loyal Americans, who was to deliver letters in Saratoga to Colonel van Vechtan, a rebel turned informer. Lovelace was captured. On receiving a report from scout Andrew Reakley, Sherwood gave full vent to his rage and sorrow:

> While Rikely was at Saratoga he saw Mr. Lovelace Hang's before Gen. Stark's door & by his order . . . This barbarous Murder of my worthy friend (& as true & brave a subject as ever left the Colonies) stings me to the heart! I hope in God His Excellency will permit us to retalliate either by hanging up some of the rascals we have prisoners from that State, or by taking and hanging on their own ground some of those inhuman butchers which I know we can do.

Then he referred to the presence of the New York emissaries for the prisoner exchange:

> I have inform'd the Captain of their Flag, on board the Trumble, of Loveless's death, & told him at the same time, that we might with as much propriety & much more Justice hang him on the bow sprit of the Vessel . . . I entreat His Excellency to Consider Mr. Loveless's poor widow & family as he was sent on secret service in which he has always been Exceedingly Useful.[76]

As usual, Haldimand refused to allow his officers to commit acts that contravened the rules of war, and Sherwood knew better than to carry out his threat. His value to the service would be ended if he disobeyed the governor, for he would not be safe under his own flags of truce.

A letter from General William Heath to George Clinton, the rebel governor of New York, showed that Stark had acted rashly:

> I am exceedingly sorry to find by General Stark's letter that he had tried at a court martial and executed Loveless, who came . . . to seize a prisoner from the neighbourhood of Saratoga in which attempt he and his party were taken . . . He having been armed, I think clearly barred the idea of his being a spy, and upon what principle he was executed I am at a loss to determine – and am apprehensive it will make some difficulty – it may be best to say as little about it at present as possible.[77]

Thus the rebels feared the very retaliation Sherwood had in mind, but the statement that since Lovelace was armed and therefore not a spy does not ring true. Loyalist agents in rebel territory generally carried firearms and tomahawks as well.

Justus Sherwood's first experience with refugees came with the arrival of his wife Sarah at Ticonderoga. Her journey was prompted by a report brought by rebels returning from Saratoga that Sherwood had been wounded before Burgoyne's surrender, and would be sent to the fort with the other prisoners of war. On October 24, 1777, Sarah went before the Council of Safety in Bennington and asked permission to join her husband in Canada. The interview took place in the Green Mountain Tavern, which belonged to Joseph Fay's father, and was the seat of what passed for government in the republic of Vermont. Joseph Fay wrote to Colonel Samuel Herrick, the Commandant of Fort Vengeance:

Whereas Capt. Sherwood's wife has applied to this Council for Liberty to go to her husband at Ticonderoga, the Council would Recommend to you, or the Officer Commanding at Pawlet or Skeensboro to convey her (by a Flagg) if you think it best, and by such person as you shall think most Expedient. Her necessary clothing and one bed to be allowed her.

Sarah sacrificed nearly everything because of her desire to see Justus, and she was in advanced stages of pregnancy when she made that journey through the cold of late autumn under grey skies. When Brigadier Powell evacuated the fort, Sarah and her two small children accompanied Justus into exile at Fort St. Johns. Ahead lay years of waiting there, and at the Loyal Blockhouse, in temporary accommodation. While Justus was bound by the Saratoga Convention, his family subsisted on a small pension, until his parole was revoked, his captain's pay restored.

Once Sherwood returned to duty he received a mission, either scouting or carrying a dispatch to the vicinity of Albany. When he returned to Fort St. Johns early in July 1778, six women and 15 children trailed after him.[78] He had hoped to bring back recruits for his depleted company of Queen's Loyal Rangers, but he could not leave the families of loyalists in distress to suffer. Most had been removed by General Schuyler when Burgoyne's army moved south in 1777, but after his surrender at Saratoga they were allowed to return to their farms. Having lost their harvests and livestock their plight was desperate, and Sherwood brought out as many as he dared so that they might be sheltered and provisioned in Canada.

Stories of the sufferings of loyalist families whose men had departed are legion. When Edward Carscallan left his farm in the Camden Valley in the autumn of 1776, his two eldest sons went with him. Soon after they left, a gang of rebels came to the house, seized his 13-year-old son George and threatened to hang him if he would not reveal his father's whereabouts. The boy was strung up and lowered three times, and when he refused to talk one of the rebels kicked him viciously – or so the story has been preserved in the Carscallan family.[79]

After John Walden Meyers departed from his farm near Coeymans, south of Albany, he made his way to New York City. In the autumn of 1778, his wife Mary and six of their seven children joined him there. Beforehand, Mary went before the Board of Commissioners for Detecting and Defeating Conspiracies in Albany, and asked for a pass. The Commissioners approved on the grounds that otherwise the Meyers family would be a charge on the public purse. The eldest son, George, was 13, and he had to remain behind. Children over 12 were potentially useful – old enough to do adult work, young enough to be brainwashed into keen little rebels. Mary went on a sloop down the Hudson with most of her household goods, the family slaves and two weeks' provisions. Later Meyers spirited George away and led him to New York City. After John became a recruiting agent for Major James Rogers, he worked from Fort St. Johns. In the spring of 1783, Mary and the seven children sailed from New York City to join John.[80]

Loyalists began coming into Canada in 1775. The stream swelled as the war progressed, while after the defeat at Yorktown, in October 1781, it became a flood. They began to suspect that their cause was lost, and their neighbours were becoming overbearing. At first most families lived around Montreal. In 1778, when Governor Haldimand decided to establish a base at Sorel for his provincial troops, he ordered houses built for refugee families across the St. Lawrence in the parish of Machiche. The wives and children would be close to their men, but, Haldimand admitted in a letter to Lord George Germain on October 15, he selected Machiche because it had very few inhabitants. He wanted as little contact as possible between loyalists and His Majesty's French-speaking subjects. Rebels might be with the refugees, sent to stir up trouble among the Canadians.

Lists of refugees were kept by various commanding officers, and those with no other means were provisioned at government expense. Haldimand was the watch dog guarding the public purse, and he tried to make sure that all who were able to care for themselves did so. An order signed by Major Richard Lernoult, the adjutant-general, on July 1, 1781, requested the senior officers to see that all women able to work and without children were struck off the provision lists.[81] In the accounts Justus Sherwood kept at the Loyal Blockhouse is an item of 11½ d. to Mrs. Walker for washing, while several small sums were paid to Widow Buck, whose husband

Plaque near site of Loyal Blockhouse recounts, inaccurately, Justus Sherwood's activities.

On a campaign or awaiting better accommodation, troops and their dependents lived in small canvas tents. Women did the housekeeping aided by their children.

had been killed while on duty.[82] Despite Haldimand's vigilence, Dr. Smyth complained about the indolence of certain men at Fort St. Johns:

> There is a Number of Active & Able Body'd Beef devourers here, eating up the King's Royal Bounty without thanking saying, God bless him – I wish his Excellency would permit anyone he pleased to adopt such bodily Exercise for those Gulp and Swallow Gentry as may keep them from Scorbutic & Indolent habits &c.

As the numbers of refugees increased, so did the need for them to have a semblance of normal life while they awaited the outcome of the war. Schools were opened at Fort St. Johns, Machiche and Montreal for the education of the children of the officers – the group most concerned that their offspring be literate. At Fort St. Johns the teacher was the Reverend George Gilmore, and the parents raised £48 per year towards his salary.[83] At Machiche, Mr. Josiah Cass, of the Queen's Loyal Rangers, taught the children, while in Montreal, after he arrived in the autumn of 1781 the Reverend John Stuart opened a classical academy for boys. At each place the parents paid what they could afford, but all three schools received grants from Governor Haldimand.

By the time the peace treaty was signed in September 1783, there were more than 7,000 American loyalists in Canada. Of these, about 2.500 were in provincial corps, not counting most of the Royal Highland Emigrants who had been recruited in Canada or Newfoundland whose homes were intact. The rest were women, children, servants and the aged, to the ratio of approximately 2.8 civilians for every soldier or officer. A return of disbanded troops and loyalists settled upon the King's lands in the 'Province of Quebec' in the year 1784, shows a total of 5,628 men, women and children.[84] This list does not include the people at Niagara and Detroit, nor those who were supporting themselves in Montreal. Adding Butler's Rangers and their dependants, and the others not accounted for on the list, a sound estimate is at least 7,000. Included on the list were 'two hundred families' that had sailed from New York City with Captain Michael Grass and the party brought by Major Peter van Alstyne, who wanted to settle near old Fort Frontenac, and had been given temporary shelter at Sorel.[85]

At the time of the disbandment of the Loyal Rangers, Sherwood held a captaincy in the corps, and Smyth was the regimental surgeon. Their work with refugees and prisoners ended soon afterward, but British regular officers received many more refugees at the various frontier posts. The Treaty of Separation, signed in Paris on September 3, 1783, recommended that individual states restore the loyalists' property. Before that treaty was signed, scouts returning to the frontier posts brought newspapers from the victorious states showing that the rebels were not in a conciliatory mood. Some of these journals were preserved by Haldimand. One began:

As Hannibal swore never to be at Peace with the Romans, so let every Whig aware – by the abhorence of Slavery – by the liberty and religion – by the Shades of those departed Fiends who have fallen in battle – by the ghosts of those of our Brethern who have been destroyed on board of Prison-ships and in loathsome dungeons. . . never to be at peace with these fiends the Refugees, whose thefts, murders, and treasons have filled the cup of woe; but shew the world that we prefer War, with all it's dreadful calamities, to giving those self destroyers of the human species a residence among us – We have crimsoned the earth with our blood to purchase peace, therefore are determined to enjoy harmomy uninterrupted with the Contaminating breath of a Tory.

The newspaper went on to report a meeting of the inhabitants of the District of Saratoga held on May 6, 1783, at which four resolutions were passed: any loyalist attempting to return to the district would be treated with severity; any who had returned would be allowed until June 10 to depart, or face the consequences; militia officers should enquire about such persons so that the inhabitants could expel them; and anyone helping a loyalist would be held in contempt. Other districts had similar meetings, and the witch hunt continued well into the 1790s. Some of these late-arriving loyalists have been accused of coming only to receive free grants of land. Information found in the papers of many such families, or handed down by word of mouth, attests to the fact that some heads of families were forced to flee to Canada nearly two decades after the Treaty of Separation.[86]

An exodus from the Green Mountains followed the Congress' decision to admit Vermont as a state in 1791. For some people the attraction was land more productive than the hills of Vermont afforded, but for others the issue was loyalty. A few people nurtured the hope that Vermont would rejoin the British Empire, and when that hope finally died, they chose to remove to Canada. One group was led by the Baptist Elder Abel Stevens, whose brother Roger had been a scout in the secret service.

Prisoner exchanges were completed soon after the proclamation on the end of hostilities in April 1783, but the migration of refugees took much longer. It began before the Declaration of Independence, and continued past the turn of the century, as relatives joined the original settlers, and some loyalists, hoping they would be undetected, were gradually hunted down and expelled. While many with loyalist sympathizers did remain unidentified, the entire loyalist migration into what became the Province of Upper Canada amounted to about 10,000 men, women and children.

The Naval Establishment

The origins of the Provincial Marine lay back in time, long before the revolution. Whenever colonies in North America were threatened, the navies of the mother countries were supplemented by colonials to help man the fleets. Remnants of the naval establishments survived until the eve of the revolution, and upon these foundations Governors Carleton and Haldimand built the Provincial Marine.[87] It had three divisions – Lake Champlain, the Great Lakes, and the Gulf of St. Lawrence – guarding the points where a rebel fleet or the French navy might attempt to penetrate Canada. The armed vessels, gunboats and bateaux were also responsible for transporting men, military supplies and trade goods to the upper posts, while on Lake Champlain the ships carried refugees picked up while patroling that waterway. After the rebel attack on Canada in 1775-76, Sir Guy Carleton took the first steps to improve his marine department, by appointing Captain René LaForce to the job he had held under the French – Commodore of the Fleet on Lake Ontario. To command the entire freshwater part of the Provincial Marine, Carleton chose Lieutenant John Schanck, Royal Navy, and bestowed on him the title of Commissioner of the Lakes. Leading the fleet on Lake Champlain was Captain Thomas Pringle, also Royal Navy.[88] Schanck's first task involved developing a dockyard and naval base at Fort St. Johns for Pringle's fleet.

When General Frederick Haldimand succeeded Carleton in 1778, he appointed Lieutenant Schanck to oversee building a naval facility at Carleton Island, and he sent Captain William Chambers, R.N. to replace Captain René LaForce on Lake Ontario.[89] That veteran commodore had had the impudence to fire on Haldimand's men in 1759 at Oswego, which His Excellency had neither forgotten nor forgiven. LaForce remained at Carleton Island making himself indispensable, and in 1779, Haldimand relented and placed him in command of the naval department there.

In 1780, Captain Chambers replaced Captain Pringle on Lake Champlain, and the command of the fleet on Lake Ontario passed to Captain James Andrews, who sailed a new ship, the *Ontario*, a vessel of 231 tons and 18 guns, built at Carleton Island. On November 10, Captain Alexander Fraser, the Indian agent on the island, described difficulties in English-French relations:

Having two Commandants in the same Department vist Captn LaForce on Shore and Andrews on Water did not answer well & was the occasion of Jealousy and the source of the inconvenience I point at – When the smallest trifle was wanted from Shore much form & ceremony was requisite to obtain it and if Captn Laforce attempted to interfere with the loading of the vessels (tho his instructions at times made it necessary) it disobliged Captn Andrews.[90]

Commanding the fleet on Lake Erie was Captain Andrew Grant and leading the fleet on the Gulf of St. Lawrence was Captain Robert Young. Grant apparently was a colonial, but Young, like Chambers and Schanck, had been seconded from the Royal Navy. Haldimand was so impressed by Schanck's talents that he secured promotions for him to commander, then captain.[91]

Information on the vessels is skimpy. The squadron led by Captain Pringle that defeated Benedict Arnold's fleet in October 1776, consisted of three schooners; the *Inflexible*, 300 tons, 18 guns; the *Maria*, 14 guns; the *Carleton*, 96 tons, 12 guns; the *Thunderer*, a large radeau or gun sketch with two howitzers, six 24-pounders and six 12-pounders; the *Loyal Convert*, a gondola with six 9-pounders, as well as twelve gunboats, each with two 24-pounders and fifty bateaux.[92]

The *Carleton* had been dismantled at Fort Chambly, transported past the rapids in the Richelieu, and reassembled at Fort St. Johns. The *Inflexible* built at Quebec City, was also taken apart and rebuilt at the fort's dockyard by John Schanck. In the spring of 1777, the frigate *Royal George* was launched, the pride of the service, 384 tons with 26 guns, some 24-pounders. The Lake Champlain fleet then included a large row galley, the *Trumble*, 199 tons, eight guns, captured from the rebels the year before.[93]

In June 1778, on Lake Ontario were three vessels, described as the snow *Haldimand*, 150 tons, 14 cannon, 12 swivels, 32 hands; the snow *Seneca*, 130 tons, 12 swivels, 45 hands; and the sloop *Caldwell*, 37 tons, 2 cannon, 6 swivels, 10 hands.[94] By 1780, the *Ontario* and the *Mohawk* had been added to this fleet. That autumn, Colonel Mason Bolton, then commandant at Fort Niagara, reported to Haldimand that the ships on Lake Erie were inactive because they lacked cables.

On November 1, the *Ontario* set sail from Niagara carrying Colonel Bolton on his way to Montreal for a leave of absence, together with a detachment of the 34th Regiment and other passengers. A storm struck about thirty miles out, and she foundered and sank with all aboard. Reporting the tragedy from Carleton Island, Captain Alexander Fraser informed Haldimand:

Her Boats and Grateings of her Hatchway, the Binnacle Compasses, Sand glasses & several Hats Caps & different wearing Apparel & Blankets were picked up along the shore by Colonel Butler on his way from Oswego to Niagara – This account is brought by Mohawk which is just arrived from above after having search'd all the South side of the Lake without having made any other discovery of the Ontario.[95]

On November 15, knowing Captain James Andrews was dead, Haldimand reappointed René LaForce, Commodore of the Fleet on Lake Ontario.

A return of the fleet on Lake Erie for 1778 listed these vessels; two small schooners, the *Hope* and the *Angelica*, each with four swivel guns; the *Gage* and the *Dunmore*, larger schooners with heavier armaments; the small sloop *Felicity*, the schooner *Faith*, and the sloop *Archangel*. Two others, the *Wyandot* and the *Ottawa* were under construction. Two other vessels mentioned in correspondence between Detroit and Michilimackinac were the *Adventure* and the *Welcome*.[96] This fleet was necessary to link the line of supply to the uppermost fort. After the Seven Years' War a dockyard was opened on Navy Island, above Niagara Falls, but all these vessels were built at Detroit, where a naval establishment was begun in 1771.

Less is known about the Provincial Marine serving in the Gulf of St. Lawrence. Haldimand had the use of several ships of the Royal Navy, but he also referred to his provincial fleet, and Captain Robert Young, his senior officer. In June 1780, the governor had taken into his provincial service a ship of 22 guns – 6 and 9-pounders – which had arrived from Liverpool. This was the *Hind*, which became Young's flagship, and he had three additional vessels in his command.[97] Haldimand mentioned other ships by name, but it is hard to tell whether these belonged to the Royal Navy, the Provincial Marine, or the trade fleet that carried supplies from Britain. In October 1778, the governor requested permission from Lord Germain for the ships *Garland*, *Triton* and *Viper* to winter at Quebec.

With the approach of each spring, Haldimand worried that the French fleet might appear off Quebec, and on June 6, 1780, he sent orders to Captain Young to be alert. If Young discovered the whereabouts of the French, he was to send messages at once to Admiral Arbuthnot, Sir Henry Clinton, and the governor of Nova Scotia. In the same letter Haldimand asked Young to choose vessels to carry despatches. On September 17, reporting to Lord Germain, he wrote that the *Wolfe* had been cast away on 'St. Peters Isle' in thick fog, and the *Hind* narrowly escaped.[98] Apparently the *Wolfe* was one of the four vessels in Captain Young's fleet.

When Captain Justus Sherwood, Loyal Rangers, was sent from Quebec City to Gaspé Bay in the summer of 1783 to begin exploring the coast for land for the loyalists' future homes, he embarked on what he called the 'Treasury Brig St Peters,' another vessel belonging to the government and therefore part of the Provincial Marine.

Captain René LaForce, sailing Lake Ontario on the *Seneca*, his flagship, served until he retired in 1783. The command of the fleet was given to Jean Baptiste Bouchette, who had won fame as the rescuer of Governor Carleton in 1775, when he spirited his charge past the rebels in a small boat, enabling him to reach Quebec City before the siege began.[99] LaForce soon came out of retirement, for he accompanied Major Samuel Holland, the Surveyor-General of Canada, to Cataraqui in June 1783, and began charting the shoreline of Lake Ontario.[100]

At Carleton Island, where John Schanck remained in charge of the naval establishment from the summer of 1778 until the end of the war, most of the carpenters were from ships of the Royal Navy, and some artificiers came from dockyards in Britain. By 1783, Schanck reported to Haldimand that he had 300 seamen from the Royal Navy serving on the lakes. This competent officer, sponsored by Carleton and Haldimand, created the Provincial Marine as a separate department distinct from the army. Another who impressed Haldimand was Captain William Chambers, for by October, 1782, he was serving as the senior captain, reporting directly to the governor.[101]

Statistics on the numbers of loyal Americans and Canadians serving under Schanck do not seem to have been kept, but in an article he wrote on the Provincial Marine, W.A.B.Douglas observed that none of the officers in Captain Schanck's service were professional naval seamen. Many, like LaForce and Bouchette, were Canadians, but there are references in muster rolls and other returns to loyalists serving with the fleets. Colonel John Peters, of the Queen's Loyal Rangers, said that his second son, Andrew, served as a midshipman on Lake Champlain. This assertion is confirmed on a return dated July 14, 1781, listing Andrew as a volunteer on that lake, while seven other men are shown as mariners on the western lakes.

In October 1779, Haldimand gave permission for Daniel Sweney to be discharged from the King's Royal Regiment of New York so that he could join 'the Lake Service,' because Sir John Johnson found him 'no great acquisition as a Soldier.' Sweney claimed to have had experience in ships, and the Provincial Marine was desperate for seamen at that time.[102] A return of disbanded troops and loyalists settled at the mouth of the Detroit River, dated December 15, 1790, shows Thomas Kelly as having served on the lakes; Adam Stoutmyre as a boatswain on Lake Erie; and James Understone as a master on the same lake.[103] Others may have left provincial corps to serve for short periods of time.

305

Writing to Haldimand on August 17, 1778, Schanck requested that more seamen be sent to Carleton Island;

> as a great deal of duty must be done here by them – For although the greatest part of the men for the Gun boats and guard boats may be composed of the Troops, yet a few seamen are absolutely necessary both for working the Guns and Sails & for steering them.

The troops with Schanck were regulars from the 47th Regiment, and some King's Royal Regiment of New York. The naval officer did not specify whether he meant regulars or provincials, and both may have been used to strengthen his crews.

The ships on the lakes were small by the standards of the Royal Navy, and those on the Gulf of St. Lawrence may have been larger, although *The Hind* had only 22 guns, fewer than *The Royal George* that plied Lake Champlain. When peace came, the ships of the Provincial Marine on the Great Lakes continued carrying supplies and trade goods, while bateaux remained in use through the stretches of rapids between the lower and upper St. Lawrence. Before the peace treaty was signed, in preparation for the day when Carleton Island might be inside United States' territory, Major John Ross evacuated the island and established a new base at Cataraqui. Captain John Schanck returned to Quebec City, and in November 1784, sailed for England in the same ship as Governor Haldimand.[104]

In his wake Schanck left skilled craftsmen, trained by his British artificers, who carried on, keeping the vessels more or less in repair. When the War of 1812 loomed on the horizon, the Provincial Marine was there to patrol the lakes until the men of the Royal Navy arrived to take over this vital work.

Part Three: Afterwards

Chapter 12: Resettlement of the Displaced Loyalists

The number of loyalists who migrated into what remained of British North America as a consequence of the American Revolution has been estimated at approximately 45,000. Of these, some 35,000 gathered at New York City, and except for the few families who chose Canada, were sent by ship to the maritime provinces.[1] Of the remaining, nearly 8,000 men, women and children, were in Canada, along the lower St. Lawrence, or receiving care at Carleton Island, Niagara and Detroit and would be joined by stragglers in the next few years. Responsible for organizing the transportation and resettlement were three governors. Sir Guy Carleton was in New York City as the commander-in-chief, making arrangements to evacuate the loyalists to Nova Scotia or Canada. Governor Frederick Haldimand in Quebec City and Governor John Parr at Halifax were to carry out the British government's orders to accommodate refugees who could not return to their homes.

Of the three, Carleton was the most compassionate and Haldimand the most efficient, while Parr, for reasons both within and beyond his control, bungled the operation so badly that the creation of the Province of New Brunswick was necessary to quell resentment among certain loyalist leaders. For several reasons Haldimand was able to do a better job than Carleton. As governor of Canada, he controlled the areas where his refugees were gathered, as well as the regions where new settlements could be planted, and the matter of acquiring good land was straightforward. Haldimand could purchase tracts from local Indians, and the number of people requiring farms was less unwieldy. Furthermore, he was not faced with a deadline when he must have all his charges moved.

From New York City Carleton had to send his people – refugee civilians and provincial corps not then disbanded – into a jurisdiction over which he had no direct control, and time was not on his side. The evacuation of the British-occupied area was supposed to end with the signing of the Treaty of Separation in September 1783, but Carleton clung to his post well into November, until the last refugee family awaiting transport had been served. Only then did he evacuate his regulars.[2] Carleton may not have realized that loyalists reaching Nova Scotia were finding a poor reception, where Governor Parr neither wanted them nor was prepared to accommodate them.

John Parr was something of a Colonel Blimp. Past 60, weighing 250 pounds, he viewed his appointment as a soft job before a comfortable retirement.[3] Having so many people dumped into his domain was something he preferred not to see happen. Before the home government had informed any of the provincial governors what provisions they were to make for the refugees, Parr reached Halifax in 1782, at the same time as an early wave of 600 loyalists. In fact, Parr had 30,000 newcomers on his doorstep before orders finally arrived.

At first the Whig Ministry was willing to abandon Nova Scotia as well as the loyalists, and to allow fishing rights to the Americans, although Lord Shelburne assured Haldimand in April 1782, of his government's determination to retain Canada.[4] The rest would be sacrificed in order to win the friendship of the United States while Britain finished the war with France and Spain. Not until the Shelburne government was replaced by the coalition under Lord North and Charles James Fox were constructive resettlement plans contemplated.

In Canada, Haldimand could afford to wait while his superiors made up their minds. The only matter really urgent was that the loyalists begin providing for themselves to reduce the pressure on government. As he made his plans the Swiss governor worked from one premise; loyalists must not settle among the Canadians. As in his native land, each language group must have its own cantons, where culture and religion would be uniform.

Initially, Haldimand thought that Cape Breton might suit the refugees, for the fishery would offer them an opportunity to prosper. This potential island province would preclude the necessity of attempting to purchase land from the Indians, and help preserve the western parts of his domain from encroachment by settlers. Upon reflection he admitted that the majority of his backwoods refugees might not adapt well to life on the seacoast. He also ruled out the lands between Montreal and the Vermont — New York boundary. That area should be reserved for the expansion of the seigneuries, which was certain to come in due course. Therefore, he sent men experienced in land colonization to investigate other territory which he thought was not under seigneurial tenure.

Plans Bureaucratic and Private

In the spring of 1783, Governor Haldimand decided to send

Captain Justus Sherwood with a party of men to explore the east coastline from Gaspé Bay to the mouth of the Miramichi River, in search of suitable land for loyalists. Sherwood left Quebec City with his men, his wife and three children on May 29, aboard the 'Treasury Brig St. Peters.' He had returned by August 12, and reported that the country was mountainous, with some good land. It would do for New Englanders, accustomed to making a living from the sea and trade, and from part-time farming, but it was less appropriate for many of the refugees in Canada – landlocked frontiersmen unable to turn to pursuits common among coastal dwellers. Sherwood also noted that land tenure would cause problems, because most of it was held by a few seigneurs, 'designing men' who in sixteen years had not permitted more than a handful of settlers to enter, lest they share 'the profits and blessings of the Salmon fishery.'[5]

Sherwood's findings were a sign of future storms which would arise in tackling the problem of land-holding throughout Nova Scotia which did not exist in the westerly parts of Canada. Another difference between the migrations to the Maritimes and Canada was that there were many more civilians in the former. In Canada, nearly all the able-bodied men and older boys had served in provincial corps. Most of the men considered civilians when the war ended had enlisted for a time before retiring to take employment around Montreal. One exception was a small group of Quakers who left the United States because the rebels had not respected their desire not to bear arms. In Maritime literature, a stronger distinction is drawn between the men of the provincial army and other refugees. Such a division has been drawn only occasionally for loyalists who came directly to the Province of Canada.

Meanwhile, on August 23, 1783, Edward Jessup wrote to Mathews requesting maps of the seigneurial grants made for the vicinity of Lake of Two Mountains, where the Ottawa River joins the St. Lawrence, so that he could determine which lands might be available for the Loyal Rangers and the King's Royal Regiment of New York. By September 11 Jessup had formulated a plan which influenced Haldimand's thinking, although he did not accept many of the proposals.

The major suggested that Sir John Johnson's two battalions and Jessup's Corps be settled in three districts on the north side of the St. Lawrence and on both sides of the Ottawa River. In this way all could have water frontage, which would avoid jealousy by ensuring that each group would not be better served than the others in the trackless wilderness where streams would be the highways. Each district should have villages and warehouses, and for the district assigned to the Loyal Rangers, Jessup recommended that a field officer with the rank of captain receive 3,000 acres, a subaltern 2,000, a non-commissioned officer 400, a private 200, and for each member of a family 50 acres.

Districts, Jessup asserted, should be divided into parishes eight or nine miles square, each with an equal number of officers and men. Officers should be awarded parishes in which to settle their men by drawing ballots. Each twentieth lot should be reserved for public use, such as a church or school. A settler who received a lot with a good mill-site should be obliged to build saw and grist mills within eighteen months, or trade the lot to someone willing to comply. Officers should receive only two thirds of their lands before the rank and file had been accommodated, and no one, except officers, should receive more than 400 acres in one piece. Soldiers' widows might be allowed 200 acres, and the same amount for their eldest sons. Left-over lots could be granted to civilians needing land.[6]

However, Haldimand had other ideas on where he would resettle the refugees, and he chose not to consider the Ottawa River as a place for the resettlement of Jessup's and Sir John Johnson's men. Even before he received Sherwood's unsatisfactory report on the east coast, Haldimand decided he would have to purchase Indian land after all, and he instructed his Surveyor-General Samuel Holland, and Deputy Surveyor-General John Collins to investigate the lands above the rapids in the St. Lawrence River. In the autumn of 1783, they were assisted by parties of loyalists, among them Sherwood. Upon receiving favourable reports, the governor authorized the laying out of townships six miles square, because he considered them 'the best to be followed as the people to be Settled there, are most used to it.'

A farm lot was to be 120 acres – 19 chains in front and 63 chains, 25 links deep, so that each township would have 25 lots across the front, plus 4 chains, 58 links for road allowances.[7] While at Cataraqui, Justus Sherwood laid out three American townships, each thirty-six miles square, and with a crew he surveyed the front row of lots facing the water, in all 75 parcels, before he left to spend the winter with his family at Fort St. Johns.[8] By November 18 Haldimand had received more explicit instructions from the Prime Minister, Lord North, enclosing a proclamation from the King – orders that disappointed him and would have appalled the loyalists had they known what they contained. Land for the refugees was to be divided into:

distinct seigneuries or Fiefs, to extend from two to four leagues in front. If situated upon a Navigable River, otherwise to be run square or in such shape and such quantities, as shall be convenient & practicable – and in each Seigneurie a Glebe to be reserved and laid out in the most convenient spot, to contain not less than 300 nor more than 500 acres; the propriety of which Seigneuries or Fiefs shall be and remain invested in Us, our Heirs and Successors.[9]

Lord North informed Haldimand that upon the expiration of ten years from the time a tenant took up his land, a quit rent of one halfpenny per acre would be exacted from him. Therefore, by order of the King, loyalists in Canada were to exist under a modified form of the French seigneurial system that prevailed in the older part of the province, hardly news that would gladden their hearts, and which Haldimand chose to conceal from them for the moment. New Englanders expected to have their grants freehold, while New Yorkers were accustomed to a quit rent of not more than 2s. 6d. per hundred acres.[10] The proposed quit rent for Canada amounted to 4s. 2d. per hundred acres – a substantial sum for a man from the ranks to sacrifice each year. Despite Sir Guy Carleton's urgent recommendations that loyalists be given their grants free of any encumbrances, as a reward for their services, the King was being ungenerous, even pig-headed, ready to repeat the bungling that had precipitated the loss of the Thirteen Colonies.

At the same time, Lord North specified the extent of certain land grants:

To every Master of a Family One Hundred Acres, and Fifty Acres to each person of which his Family shall consist.
To every Non-Commissioned Officer of our Forces reduced in Quebec Two Hundred Acres.
To every private Man reduced as aforesaid One Hundred Acres. And for every Person in their Family Fifty Acres.

A later packet included provisions for the commissioned officers:

To every field officer, 1,000 acres; every captain 700 acres, every subaltern, staff or warrant officer 500 acres; every non-commissioned officer 200 acres; every private 100 acres; and for each member of their families 50 acres.
Civilian heads of families were entitled to receive 100 acres, and 50 acres for each family member, while every single man was to receive 50 acres.

Haldimand received many recommendations from his provincial officers on the length of time loyalists would require provisions, ranging from two to three years. Through instructions from the home government dated March 17, 1784, he learned that 'they should be victualled for some time at Public Expence.' In fact it was deemed appropriate to,

victual them at two thirds Allowance to the 1st May, 1785; and from that period at one third allowance to the 1st day of May 1786, estimating the whole Ration at one Pound of Flour, and one Pound of Beef or twelve ounces of Pork and the children under 10 years of age to have a moiety of the Allowance made to grown persons. [11]

With Haldimand's instructions specifying the extent of officers' grants were orders to settle each corps together, the officers scattered among the men to provide leadership. On instructions from Whitehall the battalions and companies near the lower St. Lawrence were disbanded on December 24, and Haldimand sent orders on March 29, 1784 for the disbandment of the three battalions at the upper posts.

From New York City on June 4, 1783, Sir Guy Carleton wrote to inform Governor Haldimand that some of his loyalists preferred Canada to Nova Scotia. Then on July 5, he wrote again saying that he was enclosing a return of 200 families of distressed loyalists who had embarked and would sail in a few days. He had formed the men into eight companies of militia under officers, who would hold temporary commissions until they were under Haldimand's care. These refugees were sent under the command of Lieutenant-Colonel Stephen DeLancey, a member of the well-known New York family who had lived in Albany. His signature is on the 'Embarkation Return of Eight Companies of Loyalists Going to Canada.' Apparently DeLancey accompanied this group of loyalists, because he was known to be in Canada some months. His people were sent to Sorel, and in January 1784 they petitioned Haldimand for the bare necessities of life, pleading that some had scarcely a whole garment or a comfortable blanket.

Haldimand had at least two sets of estimates on the quantity of land required to accommodate the disbanded provincials and other refugees, which included those who had come from New York City in preference to going to Nova Scotia. One list covered Sir John Johnson's two battalions, the Loyal Rangers and King's Rangers, as well as 1,804 'Refugee Loyalists' – officers, masters of families, single men, women and children. The total number listed with the provincial corps was 3,447 all ranks and their dependents, and the grand total was 5,251 people. For these, 483,840 acres were required, twenty-one seigneuries each of 23,040 acres. Such seigneuries would be 36 square miles, the dimensions of an American township. The list is undated, but it shows the commissioned officers' allotments, and those of the rank and file. Therefore, it was compiled after Haldimand received orders for the seigneuries or fiefs.

Since a league is three miles, the amended seigneuries were to have from six to twelve miles of frontage. Ultimately, Haldimand decided on townships for approximately 100 square miles, and those fronting on the St. Lawrence and the Bay of Quinte were nine miles wide and twelve miles deep. Preceding the estimate of 483,840 acres is a 'Rough Calculation of Numbers of Loyalties to be settled And the Quantity of Land that will be wanted for Them, as follows:

	Acres
84th Regiment	77,975
1st Battn New York	88,650
2d do.	58,432
Loyal Rangers	86,050
King's Rangers	34,837
	426,523
Pensioners	29,000
Acres	455,623

This second list of estimates shows a much lower figure, and for more corps, while the odd amounts do not correspond to the acreage recommended. All should have been in multiples of 50 since this was the smallest amount recommended. The basis for its compilation is not apparent.

The surveying of townships at Cataraqui had begun in September 1783, although these would have to be enlarged and the lot lines redrawn to correspond with the orders from Whitehall. At Niagara, the laying out of lots had begun earlier. Colonel John Butler submitted an account dated April 4 1783, for the services of Allan McDonell, who had prepared lots for sixteen families. The bill was £32. 2s. 0d. rather expensive for the number of lots.[13]

During the winter of 1783-84, Joseph Brant visited Quebec City, where he arranged that some of his Mohawk people would go to the north shore of the Bay of Quinte, while others of the Six Nations would have land to the north of Lake Erie. Haldimand ordered Sir John Johnson, as Superintendent of Indians Affairs, to purchase this latter tract from the Mississauga Indians.[14] Negotiations for the purchase of a tract along Lake Ontario and the upper St. Lawrence to accommodate the loyalists were conducted by Captain William Redford Crawford of the King's Royal Regiment of New York, acting for his commanding officer. On October 9, 1783, Crawford reported to Sir John Johnson:

According to your directions I have purchased from the Mississaguas all the lands from Toniata or Onagara River to a river in the Bay of Quinte within eight leagues of the bottom of the said Bay including all the Islands, extending from the lake back as far as a man can travel in a day, the Chiefs claiming the land at the bottom of the Bay could not be got together at the present. I believe their land can be got nearly on the same terms, though this when I see them.

313

The consideration demanded by the Chiefs for the lands granted is that all the families belonging to them shall be clothed and that those that have not fusees shall receive new ones, some powder and ball for their winter hunting, as much coarse red cloth as will make about a dozen coats and as many laced hats ...

The Mississaguas appear much satisfied that the white people are coming to live among them. Three Onondaga Chiefs lately from Montreal were present and approved much of what the Mississaguas had done. Not a word was said in regard to the Mohawks. If any written obligation is wanted from them let it be sent up and I will get it executed.[15]

In March 1784, with Haldimand's approval, Sir John Johnson sent Lieutenant Walter Sutherland of his second battalion, Lieutenant William Coffin of his first battalion, and surveyor Patrick McNiff, to co-operate with surveyor Louis Kotté in laying out townships commencing at Point au Baudet, on the upper St. Lawrence. There he hoped to resettle the men of his first battalion, who had wintered at Montreal, in four or five new townships.[16]

The group of loyalists from New York City that had gone to Sorel were better received than those in Nova Scotia, despite their request for clothing and bedding. Utter chaos reigned in the other province. Sir Guy Carleton, who could not hold New York until it suited him to leave, had sent refugees and provincials still in their corps to Governor John Parr as rapidly as transports became available. Compared to the rampant disorder within Parr's domain, the task of re-establishing loyalists in Canada, while attended by some confusion and rancour, was orderly and peaceful. The difference may be attributed in part to disagreements between Carleton and Parr. The latter resented implementing promises 'bred in New York' by Carleton.[17]

Parr also disapproved of Carleton's recommendation that loyalists receive land grants free of all fees, either payment for patents or quit rents, then or at any time in the future. Carleton's plan, if allowed, would deny the government of Nova Scotia the revenues that might accrue from imposing such monetary measures.[18] Lastly, most of the good land within Nova Scotia's boundaries was held by absentee landlords, and some was occupied by Acadians who had no titles at all. Parr had to undertake escheat proceedings against landowners and move Acadians away in order to procure land that would satisfy the requirements of the grants, which were the same as those for provincials disbanded in Canada.[19] Furthermore, land granting was bedevilled by the fact that Nova Scotia's records were in incredible disarray.

One bright light was that in Nova Scotia the land was divided into townships, a practice that was to continue. These were usually 100,000 acres, a block twelve miles by thirteen – 156.25 square miles against 36 for an American township. Parr arranged for blocks approximately twelve miles square to be granted to each commander of a provincial corps, so that he could disband and resettle his regiment upon it. Most of these blocks were up the Saint John River, in the vicinity of Fredericton, while blocks for civilian refugees were set aside at the mouth of the river, now the site of the city of Saint John.

Loyalist leaders appointed by Carleton to be his agents in making agreements with Parr – men like Edward Winslow and Oliver DeLancey – were very dissatisfied with the Nova Scotia administration. Throughout stormy sessions and discontent, there arose a movement for the partition of Nova Scotia, so that loyalists could have a province where their leaders were in the majority. Two solutions presented themselves: fire Parr and appoint someone sympathetic to the newcomers, or separate the malcontents. The British government chose the latter course, and the Province of New Brunswick was established by an Act of the Privy Council dated June 18, 1784.

The first governor was Thomas Carleton, Sir Guy's younger brother. Although Thomas could not impose a seigneurial system on New Brunswick, he renamed his townships parishes in the hope that their inhabitants would emulate the more docile populace of the English parishes. The word township smacked of New England radicalism and was just too Yankee for New Brunswick's first administrator.[20] Despite Thomas Carleton's desire to exercise control over his subjects, the partition of Nova Scotia was a warning of storms to come. The loyalists being resettled in Canada would be no more willing to live under the seigneurial system than certain of those in the Maritimes had been happy putting up with Governor Parr.

In Quebec City, faced with the regulations that came late in the autumn of 1783, Governor Haldimand adjusted the dimensions of the new townships above the rapids in the St. Lawrence to comply with the King's proclamation. The approximately 100-square-mile so-called seigneuries were divided into 1,000 acre concession blocks, and sub-divided into 100-acre farm lots. At the centre of each seigneury or midway along its waterfront, if it had one, would be a town site. The governor established sixteen seigneuries at first, and he called them townships as often as the more official name. Eight were to be along the upper St. Lawrence, commencing at Point au Baudet, nine miles west of the boundary of the last French seigneury, leaving a gap as a buffer zone between anglophone and francophone. The first township inside the Province of Ontario, later named Lancaster, was surveyed in 1785 for Roman Catholic set-

Loyalist Townships along the St. Lawrence and Bay of Quinte 1784

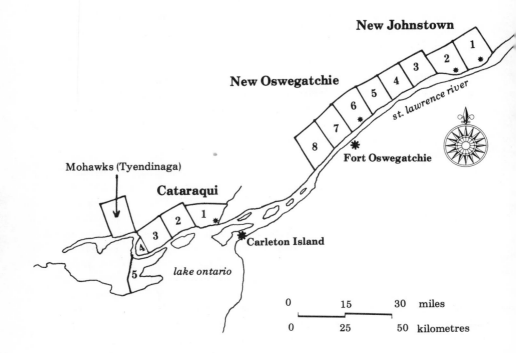

Eight townships were laid out beside the upper St. Lawrence. The lower five were the New Johnstown settlement, the upper three New Oswegatchie. The first five around the Bay of Quinte were the Cataraqui settlement. When they were named, #1 beside the St. Lawrence was Charlottenburgh, #2 Cornwall, #3 Osnabruck, #4 Williamsburgh, #5 Matilda, #6 Edwardsburgh, #7 Augusta, #8 Elizabethtown. Of the Bay of Quinte townships, #1 was Kingston, #2 Ernestown, #3 Fredericksburgh, #4 Adolphustown, #5 Marysburgh. Also shown are the first three townsites, Kingston (#1 Cataraqui), Johnstown (#6 New Oswegatchie), New Johnstown (#2 New Johnstown).

tlers, and was not one of Haldimand's original eight. Township Number 1 was Charlottenburgh, and Number 8 was Elizabethtown, although some secondary sources list these as Numbers 2 and 9.

The other eight townships were west of the rocky portion of the Canadian Shield that extends across the St. Lawrence and forms the Thousand Islands. Reporting on the quality of the land to Governor Haldimand in the autumn of 1783, Justus Sherwood branded this stretch of about forty miles unfit for cultivation. While the governor was planning to move the refugees upstream from the Montreal area, since May 1783, Butler's Rangers had been establishing themselves with their dependents on the twelve miles of frontage along the Niagara River that had been purchased from the Mississauga Indians two years before. As usual Butler was making his own arrangements, and the land his men and their families were clearing was eventually surveyed as the townships of Niagara and Mount Dorchester (later renamed Stamford).

Of the townships along the St. Lawrence, the lower five were for the first battalion, King's Royal Regiment of New York, and the upper three for the Loyal Rangers. Of those at the mouth of the Cataraqui River and westward along both sides of the Bay of Quinte, the first was for the party of loyalists from New York City commanded by Captain Michael Grass. The second was for the rest of the Loyal Rangers, and the third for the King's Rangers and the second battalion, King's Royal Regiment of New York. The fourth was for another group from New York led by Major Peter van Alstyne and some of the second battalion, King's Royal Regiment of New York, the fifth for some disbanded German soldiers who wished to remain in Canada.

For the time being these were all that Haldimand required beyond Cataraqui, and a large block was set aside as a reserve for the Mohawk Indians. Land for the three remaining townships the governor planned would be surveyed when more settlers arrived. Some loyalists would not be moving until after the 1784 season, and Haldimand suspected that the exodus from the United States was far from at an end. No land was set aside for the Royal Highland Emigrants. Many had homes to which they could return, and land grants in return for their services would be awarded later, along the Ottawa River. Those who were loyalists would be resettled among the first battalion, King's Royal Regiment of New York, or near the upper posts where they had been stationed.

By the spring of 1784, Haldimand was more or less ready to have his refugees begin their trek westward. In advance, bateaux had been constructed at Lachine, and food, clothing, tents and cooking utensils had been sent there from warehouses at Sorel by Captain John Barnes, the deputy quartermaster.[21] Sad to relate, while Haldimand's loyalists were receiving more sympathetic treatment than Parr's, not all the potential settlers in Canada were delighted with the location the governor had selected for them. Throughout the winter, winds of discontentment had been blowing through the refugee encampments and the posts where some of the disbanded provincials waited. Many wanted to stay close to Montreal, the market for their agricultural produce once they had a surplus to trade. Some anglophone seigneurs, sensing their opportunity, were actively seeking tenants among the refugees to fill their vacant lands, in the hope that their presence would induce the home government to revoke the Quebec Act and institute English civil law.[22]

On February 2, a perturbed Sir John Johnson wrote from Montreal:

> Some evil Designing persons are endeavouring to dissuade the disbanded Men and other Loyalists from taking the Lands offered them by Government, telling them if they accept them they will be as much Soldiers as ever, and liable to be called upon at pleasure; and that the terms are not as favourable as those of the Neighbouring States, where they are not prohibited from erecting Mills – and that it will be better for them to take up Lands from Signiors in the heart of the Province.

Some enterprising officers had taken initiatives that distressed the governor and the officers who had explored the land on the upper St. Lawrence and Bay of Quinte. On March 1, Sherwood wrote:

> The people of this place seem well inclin'd for Cataraqui except a number that are dictated by Captains Myers & Pritchard Lt. Ruyter Lt. Wehr and Ensn Coonrod Best, these have begun a settlement at Mississqui Bay, and (I shudder to inform you) declare that nothing but Superior force shall drive them off that land.

Although Sherwood named only Meyers and Pritchard, Colonel John Peters, still smarting because Haldimand had demoted him to a captaincy in the Loyal Rangers, had been making mischief. Haldimand's response was to order the men to leave that land. It lay too close to the border, where the presence of certain officers might provoke incidents. He was especially worried about Captain John Walden Meyers, who had conducted his one-man war around Albany. When the governor threatened to cut off provisions, Peters and Pritchard capitulated, but Meyers hung on and drove a bargain with Haldimand. Since Meyers had enough land selected to raise 1,000 bushels of corn, he could stay until he had harvested his crop, but then he must pack and take his wife and children to the lands the governor had purchased for loyalist refugees.[23]

Although Haldimand did not want any loyalists settled near Mississquoi Bay, only the senior officers left. Lieutenant John Ruiter and several of the men from Meyers' company remained and are listed as Mississquoi Bay loyalists in the Quebec Land Records.[24] Their motives were obvious. At that place on Lake Champlain lay open meadowlands where the Loyal Rangers had gone to cut hay – land that could be ploughed without having first to remove large trees. Certainly the quality of the land appealed to Meyers, a capable farmer, but Azariah Pritchard, the unscrupulous Yankee trader from Connecticut, probably hoped to smuggle goods into Canada. As for John Peters, he acted out of spite, and going to Mississquoi was not his only piece of mischief.

On May 17, 1784, Captain John Barnes wrote to Mathews, enclosing an anonymous letter attributed to Peters, calling it 'so Diabolical a rebellious piece of Business.'[25] The author of the letter accused Haldimand of being high-handed and claimed that the governor did not have the authority to dictate where loyalists should live. From his reading of the terms set forth in a proclamation from Lord North, loyalists had the right to choose where they would go.

To Sherwood, Meyers' insubordination was about what one might expect from a tenant farmer who had lived near Albany, and his real wrath was reserved for certain of his fellow Connecticut men, whom he described to Mathews as 'blowing the Coals of sedition like two furies.' Haldimand moved quickly to counteract any other independent actions, by publishing a notice in the March 4 issue of the *Quebec Gazette*. All persons – the few destined for Sorel and Chaleur Bay excepted – were to assemble at Lachine no later than April 2, to await transportation up the St. Lawrence. Many of the elderly were planning to make their homes at Sorel, where the government had purchased the seigneury in 1780. Those who were adamant could go to Chaleur Bay, and one who did was Azariah Pritchard, no doubt expecting that the location would be better for trade than the upper country. In high dudgeon John Peters took his wife and six youngest children to Cape Breton. Later he sailed to England and vented his spleen on Haldimand in at least one letter he wrote there.

In the refugee camps the rumblings refused to subside. To put an end to the hubbub, Justus Sherwood urged Haldimand to speed up his preparations. Once his people were on their farm lots, chopping down trees and striving to survive, they would have scant strength for argument. Unfortunately, Haldimand's April 2 deadline proved unreasonable. Too many people had to be moved, and the spring came very late that year. By the end of the month blocks of ice still floated in the St. Lawrence past Lachine. There was little point in moving thousands of people from their several encampments, and the stragglers still arriving at Fort St. Johns, only to confine them in other temporary quarters until the ice had melted.

Some secondary accounts refer to Colonel Stephen DeLancey, who had made the arrangements for two groups of loyalists gathered at New York City to come to Canada, as the Inspector of Loyalists in Quebec. DeLancey was the commandant of the first battalion, New Jersey Volunteers,[26] and logic would have placed him in Nova Scotia or New Brunswick, looking to the welfare of his own men. He was in Canada for a time, and in September 1784, he went to Cataraqui to make a report on conditions there.[27] Major John Ross, of Sir John Johnson's second battalion, was the commandant at Cataraqui, and he informed Governor Haldimand that he was expecting DeLancey to arrive and settle a dispute that had arisen. The groups from New York City had been making excessive demands for equipment and livestock which Haldimand could not possibly meet.

These Johnnies-come-lately were causing ill feeling because they had not been part of the Northern Department, and many of the veterans resented them. Some of DeLancey's charges were civilians who had not done any military service, and the old guard that had struggled on the pittance Haldimand had allowed them throughout the war declared that such undeserving people had no right to ask for so much. Several references in the correspondence passing between other officers and Quebec City indicate that Stephen DeLancey was responsible only for the loyalists from New York City, and for a short time the unincorporated men in Canada. For example, on January 22, 1784, Mathews informed DeLancey that he should prepare and forward to His Excellency a return of,

> those Loyalists who have not been incorporated in Corps, and who wish to avail themselves of the Provisions His Majesty had been pleased to make for them in this province. . . To make this Business more easy to you, His Excellency has directed the officers who commanded Provincial Corps to transmit to headquarters similar Returns for their respective Corps as soon as possible.

Once the settlement at Cataraqui was going smoothly, DeLancey went to Nova Scotia, where he made his home. Later he was Chief Justice of the Bahamas, and in 1791, the Governor of Tobago.[28]

In the spring of 1784, scarcely recovered from smallpox, Justus Sherwood strove to persuade his fellow loyalists to accept the location the governor had chosen for them. On March 21, Sherwood sent Mathews a letter from Josiah Cass, the schoolmaster at Machiche, expressing fears over Haldimand's plans. Mathews asked Sherwood to reassure Cass, since that officer had been on the spot:

> The objections to it that are contained in his letter proceed from ignorance of cir-

cumstances, or intentional misinformation – The journey and conveyance, you can inform him, is by no means so tedious or difficult as he conceives them to be, nor will they, in any respect, interfere with the Season nor labour when undertaken so early as His Excellency intends a sufficient number of Bateaux and Pilots will be provided at Government Expenses to convey them, their Families & Baggage to their Lands, where they will find provisions provided for them.

His Excellency, Mathews continued, could furnish only provisions and tools. Some seigneurs were offering cattle and farming utensils, or money to purchase them. Daily, loyalists were taking up land in the seigneuries, but the governor doubted that such landlords could keep their word. Also Cataraqui had advantage of climate, situation and soil over the lower St. Lawrence – the prospect of agriculture superior to the more easterly parts of the province. As Sherwood had reported in a letter to Mathews, written in the autumn of 1783: 'The climate here is very mild & good, and I think that Loyalists may be the happiest people in America by settling this Country from Long Sou to Bay Quinte.'

The Raw Land

Despite Justus Sherwood's enthusiasm and Robert Mathews' optimism, owing to the lateness of the spring of 1784, the first bateaux of settlers and their worldly goods did not leave Lachine until the middle of May. Confusion reigned as the officers sought to organize their charges. Men argued, women tried to keep children together, babies fretted and dogs howled and fought. Through all the fuss, Major Edward Jessup was overseeing the proceedings, assisted by Justus Sherwood, James Gray and James Rogers. Sir John Johnson was to have directed the migration, but he was fully occupied with his other role as Superintendent of Indian Affairs, and Jessup had stepped into his shoes, in command of doling out the supplies Governor Haldimand had authorized.

Each man and boy over 10 years was entitled to a coat, waistcoat, breeches, hat, shirt, blanket, shoe soles, leggings and stockings, while each woman and girl over 10 was to receive two yards of woollen cloth, four yards of linen, one pair of stockings, a blanket and shoe soles. Each child under 10 was allowed one yard of woollen cloth, two yards of linen, stockings and shoe soles. Two children were to share a blanket, and for the journey each five persons was provided with a tent and one cooking kettle.[29]

The families would occupy the tents until they had cabins built then these were to be returned to the quartermaster's stores in Sorel. Each family was issued with one month's provisions, and the rest of their food would be handed out when they reached the new townships. Loading the bateaux was no easy task. Family size varied, as did the quantity of household goods. Dr. Solomon Jones, of the Loyal Rangers, had a grandfather clock packed with carefully wrapped china that had come through the woods from Fort Edward slung between two horses.[30] A few families had livestock, while others lacked even such basic items as bedding. Each night on the journey the loyalists camped on the shore, cooking their meals, pitching tents. The journey to Cataraqui took about two weeks, that to the lower townships two or three days less. Adiel Sherwood, the son of Ensign Thomas Sherwood, Justus' cousin, writing at age 69 in 1868, set down a rare and valuable record of the journey through the St. Lawrence rapids:

> The river was ascended by means of small boats, called batteaux. These barques were built at Lachine, and were capable of carrying from four to five families each. Twelve boats constituted a brigade. Each rigade was placed under the command of a conductor, with five men in each boat, two of whom were placed on each side to row, with one in the stern to steer. It was the duty of the conductor to give directions for the safe management of the flotilla. When a rapid was ascended, part of the boats were left at the foot, in charge of one man, the remaining boats being doubly manned, and drawn up by means of a rope fastened to the bow, leaving four men in the boat, with setting poles, to assist. The men at the end of the rope walked along the bank, but were frequently compelled to wade in the current, upon the jagged rocks. On reaching the head of the rapid, one man was left in charge, and the boatmen returned for the balance of the brigade.[31]

As the summer progressed, deputy surveyors hired at 7s. 6d. per day laboured frantically, trying to keep ahead of the arriving settlers. Major John Ross, at Cataraqui, acted as governor of the new townships. A town plot, later named King's Town, was hastily commenced there, because the military were already on the scene. Situated beside a large harbour at that end of Lake Ontario, it was a natural location for an urban place. Beside the St. Lawrence, in the lower settlement, at the behest of Sir John Johnson, surveyors laid out the plot of New Johnstown (later Cornwall) in Township Number 2, and Williamstown – named for Sir John's father – in Township Number 1. The latter was on the Raisin River, where there was a good mill-site. In Township Number 6, Major Edward Jessup found a clearing with an old cabin that had once been used by French traders. Here some of his battalion disembarked and he ordered Justus Sherwood to lay out a town plot before people wanting to remain there turned the ground into a chaotic squatter settlement.

Sherwood must have followed Jessup's instructions, for this town plot did not reflect his own aspirations. These are evident in a town site he surveyed in 1786 in Township Number 7, where he settled. Sherwood's plan showed a common round which the public buildings would stand – a New England design drawn from his Connecticut background.[32] The 1784 town site, at first called Newtown and later Johnstown, was on a dull grid plan, a New York town. Although Jessup, too, had been born in Connecticut, he left when he was nine years old, and he did not hold dear the memories of the pretty towns of his early years. On July 2, Sherwood reported to Mathews:

> I have been continuously Employ'd here since the 5th of last month in laying out a Town half a mile square into lots of 8 rods square – and in laying out the second Concession: Giving the people the necessary oaths and their Certificates etc which has and will for some time Require my Constant attention, as Major Jessup has gone for some time to Cataraqui.

Fortunately this town did not become permanent, because the water in front was too shallow, fine for bateaux but unsuitable for schooners.

In his report, Sherwood revealed the procedure each settler went through in order to procure his lot. To prevent officers taking the best land for themselves, Haldimand ordered that pieces of paper called certificates, with lot numbers on them, be drawn from a hat, at which time each applicant had to swear an oath of allegiance. Sherwood was in charge of the townships beside the upper St. Lawrence that had been assigned to the Loyal Rangers while Edward Jessup was overseeing the awarding of certificates, tools and provisions to the Loyal Rangers who were settling in Township Number 2, Cataraqui.

On the west side of the Niagara River, Colonel John Butler and his rangers were continuing their pioneering, and other surveyors were laying out the town site that became Niagara-on-the-Lake. Mohawk Indians led by John Deserontyn and other officers of the Indian Department were settling on the reserve assigned them beside the Bay of Quinte, while Joseph Brant was leading the greater proportion of the Six Nations who had elected to go to the Grand River Valley.

Another group of disbanded provincials, notably Captain William Caldwell's company of Butler's Rangers, had decided to settle at Detroit. Hitherto this area's inhabitants consisted of French farmers and traders who occupied both sides of the Detroit River in the vicinity of the fort, some Huron and Ottawa Indians who owned land there, the British garrison and a few officers and men of the Indian Department. No attempt to establish a township was authorized by Haldimand, although there was a scuffle over land ownership.

Some Ottawa Indians ceded a tract seven miles square on the east side of the river to Jacob Scheiffelin, a secretary in the Indian Department. On October 13, 1783, Alexander McKee, the Deputy Superintendent at Detroit, informed Sir John Johnson that this was undue exploitation of the Indians, and Haldimand issued orders that private individuals were not to purchase land directly. The crown would be responsible for negotiating and ceding of the lands upon which people could be resettled. Those who qualified for land were disbanded provincials, men of the Indian Department, a few regulars who wanted to remain in Canada when their time of enlistment ended, and certain of the Detroit Volunteers. These men were local militia, mainly francophones, but included a few loyalists.

The men from Butler's Rangers who elected to settle at Detroit had been disbanded at Fort Niagara, but William Caldwell invited them to join him at Detroit. In preparation for receiving his men Caldwell journeyed to Quebec City to ask Governor Haldimand for a tract of land. When the men of Caldwell's company arrived at Detroit, they found that the only available land had been taken up by officers of the Indian Department and interpreters. Caldwell obtained a tract along Lake Erie which was known as the New Settlement, land which ultimately became the Township of Colchester.

The settlement around Detroit was more self-sufficient than the others, because of the presence of the francophone farmers from before the Seven Years' War. A census made in 1782 by the fort's commandant, Major Arent DePeyster, showed a total population of 2,191, with about 100 other men in Indian country, and 1,112 horses, 413 oxen, 807 cows, 452 heifers and steers, 447 sheep and 1,370 hogs. Of these residents, 779 were on the Canadian, or east side of the Detroit River in the parish of Assumption, the area that would soon show the greatest development because of the uncertainty over the status of the lands near the fort. The British garrison remained on duty for the time being, but this territory had been ceded to the United States by the Treaty of Separation. On the east side of the Detroit River, the village of Assumption, later named Sandwich, was becoming the administrative centre, and a few miles to the south, a fort was planned, at what would soon become the village of Amherstburg.[33]

Everywhere else there were severe shortages. Colonel Butler had asked repeatedly for blacksmith's tools, and the parts needed to construct a mill at Niagara. Some of Justus Sherwood's complaints were more specific. He said he had received 487 axes, 110 hoes, 20 bush hooks, 13 grindstones, 39 frows (a tool for splitting shingles) and some knives. He asked for more of all these items, and two sets of blacksmith's tools, two sets of carpenter's tools, and one set of each for the Loyal Rangers settling at Cataraqui, as well as half a dozen whip saws and as many crosscut saws with whatever glass and nails Haldimand was allowing for people's huts adding; 'the Bush Hooks should be in the form of short Scythes.' He begged that rations not be reduced, since his people would be incapable of hard labour without adequate food,

> as they have no milk or butter nor any kind of vegetable whatever, no fresh meat nor fish except now and then by Chance a few small pan fish taken with hook and line and even this trifling resource must fail in the winter season.[34]

Apparently the muskellunges eluded the loyalists' hooks and lines more effectively than those of more recent anglers. A fish that could measure seven feet and weigh sixty pounds required a large pan and would compare favourably with anything brought into a Connecticut fishing port.

At the time Sherwood was writing, other officers were in Vermont and the Mohawk Valley in quest of seed corn. Mathews warned them to be discreet that they were shopping on behalf of the British government lest the Americans refuse to sell to them, or raise their prices. At Cataraqui, Major John Ross was also requesting help with supplies, and his difficulties were compounded because of a stream of refugees coming to Carleton Island from New York and Pennsylvania who had not been equipped and provisioned at Lachine before they reached the new townships. Ross also blamed Sherwood for some of the deficiencies:

> There is scarce a turnip seed, if it was Sent it was embezzled on the road, they have no seed wheat, and many not so much as a blanket to cover them in Winter, and the wish of a great part is to return at all hazard, in Short Axes and Hoes have not yet come up for half of them, it is said Ct. Sherwood Stopp'd more than his portion at Oswegatchie.[35]

Further on Ross observed:

> Disputes amongst the Loyalists frequently arise, and most material as yet between Master & Servant where Severe Correction Seems to take place, an Evil which requires a Speedy remedy, and what I do not think myself at liberty to pronounce judgment upon; many more may be expected to ensue; Strange is the Collection of people here.

The loyalists from the frontiers of the northern states were an unruly group. Ross was a Scotsman, whose own countrymen were not noted for their peacable qualities. However, his letter soon bore fruit. On August 3, Governor Haldimand appointed Ross, Lieutenant Neil Maclean and Justus Sherwood to be magistrates for the settlers at Cataraqui and in the three townships beside the St. Lawrence being settled by Loyal Rangers. These settlements were being called New Oswegatchie, and Major Jessup had received the same appointment on November 27, 1783.[36] On his return from Cataraqui to New Oswegatchie, Jessup was very ill, and in September he set out for Sorel, where he had left his family. In his absence another magistrate was needed, and Sherwood was the logical choice.

Steadily the settlers made progress, despite the shortages,

building cabins and clearing land – more then sufficient for the quantities of seed rationed out to them. Writing prior to 1890, J.F. Pringle of Cornwall compiled a description of the first dwellings from information supplied by members of the generation who were children when they lived in them.

Settlers banded together and built small houses, the largest not more than '20 feet by 15' of rounded logs, notched at the corners and laid one upon the other to a height of seven or eight feet. The roof was of elm bark. Each cabin had an opening for a door and one for a window, and the floor was of split logs, the hearth of flat stones. Chimneys were of field stones fastened with clay for mortar to the same height as the walls, and above them of small sticks plastered with clay. The logs were chinked with a mixture of sticks and clay, and a blanket served for a door until the owner had time to cut boards with a whip saw. Each window was fitted with a rough sash and four pieces of glass, the panes 7½ inches by 8½.[37]

By July 10, 3,776 people were in the new townships west of Point au Baudet and at Cataraqui, being provisioned by government. Nearly all of them had been brought by bateau from Lachine and were on their lands, or awaiting their certificates. Other loyalists were at Montreal, Fort St. Johns, Fort Chambly, Lachine and Chaleur Bay. The overall total being provisioned was 5,628.[38]

There were, however, more loyalists and their families in Canada than the provision lists indicated. Some men who had served in provincial corps early in the war had retired and were supporting themselves and their dependants in Montreal and other centres. Nor does the last figure include Butler's Rangers and the other refugees at Niagara, the few at Detroit, or the ones who had left their encampments and accepted the enducements of the anglophone seigneurs to become tenants. Altogether, more than 7,000 people had left the American states and taken refuge in Canada, or at her frontier posts, since the outbreak of the revolution. More would follow as the persecution in the victorious United States continued.

Throughout the summer and autumn of 1784, reports from the new townships reached Governor Haldimand's headquarters in Quebec City. The settlement at Niagara was the most advanced, because all persons who could be spared had been working on the land for some time. A survey dated August 25, 1783, showed that 236 acres had been cleared, and there were 49 horses, 42 cows, 30 sheep and 103 hogs at that post.[39] By July 1784, 250 officers and men with their families, in all 620 people, had decided to stay, and in fact very few of the uncommitted departed once they learned that they were entitled to grants of land.[40]

In contrast with Niagara, Major Edward Jessup reported on September 14, 1784, that at New Oswegatchie – Townships Numbers 6, 7, and 8 along the St. Lawrence – there were 6 horses, 8 oxen and 18 cows to be shared among 600 people. At Cataraqui, Major John Ross continued his pleas for more supplies and equipment, while from New Oswegatchie Captain Justus Sherwood's letters were more optimistic. On July 23, he informed Mathews:

The people have all got their farms to work they are universally pleas'd and seem to Emulate each other in their Labour, insomuch that almost every lot in the front of our three Townships and many of the back Concessions have already Considerable improvements and the Country begins to wear a very promising appearance.

On October 17, he reported again,

Our people have made a very rapid progress in Settlement but they are now much disheartened at not having received any seed wheat altho' they had sufficient Ground Clear'd I don't know what we shall do for bread another year but hope Gov't will lengthen our provisions.

The Savages begin to steal & kill our Cattle & to threaten our women and children pray represent this to the Commander in Chief, mentioning at the same time that it is owing to the rum they get at Oswegatchie for which they give all their provisions and then are induc'd to steal from us.

The Indians he mentioned were living on the south shore of the St. Lawrence, descendants of some Iroquois who had been lured into the neighbourhood by the French, who had built a mission at the fort at the mouth of the Oswegatchie River in 1749.

In 1784, local government was almost non-existent. As in New Brunswick, where Governor Thomas Carleton had postponed calling an election and establishing a legislative assembly, all decision-making was in the hands of the military governors, whose appointed legislative councillors could advise but not dictate, and the justices of the peace. Canada was divided into two districts for administrative purposes – Quebec and Montreal. The first was ruled directly by the governor-in-chief in Quebec City; the second by the commanding officer at Montreal. When the war ended the latter was Brigadier Barry St. Leger, who, as the commandant of Fort St. Johns, had known many loyalists during the revolution.[41]

The officers in the new townships were subject to Major John Ross at Cataraqui, who in turn was subordinate to St. Leger. On November 16, 1784, Frederick Haldimand left Canada never to return. He remained the governor until 1786, when a successor was chosen, and was made a Knight of the Bath for the service he performed in Canada. For the next eighteen months, two lieutenant-governors would rule in his stead. The first was Henry Hamilton, the lieutenant-governor at Detroit until his capture by the rebels, who was freed at the conclusion of hostilities; the second was Sir Henry Hope.[42]

The May 18, 1785 issue of the *Quebec Gazette* showed that Sir John Johnson, then at Montreal, James Baby of Detroit, and Justus Sherwood of New Oswegatchie had been appointed legislative councillors to represent the District of Montreal. This was meagre local government for a sprawling area that needed roads, schools, churches, draft animals, food supplies and clothing for new arrivals, as well as for the first settlers. In desperation the pioneers held town meetings in order to attempt to solve some of their problems, long before such gatherings were authorized. New Englanders were accustomed to arriving at consensus by this method, while New Yorkers had had recourse to a court leet, which differed from the New England town meeting in that the presiding judge was the steward of the manor – the system that prevailed in England. In Connecticut, where most of the Yankee settlers had originated, this officer was elected.

With the coming of the spring of 1785, more loyalists from the Montreal area arrived to take up land in the new townships. Some had wintered there, but a thin stream of refugees fleeing their homes continued reaching the various British outposts. One who came to Cataraqui with his family that season was Captain John Walden Meyers, keeping the promise he had made to Governor Haldimand that he would quit Mississquoi Bay. In the new townships the settlers struggled forward, existing in their woodland homesteads, having only the barest necessities for survival. Through the long frigid winter, they longed for the day when they would have a constitution that would meet their needs, and they solved their day-to-day problems as best they could.

Late comers joined them to take their turn at cabin building and forest clearing, and in the desire for a few public institutions – and the right to effective local government. They were in a kind of limbo, but relief was on the way in the form of Sir Guy Carleton. Now, however, his subjects would have to accustom themselves to calling him Lord Dorchester.

The Dorchester Interlude

Sir Guy Carleton was created 1st Baron Dorchester for the services he had rendered evacuating the New York City area in 1783. Early in 1786, His Lordship accepted the appointment for a second tour of duty as governor-in-chief of Canada, arriving in June at Quebec City.[42] With him as his aide-de-camp came Major Robert Mathews, whose letters shed so much light on the affairs of the provincial corps during the revolution.

Soon after he reached Canada, Dorchester addressed himself to the need for a new constitution to accommodate the changes wrought by the presence of the loyalists – one that would suit both anglophone and francophone in his domain. In November, he called a council upon state business and struck four committees. These were to report on the courts of justice; the militia, highroads and communications; population and agriculture; and external and internal commerce and the regulation of the police.[43] The Quebec Act, which the governor had shepherded through both houses of the British Parliament, was outmoded, particularly with respect to civil law and land tenure.[44] Despite his background as a large landowner in New York, Sir John Johnson would give leadership in the struggle for English civil law and freehold tenure. On December 19, 1786, several half-pay officers at New Oswegatchie wrote to Johnson requesting his help in obtaining changes in the government. Specifically they asked that they might hold their lands 'by Grants free from any Seigneurial claims or any other incumbrances whatever, the King's Quit rent excepted.'[45]

Under the conditions set forth in the crown's instructions, dated July 16, 1783, after a tenant had been on his land for ten years, a quit rent of one halfpenny per acre was to be levied.[46] Since this was a substantial increase over the rents paid in New York before the revolution, the officers who signed the petition may not have been very enthusiastic about that measure. They also requested that the country be divided into counties with courts at convenient places, and they appealed for encouragement in the preaching of the Gospel and the establishment of schools, and a prohibition on the importation of lumber from the United States that was a threat to this vital source of income in the new townships. The letter was signed by James Campbell, Elijah Bothum, Thomas Sherwood, Daniel Jones, William Lamson, Allan MacDonell, a second Allan MacDonell, Justus Sherwood, William Fraser, Joseph White, John Jones, Peter Drummond, Thomas Fraser and John Dulmage.

When Dorchester arrived the only local government was the District of Montreal, while the new townships were represented on the legislative council by their three appointed members. All other matters were handled by the magistrates, selected from the senior half-pay officers and the corps commanders. As well as maintaining law and order these justices of the peace performed marriages, which the Reverend John Stuart, the Anglican chaplain to the second battalion, King's Royal Regiment of New York, deplored in a letter he wrote to the Society for the Propagation of the Gospel from his cabin at Cataraqui:

> As to marriages he is seldom employed, it having been customary during the War for Officers and magistrates to perform that ceremony and also to baptise; the latter, indeed, is discontinued since his arrival, but he had not been able to check the former practice.[47]

He added, disapprovingly, that the inhabitants were mostly Presbyterians, Anabaptists, Dutch Calvinists or New England 'Sectaries.' He also noted that dissenters were much encouraged by the allowance of £50 to the Presbyterian minister John Bethune, the retired chaplain to the Royal Highland Emigrants, then residing in Williamstown. Stuart's letter was a warning of an approaching storm – the unsuccessful attempt to make the Church of England the established church in Upper Canada. Both Stuart and Bethune were soon busy baptizing, for once the loyalist families knew they were secure, the birth rate went up rapidly. A social phenomenon evident in several families showed that even where wives were close at hand, no babies were born during the time of displacement in refugee accommodation. Husbands must have practised a form of birth control. At that time men used dried sheep's gut as a condum, specifically to prevent venereal disease, but equally effective as a contraceptive.[48]

For example, Thomas Sherwood and his wife Anna had three children born near Fort Edward by 1779, the year he brought his family to Fort St. Johns. Their next child, James, was born at New Oswegatchie in September, 1784, conceived after the signing of the peace treaty, by which time Thomas knew he would be receiving help to settle somewhere in Canada.[49] A similar gap is found in the families of Justus and Samuel Sherwood.

A month before Lord Dorchester reached Canada, the Reverend John Stuart opened an academy in Cataraqui, and he reported that Sir Henry Hope had:

> erected a convenient School-house (which is almost finished) allowing a salary for an Assistant till something permanent may be fixed; and he has committed the sole direction of the school to Mr. Stuart and likewise the choice of an Assistant. That he opened the School in May last, the number of Pupils is more than 30 at present. The Poor are taught gratis, and those who are able to pay a moderate sum for tuition.[50]

Few of the rank and file loyalists were interested in education. With so much work to be done the labour of all family members was necessary. Beside, most were illiterate and gave schooling a low priority.

Methodism soon became the most popular religious denomination. Barbara Beck and her husband Paul came to New Oswegatchie in 1785, after Paul had worked in Montreal for some years since retiring from Samuel McKay's unit. Barbara organized classes in her cabin, and open-air meetings where people could gather to hear itinerant preachers.

In April 1787, men calling themselves the Western Loyalists sent a petition to Lord Dorchester, listing eleven requests. They wanted to live under the blessings of the British constitution and have the British system of land tenure. They asked for help in establishing Churches of England and Scotland, schools in New Johnstown, New Oswegatchie, Cataraqui and Niagara, and the stimulation of the manufacture of potash and the growing of hemp. They needed a loan of three months' supply of pork, and clothing for those who had arrived since the distribution had been made to the first settlers. They asked that the surveying of townships be hastened, and that a post road be built from Montreal to Cataraqui, with post offices along it. They also requested that trade with the Western Indians be encouraged and supervised, and they needed depots where the government would receive their surplus grain. Lastly, they asked that commissioners then in Montreal to settle loyalist claims for compensation be sent to the settlements. Many people were unable to go to that city to present their claims because the journey was too expensive. The petition was signed:

Township No. 1 Alex. McDonell
Township No. 2 S Anderson
Township No. 3 John McDonell
Township No. 4 Richard Duncan
Township No. 5 John Munro
Township No. 6 William Fraser
Township No. 7 Justus Sherwood
　　　　　　James Campbell
　　　　　　John Jones
Township No. 8 Thomas Sherwood
　　　　　　Peter Frul
Township No. 1 Cataraqui John Everitt
Township No. 2 Cataraqui Henry Simmons
Township No. 3 Cataraqui George Simmons
Township No. 4 Cataraqui Peter Van Alstyne
Township No. 5 Cataraqui Archibald McDonald[51]

Most townships were satisfied with one signature, but two – those where there was a congregation of New Englanders – needed more, an indication that emotions ran high among the Yankees. Many of these requests were embodied in the Constitutional Act of 1791. The commissioners did journey up the St. Lawrence and as far as the Niagara settlement, to record the claims of the disbanded officers and men and the civilians. The compensation paid was usually less than requested, but in time generous land grants would help soften the blow. Meanwhile, the spring and summer were very dry, and the harvest promised to be less than necessary to support the settlers through the coming winter. This was serious. Only two years had passed since they had been provisioned by government, and most families had enough land cleared if the harvest was normal. New arrivals may have received provisions for the first two years, but the record is vague. Equally well, the government may have expected them to be helped by the earlier residents.

In the midst of the drought, Lord Dorchester sent John Collins and William Dummer Powell to investigate complaints that were causing unrest in the new townships. They addressed their report from Kingston, in perhaps the oldest known document to use the modern name for Cataraqui:

> In the course of our Enquiry we were led from Public Rumour to expect much complaint in the 5th Township, New Oswegatchie of the Conduct of Justus Sherwood Esquire in the 3rd Township of Cataraqui against Jeptha Hawley Esqr as tradeing Justices, but to our great surprise not a Complaint was heard in either Township and from our personal Knowledge of the Parties we are apprehensive that Complaint has been suppressed by what means however which we cannot account for.[52]

Jeptha Hawley, another old Green Mountain Boy, may have been guilty of taking bribes, but significantly, the complaint against Justus Sherwood originated in Township Number 5 – more correctly New Johnstown – where dwelt John Munro, the onetime magistrate in the New Hampshire Grants on behalf of Governor Tryon of New York. Munro was being vicious, venting his hatred upon Sherwood, one of the few former Green Mountain Boys who was vulnerable. Fortunately for Sherwood, Lord Dorchester knew him and did not take the report seriously.

That summer, Robert Mathews, made a voyage to Detroit and kept a journal.[53] He left Quebec City on May 13, and at Montreal he took aboard presents for the Indians to the west. On the 18th, he had reached Point au Baudet, where one McGee of the King's Royal Regiment of New York had a settlement and was making good progress. On the 19th, Mathews' party landed and walked to 'Captain Alexander McDonell's' house for breakfast. Then they went on to a Mr. Wilkinson's who had a planing mill, and from there to Major James Gray's property, where Mathews found the soil very rich. The following day he went to Captain Richard Duncan's, Captain John Munro's, and Lieutenant Malcolm McMartin's, and on to Ensign Timothy Thompson's.

On the 21st, he reached Major Edward Jessup's opposite Fort Oswegatchie. Jessup, who had not yet built a house, came aboard the bateau as far as Justus Sherwood's, four miles on. Sherwood had built a 'very tolerable house' on the townsite of New Oswegatchie, which he had surveyed in 1786, that was some distance from his farm. 'He has Potash going forward. We did not find him at home.' After wasting half an hour waiting for Sherwood, Mathews went on to Lieutenant James Campbell's and stayed the night with a man who had been a sergeant in the Loyal Rangers, who had 'made a good beginning.' There the widow of Lieutenant Solomon Johns, King's Rangers, brought a petition for Lord Dorchester. Lieutenant Johns, whom Mathews remembered as 'a gallant, active worthy Young Man' had done wonders with his farm, but had been killed 'last March' by a falling tree, and his wife and children were destitute.

By May 22, Mathews was at Carleton Island, and he watched the *Seneca* sail for Niagara with two companies of the 65th Regiment aboard. From there he went to visit Cataraqui, where Lieutenant Charles Southouse and a detachment of the 29th Regiment were on duty. On the 25th, he returned to Carleton Island and took a ship's boat to Lake Ontario. Two days later he met with some Six Nations at Buffalo Creek, but he missed seeing Joseph Brant, who was at the Grand River settlement at the time. Late in the day Mathews reached Fort Niagara, which he thought very vulnerable to attack. Colonel John Butler informed him that an American visitor named Chapman was there, wanting help in purchasing land from the Indians. Mathews called him an impudent New Englander, and was present at an interview during which neither Butler nor the fort's commandant, Major Archibald Campbell, 29th Regiment, gave Chapman any encouragement.

While at Fort Niagara, Mathews wrote to Joseph Brant, since he would not be seeing him, and in the journal he reported that Colonel Butler was very upset. Few presents had been sent for the Indians since Sir John Johnson had left on a visit to England. Sadly Mathews noted 'there never was since I have known them a cordiality between Sir John & Colo Butler.' The former ranger leader had not yet received any half pay, and, distressed at the way Johnson was treating him, he wanted to be dependent only on the commander-in-chief and the commandant of Fort Niagara. Nonetheless, Mathew found the settlement thriving and most of the people honest.

Butler told Mathews that some people were unhappy over the government, and asking to elect their commissioners of the peace – shades of Connecticut. Also, the loyalists at Niagara had received less clothing and utensils than those in other settlements, and all disliked the Canadian system of land-holding. Dorchester had asked his aide to report on safe anchorages, for Mathews noted that the best place for debarkation of vessels near Niagara was Toronto. Burlington Bay he described as barred by a large shoal, and Carleton Island as the best harbour on the lake.

On June 1, Mathews went to Chippawa Creek, where 'Justice Birch' was settled, and after looking around 'the Forty' he found it as 'I left it 8 years ago.' From there he went to Fort Schlosser, where Major Thomas Ancrum was in command, and by the 10th, he had reached Detroit. There he met with Captains Henry Bird, William Caldwell and Mathew Elliot. Progress at Detroit was slow, because of the difficulty the officers had had in settling their tract. At first it had been intended for Indians. The settlement Mathews thought very primitive, and sorely in need of courts. Before taking his leave, he had an interview with Alexander McKee, the Deputy Superintendent of Indian Affairs. Mathews had returned to Quebec City by July 15.

The winter of 1787-88 went down in local history as the Hungry Year. Food was scarce, with little relief in sight. The tales of how people survived are legion, from the soup bone that passed from cabin to cabin to the faithful cat who brought home a rabbit daily until the famine passed. Those who had livestock butchered it to survive, although there is no evidence that even in those desperate days anyone ate horses. When the spring came no one had any seed potatoes or grain to plant, for it had been consumed. Despite the cruel times, the half-pay officers sent a public letter to Dorchester that appeared in the February 28 issue of the *Quebec Gazette*, asking for English civil law.

Aware of his subjects' plight, Dorchester informed the home government of the famine and received permission to obtain relief supplies where he could find them. Some livestock and seed may have been purchased in the southern United States, where the drought was less severe. Good climatic conditions prevailed during the growing season of 1788, but shortages persisted because all seed was imported and rationed.

On July 24 Dorchester issued a proclamation of importance. He was instituting more local government. The area west of the Ottawa River he divided into four new districts. Luneburg extended from the last French seigneury to the Gananoque River. West of Luneburg lay Mecklenburg, centred on Kingston and extending to the Trent River, while Nassau was basically the Niagara settlement, and Hesse that opposite Detroit. Dorchester chose German names to humour the King and from the same motives named townships in honour of the numerous royal progeny until those ran out: Charlottenburgh, Williamsburgh, Matilda, Edwardsburgh, Augusta, Elizabethtown, Ernestown, Fredericksburgh, Adolphustown, Sophiasburgh, Ameliasburgh and Marysburgh.

Each district had Courts of Common Pleas to handle civil matters. For criminal cases there would be Courts of Quarter Sessions of the Justices of the Peace, and of Oyer and Terminer and General Gaol Delivery. At criminal trials, a quorum would be six magistrates, but under certain circumstances two would be sufficient. Each district was to have a land board to award grants to settlers, additional ones to officers and others entitled to receive them.[54]

That autumn Dorchester toured the new townships, and was generally pleased with what he found. The settlements were flourishing, and many loyalists assured the governor that they were better off than before the revolution. The Hungry Year is often dated 1789 because the crop at Niagara was poor and a drought struck the lower St. Lawrence. Dorchester's report confirms that of Thad Leavitt, who, in his *History of Leeds and Grenville Counties*, wrote that the worst of the famine was over by the autumn of 1788. When Dorchester visited, people were recovering, but the half-pay officers had a universal complaint. The officers of the 84th Regiment, Royal Highland Emigrants, had received larger land grants than those in provincial corps. This was unfair, and the governor solved this most satisfactorily by raising all grants to match those given the 84th. Each field officer was then entitled to 5,000 acres, each captain to 3,000, each subaltern to 2,000 acres, each private 200 acres extra.[55] Here was salve for wounds left by the niggardly sums awarded for property and homes some had lost in the United States.

On November 9, 1789, Dorchester went a step further. The minutes of a meeting of his Executive Council quoted him saying:

that it was his wish to put a mark of honour upon the families who had adhered to the Unity of Empire, and joined the Royal Standard in America before the Treaty of Separation in the Year 1783.

The Council concurring with his Lordship, it is accordingly ordered that the several Land-Boards take a course of preserving a Registry of the names of all persons falling under the description aforementioned, to the end that their posterity may be discriminated from future settlers in the Parish Registers and Rolls of the Militia in their respective Districts . . .

And it is also ordered, that the said Land-Boards may in every such case, provide not only for the Sons of those Loyalists as they arrive to full age, but for their Daughters also of that age, or on their marriage, assigning to each a Lot of two hundred Acres more or less . . .

This was the famous U.E., considered the first indigenous Canadian honour. The list is also the basis for membership in the United Empire Loyalists' Association of Canada – and the cause of much dissent, because no similar list was compiled for Maritime loyalists. One reason may be that the various lieutenant-governors did not wish to differentiate loyalists from others, in order to make every petitioner pay a patent fee to have land registered – a source of revenue.

Once the Hungry Year was behind, the settlers began to progress rapidly, but the four districts Dorchester created remained nearly devoid of such trappings of civilization as roads, churches, schools, public buildings other than taverns, and the restrictions of French civil law and the hated seigneurial tenure rankled. By 1790, Dorchester was proposing that Canada be divided into two parts, to accommodate the aspirations of the loyalists. While it was neither feasible nor desirable to revoke the Quebec Act that gave French-speaking Canadians their rights, it was practicable to establish a separate province in the western wilderness. To everyone's satisfaction, the governor was proposing Sir John Johnson as the lieutenant-governor of the new province.

The division of Canada occurred during Dorchester's term, but most of the credit must go to Frederick Haldimand. His insistence that the main body of loyalists go to the lands he purchased made the division possible. Had he permitted large numbers of people to take up land in the seigneuries along the lower St. Lawrence, and scattered more of them at Sorel, Mississquoi Bay and Chaleur Bay, there could have been no territorial separation. Dorchester did not draft the Constitutional Act, nor did he get his way over the choice of the first lieutenant-governor. Sir John Johnson lived at Lachine, but he was often in the areas where the men of his corps had settled, for he had large land grants in the wilderness and a manor house at Williamstown. He commanded the respect and affection of many people in the new province, but the British government selected John Graves Simcoe. With his arrival, Dorchester no longer ruled the new settlements directly. Thus the loyalist settlers lost the services of both Lord Dorchester and Sir John Johnson, men many felt had cared for them with compassion and understanding.

Founding Fathers

The history of the Provincial Corps of the Northern Department ended with their disbandment and the resettlement of those who had been forced to accept exile in Canada. No account would be complete without some word on the impact these veterans and their dependants had on the history of Ontario, the province they founded. When John Graves Simcoe became the first lieutenant-governor, the heads of families in his new province were nearly all loyalists who had served in provincial corps. The others were the francophones opposite Detroit; the few who had come from New York City by choice; the various unincorporated loyalists; the few civilians; and discharged German regulars. For the years of Simcoe's reign, his domain could with justification be called a loyalist province.

Following the governor's arrival, some of the men from his Queen's Rangers who had been disbanded in New Brunswick uprooted and made their trek to Upper Canada to join their former commander. Then, because the province needed people, Simcoe informed the home government that many in the United States longed to live under the benefits of the British crown, and ought to be encouraged to leave the new republic. Some who departed for Upper Canada during Simcoe's term in office were genuine loyalists, among them Quakers happy that the governor promised they would never be expected to bear arms. Others who left may have been motivated more by the prospect of cheap land than by ideology[56]; also, after 1791, the year Vermont was admitted to the Congress, another exodus of loyalists occurred. Again some were genuinely loyal – people who had clung to the forlorn hope that Vermont might rejoin the British Empire, while others were attracted by cheap land. All loyalists were entitled to free grants, which Simcoe raised to 200 acres per head of family. Even those who could not prove that they had served the King were allowed 200 acres in return for a small fee to have it registered, provided they appeared to be of good character.

In 1796, as Simcoe was leaving the province, the British garrisons were withdrawn from most of the upper posts. Under the terms of Jay's Treaty, Michilimackinac, Detroit, Niagara, Oswego, Oswegatchie, Pointe au Fer, and the Loyal Blockhouse were handed over to the Americans. Near Carleton Island the boundary was in doubt, and this base continued in British hands. Simcoe wanted the border to run south of the base, through the narrow channel in the St. Lawrence, but the Americans expected it would be drawn to the north of the island. (By 1812, the garrison consisted of three people, when some Americans seized the fort and held it until the boundary was settled, to run north of the base. Carleton Island was the only territorial gain the United States achieved from that war.)

When Simcoe departed he left a developing province, wherein new townships had been surveyed to accommodate incoming settlers. On the east side of the Detroit River, the village of Sandwich – later the city of Windsor – was taking root. The village was the old parish of Assumption, where a Roman Catholic church was erected in 1787. Its congregation was much older, for the parish had begun as a mission to the Indians during the French regime. The Honourable James Baby, of the Legislative Council, was operating a mill. Among the prominent settlers were William Caldwell and the men of his company, Butler's Rangers, Mathew Elliot and Alexander McKee of the Indian Department, and Simon, George and James Girty, as well as some disbanded regulars.[57] Governor Haldimand had neglected the Detroit area in his planning because the number of loyalists settling there was small. By order of Simcoe; the township of Malden, the first in that neighbourhood, was surveyed in 1793.[58]

At Niagara, John Butler and his disbanded rangers established a settlement across the river from the fort. The rangers founded two townships, one below the escarpment over which the great cascade tumbles, the other above. The first was called Niagara, the second Mount Dorchester (later changed to Stamford.) A village took root to the north of the lower landing on John Butler's own land. He named it Butlersbury after his home in the Mohawk Valley, although some called it Niagara, and others spelled it Butlersburg. There Butler built his house, and he gave leadership in the new community.

He served as a judge of the Nassau District Court and as Deputy Superintendent of Indian Affairs. In 1791, he organized three small battalions of militia, in all 835 rank and file.[59] Butler died in 1796, at age 71, and was laid to rest in Butler's Burying Ground, now an historic site with a plaque in memory of his rangers. His grave is unmarked, which is typical of first-generation loyalists, and one of the earliest headstones is that of his son Thomas. A building nearby is known as Butler's Barracks, and it is similar to the one that sheltered the rangers during the revolution. Some people think that Butler's men occupied it, but records show that it dates from about 1820.[60]

When, in 1792, Governor Simcoe chose Butlersbury as his first capital he renamed it Newark, but the original plan for the town was John Butler's, and it showed his Connecticut origin. He intended to create a New England town, with a square round which public buildings would stand. Unfortunately the first public buildings were built along the Niagara River and his plan for a square was lost. The village evolved on a grid plan but because well-to-do civil servants built the first houses it grew into a very pleasant place. In 1807, a traveller named George Heriot observed:

The houses are in general composed of wood, and have a neat and clean appearance; their present number may amount to near two hundred. The streets are spacious, and laid out at right angles to each other, so that the town when completed will be healthful and airy.[61]

During the War of 1812-1814, Butler's town was burnt by the Americans, and many of the houses Heriot admired were destroyed. One that survived was the home of Lieutenant Ralfe Clench. His wife, Elizabeth, was a daughter of Sir William Johnson by Caroline Peters.[62] Nevertheless, a visitor who saw the town in 1824 noted:

> Excepting Brockville, it is the neatest village in the Province, and, on account of its healthy situation and proximity to the falls of Niagara has become a fashionable place of resort, during the summer months.[63]

Now known as Niagara-on-the-Lake, Butler's village evokes a mood similar to Williamsburg, Virginia, and for similar reasons. Both began as provincial capitals that lost function and continued as backwater communities, with charming consequences. Williamsburg has been restored as a museum depicting life in colonial America. Thus far Niagara-on-the-Lake has been restored privately, but the back streets resemble those in Williamsburg, with the added advantage that it is a living community.

The first village above the escarpment at what was called the upper landing was Chippawa, and now the tourist city of Niagara Falls has all but absorbed the older community. The two townships have vanished from maps, swallowed when regional government was introduced on the Niagara peninsula. The 100 and 200 acre lots farmed by rangers below the escarpment were soon subdivided into smaller holdings as the value of the light, sandy soil and gentle climate for tender fruit growth became apparent. Yet a few traces of the rangers remain. The house John Butler built was torn down to make way for a modern road, but in the Mohawk Valley the house he lost is protected by law, and can not be altered or demolished. Although it is privately owned, visitors make their way to it and see the wooden sign that reads 'Butlersbury 1742.'

Across Lake Ontario from Niagara, another population nucleus was forming at the new capital, York. Lord Dorchester had originally intended it as a naval base, probably on the strength of Mathews' report on the quality of the harbour at the Toronto Carrying Place. Farther east, overlooking the Bay of Quinte, a village called Meyers' Creek, in honour of John Walden Meyers, and later renamed Belleville, was growing as a squatter settlement on an Indian reserve. The lot had two good waterfalls on the Moira River and should never have been set aside for Indians needing a place to camp. Someone in authority should have realized that people would not leave that lot alone when they needed mill-sites. Belleville was purchased from the Mississauga Indians in 1818, making the survey of the town plot an afterthought, which accounts for a lack of form today in the older parts of the city.

Eastward again, Kingston, whose town site was established by Major John Ross, was the mercantile centre of the province. There, Richard Cartwright, Colonel Butler's secretary at Fort Niagara for a time during the war, was the leading merchant and public servant. Nearby, in the third township (Fredericksburgh) Major James Rogers and his family lived among the men of his disbanded King's Rangers. Rogers and his wife Margaret had five children, James Jr., David McGregor, Mary, Margaret and Mary Ann, who married John Peters Jr. After the war James Sr. went to New Hampshire and fetched all the members of his family except James Jr. and Mary. His elder son was already in Canada, and Mary remained behind because she had married the year before. Later she came with her husband and the family was reunited.[64]

For some years Rogers supervised the needs of the disbanded second battalion, King's Royal Regiment of New York, as well as his own rangers, at the request of Sir John Johnson. Apparently Major Robert Leake, who should have cared for the men, remained in England following the revolution. Soon James' health began to fail, and he died on September 25, 1790, at age 64.[65] All of his children married and had issue, and he left a substantial number of descendants, many of whom still live along the Bay of Quinte. A plaque entitled 'Lieutenant-Colonel James Rogers' stands in the grounds of St. Paul's Church, Sandhurst. With charming exaggeration it proclaims that Rogers commanded the second battalion, King's Rangers.

Of the Peters family, only John Jr. settled in the townships Governor Haldimand had chosen for the loyalists. He went to Cataraqui, and because he married Mary Ann Rogers he settled later in Sophiasburgh, the sixth township surveyed along the Bay of Quinte. John Peters Sr., still smouldering at the way Haldimand had treated him, removed himself from that governor's jurisdiction in the autumn of 1784. Two years later he wrote:

> I and my family left Canada October 17th, with many others to get rid of such a petty tyrant, and we arrived at Cape Breton. Here I left my wife and children in a fisherman's house under the protection of Peter the Indian King of Cape Breton (who had more honour than two Swiss governors) and I went to Halifax.[66]

While Peters inferred that all his family went to Cape Breton, John Jr. and Andrew did not accompany him. Several letters in the Rogers Papers give information on the later years of the Peters family. One, dated May 4, 1785, is of particular interest. Writing from Lachine to his father, John Jr. said he had no success in his business in the 'colonies' nor was he able to get passage to Cape Breton, for he had no money. He was planning to go to Cataraqui in quest of a land grant, but he longed to settle 'with my family.' Andrew, he reported, was still in 'the colonies' and John Jr. had left 'papers & books with him, but brought my Mama's Bible & Prayer Books.'

The following year, John Sr. went to England to press his claim for reimbursement of the money he had expended on the Queen's Loyal Rangers, and he never rejoined his family.

John Jr. sent other letters, which mention a brother, D.W., in Boston, and Andrew, who settled in the Saint John Valley, in New Brunswick. Samuel stayed in Cape Breton with his mother, Joseph and Ann. The Peters had eight children, and the name of one son has been lost, but John Jr. referred to another brother, Edmund Fanning Peters, called Fanning, who was the cause of much heartache. On February 6, 1795, Fanning wrote to his eldest brother from Quebec City telling him that he was miserable serving with the 60th Regiment, and wanted a discharge.

Writing on January 21, 1797, from Sophiasburgh to his mother in Sydney, Cape Breton, John Jr. told of the sad fate that befell young Fanning Peters, named for his father's colleague of Yale College days, Edmund Fanning, then the lieutenant-governor of Prince Edward Island. After saying that he had not heard from any of the family except Andrew for more than a year, John Jr. alluded to Fanning's having deserted from Oswego. The young man had been posted there some time in November 1796, and he had vanished only a day or two before a commission arrived for him, obtained through the good offices of Governor Fanning, who may have been his namesake's godfather. If only this brother had been patient a little longer, John Jr. lamented, their father's old friend might have helped him leave the army. Since then, no one had any idea where Fanning Peters was hiding. In closing, John Jr. added that the country was full of fever and ague, and he would move to Halifax if he could get any 'Public business.' He mentioned his son John and a daughter, and sent his love to Samuel, Joseph and Ann.

John Peters Sr. died in Paddington, near London, some time after 1786, still trying to get compensation. Gout in the head and stomach were believed to have carried him off. The letter that was the source of much information about him is dated June 4, 1786, from Duke's Row, No. 3, Pimlico, and addressed to 'a Friend in London.' His closing remarks are touched with the bravado characteristic of the man, yet they reveal his tendency to exaggerate, and a thinly disguised fury at the way fate had dealt with him.

I cannot say I look back with regret at the part I took from motives of loyalty and from a foresight of the horror and miseries of independency, though I never imagined they would be so great as they are now, yet I thought the part I took right and I certainly think so still, from love of my country as well as duty to my sovereign; and notwithstanding my sufferings, and services, and scandalous treatment by General Haldimand I would do it again, if there was occasion.

He was also chagrined at the way certain less deserving souls were being received as friends by the people of Britain:

> It is true I see persons who were notorious on the rebel side who are now here and taken notice of and advanced, while I am neglected and deprived of what is justly due me, but with the consciousness of having done right I can look with disdain at the triumph of successful villainy.

John Peters lies in a grave far from the place he held dear. He would have preferred to rest in the Connecticut Valley, rather than in the soil of Canada, or a mother country which, in his view, had not treated him with kindness.

Along the St. Lawrence, the upper townships, numbers 6 (Edwardsburgh), 7 (Augusta), and 8 (Elizabethtown), occupied by disbanded Loyal Rangers, were being called New Oswegatchie. Johnstown, the townsite in Edwardsburgh, was a failure. The harbour was shallow, adequate for bateaux that brought supplies and produce through the rapids, but not for the schooners that plied between Lake Ontario and the head of the Galops Rapids. Nor did the townsite Justus Sherwood surveyed in 1786 in the centre of Augusta develop. Again the water was shallow, and the only public building to overlook Sherwood's green was the Blue Church. Although Sherwood built his own house on the town plot few people followed his example.

In all, Justus and Sarah Sherwood had six children, for three daughters were born in Augusta. Their father was a leader in New Oswegatchie because Edward Jessup went to England and stayed for some time. Sherwood was a magistrate and a member of the Legislative Council. In 1786, Lord Dorchester appointed him to the Luneburg District Land Board.

With the arrival of Governor Simcoe, Sherwood's name all but disappears from the public record. For some reason Simcoe disapproved of him. Three appointments that might have gone to him were given to other men. Simcoe did not appoint him to his Legislative Council, although as a member of the earlier council Sherwood had every right to expect that he would be on the new council as a matter of course. Instead, Simcoe appointed John Munro, a slap on the wrist for Sherwood. Then Simcoe chose Captain Peter Drummond as his county lieutenant to raise a militia battalion, despite the fact that Sherwood's military experience was superior to Drummond's. When Simcoe wanted a district court judge he selected John Munro.[67]

Perhaps Sherwood, the Connecticut Yankee, had been too vocal on the need for people to have some say in running their affairs. Accustomed to responsible government and freehold tenure, Sherwood had petitioned for the abolition of seigneurial tenure.[68] Someone may have passed Sherwood's opinions on to Simcoe and the governor wanted no part of him.

Sherwood had to be content with making a fortune that left his family secure. He did a lot of surveying and took part in the timber trade, rafting his logs to Quebec City. He instilled a mixture of ambition and philanthropy in his two sons. Samuel was one of the first lawyers in Upper Canada, while Levius was a member of the Legislative Council and a judge of the Court of King's Bench. Their father did not live to see how successful they became. He died in 1798, aged 51, at Trois Rivières, on his way to Quebec City with his timber rafts.[69]

While other loyalists were migrating up the St. Lawrence in 1784, Dr. and Mrs. George Smyth went to live in Sorel, for life in the new settlements would be too severe for them. Both Terence and Thomas went to Elizabethtown and later received grants of land along the Rideau River. The date of Hudibras' death is not certain, but one source suggest that he died between October 1788 and June 1789.[70] Terence is thought to have built the earliest mill at the site of Burritts Rapids, while Thomas owned the land and operated a sawmill at the cataract later named Smiths Falls. For a time the village was known as Smyth's Falls and later the spelling was altered. Thus Smiths Falls stands as a monument to the Smyth family, and to Hudibras' erractic contribution to the security of Canada and the conduct of refugees to her territory.

While Sherwood's town plot in the centre of Augusta was withering on the vine, to the east, on land owned by Edward Jessup, was one of the best harbours on the upper St. Lawrence. There the town soon to be called Prescott was growing under Jessup's patronage after a late start. He had been preoccupied with his problems over getting compensation for the property he lost in New York state. He had sailed for England in the autumn of 1784 with his brother Ebenezer to present their claims before commissioners appointed to enquire into the losses and services of American loyalists. Although the commissioners were expected in Canada eventually, the Jessups felt their need was urgent. Edward's claim, dated March 29, 1785, set his losses at £10,160. 6s. 9d., but in a letter written in London in May, he estimated his losses at £11,172. 16s. 9d.[71]

Edward remained in England until late in 1786. A letter written by Major Mathews on January 22, 1787, implied that Jessup had arrived in Canada recently. That spring Edward took his family to Augusta, where he had received lots 1, 2 and 3 in the first concession. He played a decisive role in the development of the community, serving as a magistrate. Then he was commissioned the lieutenant-colonel commandant of a battalion of militia for the three townships of New Oswegatchie. He made another visit to England in 1789 in the hope of receiving compensation for his losses.

Jessup must have left all his land deeds and other papers in Queensbury before he fled to Crown Point in 1776, and he was never able to recover them to offer as proof of his holdings. The British government sent John Anstey as a commissioner to the United States from 1785 until 1787, to search for documents supporting loyalists' claims, and he found some Charlotte County records.[72] None of Edward's land titles was found among them.

While he was in London on his second visit Edward was challenged to a duel on August 12, 1789, by Levi Allen, visiting at the same time. Levi was one of Ethan Allen's brothers, who earned some repute as a loyalist because, following a quarrel, Ethan arranged to have his property confiscated. This gave Levi an aura of respectability.[73] Jessup refused to oblige, claiming he had said nothing unflattering. He probably had provoked Allen. Few former officers of provincials could have resisted making snide remarks about any of the Allen brothers. Jessup backed away because Levi could be as mean a man with sword or pistol as any of the feuding Allens.

Back in Canada, Edward devoted himself to developing a town beside the harbour on his land. As at Johnstown he was content with a dull grid plan. In 1800, he was still trying to get compensation, and on May 3, he wrote a memorial stating that he had lost 110,000 acres of uncultivated land. There is no evidence that he ever received any compensation other than land and half pay. By that time he owned 5,000 acres in the Johnstown District, which was separated that year from the Eastern District (formerly Luneburg until Simcoe changed all the district names.) Jessup died in 1816, at age 81, and was buried in the hilltop cemetery that now has a memorial known as the Jessup Steps. One house still standing was built by Edward, and several streets – Dibble, Edward and Jessup, commemorate the family.

When a branch of the United Empire Loyalists' Association of Canada was formed in the Prescott area, the members named it the Colonel Edward Jessup Branch. Typical of descendants, they chose Jessup's militia rank – the higher one – in preference to the rank he held as a loyalist officer. Such decisions help perpetuate the notion that Ontario was founded by half-pay colonels.

Of Edward's brothers less is known. Ebenezer remained in England, where one source states that he died in 1789. Another contends that he went to India and lived until 1818.[74] His only son, Henry James, practised law in Quebec City. Joseph Jessup stayed at Sorel for a time, then he moved to Elizabethtown, where he may have owned mills. He died in 1821 and was buried in the family plot at Prescott, not far from his elder brother Edward.[75]

Edward Jessup Jr. was a captain in the militia under his father, and in 1798 he was elected to the Legislative Assembly, and served as clerk of the peace for the District of Johnstown. His son, Hamilton Dibble Jessup, was a captain of militia at the Battle of the Windmill in 1838.[76]

Despite Edward Jessup Sr.'s insensitivity as a town builder, and Justus Sherwood's disappointment that his townsite was a failure, New Oswegatchie was not to be without its Yankee symbol. In 1808, a few miles to the west, in Elizabethtown, another Connecticut Yankee, Ensign William Buell, had a townsite surveyed on his land by Reubin Sherwood, Ensign Thomas' son. Named Brockville in 1812, Buell made sure that his town had a square as its focal point. He set aside four acres for a green, court house and gaol, on a hill overlooking the St. Lawrence. Around the green public buildings were erected, and at each corner a church. Brockville is a New England town, the only one in Ontario, and described by one traveller in the 1830s as 'the prettiest town I saw in Upper Canada.'

New England loyalists were scattered throughout all the townships, but many congregated in New Oswegatchie, among them James and David Breakenridge, William Buell and Solomon Johns. All had been officers in the King's Rangers, but they settled in these townships, rather than with James Rogers in the township that had been assigned to their regiment. In having a New England townsite surveyed, Buell had done what came naturally. His square reflected the political tradition that bred him, and many of the other settlers in New Oswegatchie. The green was to be the place where men gathered to discuss the affairs of the country, to argue and occasionally settle their differences with fisticuffs.

The Buells remained true to their New England origins. The founder entered the Legislative Assembly in 1800, to work for reform, years before a political party of that persuasion had evolved. By the 1830s William Buell Jr. was the editor of the *Brockville Recorder*, and he made his newspaper the voice of moderate reform in the eastern part of the province. When Mackenzie's rebels marched down Toronto's Yonge Street the younger Buell deplored such violence. 'We are an advocate of Reform so far as is consistent with the true principles of the British Constitution. We go no further.'

Reform must come through discussion in the legislature in the New England manner. The people in the Johnstown District

Sir John Johnson's manor house in Williamstown stands near the remains of his mills on the Raisin River.

Home of the Reverend John Bethune, chaplain, Royal Highland Emigrants, in Williamstown, belongs to the Ontario Heritage Foundation. Courtesy: Ontario Heritage Foundation.

agreed, for in 1837 only eight were arrested and no one was charged.[77] In districts to the west the lists of men arrested show a generous sprinkling of loyalist names. Those of New York background were more likely to boil over when their frustrations became unbearable. Three of John Walden Meyers' grandsons were arrested, while Peter Mathews, a New York loyalist's son, was hanged for his part in the Mackenzie uprising.

Another reason why the people of the Johnstown District were more content was because the front row of townships was filled up before the clergy and crown reserves were established. With few vacant lots to interfere with the progress of their settlement people had less cause for complaint. The same was true of the five townships called New Johnstown where the first battalion, King's Royal Regiment of New York settled.

In the second township (Cornwall) the village of New Johnstown, which Sir John Johnson's surveyors had selected, would become the city of Cornwall. Williamstown, in the first township (Charlottenburgh), was a hive of activity, with mills on the Raisin River, but destined to decline when the era of water power passed. There Johnson had an estate close to the town plot. His white clapboard manor house is still standing, overlooking the river. A few steps away is the house built by the Reverend John Bethune, the chaplain of the Royal Highland Emigrants. St. Andrew's Church, which Bethune founded, is still there, although the original building has been replaced.

Sir John Johnson had a second estate on the south shore of the St. Lawrence opposite Montreal which he called Mount Johnson, but he lived most of the time in Montreal with Polly and his growing family. He continued taking part in public life, representing the District of Montreal on the Legislative Council.[78] He was also colonel-in-chief of the militia for the Eastern Townships, an honorary position. He was compensated to the extent of £47,000 and substantial grants of land.[79] He was frequently in the townships along the St. Lawrence and the Bay of Quinte where his men had settled.

The years were passing, but Johnson had never forgotten Clarissa Putnam and his two eldest children, William and Margaret, who lived in Schenectady. In 1809, when Lady Johnson paid a visit to England on her own, Sir John invited Clarissa to come to Montreal. She did, and the two aging lovers had a quiet reunion. Johnson gave her a house in Schenectady and an annuity of £1,000 per annum.[80]

When war broke out in 1812, Johnson was 70 years old but eager to do his part. He advised Sir George Prevost, the commander-in-chief and one with feet of clay, that if Indians and rangers could lay waste to the lands behind the advancing Americans, the climate would defeat them. This letter is on display at the Crysler's Farm Battlefield Park near Morrisburg, loaned by another Sir John Johnson, the Sixth Baronet of New York.

The Johnsons had ten children, but several predeceased them. By 1812, William, who had survived Polly's trek to New York City in 1776, had died of natural causes. Their second son had died in Polly's arms towards the end of her epic journey. Anne, the eldest daughter, married Colonel MacDonell, a deputy quartermaster-general of Canada. The third son, Adam Gordon, became the heir and was the Third Baronet of New York. James Stephen, the fourth son, was killed at Badajoz, Spain, in 1808. Marie Catherine, the second daughter, married Major-General Sir Henry Foord Bowes, the hero of Badajoz where James Johnson died. She was widowed when Sir Henry fell at the seige of Salamanca. The fifth son, Robert Thomas, drowned in Canada, and the sixth, Warren, a major in the 60th Regiment, died of yellow fever while on active service.

Three sons outlived the Johnsons, Adam Gordon, John Jr., whose son was the Fourth Baronet, and Charles Christopher, commissioned in the 9th Lancers, who married Susan, a daughter of Admiral Sir Edward Colpoys. The present holder of the title is the Seventh Baronet, Sir Peter Colpoys Johnson, a descendant of Charles Christopher.[81] The family was founded by a likely Irish youth who came to the Mohawk Valley and received the baronetcy for taking good care of the interests of the Lords of Trade in London. The Second Baronet, through fortunes of war, moved to Canada. Because his sons were educated in England some felt at home there and remained. Despite their beginnings – an Irish commoner and a German indentured servant girl – some joined the British aristocracy and the title now belongs to an Englishman.

Polly died in 1815, and Sir John was alone. Of the other members of his family, Guy Johnson died in England in 1788, trying to obtain the compensation he thought he deserved. His wife Mary and daughters Mary and Julia were with him. Like Sir John, Daniel Claus made his home in Montreal. His wife Ann had died at Oswego in 1775,[82] but his son William and daughter Catherine were with him. William Claus had served as a lieutenant in the first battalion, King's Royal Regiment of New York, and he became a Deputy Superintendent of Indian Affairs, a colonel in the militia, and the Lieutenant of Oxford County.[83]

Of Sir John's Mohawk kinsmen, his stepmother, Brown Lady Johnson, whom British officers called Miss Molly Brant although

348

she was legally married to Sir William, spent her remaining years in Kingston. Most of her daughters married white men and their descendants lost their identity as Mohawks. Sir John's half-brother, Peter Warren Johnson, was killed at the Battle of Long Island in 1776. George, the youngest half-brother, married a Cayuga women and went to live among her people beside the Grand River.[84] Of William of Canajoharie, Caroline Peters' son, less is known.

More than Molly's children, William was the son of the longhouse. Until he was 18 William lived with his mother at Canajoharie, when Sir William sent him to Lancaster, Pennsylvania, to be educated by the Reverend Thomas Barton. The youth was miserable in Lancaster, where people resented his appearance, a reminder of the Indian menace.[85] After this attempt to introduce him to European ways, William returned to his mother's people. During the revolution he served with the Indians, and the rebels twice claimed that he was killed in action, first near Fort St. Johns in 1775, and again at Oriskany in 1777. Yet William signed a letter warning the rebels that the Indians would not tolerate the burning of their villages, citing the Cherry Valley raid of 1778 as the kind of vengeance they could expect.[86] He perished later in the war at an unknown time and place.

Sir John died in 1830, nearly 88 years old, and his funeral was remembered for its size and magnificence. The hearse was drawn by four black horses, the coffin draped with the insignia of a brigadier-general. The procession was led by the 24th Regiment, followed by relatives and friends. Next came the officers of the Masonic Lodge, of which Sir John had been Provincial Grand Master. After the Freemasons marched hundreds of Indian men and women from the reserves at Caughnawaga, St. Regis and Lake of Two Mountains. The service was held at the Episcopal Church on Notre Dame Street, and afterward the cortege passed along the streets to the bank of the St. Lawrence, where a boat waited to take the remains across the water.

As the boat pulled away, troops lining the shore fired a salute that was echoed by the guns from the batteries on St. Helen's Island.[87] Sir John was laid to rest beside Polly in the family vault at Mount Johnson, gone but not forgotten. On June 24, 1961, at the Crysler's Farm Battlefield Park, three plaques were unveiled by the Sixth Baronet of New York, Sir John Johnson. One was to the heroes of the 1813 battle; the second to the men of the Royal Highland Emigrants, King's Royal Regiment of New York, King's Rangers and Loyal Rangers; the third to the memory of Sir John Johnson, the Second Baronet of New York. Above them flies the Union Jack –

lacking the cross of St. Patrick that was not added until 1802. The plaque reads:

```
THE UNION JACK FLOWN FROM THIS POLE

FLAG OF THE BRITISH EMPIRE

AT THE TIME OF THE AMERICAN REVOLUTION

COMMEMORATES

SIR JOHN JOHNSON

KNIGHT AND SECOND BARONET OF NEW YORK

Major-General of Militia in New York Province

Lieutenant Colonel Commandant of the

King's Royal Regiment of New York

Superintendent General and Inspector General

of the Six Nations Indians

Superintendent of Refugee Loyalists

Colonel-in-Chief of Militia of the Eastern Townships

Member of the Legislative Council of Lower Canada

Born - Mount Johnson, N.Y., Nov. 5, 1742

Died - Montreal, Jan. 4, 1830

THIS PLAQUE

WAS PRESENTED AND THE FIRST FLAG RAISED BY

SIR JOHN JOHNSON

SIXTH BARONET OF NEW YORK

June 24th, 1961.
```

Legacy and Myth

From the loyalists Ontario has inherited pretty towns, houses that resemble those of the same period in northern New York and New England, and two views of politics. Most loyalist architecture that has survived is Georgian and symmetrical. Houses, whether of stone, brick or wood, have clean lines and simple but often artistic detail, devoid of the extravagances of the Victorian era.

Examples in public ownership are the French-Robertson house and the exterior of the Loucks house in Upper Canada Village, or Homewood, to the west of Prescott, built by Dr. Solomon Jones, the surgeon's mate in the Loyal Rangers. The stone house built by William Buell in Brockville, and John Walden Meyers' brick house in Belleville, both demolished, were smaller copies of Johnson Hall in the Mohawk Valley and Philip Schuyler's mansion in Albany; the latter two are now museums. The many sturdy stone farmhouses in eastern Ontario further express the loyalists' delight in Georgian forms.

These are the physical expression of the values held by founding families, refugees who brought their notions of town building and architecture with them and re-established the kinds of communities they had left. They brought an emotional tradition, too – Yankee politics and New York indifference to government. Thus families of New England origin such as the Buells longed for responsible government and tended to support the Reform Party. Representing the traditions of feudal New York were the descendants of Ephriam Jones, the commissary for the below-strength corps commanded by John Nairne before Governor Haldimand tidied up his records and formed the Loyal Rangers. Jones' sons and daughters became the backbone of the Family Compact, the little oligarchy opposed by William Lyon Mackenzie.

The greatest impact the loyalists made was by their sheer presence, their need for accommodation where their familiar institutions could be given them. Such could not be met in a province where the conditions laid down under the Quebec Act prevailed. Unfortunately, the history of the settlement of the loyalists and the creation of Upper Canada, so straightforward, has since become obscured by myth-makers.

By the mid nineteenth century there had arisen what some historians call the loyalist cult. Myth-makers distorted the picture of the loyalist founders into defenders of their version of the British Empire, failing to recognize that the empire of Queen Victoria was a different creature from that of George III. Loyalist families from the revolutionary era were recast as staunch defenders of empire, men standing shoulder to shoulder during the War of 1812-1814, and later during the 1837 rebellion. The myth-makers felt honour bound to portray this kind of solidarity during the War of 1812 because it expiated the effects of the revolution. Loyalists emerged from that conflict as sorry losers, but by their successful defence of Upper Canada, they became the victors over the Americans who had driven them out of their country.

In a paper given to the annual convention of the United Empire Loyalists' Association of Canada in May 1979, Dennis Duffy claimed that the War of 1812 was a godsend:

> If there had been no 1812, it would have been necessary to have invented one; . . . as an historical event that formed the cornerstone for a tribal mythology, 1812 liberated a culture from a sense of defeat and bitterness . . . 1812 formed an Easter that followed the Good Friday of the Revolutionary War, giving to Upper Canadian Loyalism a confidence in its own recuperative powers . . . To achieve this good, the events of the war would have to be reshaped.[88]

This was done, to create an impression that loyalists drove the hated Americans out of their new homeland. Mythology aside, some loyalists had returned to the United States, disillusioned by the unrepresentative form of government and the restrictions that impeded the development of Upper Canada, especially when compared with the progress possible in the land that had rejected them.

Others were unco-operative. John Walden Meyers was so surly that a Scots immigrant named James McNabb who supported the Family Compact had him charged with treason.[89] Without British regulars standing firm in the battles fought in Upper Canada, loyalists who served in the militia would not have been very effective against the Americans.

When rebellion flared in 1837, as in the American Revolution there were rebels and loyalists. Myth-makers have pretended that the loyalist families of the revolution were firm supporters of the Family Compact. However, the loyalists of this later conflict were not necessarily the families who had been loyal during the earlier struggle for self-government.

Finally the myth affirmed that loyalists were the cream of American colonial society – the Harvard and Yale graduates, the aristocracy, the civil servants, the owners of vast holdings in land and other property. Some were, but the typical Ontario loyalist founder was an illiterate frontiersman. Only four field officers – John Butler, Edward Jessup, James Gray and James Rogers – settled in the province. Only certain of the commissioned officers could count their lost acreages in the thousands and had lost substantial properties. The claims filed by most of Ontario's founders show that they were men of modest means, who requested compensation for less than £200 and signed their petitions with a cross.

Mythology that shows loyalists only as pioneers and upholders of empire has allowed them to be an anachronism – an humiliation in an age when the British Empire is gone. In the process of converting loyalists from vanquished into victor – and in the north they never were vanquished – the fascinating time in their lives had been buried. Addressing the annual dinner of the Ontario Historical Society in June 1972, John Morgan Gray said:

Research on the Loyalists has been diffused and spotty; records are lacking for many parts of the Loyalists' history. But there is one fundamental fact about many of them that needs no research; for five, six, seven years they had been soldiers, they had become something different – a special sort of man. And wars change, but soldiers do not . . .

In very truth, Old Soldiers Never Die. The early history of Ontario and of Ontario's response to events was probably most influenced, and could have been predicted with some accuracy, from that single condition. The Loyalists had been soldiers and soldiers' wives and soldiers' children.

The image of men serving in provincial corps for the defence of Canada, and in action against the rebels is the valorous portrait. Loyalists are Ontario's archetypal heroes.

Bibliographical Essay

While I have made use of many reliable secondary sources, as listed in the bibliography that follows, most of the material I have used is found in two sources. One is the wealth of material transcribed by the Late Brigadier E.A. Cruikshank, without whose dedication my task would have required many more years of research in handwritten, difficult to read documents. The other is the Haldimand Papers, which were donated to the British Museum in London by Sir Frederick's nephew. I have shown three different sets of references for this one collection, because I examined these papers in three different places.

While visiting the British Museum I selected a sampling in order to have some of the authors' original handwriting. The Ontario Archives has a small collection of the papers from the Public Archives of Canada's copies, on photostats. Since I live in Toronto, I studied these copies before going to Ottawa to see the rest of the Haldimand collection. As well as the Ontario Archives, my footnotes refer to the Public Archives and the British Museum. This was necessary owing to a change in policy at the Public Archives mid stream in my research.

The collection known as the Haldimand Papers, Series B. in the Public Archives consists of hand written transcripts of the originals in the British Museum, with different page numbers. Over the years I have collected copies of hundreds of these papers. On my more recent visits to Ottawa, I have found that these large, leather-bound volumes are now in storage to preserve them, and I have had to read the microfilm reels which the archives purchased from the British Museum. Since these reels are photographs of the originals, they have the Museum's numbering system. After one wild goose chase with the microfilm in an effort to have all my footnotes conform to the British Museum's numbers, and considerable eyestrain, I resolved to use the B references from the handwritten transcripts, and to use the British Museum numbers for the material I collected subsequent to the decision to preserve the old volumes.

Other repositories of value are, the Ontario Department of Public Records and Archives, and the Public Record office in London. Notable in the first are the Jessup, F.J. French, Canniff and Rogers Papers; in the second the Audit Office records where all copies of the Loyalists' claims for compensation are kept, and the War Office records. At the Public Archives of Canada, in addition to the Haldimand collections, are the papers of Daniel Claus, and copies of the

War Office and the Colonial Office records.

I also consulted the Glen Papers, and the Colden Letter Books in the New York Public Library, the Schuyler Papers and the Sir William Johnson collections in the New York State Library in Albany, and the Winslow Papers at the University of New Brunswick. I am fortunate to live in Toronto, in that the Metropolitan Central Library has a superb collection of reference books – nearly all the works listed as secondary sources are there. The exception is the old histories of Vermont, which I read in the libraries of the Bennington Museum and the Vermont Historical Society in Montpelier.

Footnotes

Part I: Background and Perspective
Chapter 1: Circumstances Surrounding the Revolution

Chapter 2: British Administration in Canada

1. W.O. Raymond, *Loyalists in Arms*, New Brunswick Historical Society Collections, 5 (1904) p. 190.
2. Paul H. Smith, *Loyalists and Redcoats, A Study of British Revolutionary Policy* (Chapel Hill, N.C. 1964), pp. 63-5.
3. Ibid., p. 74, quoted from Germain to Clinton, Jan. 23, 1779, Sir Henry Clinton Papers, University of Michigan, Ann Arbor, Mich.
4. Sir John Fortesque, ed., *Correspondence of George III.* (London, 1927-28), vol. 4, No. 2110, George III to Lord North, Dec. 18, 1777.
5. Philip Katcher, *The American Provincial Corps, 1775-1784*, Osprey Men-at-Arms Series (Reading, England, 1973), pp. 17-18.
6. *A List of General and Field Officers.* (London) more often called The Army List. After 1785, this regiment's officers are on the half pay lists of the Irish Establishment.
7. Sir Leslie Stephen and Sir Sidney Lee, eds. *The Dictionary of National Biography* (London, 1921-1964). Vol. III, p. 1002. According to this account, Carleton was at Louisbourg with General Amherst, but Carleton's biographer, A.G. Bradley, disagrees.
8. A.G. Bradley, *Lord Dorchester*, Makers of Canada Series, Vol. III (Toronto, 1926), pp. 29-33.
9. A.L. Burt, *Guy Carleton, Lord Dorchester*, 1724-1808, Canadian Historical Association, Booklet No. 5 (1955), pp. 6-7.
10. Ibid. pp. 10-11.
11. J.N. McIlwraith, *Sir Frederick Haldimand*, Makers of Canada Series, Vol. III (Toronto, 1926), pp. 6-11, 17.
12. Ibid., p. 27.
13. Ibid., pp. 41, 83.
14. Ibid., pp. 89-09.

15. Public Archives of Canada, Haldimand Papers, B 54, p. 30, Haldimand to Germain, Oct. 15, 1778.
16. Lieut.-Col. H.M. Jackson, *Rogers' Rangers*, published privately, 1953, pp. 181-2.
17. Haldimand Papers, British Museum, Add. Mss. 21819, p. 125, Haldimand to Sir John Johnson, Aug 10, 1780
18. McIlwraith, pp. 279-84.
19. J.J. Talman, *Loyalist Narratives from Upper Canada*; Champlain Society (Toronto, 1966), P. 396, Narrative of Alexander McKee.
20. Ontario Archives, Jessup Papers, Military Order Book, orders for Oct. 21, 1782.
21. Arthur Pound and Richard E. Day, *Johnson of the Mohawks.* (New York, 1930), p. 104.
22. Barbara Graymont, *The Iroquois in the American Revolution* (Syracuse, N.Y., 1972), p. 29.
23. Richard E. Day, ed., *Papers of Sir William Johnson*, 14 vols. Vol. 1, pp. 465-66, Commission of William Johnson, Apr. 15, 1755.
24. PAC, Colonial Office Records, Series 'Q', vol. 20, p. 305, Haldimand to Lord Townsend, Oct. 25, 1782.
25. PAC, Haldimand Papers, B 167, p. 371, Return of Officers in the Indian Department.

Part II: The Provincial Corps, Northern Department

Chapter 3: The Role of the Provincials

1. Esther C. Wright, *The Loyalists of New Brunswick* (Fredericton, 1955), p. 18, taken from the Carleton Papers, New Brunswick Historical Society.
2. PAC, Haldimand Papers, B 105, pp. 295-380, Dec. 1, 1783, and B 110, p. 103.
3. Ontario Bureau of Archives, *Third Report* (1905), p. 88. *A List of Disbanded Troops and Loyalists Settled on the North Side of Lake Erie.* Opposite some names is Detroit Volunteers; opposite others, Butler's Rangers, Indian Department or regular regiments.
4. Lawrence Elliot, *The Long Hunter; a new life of Daniel Boone.* (New York, 1976).
5. Haldimand Papers, Br. Mus. Add. Mss. 21819, p. 185, Haldimand to Sir John Johnson, Apr. 12, 1781.

Chapter 4: The Royal Highland Emigrants (84th Foot)

1. PAC, War Office 28, vol. 10, part 4, p. 486.
2. J.R. Harper, 'The Fraser Highlanders' Historical Publication 4. The Montreal Military and Maritime Museum, manuscript, p. 363.
3. Extract of a letter in Torloisk House, Isle of Mull, Scotland. The original is listed as Family Documents, Castle Ashby, Northampton, England, No. 1340.
4. Dictionary of National Biography. Vol. XII, p. 643
5. Seanachie, *Account of Clan Maclean* (London, 1838), p. 356.
6. E.A. Cruikshank, *Butler's Rangers*, Lundy's Lane Historical Society (Welland, 1893), p. 112.
7. PAC, Haldimand Papers, B 102, p. 196-9, Memorial of Allan Maclean, undated.
8. PAC, War Office 28, vol. 4, p. 212, Commission to Allan Maclean.
9. Harper, 'Fraser Highlanders', p. 370
10. George F.C. Stanley, *Canada Invaded, 1775-1776.* (Ottawa, 1973), Appendix I,
11. E. Ryerson, *The Loyalists of America*, 2 volumes, (Toronto, 1880). Vol. 2, p. 262. The Officers of the 1st. Battalion, Royal Highland Emigrants, 1779, with dates of

their commissions.

12. E.A. Cruikshank, *The King's Royal Regiment of New York*, Ontario Historical Society Papers and Records, Vol. 27, (1930), p. 198.

13. PAC, *Quebec Gazette*, Sept. 14, 1775.

14. Harper, 'Fraser Highlanders,' p. 367.

15. Quebec Gazette, Sept. 14, 1775.

16. E.A. Cruikshank, *Memoir of Lt.-Col. John Macdonell*, Ontario Historical Society Papers and Records, Vol. 22, 1927, p. 24.

17. The preceding, and much of what follows in this section has been compiled from several reliable secondary sources and two primary ones. Some of the detail is drawn from Bradley's biography of Carleton, and from Stanley's *Canada Invaded, 1775-1776*. Primary sources are J. Samuel Walker, *The Perils of Patriotism*, an account of John Joseph Henry, who was a private in the Lancaster, Pennsylvania, riflemen, first published in 1812, and Sheldon S. Cohen, *Canada Preserved: The Journal of Captain Thomas Ainslie*, who served in the British militia at Quebec, 1775-76.

18. Ainslie, p. 24.

19. PAC, Colonial Office Records, Series 'Q', Vol. 12, p. 344.

20. Ibid., Vol. 12, p. 69. Maclean to a friend, May 25, 1776.

21. Ibid.

22. Herbert W. Debor, *German Regiments in Canada, 1776-1783*, German Canadian Yearbook, vol. 2 (Toronto, 1975), p. 34-36.

23. PAC, Colonial Office Records, Series 'Q', Vol. 13, pp. 26-27, Carleton to Germain, quoted by Cruikshank in *A History of the Origin and Services of the Military and Naval Services of Canada from the Peace of Paris in 1763 to the Present Time*, 3 vols. (Ottawa, 1919-1920), Vol. 2, p. 196.

24. Cruikshank, *John MacDonell*, p. 22.

25. Cruikshank, King's Royal Regiment of New York, p. 206.

26. Lieutenant-General John Burgoyne, *A State of the Expedition from Canada* (London, 1780), Appendix, p. iii.

27. Stanley, *Canada Invaded*, p. 130.

28. PAC, Haldimand Papers, B 105, p. 84, Maclean to Haldimand, July 1, 1778.

29. PAC, War Office 28, vol. 4, p. 223. Muster of the Emigrants Ending 25th Decem 1777.

30. Ibid., p. 233, list dated at Quebec, Dec. 19, 1778.

31. PAC, Haldimand Papers, B 50, p. 20, Haldimand to Germain, Apr. 16, 1779.

32. The Army List, 1773, p. 188.

33. PAC, Haldimand Papers, B 54, p. 29, Haldimand to Germain, Oct. 14, 1778.

34. Ibid., B 58, p. 83. List of the Officers in the Corps of Rangers Commanded by Lieut. Colonel John Butler, Aug. 25, 1783. MacDonell's commission is dated Aug. 1, 1778, when Butler was still a major.

35. Haldimand Papers, Br. Mus. Add. Mss. 21827, pp. 348-349, A list of the officers in Butler's Rangers.

36. The Army List, 1779, p. 150, a list of officers in the 84th Regiment.

37. C.J.J. Bond, *The British Base at Carleton Island*, Ontario Historical Society, Papers and Records, vol. 52, no. 1 (1960), p. 17, quoted from Haldimand, B 128, p. 13.

38. The Army List, 1781, p. 150.

39. Ontario Archives, Canniff Papers. Notes on the Goring Family, Francis Goring to Robert Cruikshank, silversmith in Montreal, Sept. 14, 1779.

40. PAC, Haldimand Papers, B 54, p. 266-9, Haldimand to Germain, explaining that he could then authorize the raising of two other provincial corps because the 84th was at strength.

41. Lt. John Enys, *The American Journals of Lt. John Enys*, Elizabeth Cometti, ed. (Syracuse, N.Y., 1976), p. 35.

42. PAC, War Office 28, vol. 3, p. 185, Maclean to Haldimand, Oct. 19, 1781.

43. Harper, 'Fraser Highlanders', p. 372-72.

44. Cruikshank, King's Royal Regiment of New York, p. 275.

45. William Leete Stone, *Life of Joseph Brant*, 2 vols. (Cooperstown, N.Y., 1845). vol. 2, p. 186, Stone gives Almon's Remembrancer, Vide Letter of Col. Willett to Lord Stirling as his source.

46. Cruikshank, King's Royal Regiment of New York, p. 283.

47. Ibid., p. 287.

48. PAC, Haldimand Papers, B 45, p. 115, Lord North to Haldimand, Aug. 8, 1783.

49. Ontario Bureau of Archives, *Third Report* (1905), Hesse District Land Board Lists of Petitions, p. 88, shows several men of the 84th on this list.

50. Fortesque, *Correspondence of George III*, vol. 3, No. 1632.

51. Ontario Bureau of Archives, *Third Report* (1905), Book of Official Instructions to the Land Surveyor of Upper Canada, p. 448.

52. M.E. Beacock, 'North Mull,' M.A. Dissertation, Edinburgh University, 1954, p. 25.

53. Ontario Archives, Jessup Papers, Military Order Book, item for Oct. 17, 1782.

Chapter 5: The King's Royal Regiment of New York

1. Pound and Day, *Johnson of the Mohawks*, pp. 496-97.

2. Ibid., p. 434.

3. Sir John Johnson, *The North American Johnsons* (London, 1963), p. 43.

4. Pound and Day, *Johnson of the Mohawks*, p. 381.

5. Ibid., p. 434-46.

6. Ibid., pp. 437-38.

7. Cruikshank, King's Royal Regiment of New York, pp. 195-99.

8. Talman, *Loyalist Narratives*, p. 382, Memorial of Abraham Cuyler.

9. Graymont, *Iroquois in the American Revolution*, p. 82.

10. Stone, *Life of Brant*, vol. 1, chapter 6. The foregoing is a precis of Stone's account.

11. Cruikshank, King's Royal Regiment of New York, p. 201.

12. Johnson, *North American Johnsons*, p. 55-6.

13. Mary Q. Innis ed., Mrs. Simcoe's Diary (Toronto, 1965), p. 66. She described Sir John's house as she saw it in 1792.

14. A description of this campaign can be found in Cruikshank, *King's Royal Regiment of New York*, pp. 201-13.

15. The uniform coat of Lieutenant Jeremiah French, of the second battalion, is on display at the Hamilton Military Museum, Dundurn Castle. It is red, with blue facings, trimmed with gold lace and gold buttons stamped R.R.N.Y.

16. *Orderly Book of Sir John Johnson During his Campaign Against Fort Stanwix from Nov. 4th 1776 to July 30th 1777* (New York, 1881), annotated by William Leete Stone, p. 3, Nov. 7, 1776, pp. 62-96.

17. PAC, Colonial Office Records, Series 'Q', vol. 13, p. 329. A List of Officers Employed in the Indian Department with their Rank and Pay, June 15, 1777, p. 60 pt 1.

18. J. Almon, ed., *The Remembrancer or Imperial Repository of Political Events*, 17 vols. (London, 1775-1784), vol. 5, p. 392.

19. Ontario Bureau of Archives, *Second Report* (1904), p. 970. Claim of Mary Hare, widow of John, who fell at Oriskany, mother of William Hendrick Hare of Butler's Rangers.

20. PAC, Colonial Office Records, Series 'Q', vol. 14, pp. 153-5, Butler to Carleton, Aug. 15, 1777.

21. Graymont, *Iroquois in the American Revolution*, p. 135. The orderly book remained in American hands and was published in New York in 1881.

22. John R. Brodhead, ed., *Documents Relating to the Colonial History of New York*, 15 vols., (Albany, N.Y., 1853-1887), vol. 8, pp. 718-23, Claus to Knox, Oct. 16, 1777.

23. PAC, Colonial Office Records, Series 'Q', vol. 15, p. 261.

24. PAC, Haldimand Papers, B 154, pp. 2-4.

25. Bond, *British Base at Carleton Island*, p. 4.

26. Enys, *Journals*, p. 23.

27. These campaigns are described in detail by Cruikshank in *King's Royal Regiment of New York*, pp. 216-56.

28. E.A. Cruikshank, *Captain John Walden Meyers, Loyalist Pioneer*, Ontario Historical Society Papers and Records, vol. 31 (1936). p. 12.

29. The Army List, 1773, pp. 185-6. Half Pay List, 60th Regiment.

30. Haldimand Papers, Br. Mus. Add. Mss. 21819, pp. 17-19, Haldimand to Sir John Johnson, May 17, 1779.

31. Cruikshank, *John Walden Meyers*, p. 15.

32. Haldimand Papers, Br. Mus. Add Mss. 21819, p. 83, Haldimand to Sir John Johnson, Apr. 17, 1780.

33. Cruikshank, King's Royal Regiment of New York, p. 233, part of Sir John's letter to Haldimand, June 3, from Fort St. Johns.

34. Haldimand Papers, Br. Mus. Add. Mss. 21819, pp. 129-30; Haldimand to Sir John Johnson, Aug. 24, 1780.

35. Ibid., p. 133, Haldimand to Sir John Johnson, Sept. 1, 1780.

36. Gavin K. Watt, 'The King's Royal Regiment of New York, Johnson's Royal Greens,' mimeographed manuscript, 1975, p. 13.

37. PAC, Haldimand Papers, B 159, pp. 170-8. Report of Sir John Johnson to Haldimand, Oct. 31, 1780.

38. Cruikshank, King's Royal Regiment of New York, pp. 247-8.

39. PAC, Haldimand papers, B 167, pp. 403-5. List of Officers of the Second Battalion, King's Royal Regiment of New York.

40. Ira Allen, *The National and Political History of the State of Vermont* (London, 1798), pp. 27, 31-35.

41. Ryerson, *Loyalists of America*, vol. 2, p. 262. Certificate of Brigadier-General Allan Maclean on behalf of John Munro.

42. These campaigns are described in detail by Cruikshank, *King's Royal Regiment of New York*, pp. 259-323.

43. Haldimand Papers, Br. Mus. Add. Mss. 21819, pp. 184-5, Haldimand to Sir John Johnson, Apr. 12, 1781.

44. Innis, ed., Mrs. Simcoe's Diary, p. 67.

45. Haldimand Papers, Br. Mus. Add. Mss. 21819, p. 202, Haldimand to Sir John Johnson, July 16, 1781.

46. Ibid., p. 204, Haldimand to Sir John Johnson, July 30, 1781, and p. 206, Haldimand to Sir John Johnson, Aug. 9, 1781.

47. Watt, 'Johnson's Royal Greens,' p. 14; also Stone, *Life or Brant*, vol. 2, p. 186, footnote refers to Walter Butler's pocketbook, which mentions the 36 Royal Highland Emigrants.

48. Ernest Green, *Gilbert Tice, U.E.*, Ontario Historical Society Papers and Records, vol. 21 (1924), p. 196. Green referred to Haldimand Papers, B 107, p. 301 onward for Tice's journal.

49. PAC, Haldimand Papers, B 124, pp. 24-33, Ross to Haldimand, dated Oct. 7, 1781.

50. Hugh Hastings, ed., *George Clinton Papers*, 10 vols. (Albany, 1900-1914), vol. VII, pp. 472-75, Willett's report to Governor Clinton.

51. Victor Hugo Paltsitz, *Minutes of the Board of Commissioners for Detecting and Defeating Conspiracies* (Albany, 1901). This work contains many references to wives amd families being sent to the British lines to alleviate the strain on government funds.

52. PAC, Haldimand Papers, B 55, pp. 201-3, Haldimand to Lord Shelburne, July 17, 1782.

53. Cruickshank, *King's Royal Regiment of New York*, pp. 287-8.

54. H.M. Jackson, *Justus Sherwood, Soldier, Loyalist and Negotiator*, published privately, 1958, p.51.

55. Ontario Archives, uncatalogued documents, a recent acquisition from a descendant of Captain Archibald MacDonell.

Chapter 6: Butler's Rangers

1. Robert Rogers, *Journals* (London, 1769 edition), pp. 50-70.

2. John Knox, *Historical Journal of the Campaign in North America for the Year 1757, 1758 and 1760*, Arthur G. Doughty, ed., 3 vols. Champlain Society (Toronto, 1914), vol. 1, p. 34, gives a description of ranger dress and equipment.

3. Rogers, *Journals*, pp. 56-70.

4. The main source of information for this chapter is E.A. Cruikshank, *Butler's Rangers*, Lundy's Lane Historical Society (Welland, Ont., 1893), pp. 11-113.

5. Hazel C. Mathews, *The Mark of Honour* (Toronto, 1965), p. 36.

6. The information on the Butler children was supplied by a descendant, Lorne Butler of Toronto.

7. Graymont, *Iroquois in the American Revolution*, pp. 81-2.

8. PAC, Colonial Office Records, Series 'Q', vol. 13, pp. 329-31.

9. Ibid., vol. 14, p. 159. Beating Order, Sept. 15, 1777.

10. PAC, War Office 28, vol. 4, p. 6. Subsistence wanting for the Corps of Rangers Commanded by John Butler Esqr. Major Commd from the 25th October, 1778 to the 24th May following both including 212 days.

11. Hugh Hastings, ed., *The Public Papers of George Clinton*, 10 vols. (Albany, N.Y., 1900-1914), vol. 3, pp. 203-4. Claim of Richard Cartwright.

12. Brodhead, *Documents*, vol. 8, p. 752, Guy Johnson to Germain, Sept. 10, 1778.

13. Graymont, *Iroquois in the American Revolution*, p. 168. Compiled from Blacksnake Conversations, Draper Mss. 4S27-28. State Historical Society of Wisconsin.

14. PAC, Haldimand Papers, B 100, p. 38, Butler to Bolton, July 8, 1778.

15. PAC, Colonial Office Records, Series 'Q', vol. 15, pp. 225-7. Articles of Capitulation.

16. Ontario Bureau of Archives, *Second Report*, p. 990. Claim of James Ramsey and William McClellan.

17. Cruikshank, *Butler's Rangers*, pp. 57-8, quotes Walter's letter in full.

18. PAC, Haldimand Papers, B 85, p. 83. List of Officers in the Corps of Rangers Commanded by Lieut. Colonel John Butler.

19. Haldimand Papers, Br. Mus. Add. Mss. 21827, p. 349, Return of the Officers of the Corps of Rangers Commanded by Lt. Col. John Butler.

20. PAC, Haldimand Papers, B 96-1, pp. 148-50, copy of the bill Butler sent Haldimand.

21. B. Lancaster and J.H. Plumb, *The American Heritage Book of the Revolution* (New York, 1958), pp. 277-8.

22. Cruikshank, *John Walden Meyers*, p. 12.

23. Cruikshank, *Memoir of Lieutenant-Colonel John MacDonell*, p. 29.

24. PAC, Haldimand Papers, B 96-1, pp. 165-7, Haldimand to John Butler, Aug. 1, 1779; also R.G. 10, series 2, vol. 12, p. 14.

25. Graymont, *Iroquois in the American Revolution*, p. 200, from Draper Mss. 8F21, 28, Historical Society of Wisconsin; Fitspatrick, *Writings of George Washington*, Washington to Sullivan, Aug. 1, 1779, in vol. 14, pp. 29-30.

26. Mathews, *Mark of Honour*, p. 64, from the William Merrett Papers, vol. 19, Goring Papers, copy of a letter to Mr. Robert Hamilton, 1779.

27. Graymont, *Iroquois in the American Revolution*, pp. 216-7.

28. Ontario Archives, Canniff Papers, Notes on the Goring Family. Goring to Robert Cruikshank, Sept. 1, 1779.

29. Cruikshank, *King's Royal Regiment of New York*, p. 221, Johnson to Haldimand, Sept. 6, 1779.

30. Cruikshank, *John Walden Meyers*, pp. 25-6.

31. Haldimand Papers, Br. Mus. Add. Mss. 21821, Andrew Bradt to Brigadier Powell, Sept. 29, 1781.

32. PAC, Haldimand Papers, B 109, p. 80, Bolton to Haldimand, Feb. 6, 1780.

33. Public Record Office, AO 13-19, Claim of Thomas McMicking, Sept. 18, 1794.

34. PAC, Haldimand Papers, B 127, pp. 117-21, Report of Captain Alexander Fraser, the Indian agent, to Haldimand, May 21, 1780.

35. Ontario Archives, Haldimand Papers, envelope 7, pp. 471-4, Bolton to Haldimand, Sept. 30, 1780.

36. PAC, War Office 28, vol. 4, p. 10. Monthly Return of Lieutenant Colonel John Butlers Corps of Rangers, Niagara, on 6th Oct. 1780.

37. McIlwraith, *Sir Frederick Haldimand*, p. 223.

38. PAC, Haldimand Papers, B 85, p. 83. A list of officers in Butler's Rangers, with dates of their commissions.

39. Graymont, *Iroquois in the American Revolution*, p. 238; Colonial Office Records, Series 'Q', vol. 18, pp. 212-5, Guy Johnson to Germain, Nov. 20, 1780.

40. PAC, Haldimand Papers, B 101, p. 66, Powell to Haldimand, May 9, 1781.

41. PAC, Claus Papers, p. 139, John Macomb to Claus, Sept. 14, 1781.

42. Ontario Archives, Haldimand Papers, envelope 7, p. 86, Haldimand to Germain, Oct. 23, 1781.

43. Graymont, *Iroquois in the American Revolution*, pp. 248-9

44. Stone, *Life of Brant*, vol. 2, pp. 191-3.

45. Ontario Archives, Haldimand Papers, envelope 8, pp. 144-5, Haldimand to von Speth, Dec. 27, 1781.

46. PAC, Haldimand Papers, B 102, pp. 14-15, Simon Girty to De Peyster, Apr. 12, 1782.

47. Ibid., p. 86, Caldwell to De Peyster, June 13, 1782.

48. Elliott, *The Long Hunter*, pp. 162-4.

49. Ibid., p. 167, from Draper Mss. Historical Society of Wisconsin.

50. PAC, Haldimand Papers, B 54, pp. 115-20, Lord North to Haldimand, Aug. 8, 1783.

Chapter 7: The King's Loyal Americans

1. PAC, Haldimand Papers, B 39, p. 544, Carleton to St. Leger, June 19, 1777.

2. Ibid., B 167, p. 11, Leake's Subsistence Account.

3. Rev. H.G. Jessup, *Edward Jessup of West Farms, Westchester County, and His Descendants* (Cambridge, 1887), pp. 202-4.

4. Talman, *Loyalist Narratives*, p. 393, Memorial of Edward Jessup.

5. L.J. Cappon, ed., *Atlas of Early American History: The Revolutionary Era, 1760-1790* (Princeton, N.J., 1976). p. 4.

6. E. Rae Stuart, *Jessup's Rangers as a Factor in Loyalist Settlement, Three History Theses, 1939* (Toronto, 1961), p. 15.

7. Hazel C. Mathews, *Frontier Spies* (Fort Myers, Fla., 1971), p. 11.

8. Lieutenant James M. Hadden, *Journal and Orderly Books* (Albany, N.Y., 1884), pp. 67-8, footnote.

9. Higgins, Ruth L. *Expansion in New York with Special Reference to the Eighteenth Century* (Columbus, Ohio, 1931), p. 92.

10. Dr. Holden, *History of the Town of Queensbury*, cited in Hadden's *Journal and Orderly Books*, pp. 67-8.

11. Hadden, *Journal and Orderly Books*, p. 69, Carleton to Brigadier William Phillips, Oct. 29, 1776.

12. U.E.L. Association of Ontario, *Annual Transactions, 1909-1902*, p. 36, Memorial of Ebenezer Jessup.

13. Ontario Archives, French Papers, Pkg. 4, p. 10.

14. PAC, Haldimand Papers, B 158, p. 9, Gray to Carleton, Jan. 12, 1777; Ontario Archives, Jessup Papers. Receipt Book, Edward Jessup's Corps of King's Loyal Americans, 1777-1780. Receipt for James Hume, paid 6d. per day Halifax, from Nov. 4, 1776 to Apr. 24, 1777.

15. Stuart, *Jessup's Rangers*, Appendix B. pp. 123-8, from PAC, Haldimand Papers, B 167, p. 5 onward, copied by Dr. H.C. Burleigh.

16. PAC, Haldimand Papers, B 167, p. 141, List of Officers of the King's Loyal Ameri-

cans, June 7, 1777; p. 14, a list of Captain Munro's company; p. 122, Strength of Jessup's Corps on Burgoyne's Campaign, 1777.

17. Ibid., B 158, p. 22, Gray to Captain Foy, Apr. 20, 1777.

18. Burt, *Guy Carleton*, pp. 10-14.

19. Ibid. The same is stated in John Lunt, *John Burgoyne of Saratoga* (London, 1957), pp. 121-32.

20. Zadock Thompson, *History of Vermont, Natural, Civil and Statistical* (Burlington, Vt., 1842), Part III, p. 92.

21. Lieutenant-General John Burgoyne, *A State of the Expedition from Canada, as laid before the House of Commons* (London, 1780), p. 36 of the Appendix.

22. Stuart, *Jessup's Rangers*, p. 31; PAC, Haldimand Papers, B 161, p. 10, muster roll, Oct. 7, 1777.

23. Ibid, B 214, p. 26, Jessup to Burgoyne, July 17, 1778, quoted in Stuart, p. 30.

24. Ibid., B 167, p. 14 onward, quoted in Stuart, *Jessup's Rangers*, Appendix B, pp. 123-8.

25. Ibid., B 161, p. 122, undated, other letters in this bundle are all for the year 1780.

26. PAC, Colonial Office Records, Series 'Q', vol. 13, pp. 142-6. *Report of Samuel McKay on his reconnaissance, Feb. 28-Mar. 31, 1777*; Talman, *Loyalist Narratives*, p. 399, *Memorial of Justus Sherwood*.

27. Abby M. Hemenway, *The Vermont Historical Gazetteer: a magazine embracing a history of each town, civil, ecclesiastical, biographical and military.* Published between 1867 and 1891 at various places in Vermont, vol. I (Burlington, 1867), p. 749.

28. R.E. Dupuy and T.N. Dupuy, *The Compact History of the Revolutionary War* (New York, 1963). This is a useful account, concise with the basic facts and dates. The interpretation as to where Burgoyne failed is the author's.

29. Lt. Thomas Anbury, *Travels through the Interior Parts of America* (London, 1789), 2 vols., vol. 1, pp. 369-70.

30. George F.C. Stanley, *For Want of a Horse* (Sackville, N.B., 1961), pp. 139, 147, 156.

31. Ontario Archives, French Papers, Pkg. 3. Certificate of John Shank. (sic)

32. PAC, War Office 28, vol. 4, p. 266. Present State of Several Detachments of Royalists who returned from Lieutenant General Burgoyne's Army to Canada after the Convention. Head Quarters at Quebec, 1st. May, 1778.

33. Lunt, *John Burgoyne*, pp. 208-10.

34. PAC, Haldimand Papers, B 167, pp. 141, 144, 159. Muster rolls dated Jan. 29, 1778; B 214, p. 26, Ebenezer Jessup to Burgoyne, July 17, 1778.

35. *Proceedings of the Vermont Historical Society*, June 3, 1938, p. 89.

36. E.B. O'Callaghan, ed., *Orderly Book of Lieut.-Gen. John Burgoyne* (Albany, N.Y., 1860), Series VII, p. 153.

37. PAC, War Office 28, vol. 4, p. 266. Present State of the Several Detachments of Royalists who returned from Lieutenant Genl Burgoyne's Army to Canada after the Convention. Head Quarters at Quebec, 1st May, 1778.

38. PAC, Haldimand Papers, B 54, pp. 266-9, Haldimand to Germain, Nov. 1, 1779.

39. Ontario Archives, Jessup Papers, Military Order Book, Jan. 29, 1780.

40. Haldimand Papers, Br. Mus. Add. Mss. 21827, pp. 230-1, the findings of the Board of Officers, dated Feb. 1781. The decision on some of Ebenezer's men was made at an earlier date.

41. PAC, War Office 28, vol. 10, part 2, p. 228.

42. Hemenway, vol. 1, p. 51. Statement of John Chipman.

43. Ontario Archives, Jessup Papers, Military Order Book, Jan. 24, 1781, to Aug. 23, 1781.

44. PAC, Haldimand Papers, B 83, p. 180, A list of officers appointed in the corps under Major Edward Jessup, with dates of appointment, Nov. 12, 1781.

Chapter 8: The Queen's Loyal Rangers

1. Toronto *Globe*, July 16, 1877. 'A Narrative of John Peters, Lieutenant-Colonel in

362

the Queen's Loyal Rangers in Canada Drawn by Himself in a Letter to a Friend in London.' This is a lenghty letter in such small print that it is all on a single page of the newspaper. Although the information contained in this document should be treated with circumspection, I have drawn on it for some of the biographical detail in this chapter.

2. Burgoyne, *A State of the Expedition from Canada*, Appendix, p. 36, Burgoyne to Germain, July 11, 1777.

3. PAC, War Office 28, vol. 4, p. 271, officers' certificates.

4. Public Record Office, AO 13-14. Memorial of John Wilson.

5. Stuart, *Jessup's Rangers*, p. 24.

6. Hemenway, *Vermont Gazetteer*, vol. 1, p. 749.

7. *The Concise Illustrated History of the American Revolution* (Gettysburg, Pa.. 1976), p. 23.

8. PAC, Haldimand Papers, B 167, pp. 102, 378 and 398.

9. Eula C. Lapp, *To Their Heirs Forever* (Picton, Ont., 1790), p. 154.

10. Almon, *Remembrancer*, vol. 5, p. 392, Burgoyne's instructions to Colonel Baum.

11. Joseph R. Parke, *The Battle of Bennington* (Bennington Museum, 1976)

12. Katcher, *American Provincial Corps*, p. 11.

13. Several sources mention only a Tory officer. Almon's *Remembrancer*, vol. 5, p. 392, in Burgoyne's instructions to Baum refers to Sherwood.

14. Hadden, Journal and Orderly Books, p. 114.

15. B.F. Stevens, *Facsimilies of Manuscripts in European Archives Relating to America, 1773-1783* (London, 1889-1895), Skene to Lord Dartmouth, Aug. 30, 1777.

16. Burgoyne, *Orderly Book*, p. 153.

17. *The Concise Illustrated History of the American Revolution*, p. 23.

18. Lapp, *To Their Heirs Forever*, pp. 4, and 130-1. The letter is a muster roll of Sherwood's company, taken from a photostat from the New York State Library, Albany. MSS 3591.

19. I.C.R. Pemberton, 'Justus Sherwood, Vermont Loyalist,' Doctoral dissertation. University of Western Ontario (London, Ont., 1972), p. 57.

20. PAC, War Office 28, vol. 4, p. 103.

21. Ibid.

22. Hadden, *Journal and Orderly Books*, fn., p. 72.

23. Ibid., Appendix 14, p. 480. Memorial of John Peters to the Lords of Treasury.

24. PAC, War Office 28, vol. 10, part 2, p. 228. List of officers, dated Aug., 1780.

25. Sir Henry Clinton Papers, William L. Clements Library, University of Michigan. 2019. Deposition of Andrew Stephenson, who reported Sherwood's boast that if he did not have enough prisoners to exchange for French and other 'worthy gentlemen' he would go out and catch some.

26. PAC, War Office 28, vol. 4, p. 280. Muster Roll of the Corps of Royalists Commanded by John Peters Esquire, July 14, 1781.

27. PAC, Haldimand Papers, B 83, p. 180. A list of officers appointed to the corps under Major Edward Jessup, with dates of appointment. Nov. 12, 1781.

28. Ibid., B 167, p. 398. A Return of Officers in the Loyal Rangers, made after disbandment, Dec. 24, 1783.

Chapter 9: The Loyal Rangers

1. Ontario Archives, F.J. French Papers, Pkg. 4, p.3.

2. Ibid., Jessup Papers, Military Order Book, Nov. 12, 1781. Order for the appointment of Officers for the Loyal Rangers; signed by Richard B. Lernoult, Adjutant-General, refers to one company of artificers.

3. Cruikshank, *John Walden Meyers*, p. 37.

4. Ontario Archives, Jessup Papers, Military Order Book, Nov. 4, and Oct. 4, 1782.

5. PAC, Haldimand Papers, B 167, p. 398. A Return of Officers of the Loyal Rangers.

6. PAC, War Office 28, vol. 10, part 4, pp. 441-61.

7. *Centennial of the Settlement of Upper Canada by the United Empire Loyalists: 1784*

1884 (Toronto, 1885). Appendix B is a list from the land board records in alphabetical order. Samuel Sherwood is shown as a lieutenant in the Loyal Rangers.

8. PAC, Haldimand Papers, B 137, p. 253, Jessup to Mathews, Aug. 15, 1782.

9. Stuart, *Jessup's Rangers*, fn. p. 36.

10. PAC, Haldimand Papers, B 173, p. 124. State of the garrison at Isle aux Noix and its dependencies, Aug. 1. 1783.

11. Public Record Office, AO 13-22. Memorial of Thomas Sherwood, Aug. 29, 1787, at New Oswegatchie.

12. Marjorie E. Lyons, 'Elizabethtown. Some Phases of its Settlement and Development to 1850.' M.A. Thesis, Queen's University, 1935, p.12.

13. PAC, Haldimand Papers, B 169, pp. 121-1. A list of the officers and men of the Loyal Rangers and their dependents.

14. Ontario Bureau of Archives. *Second Report* (1904). This volume consists of thousands of loyalists' claims, and many of the officers from the Loyal Rangers mentioned that they were drawing half pay.

Chapter 10: The King's Rangers

1. S.M. Pargellis, *Dictionary of American Biography* (New York, 1935), vol. 8, pp. 108-9

2. R.A. Preston, *Kingston Before the War of 1812*, Champlain Society (Toronto, 1959), p. 74 fn.

3. John R. Cuneo, *Robert Rogers of the Rangers* (New York, 1959), pp. 4-5; H.M. Jackson, *Rogers' Rangers*, published privately, 1953, p. 1.

4. Talman, *Loyalist Narratives*, Narrative of Stephen Jarvis, p. 159.

5. PAC, War Office 28, vol. 10, part 3, p. 270.

6. Franklin B. Hough, ed., *Journals of Robert Rangers* (Albany, N.Y., 1883), p. 14; Jackson, *Rogers' Rangers*, pp. 29, 36.

7. Cuneo, *Rogers of the Rangers*, gives this form of the name, although in some sources it is Spikeman.

8. Hough, *Journals*, pp. 45, 79; *Talman, Loyalist Narratives*, Narrative of Susan Burnham Greeley, James Rogers' granddaughter, p. 80.

9. Hough, *Journals*, pp. 80-2. List of the men detached for service with the rangers.

10. Ibid., pp. 111-2.

11. Alan Everest, *Moses Hazen and the Canadian Refugees during the American Revolution* (Syracuse, N.Y., 1976), p. 12.

12. Hough, *Journals*, p. 9, introduction.

13. Collections of the New York Historical Society, New York. *The Colden Letter Books*, vol. 1, 1760-65. Colden to Amherst, July 2, 1762, pp. 95-6.

14. Burt G. Loescher, *Rogers' Rangers*, 2 vols., published privately, 1969, vol. 2, pp. 154-9.

15. The Army List, 1773, p. 197. Captain Robert Rogers is on this list, and on p. 219 he is shown as on half pay from the American Rangers.

16. Jackson, *Rogers' Rangers*, p. 152.

17. Calendar of Sir William Johnson Manuscripts in the New York State Library, Albany, 1849. Compiled by Richard E. Day, University of the State of New York. Johnson to Gage, Jan. 23, 1766.

18. D. Armour, ed., *Treason? at Michilimackinac*, Mackinac Island State Park Commission, 1967, p. 4: Commission of Jonathan Carver from Robert Rogers, p. 47; Carver to James S. Goddard, p. 49; Carver to Captain James Tute, pp. 50-4. This booklet consists mainly of documents published verbatim from the originals on events at Michilimackinac and later at Montreal.

19. PAC, Colonial Office Records, Ser. 5; 85, M. 224, p. 284.

20. Armour, *Treason?* , p. 94; also PAC, Colonial Office Records, Series 'Q', vol. 2, part 2, p. 33. Spiesmacher to Gage, Feb. 24, 1768.

21. PAC, Haldimand Papers, B 18, p. 99, Spiesmacher to Carleton, no date.

22. PAC, Treasury Solicitors Papers, General Series, Bundle 4957. Proceedings of a

General Court Martial held at Montreal in October, 1768 for the Trial of Robert Rogers.

23. Talman, *Loyalist Narratives*, Narrative of Susan Burnham Greeley, p. 79.
24. O'Callaghan, *Documents Relative to the Colonial History of New York*, vol. 7, p. 687, Tryon to Germain, Sept. 27, 1776.
25. Raymond, *Loyalists in Arms*, pp. 198-9, and 202.
26. Hough, *Journals*, Appendix E, pp. 275-8.
27. Raymond, *Loyalists in Arms*, p. 202
28. Haldimand Papers, Br. Mus. Add. Mss. 21820, p. 13. List of officers belonging to R. Rogers' regiment. Signed by James Rogers, Major of the regiment.
29. Jackson, *Rogers' Rangers*, p. 182.
30. Ontario Archives, Jessup Papers, Military Order Book, Jan. 29, 1780. The Board of Officers was ordered to meet on Feb. 8, 1780.
31. Haldimand Papers, Br. Mus. Add. Mss. 21810, p. 83, is a muster roll dated Sept. 8, 1780, showing 1 lieutenant, 1 sergeant, and 2 privates on secret service, from a roster of 49 all ranks.
32. Ibid.
33. Jackson, *Rogers' Rangers*, p. 187.
34. Haldimand Papers, Br. Mus. Add. Mss. 21820, p. 100, J. Rogers to Mathews, Dec. 16, 1780.
35. PAC, Haldimand Papers, B 167, p. 285. Memorial Against Major James Rogers; also p. 328, Findings of the Board of Officers.
36. Ontario Archives, Jessup Papers, Military Order Book, Nov. 25, 1781. The appointments were made in September.
37. Haldimand Papers, Br. Mus. Add. Mss. 21820, pp. 106-7, J. Rogers to Mathews, Jan. 5, 1781.
38. M.B. Fryer, *Loyalist Spy* (Brockville, 1974), pp. 111-12, and 117.
39. Preston, *Kingston*, p. 61.
40. PAC, Haldimand Papers, B 179-2, p. 181, Mathews to Sherwood, Feb. 14, 1782.
41. Ibid., B 178, pp. 15-16, Thomas Smyth to Mathews, Jan. 9, 1783.
42. Jackson, *Rogers' Rangers*, p. 50.
43. PAC, Haldimand Papers, B 169, pp. 15-30. Sherwood's Journal, beginning on Sept. 19, 1783, of which pp. 26-8 contain Lieutenant Johns' own report while exploring with a small party.
44. Haldimand Papers, Br. Mus. Add. Mss 21820, pp. 203-7. Muster rolls dated Jan. 1784, after disbandment.
45. PAC, Haldimand Papers, B 168, p. 43. The list is marked July, 1784.
46. Ontario Bureau of Archives, *Second Report* (1904). In making their claims, several of the officers said that they were receiving half pay.
47. University of New Brunswick Archives, Microfilm Reel 104. Guides and Pioneers, no page number.
48. Haldimand Papers, Br. Mus. Add. Mss. 21820, pp. 219-20. Return of Officers from New York under the Command of Major James Rogers.
49. E.C. Wright, *The Loyalists of New Brunswick*, p. 332.
50. Preston, *Kingston*, p. 239, fn.

Chapter 11: Special Services

1. Mathews, *Frontier Spies*, pp. 28-30.
2. PAC, Haldimand Papers, B 55, pp. 4, 142, Haldimand to Germain, Nov. 28, 1781. Haldimand said he was indebted to rebel papers captured and taken to Niagara for knowledge of Cornwallis, and he had not heard from Sir Henry Clinton since a letter dated Aug. 2, 1781.
3. Richard L. Bushman, *From Puritan to Yankee* (Cambridge, Mass. 1976). p. 45.
4. Pemberton, 'Justus Sherwood,' p. 31.
5. The author viewed both tracts of land while visiting Vermont in 1975.
6. F.F. Van De Water, *The Reluctant Republic, Vermont, 1724-1791* (Taftsville, Vt.,

1974), pp. 79-95.

7. A.J. Coolidge and J.B. Mansfield, *History and Description of New England, General and Local,* 2 vols., (Boston, 1859), vol. 1, p. 110.

8. Public Record Office, AO 13-22, pp. 35-39. Memorial of Justus Sherwood.

9. Mathews, *Frontier Spies,* p. 42.

10. H.P. Smith, *History of Addison County, Vermont,* pp. 525-6, extract sent by the Vermont Historical Society, Montpelier, Vt.

11. Memorial of Justus Sherwood.

12. Ibid.

13. E.P. Walton, *Records of the Council of Safety, State of Vermont* (Montpelier, Vt., 1873), vol. 1, p. 192.

14. Levius's date of birth was from the Sherwood family records. His name is sometimes spelled Livius, but on a deed in the Sherwood Family Papers, PAC, the signature is Levius P. Sherwood.

15. H.S. Wardner, *The Birthplace of Vermont, A History of Windsor to 1781* (New York, 1927), p. 489.

16. PAC, Haldimand Papers, B 83, p. 97. Order from Headquarters, June 1, 1778.

17. PAC, Haldimand Papers, B 176, pp. 142-3, Sherwood to Mathews, July 1, 1781. At the time Sherwood was on the site of the Loyal Blockhouse with 23 men and boys.

18. Ontario Bureau of Archives, *Second Report* (1904), p. 364, Claim of George Smyth; p. 377, Claim of Patrick Smyth.

19. Dorothy Barck, *Minutes of the First Commission for Detecting Conspiracies, 1776-1778,* 2 vols. (New York History Collections, 1924-1925), vol. 1, p. 219.

20. Ontario Bureau of Archives, *Second Report,* pp. 364 and 377.

21. PAC, Haldimand Papers, B 176, p. 13, Smyth to Haldimand, June 15, 1781; B 182, Smyth to Sir John Johnson, Sept. 30, 1780.

22. Paltsits, *Minutes of the Commissioners,* vol. 2, pp. 479, 545-6, 549, 561.

23. Public Record Office, AO 13-15, p. 415, Memorial of Patrick Smyth.

24. Paltsits, *Minutes of the Commissioners,* vol. 3, pp. 726 and 730.

25. E.A. Cruikshank, 'Some Loyalists from New York Expatriated to Canada.' United Empire Loyalists' Association, Sesquicentennial Number, 1935, pp. 68-9. Memorial of Mathew Howard of Pits Town.

26. Paltsits, *Minutes of the Commissioners,* vol. 3, p. 759.

27. PAC, Haldimand Papers, B 177-1, p. 28, Report of Terence Smyth.

28. Mathews, *Frontier Spies,* p. 28, from Sir Henry Clinton Papers. Information on Joseph Bettys, Oct. 26, 1777.

29. Cruikshank, *King's Royal Regiment of New York,* p. 229.

30. Cruikshank, *John Walden Meyers,* pp. 11-15.

31. PAC, Vermont Papers, intercepted letters.

32. Mathews, *Frontier Spies,* p. 17

33. John Pell, *Ethan Allen* (Boston, 1929), p. 39.

34. PAC, Haldimand Papers, B 175, p. 19, Robinson to Ethan Allen, Mar. 30, 1780.

35. PAC, Vermont Papers.

36. Pell, *Ethan Allen,* p. 188, quoted from PAC, Colonial Office Records, Series 'Q', no other reference numbers.

37. PAC, Haldimand Papers, B 180, pp. 42-58, Sherwood's journal, Oct. 26 to Nov. '31st.'

38. Ibid.

39. Ontario Archives, Haldimand Papers, Envelope 7, p. 158, Haldimand to Major Carleton, Nov. 9, 1780.

40. PAC, Haldimand Papers, B 180, pp. 4-6, Sherwood to Mathews, Mar. 10, 1781.

41. Ibid., p. 7, Peters to Sherwood, Mar. 20, 1781.

42. PAC, Haldimand Papers, B 175, p. 79, Sherwood to Mathews, May 9, 1781.

43. PAC, Vermont Papers, letter of Micah Townsend to the Congress, Apr. 10, 1781.

44. PAC, Haldimand Papers, B 133, pp. 161-2, Major Carleton to Haldimand, May 17, 1780.

45. Jackson, *Justus Sherwood,* p. 17.

46. PAC, Haldimand Papers, B 176, pp. 189-90, Memorandum by Captain Sherwood, July, 1781; B 179-2, p. 57, Mathews to Sherwood, July 14, 1781, and p. 304-5, a list of the parties to be sent.

47. Ibid., B 135, p. 234-5, Haldimand to St. Leger, July 5, 1781.

48. Ibid. p. 284, a list of the men, regiments and ranks and civilians captured with Mathew Howard.

49. Cruikshank, *John Walden Meyers*. Commencing on p. 11, Cruikshank quoted various letters that dealt with the silver.

50. PAC, Haldimand Papers, B 176, pp. 289-90, Smyth to Mathews, Sept. 25, 1781; B 178, p. 102, Deposition of Mathew Howard, Mar. 1, 1783.

51. PAC, War Office 28, vol. 5, p. 168, St. Leger's list.

52. PAC, Haldimand Papers, B 176, p. 264. Secret Intelligence, Sept. 2, 1781.

53. Jackson, *Justus Sherwood*, p. 33-4.

54. PAC, Haldimand Papers, B 176, p. 326, Sherwood to Mathews, Nov. 2, 1781; Jackson, *Justus Sherwood*, p. 35.

55. Ibid.; Pell, *Ethan Allen*, p. 281.

56. Ibid. pp. 218-9.

57. PAC, Haldimand Papers, B 176, p. 331, Smyth to Mathews, Nov. 7, 1781.

58. Ibid., B 179-2, p. 205, Mathews to Sherwood, Feb. 20, 1782.

59. Ibid., B 63, p. 239, Mathews to Sherwood, Apr. 26, 1784.

60. Ibid., B 177-2, p. 388, Smyth to Mathews, May 9, 1782.

61. Ibid., B 177-1, p. 443, Report of John Lindsay, Aug. 17, 1782.

62. Public Record Office, AO 12, Claim of Jeremiah French, with a letter by Sherwood supporting his claim, and describing the Absentee Act.

63. PAC, Haldimand Papers, B 177-1, p. 601, Sherwood to Mathews, Nov. 26, 1782.

64. Haldimand Papers, Br. Mus. Add. Mss. 21821, p. 421, Proceedings of the court martial, Dec. 3, 1782, written by Thomas Sherwood.

65. Jackson, *Justus Sherwood*, pp. 52-3.

66. PAC, Haldimand Papers, B 176, p. 293, Smyth to Mathews, Sept. 29, 1781.

67. John Bakeless, *Turncoats, Traitors and Heros* (Philadelphia, 1959), p. 28.

68. Bradley, *Lord Dorchester*, p. 231.

69. Samuel Walker, *The Perils of Patriotism* (Lancaster, Pa., 1976). p. 31.

70. Talman, *Loyalist Narratives*, p. 338, letters of John Stuart.

71. Cruikshank, *King's Royal Regiment of New York*, p. 264.

72. H.C. Burleigh, *Samuel Sherwood's Account Book* (Kingston, 1975), Preface.

73. Walton, *Records*, vol. 1, pp. 36 and 39.

74. PAC, Haldimand Papers, B 176, pp. 211-13, Smyth to Haldimand, Aug. 13, 1781.

75. Ibid., p. 205, Sherwood to Mathews, Aug. 9, 1781.

76. Ibid., pp. 314-5, Sherwood to Mathews, Oct. 18, 1781.

77. Mathews, *Frontier Spies*, pp. 115-6, from Sir Henry Clinton Papers, 4061, General Heath to Governor George Clinton, Oct. 11, 1781.

78. PAC, Haldimand Papers, B 181, p. 106, Sherwood to Carleton, July 10, 1778.

79. Lapp, *To Their Heirs Forever*, p. 129. The author is a descendant of Edward Carscallan.

80. Fryer, *Loyalist Spy*, pp. 56-58, 94, 98, 178.

81. Ontario Archives, Jessup Papers, Military Order Book, July 1, 1781.

82. Justus Sherwood's Account Book, Baldwin Room, Metropolitan Toronto Central Library.

83. McIlwraith, *Haldimand*, p. 235.

84. PAC, Haldimand Papers, B 168, p. 100, List of disbanded troops and loyalists settled upon the King's lands, 1784.

85. Ibid., B 146, pp. 63-4, 158; B 148, pp. 161-2, letters passing between Carleton and Haldimand concerning Michael Grass's party.

86. One late arrival was the author's great-great-great-grandfather, Caleb Seaman, who was arrested in Schenectady in 1789. His petition for land, and information preserved in the family, show the kind of persecution that continued after the revolution.

87. W.A.B. Douglas, 'The Anatomy of Naval Incompetence; the Provincial Marine in Defence of Upper Canada before 1813.' *Ontario History*, March, 1979, p.4.
88. Haldimand Papers, Br. Mus. Add. Mss. 21801, re Schanck; Stanley, *Canada Invaded*, p. 137, re Pringle.
89. PAC, Haldimand Papers, B 54, p. 46, Haldimand to Germain, Oct. 14, 1778, re Schanck; Preston, *Kingston*, pp. 15-17, re Chambers.
90. PAC, Haldimand Papers, B 123, p. 466, Jehu Hay to Haldimand, July 22, 1784.
91. Douglas, 'Naval Incompetence,' p. 5.
92. Jackson, *Justus Sherwood*, pp. 5, 26 and 34.
93. PAC, Colonial Office Records, Series 'Q', vol. 15, p. 45, Return of His Majesty's Armed Vessels on the Lakes, 26 June, 1778.
94. Ontario Archives, Haldimand Papers, Envelope 7, pp. 471-4, Bolton to Haldimand, Sept. 30, 1780.
95. Preston, *Kingston*, p. 16, fn. 33.
96. Milo M. Quaife, 'The Royal Navy of the Upper Lakes,' Burton Historical Collection, *Leaflet II, no. 5*, May 1924, pp. 58-60.
97. PAC, Haldimand Papers, B 54, pp. 284-9, Haldimand to Germain, July 12, 1780; pp. 120-1, Haldimand to Germain, June 6, 1780.
98. Ibid, copy of the order to Young is included; pp. 326-7, Haldimand to Germain, Sept. 17, 1780.
99. Ontario Archives, Haldimand Papers, envelope 10, no page number, Maclean to Haldimand, May 2, 1783. He refers to Bouchette aboard the *Seneca*.
100. PAC, Haldimand Papers, B 124, pp. 34-8, Holland to Haldimand, June 26, 1783.
101. Ontario Archives, Jessup Papers, Military Order Book, orders for Oct. 21, 1782.
102. Haldimand Papers, Br. Mus. Add. Mss. 21819, Haldimand to Sir John Johnson, Oct. 17, 1779.
103. PAC, R.G. 1, L 4, vol. 2, p. 208.
104. PAC, Quebec Gazette, Nov. 28, 1784.

Part Three: Afterwards

Chapter 12: Resettlement of the Displaced Loyalists

1. W.S. MacNutt, *New Brunswick: A History*, 1784-1867 (Toronto, 1963), p. 21.
2. Bradley, *Lord Dorchester*, p. 218-9.
3. MacNutt, *New Brunswick*, p. 26.
4. McIlwraith, *Haldimand*, p. 188
5. PAC, Haldimand Papers, B 169, pp. 6-14, Sherwood's journal, commencing on May 29, 1783.
6. Ibid., B 162, p. 99, Jessup to Haldimand, Sept. 11, 1783.
7. Ibid., B 126, pp. 42-44, Haldimand to Collins, Sept. 11, 1783
8. PAC, Map Division, 400, 1783-1784.
9. E.A. Cruikshank, ed., *The Settlement of the United Empire Loyalists on the Upper St. Lawrence and Bay of Quinte in 1784*, Ontario Historical Society (Toronto, 1934). pp. 34-5.
10. Stuart, *Jessup's Rangers*, p. 5.
11. Talman, *Loyalist Narratives*, Introduction, p. xlviii.
12. PAC, Haldimand Papers, B 169, pp. 120-2, undated.
13. Ibid., p. 135, Account of Allan McDonell, Apr. 4, 1783.
14. Ibid., pp. 131-4, Substance of Captain Brant's wishes respecting a settlement of the Mohawk & others of the Six Nations upon the Grand River &ca.
15. Cruikshank, King's Royal Regiment of New York, p. 302.
16. Ibid., p. 307.
17. University of New Brunswick Archives, Winslow Papers, Thomas Knox to Edward Winslow, July 25, 1784, p. 215.
18. PAC, Haldimand Papers, B 146, pp. 63-4, Carleton to Haldimand, July 5, 1783.
19. E.C. Wright, *Loyalists of New Brunswick*, p. 173. A footnote refers to the Colonial Office Records, no. 217.
20. MacNutt, *New Brunswick*, pp. 40-5, 56.
21. PAC, Haldimand Papers, B 138, p. 360-3, Barnes to Haldimand, from Sorel, May 24, 1784.
22. Ibid., B 178, p. 293, Sherwood to Mathews, Mar. 1, 1784.
23. Cruikshank, *John Walden Meyers*, pp. 40-1.
24. PAC, Quebec Land Records.
25. PAC, Haldimand Papers, B 45, p. 351, Barnes to Mathews, May 17, 1784. Peters' letter follows, no page number or date.
26. E.C. Wright, *Loyalists of New Brunswick*, p. 41.
27. PAC, Haldimand Papers, B 126, p. 122, Ross to Haldimand from Cataraqui, Sept. 10, 1784.
28. Dictionary of National Biography, vol. 5, pp. 754-5, in the biography of Sir William Howe DeLancey, Stephen's son.
29. PAC, R.G. 4, S 28, p. 116. A list signed by Captain John Barnes, Deputy Quartermaster-General at Sorel.
30. Thad. Leavitt, *History of Leeds and Grenville* (Brockville, 1879), p. 92, in a biography of Solomon's son, Dunham Jones. The clock and china are still in the possession of the Jones family.
31. Ibid., p. 18, Memoir of Adiel Sherwood.
32. PAC, Map Collection, F/412 – 1783. A note on the back incorrectly identifies this as a plan of Maitland, but the shoreline does not match.
33. C.S.B. Lajeunesse, ed., *The Windsor Border Region*, Champlain Society (Toronto, 1960), pp. cii-cxxi, 69-73.
34. PAC, Haldimand Papers, B 162, pp. 338-9, Sherwood to Mathews, July 23, 1784.

35. Cruikshank, *King's Royal Regiment of New York*, p. 313, Ross to Mathews, July 7, 1784.
36. Ontario Archives, Jessup Papers, item for Nov. 27, 1783.
37. J.F. Pringle, *Lunenburgh or the Old Eastern District* (Cornwall, 1890), pp. 35-6.
38. PAC, Haldimand Papers, B 168, p. 42. A Return of Loyalists Receiving Provisions, July 10, 1784; p. 100, Return of Disbanded Troops and Loyalists settled upon the King's Lands in the Province of Quebec in the Year 1784.
39. Ibid., B 169, p. 1, survey date is Aug. 25, 1783.
40. Cruikshank, *Butler's Rangers*, p. 113.
41. Quebec Gazette, May 18, 1785.
42. Bradley, *Lord Dorchester*, p. 221.
43. Ibid., p. 323.
44. Stuart, *Jessup's Rangers*, p. 109.
45. A. Shortt and A.G. Doughty, *Documents Relating to the Constitutional History of Canada, 1759-1791*. Revised Edition (Ottawa, 1918), Part II, p. 945.
46. Cruikshank, *Loyalist Settlement*, p. 35. Additional Instructions to Governor Haldimand.
47. Preston, *Kingston*, pp. 120-1, Stuart to the Society for the Propagation of the Gospel, Aug. 15, 1787.
48. Francis Grose, *Dictionary of the Vulgar Tongue, 1811* (Northfield, Ill., 1971), (revision of *A Classical Dictionary of the Vulgar Tongue, 1785-1788.)*
49. Ontario Archives, biographical card catalogue, also Leavitt, *Leeds and Grenville*, pp. 20, 31.
50. Preston, *Kingston*, p. 118, Stuart to the Society for the Propagation of the Gospel, Sept., 1786.
51. Shortt and Doughty, *Documents*, p. 949, from Colonial Office Records, Series 'Q', 27-2, p. 989.
52. Preston, *Kingston*, p. 123, Report of John Collins and William Dummer Powell to Lord Dorchester on Loyalists' Grievances, Aug. 18, 1787.
53. PAC, M.G. 23 J 9, Mathews' journal, pp. 6-7, 12, 16-17, 20-25.
54. PAC, R.G. 1, May 14, 1788, p. 33, draft patent for forming new districts.
55. G.M. Craig, *Upper Canada, the Formative Years* (Toronto, 1963), pp. 12-13.
56. E.A. Cruikshank, *Simcoe Correspondence*, 5 vols. (Toronto, 1923-1931), vol. 1, pp. 108-9; Craig, *Upper Canada*, pp. 24-5.
57. Ontario Bureau of Archives, *Third Report* (1905), p. 88. A list of disbanded troops and loyalists settled on the north side of Lake Erie.
58. Ibid., pp. 222-3; LaJeunesse, *Windsor Border*, p. 161.
59. Cruikshank, *Simcoe Correspondence*, vol. 1, p. 24, Return of the Nassau Militia, May 2, 1791.
60. The information on Butler's Barracks was obtained from Peter J. Stokes, a restoration architect who resides in Niagara-on-the-Lake, and an expert on its early buildings.
61. Peter J. Stokes, *Old Niagara on the Lake* (Toronto, 1971), title page, from George Heriot, *Travels through the Canadas* (London, 1807).
62. Ibid. p. 24. Stokes identifies Mrs. Clench as Sir William's granddaughter, but the ages of Clench and his wife suggest that she was Sir William's daughter.
63. Ibid., title page.
64. Talman, *Loyalist Narratives*, Narrative of Susan Burnham Greeley, p. 83.
65. Ontario Archives, The Langhorn Parish Register, p. 60.
66. Toronto Globe, *Narrative of John Peters*.
67. Fred H. Armstrong, *Handbook of Upper Canadian Chronology and Territorial Legislation* (London, Ont., 1967), p. 104.
68. Shortt and Doughty, *Documents*, Part II, p. 945.
69. Ontario Archives, Biographical Card Catalogue.
70. Preston, *Kingston*, p. 62.
71. Ontario Archives, F.J. French Papers, Pkg. 4, p. 8.
72. E. Wright, ed., *Red, White and True Blue* (New York, 1976), p. 141, quoted in L.F.S. Upton's article 'The Claims: The Mission of John Anstey,' from Public Record

Office, Audit Office, 12/113, Anstey to Forster, Sept. 25, 1786, ff. 44-51.

73. Stuart, *Jessup's Rangers*, p. 117.

74. Jessup gives the date of Ebenezer's death as 1789, on p. 202-3. Mabel Pitkin Shorey, the author of *The Early History of Corinth, once known as Jessup's Landing* (Corinth, N.Y., 1959), states that Ebenezer went to India and died there in 1818, p. 16.

75. Jesup, *Edward Jessup*, pp. 203, 233.

76. Ontario Archives, Papers of F.P. Smith, Pkg. 3, Sketch of H.D. Jessup.

77. Leavitt, *Leeds and Grenville*, pp. 44, 63, 181.

78. PAC, Quebec Gazette, May 18, 1785.

79. Johnson, *North American Johnsons*, p. 72.

80. Ibid., p. 45.

81. Ibid., pp. 71-2.

82. Pound and Day, *Johnson of the Mohawks*, p. 430.

83. Cruikshank, *King's Royal Regiment of New York*, p. 322, fn. 14.

84. Ontario Bureau of Archives, *Second Report* (1904). Enquiry into U.E.L. Losses and Services, p. 472, Claim of Molly Brant; information on Peter and George Johnson from Helen Caister Robinson, author of a forthcoming biography of Molly Brant.

85. Pound and Day, *Johnson of the Mohawks*, p. 420.

86. Hastings, *George Clinton Papers*, vol. 4, no. 1970. Letter of Joseph Brant, dated December 13, 1778, to Colonel John Cantine of Mormeltown, signed by Captain William Johnson and others.

87. The batteries were there at the time for the fort was built in 1821.

88. Dennis Duffy, 'Two Wars Struggling to Form the Conscience of a Single State: Upper Canadian Loyalism, 1776-1812.' Address given May 25, 1979, to the United Empire Loyalists' Association of Canada, at Toronto.

89. Ontario Archives. List of Persons Accused of Treason, 1812-1814.

371

Secondary Sources

Ainslie, Captain Thomas. *Journals.* (edited by Sheldon S. Conen, and published under the title *Canada Preserved*). Toronto, 1968.

Allen, Ira. *The Natural and Political History of the State of Vermont.* London, 1798.

Almon, J. ed. *The Remembrancer or Imperial Repository of Political Events.* 17 volumes, London, 1775-1784.

American Heritage Series. *The Concise Illustrated History of the American Revolution.* Gettysburg, Pa., 1976.

Anburey, Lieutenant Thomas. *Travels Through the Interior Parts of America.* 2 volumes, London, 1789.

Armour, D. ed. *Treason? At Michilimackinac.* Mackinac Island State Park Commission. 1967.

Armstrong, Fred. H. *Handbook of Upper Canadian Chronology and Territorial Legislation.* London, Ont. 1967.

Bakeless, John. *Turncoats, Traitors and Heroes.* Philadelphia, 1959.

Barck, Dorothy, ed. *Minutes of the Committee and First Comission for Detecting Conspiracies, 1776-1778.* 2 volumes. New York Historical Collections, 1924-1925.

Bartlett's Canada. Toronto, 1968.

Beacock, M.E. 'North Mull.' M.A. Dissertation, Edinburgh University, 1954.

Bond, C.J.J. 'The British Base at Carleton Island.' *Ontario History*, March 1960.

Bradley, A.G. *Lord Dorchester.* The Makers of Canada Series, volume III. Revised Edition, Toronto, 1926. Preface by A.L. Burt.

Bredenberg, Oscar E. *Military Activities in the Champlain Valley After 1777.* Champlain, N.Y. 1962.

Brodhead, John R. ed. *Documents Relating to the Colonial History of New York.* 15 volumes. Albany, N.Y., 1853-1887.

Burgoyne, Lieutenant-General John. *A State of the Expedition from Canada.* London, 1780.

Burleigh, H.C. *Samuel Sherwood's Account Book.* Kingston, 1975.

Burt, A.L. *Guy Carleton – Lord Dorchester, 1724-1808.* Canadian Historical Association. Historical Booklet No. 5, 1955.

Bushman, Richard L. *From Puritan to Yankee.* Cambridge, Mass., 1976.

Cappon, L.J. ed. *Atlas of Early American History: The Revolutionary Era, 1760-1790.* Princeton, N.J., 1976.

Catholic World, Dec., 1880.

Centennial of the Settlement of Upper Canada by the United Empire Loyalists, 1784-1884. Toronto, 1885.

Clarke, J. *The Life and Times of George III.* London, 1972.

Clinton, Sir Henry. Sir Henry Clinton Papers. William L. Clements Library, University of Michigan, Ann Arbor, Mich.

Coolidge, A.J. and Mansfield, J.B. *History and Description of New England, General and Local.* 2 volumes, Boston, 1859.

Craig, Gerald M. *Upper Canada, the Formative Years.* Toronto, 1963.

Cruikshank, Brigadier E.A. *The Activities of Abel Stevens as a Pioneer.* Ontario Historical Society Papers and Records, volume 31, 1936.

Cruikshank, *Butler's Rangers*. Lundy's Lane Historical Society, Welland, Ontario, 1893.

Cruikshank, *The King's Royal Regiment of New York*. Ontario Historical Society Papers and Records, volume 27, 1931.

Cruikshank, *Memoir of Lt.-Col. John MacDonell*. Ontario Historical Society Papers and Records, volume 22, 1927.

Cruikshank, *Captain John Walden Meyers, Loyalist Pioneer*. Ontario Historical Society Papers and Records, volume 27, 1931.

Cruikshank, *Some Loyalists from New York Expatriated to Canada*. Sesquicentennial Number, United Empire Loyalists' Association, 1935.

Cruikshank, *The Settlement of the United Empire Loyalists on the Upper St. Lawrence and Bay of Quinte in 1784*. Ontario Historical Society. Toronto, 1934.

Cruikshank, Ed. *Simcoe Correspondence*. 5 volumes. Toronto, 1923-1931.

Cruikshank, Ed. *A History of the Organization, Development and Services of the Military and Naval Forces of Canada from the Peace of Paris in 1763 to the Present Time*. 3 volumes, Canada Department of Militia and Defence, 1919-1920.

Cuneo, John. *Robert Rogers of the Rangers* New York, 1959.

Day, Richard E. *Calendar of Sir William Johnson Manuscripts in the New York State Library*. Albany, 1849.

Day, et al. *Papers of Sir William Johnson*. 14 volumes. Albany, 1921-1965.

Debor, Herbert W. *German Regiments in Canada, 1776-1783*. German Canadian Yearbook, volume 2. Toronto, 1975.

Douglas, W.A.B. 'The Anatomy of Naval Incompetence; the Provincial Marine in Defending Upper Canada before 1813.' *Ontario History*, March 1979.

Dupuy, R.E. and Dupuy, T.N. *The Compact History of the Revolutionary War*. New York, 1963.

Elliot, Lawrence. *The Lone Hunter, a new life of Daniel Boone*. New York, 1976.

Enys, Lt. John. *The American Journals of Lt. John Enys*. Elizabeth Cometti, ed. Syracuse, 1976, for the Adirondack Museum.

Everest, Allan S. *Moses Hazen and the Canadian Refugees in the American Revolution*. Syracuse, N.Y., 1976.

Fortesque, Sir John, ed. *Correspondence of George III*. London, 1927-1928.

Fryer, M.B. *Loyalist Spy*. Brockville, Ontario, 1974.

Fryer, M.B. and Ten Cate, A.G. *Pictorial History of the Thousand Islands*. Brockville, Ontario, 1977.

Graymont, Barbara. *The Iroquois in the American Revolution*. Syracuse, New York, 1976.

Green, Ernest. *Gilbert Tice, U.E.* Ontario Historical Society Papers and Records, volume 21, 1924.

Grose, Francis. *A Classical Dictionary of the Vulgar Tongue; 1785-1788*. Revised edition, 1811, republished in Northfield, Minn., in 1971.

Hadden, Lieutenant James M. Royal Artillery. *Journal and Orderly Books*. Albany, New York, 1884.

Harper, Colonel J.R. 'The Fraser Highlanders.' Historical Publication No. 4. The Montreal Military and Maritime Museum, manuscript.

Hastings, Hugh, ed. et al. *Public Papers of George Clinton*. 10 volumes. Albany, 1900-1914.

Hemenway, Abby Maria. *The Vermont Historical Gazetteer, a magazine embracing the history of each town, civil, ecclesiastical, biographical and military. 5 volumes, 1867-1891, published at several places in Vermont*.

Higgins, Ruth L. *Expansion in New York with Special Reference to the Eighteenth Century*. Columbus, Ohio, 1931.

Hough, Franklin B. ed. *Journals of Robert Rogers*. Albany, New York, 1883.

Innis, Mary Quayle, ed. *Mrs. Simcoe's Diary*. Toronto, 1965.

Jackson, Lieutenant-Colonel H.M. *Rogers' Rangers*. Published privately, 1953.

Jackson, *Justus Sherwood, Loyalist, Soldier and Negotiator*. Published privately,

1958.

Jesup, the Reverend H.G. *Edward Jessup of West Farms, Westchester County, New York and His Descendants.* Cambridge, Mass. 1887.

Johnson, Sir John. *Orderly Book of Sir John Johnson During his Campaign Against Fort Stanwix, From November 4th, 1776 to July 30th, 1777.* Annotated by William Leete Stone. New York, 1881.

Johnson, Sir John, Sixth Baronet of New York. *The North American Johnsons*, London, 1963.

Jones, Thomas. *History of New York During the Revolutionary War.* New York Historical Society. 2 volumes, New York, 1879.

Katcher, Philip. *The American Provincial Corps, 1775-1784.* Osprey Men-at-Arms Series. Reading, England, 1973.

Knox, John. *Historical Journal of the Campaign in North America for the Years 1757, 1758 and 1760.* Arthur G. Doughty, ed, 3 volumes. Toronto, 1914, for the Champlain Society.

Lajeunesse, C.S.B. ed. *The Windsor Border Region.* Toronto, 1960, for the Champlain Society.

Lancaster, Bruce, and J.H. Plumb. *The American Heritage Book of the Revolution.* New York, 1958.

Lapp, Eula C. *To Their Heirs Forever.* Picton, 1957.

Leach, D.E. *Arms for Empire.* New York, 1973.

Leavitt, Thad. *History of Leeds and Grenville.* Brockville, 1879.

Leggett, Robert. *Rideau Waterway.* Toronto, 1955.

Loescher, Burt G. *Rogers' Rangers.* 2 volumes. Published privately, 1969,

Lunt, John. *John Burgoyne of Saratoga.* London, 1957.

Lyons, Marjorie E. 'Elizabethtown. Some Phases of its Settlement and Development to 1850.' M.A. thesis, 1935, Queen's University.

Mathews, Hazel C. *Frontier Spies.* Fort Myers, Florida, 1971.

Mathews, *Mark of Honour.* Toronto, 1966.

MacNutt, W.S. *New Brunswick: A History, 1784-1867.* Toronto, 1963.

McIlwraith, Jean N. *Sir Frederick Haldimand.* The Makers of Canada Series, Volume III, Revised edition, 1926, with a foreword by A.L. Burt.

Mitchell, Dugald. *A Popular History of the Highlands and Gaelic Scotland.* Paisley, Scotland, 1900.

O'Callaghan, E.B. ed. *Orderly Book of Lieut.-Gen. John Burgoyne.* Munsell Historical Series, VII. Albany, New York, 1860.

Ontario Bureau of Archives. *Second Report* (1903), *Third Report* (1904), and *Fourth Report* (1906)

Paltsits, Victor Hugo, ed. *Minutes of the Board of Commissioners for Detecting and Defeating Conspiracies.* Albany, 1901.

Pargellis, S.M. *Dictionary of American Biography.* New York, 1935.

Parke, Joseph W.R. *The Battle of Bennington.* Bennington Museum pamphlet, 1976.

Pell, John. *Ethan Allen.* Boston, 1929.

Pemberton, Ian C.R. 'Justus Sherwood, Vermont Loyalist.' Doctoral Dissertation, University of Western Ontario. London, Ontario, 1972.

Pound, Arthur, and Day, Richard E. *Johnson of the Mohawks.* New York, 1930.

Preston, R.A. *Kingston Before the War of 1812.* Toronto, 1959, for the Champlain Society.

Pringle, J.F. *Lunenburgh or the Old Eastern District.* Cornwall, Ontario, 1890.

Quaife, Milo M. *The Royal Navy of the Upper Lakes.* Burton Historical Collection. Leaflet II, 5, Detroit, May, 1924.

Raymond, W.O. *Loyalists in Arms.* New Brunswick Historical Society Collections. No. 5, 1904.

Rogers, Robert. *Journals.* London, 1769.

Ryerson, Egerton. *The Loyalists of America.* 2 volumes, Toronto, 1880.

Seanachie. *Account of Clan Maclean.* London, 1838.

Shorey, Mabel Pitkin. *The Early History of Corinth once known as Jessup's Landing.*

Corinth, New York, 1959.

Shortt, A. and Doughty, A.G. *Documents Relating to the Constitutional History of Canada, 1759-1791.* Revised Edition, Ottawa, 1918.

Smith, H.P. *History of Addison County, Vermont.* The information used was sent by the Historical Society of Vermont.

Smith, Paul. *Loyalists and Redcoats. A study of British Revolutionary Policy.* Chapel Hill, North Carolina, 1954.

Stanley, George F.C. *Canada Invaded, 1775-1776.* Ottawa, 1973.

Stephen, Sir Leslie, and Lee, Sir Sidney, eds. *The Dictionary of National Biography.* London, 1921-1964.

Stevens, B.F. *Facsimilies of Manuscripts in European Archives Relating to America, 1883-1783.* London, 1889-1895.

Stokes, Peter J. *Old Niagara on the Lake.* Toronto, 1971.

Stone, William Leete. *Life of Joseph Brant,* 2 volumes. Cooperstown, New York, 1845.

Stuart, E. Rae. *Jessup's Rangers as a Factor in Loyalist Settlement.* Three History Thesis, 1939. Toronto, 1961.

Talman, J.J. *Loyalist Narratives from Upper Canada.* Toronto, 1966, for the Champlain Society.

Thompson, Zadock. *History of Vermont, Natural, Civil and Statistical.* Burlington, Vermont, 1842.

Toronto *Globe,* July 16, 1877. *A Narrative of John Peters, Lieutenant-Colonel in the Queen's Loyal Rangers in Canada. Drawn by Himself in a Letter to a Friend in London.*

Upton, Leslie F.S. *The Diary and Selected Papers of Chief Justice William Smith, 1784-1793.* Toronto, 1965, for the Champlain Society.

United Empire Loyalists' Association of Ontario. *Annual Transactions,* 1901-1902.

Van De Water, Fred. F. *The Reluctant Republic, Vermont, 1724-1791.* Taftsville, Vermont, 1974.

Vermont State Library. *Manuscripts Relating to Ethan Allen.*

Walker, J. Samuel. *The Perils of Patriotism. John Joseph Henry and the American Attack on Quebec, 1775.* Lancaster, Pennsylvania, 1975.

Walton, E.P. ed. *Records of the Council of Safety, State of Vermont.* Montpelier, Vermont, 1873.

Wardner, H.S. *The Birthplace of Vermont. A History of Windsor to 1781.* New York, 1927.

Watt, Gavin K. 'The King's Royal Regiment of New York, Johnson's Royal Greens.' Mimeographed text, 1975.

Wright, E. ed. *Red, White and True Blue.* New York, 1976. A series of articles on loyalists.

Wright, Esther Clark. *The Loyalists of New Brunswick.* Fredericton, 1955.

Index

Hawley, Jephtha. 332
Hay, Sgt. John. 57
Hazen, Moses. 22-3, 237, 241, 282
Heath, Gen. William. 296
Hebron, Conn. 206, 207
Heck, Barbara. 212, 330-1
Heck, Paul. 212, 330
Heriot, George. 338
Herkimer, Hon Jost. 32
Herkimer, Gen. Nicholas. 32, 61
Herrick, Col. Samuel. 278, 297
Hewson. 109, 271
Hiadagoo (Seneca) 142
Hill, Aaron (Mohawk). 145
Hogel, Capt. Francis. 209, 212, 225
Hogs. 324, 326
Holland, Surveyor-General Samuel. 305, 310
Hoosic, N.Y. 271, 285
Hope, Sir Henry. 327, 330
Horses. 90, 94, 98, 102, 103, 116, 118, 122, 138, 144, 153, 159, 160, 162, 165, 166, 167, 168, 187, 192, 194, 212, 213, 214, 215, 217, 220, 223, 233, 279, 324, 326, 327, 334
Hospitals. 16, 125, 259, 270, 273
Hostages. 70, 71, 136, 294
Houses, of Settlers. 324-5, 326, 328, 332, 350
Howard, Lieut. Mathew. 271-2, 284-5, 286
Howe, Gen. Sir William. 14, 22, 27, 40, 53, 71, 186, 209, 244, 245, 276, 294
Hoyes, Capt. Robert. 79, 178
Hubbardtown. 209; Battle of, 211; 212
Hudson River. 71, 80, 165, 181, 182, 192, 212, 220, 223, 247, 263, 264, 269, 287, 298
Hudson Valley. 193
Hungry Year. 331-2, 334, 335, 336
Hurlburt, Lieut. Philo. 209, 227
Hurlburt, Moses. 255
Huron Indians. 323

Ile Jesus. 119, 126
Independent Companies. 23, 86, 156, 202, 204, 227, 231, 254
Indian Agents. 27, 28
Indian Allies of Britain. 42, 63, 70, 77, 82, 85, 86, 87, 90, 93, 96, 100, 101, 102, 104, 105, 113, 114, 116, 117, 118, 120, 121, 122, 123, 125, 135, 136, 137, 138, 139, 145, 146, 149, 150, 152, 153, 155, 159, 160, 161, 163, 165, 166, 167, 168, 170, 172, 173, 174, 175, 212, 214, 215, 234, 241, 251, 279, 324, 327, 332, 333, 334, 348, 349
Indian Department. 26, 27, 28, 32, 63, 68, 69, 74, 76, 78, 80, 84, 134, 135, 137, 138, 139, 143, 145, 146, 159, 160, 161, 164, 166, 168, 170, 172, 323, 324, 337, 338
Indians, Canadians. 90, 93; with Burgoyne, 186; 308

Iroquois Indians (Confederacy of Six Nations). 21, 29, 50, 55, 65-6, 78, 82, 85, 86, 87, 90, 91, 93, 96, 123, 125, 133, 135, 136, 138, 139, 148, 149, 150, 153, 154, 155, 156, 162, 169, 313, 323, 333
Iroquois Villages. 86, 146, 148, 149, 150
Isle aux Noix. 27, 51, 53, 56, 57, 80, 101, 110, 126, 230, 234, 237, 250, 278, 280, 281, 292
Isle la Motte. 207

Jacobites. 36, 52
Jarvis, Stephen. 239
Jay's Treaty. 337
Jessup, Abigail (Wife of Edward). 181, 325
Jessup, Abigail (Dau. of Edward). 181, 325
Jessup, Deborah (Dau. of Ebenezer). 181
Jessup, Col. Ebenezer. 73, 108, 179-82, 183, 184, 185, 187, 188, 192, 193, 194-5, 196-7, 198, 199, 200, 203, 204, 209, 225, 227, 233, 235, 247, 248, 252, 343-4
Jessup, Maj. Edward. 56, 73, 96, 179-83, 184, 185, 188, 193, 194, 195, 198, 202, 203, 204, 225, 227-8, 230, 231, 233, 234, 235, 255, 258, 278, 309-10, 321, 322, 323, 325, 327, 332, 342, 343-4, 352
Jessup, Edward Jr. 181, 228, 325, 345
Jessup, Elizabeth (Wife of Ebenezer). 181
Jessup, Elizabeth (Dau. of Ebenezer). 181
Jessup, Hamilton Dibble. 345
Jessup, Henry James (Son of Ebenezer). 181, 344
Jessup, Capt. Joseph. 73, 179-82, 185, 188, 194, 195, 235, 344-5
Jessup, Joseph Sr. 180, 182
Jessup, Leah (Dau. of Ebenezer). 181
Jessup, Mary-Ann-Clarenden (Dau. of Ebenezer). 181
Jessup, Sarah (Dau. of Ebenezer). 181
Jessup's Falls. 182
Jessup's Landing (Corinth, N.Y.) 182
Johns, Lieut. Solomon. 84, 253, 259, 260, 333, 345
Johnson, Adam Gordon (Son of Sir John). 348
Johnson, Ann (Mrs. Daniel Claus). 64, 348
Johnson, Anne (Dau. of Mary Brant). 29
Johnson, Anne (Dau. of Sir John). 348
Johnson, Brown Lady. See Mary Brant.
Johnson, Charles Christopher (Son of Sir John). 348
Johnson, Elizabeth (Dau. of Caroline Peters). 339
Johnson, Elizabeth (Dau. of Mary Brant). 29
Johnson Family. 34, 29, 64-72, 112, 134, 136, 182, 348
Johnson, George. 29, 349
Johnson, Col. Guy. 29, 39, 64, 66, 68, 69, 94,

382

383

387

Rawden, Lord, 246
Reakley, Andrew. 296
Rebel Fleet. 72
Rebel Patrols. 93
Rebellion of 1837. 345-7, 352
Recollets. 45, 48
Recruiting, Agents, Parties. 34, 38, 42, 97, 111, 114, 139, 156-7, 163, 200, 212, 224, 227, 241, 248, 250, 252, 255, 258, 293, 297
Red Jacket (Seneca) 142, 162
Reform Party, Reformers. 345-6, 351
Refugees. 23, 31, 32, 77, 90, 112, 120, 126, 127, 137, 147, 160; provincials in Canada after Burgoyne's surrender, 212, 248, 250, 268, 272, 274, 275, 280, 287, 289; sanctuary in Vermont, 291; 292, 293-301, 307, 308, 312, 314, 317, 318, 319, 325, 351
Reserves. Clergy and crown, 347; Indian, 317, 323, 339; Public use, 310-11
Rhode Island. 12
Richelieu River. 12, 27, 49, 42, 51, 54, 81, 84, 135, 186
Rideau River. 343
Riedesel, Gen. the Baron Friedrich von. 28, 49, 50, 156, 157, 187, 211, 212, 220, 233-4, 282
Riflemen, British. 213, 233
Riflemen, German. 76, 81, 90, 98
Rifles. 147, 175
Rivière du Chene. 27, 51, 230, 233
Roads. 328, 329, 331, 336
Roberts, Capt. Benjamin. 243
Robertson, Ensign Neil. 183, 188, 200, 204
Robins, James 185, 231
Robins, John. 247, 261
Robinson, Col. Beverley. 276-7
Rochester, N.Y. (Ulster County). 165
Rockingham, Prime Minister Lord. 121, 289
Rogers, David McGregor (Son of James). 340
Rogers, Elizabeth (Wife of Robert). 242, 243, 244
Rogers, Maj. James. 56, 199, 233, 234, 237-44, 246, 247-8, 249, 250, 251, 252, 253, 254, 255, 256-7, 258, 259, 260, 261, 262, 274, 278, 281, 292, 298, 321, 340, 345, 352
Rogers, James Jr. 256-7, 340
Rogers, Margaret (Wife of James). 244, 256, 340
Rogers, Margaret (Dau. of James). 340
Rogers, Mary (Dau. of James). 340
Rogers, Mary Ann (Dau. of James). 340
Rogers, Richard (Bro. of James and Robert). 237, 240, 241
Rogers, Col. Robert. 129-30, 237-44, 245-6, 247, 248-9, 250, 251, 253, 254, 258, 260, 261, 262
Roger's Rangers (1st Regt. of Queen's Rangers). 23, 129-31, 237, 240-2

Roman Catholics. 18, 34, 68, 315-7, 337
Ross, Maj. John. 57, 59, 96, 97, 107, 109, 110, 113-8, 119, 120, 121, 122, 123, 124, 125, 126, 127-8, 167, 168, 169, 203, 204, 287, 292, 306, 320, 322, 325, 327, 339
Rouville, Capt. René de. 74, 76, 179
Royal Artillery. 44, 76, 78, 79, 98, 101, 186, 192
Royal Greens. See King's Royal Regiment of New York.
Royal Yorkers. See King's Royal Regiment of New York.
Royal Highland Emigrants (84th Foot) 1st Battalion. 16-7, 22, 31, 34-62, 69, 72, 74, 85, 101, 107, 108, 114, 122, 143, 149, 153, 196, 198, 199, 203-4, 227, 251, 300, 312, 318, 335, 349
Royal Highland Emigrants (84th Foot) 2nd Battalion. 40
Royal Navy. 33, 205, 302, 304, 305, 306
Royal Proclamation, 1763. 174
Ruiter, Capt. Henry. 253, 259-60
Ruiter, Lieut. John. 231, 318-9
Ryckman, Lieut. John. 117

Sacondaga, N.Y. 102
Sacandaga River. 182
Safe Conducts. 268, 287
Sagarithra (Tuscarora). 140
St. Croix River. 249, 263
St. Helen's Island. 42, 349
St. John Gate (Quebec City). 47
Saint John, N.B. 315
Saint John River. 247, 315
Saint John Valley. 241, 248, 263, 341
St. Lawrence, Gulf of. 303, 304, 306
St. Lawrence River. 21, 22, 27, 34, 39, 40, 42, 43, 59, 65, 69, 80, 81, 87, 91, 119, 120, 128, 139, 203, 207, 211, 260, 291, 298, 301, 306, 307, 309, 310, 312, 313, 314, 315, 317, 318, 319, 321, 322, 323, 325, 327, 331, 333, 336, 337, 342, 343, 345, 347, 349
St. Leger, Brig. Barry. 28, 32, 74, 76, 77, 78, 80, 81, 114, 127, 137, 139, 164, 186, 200, 204, 234, 236, 252, 255, 256, 280, 281, 284, 285, 286, 287, 288, 290, 327
St. Leger Expedition. 74-81
St. Louis Gate, Quebec City. 47, 48
St. Maurice River. 21
St. Regis. 91, 94, 349
St. Roch, Suburb of. 45, 47
Salem, Delaware Village. 170-2
Sandhurst. 340
Sandusky, O. 166, 173
Sandusky River. 166, 170
Sandwich (Assumption). 324, 337
Sang-blanc, French Agent. 134
Saratoga, N.Y. 16, 81, 101, 106, 125, 139, 179, 194, 195, 196, 204, 209, 222, 224, 234,